# Translated Texts 1

This series is designed to meet the needs of students of ancient and medieval history and others who wish to broaden their study by reading source material, but whose knowledge of Latin or Greek is not sufficient to allow them to do so in the original language. Many important Late Imperial and Dark Age texts are currently unavailable in translation and it is hoped that TTH will help to fill this gap and to complement the secondary literature in English which already exists. The series relates principally to the period 300–800 AD and includes Late Imperial, Greek, Byzantine and Syriac texts as well as source books illustrating a particular period or theme. Each volume is a self-contained scholarly translation with an introductory essay on the text and its author and notes on the text indicating major problems of interpretation, including textual difficulties.

Front cover: The bust of a philosopher by Gail Heather, based on an original found in a fifth-century philosopher's school at Aphrodisias in Asia Minor.

A full list of published titles in the Translated Texts for Historians series is available on request. The most recently published are shown below.

For full details of Translated Texts for Historians, including prices and ordering information, please write to the following:
**All countries, except the USA and Canada:** Liverpool University Press, 4 Cambridge Street, Liverpool, L69 7ZU, UK (*Tel* +44-[0]151-794 2233, *Fax* +44-[0]151-794 2235, *Email* J.M.Smith@liv.ac.uk, http://www.liverpool-unipress.co.uk). **USA and Canada:** University of Pennsylvania Press, 4200 Pine Street, Philadelphia, PA 19104-6097, USA (*Tel* +1-215-898-6264, *Fax* +1-215-898-0404).

Translated Texts for Historians
Volume 36

# Politics, Philosophy, and Empire in the Fourth Century

## Select Orations of Themistius

Translated with an introduction by
PETER HEATHER and DAVID MONCUR

Liverpool
University
Press

First published 2001
Liverpool University Press
4 Cambridge Street
Liverpool, L69 7ZU

Copyright © 2001 Peter Heather and David Moncur

British Library Cataloguing-in-Publication Data
A British Library CIP Record is available
ISBN 0–85323–106–0

Set in Monotype Times by
Wilmaset Ltd, Birkenhead, Wirral
Printed in the European Union by
Bookcraft Ltd, Midsomer Norton

# TABLE OF CONTENTS

# ABBREVIATIONS

| | |
|---|---|
| AE | *L'Année Epigraphique* |
| CM | *Chronica Minora*, 3 vols., ed. Th. Mommsen, M.G.H., A.A. ix, xi, xiii (Berlin, 1892, 1894, 1898). |
| Cons. Const. | Consularia Constantinopolitana |
| *C. Th.* | *Codex Theodosianus*, 2nd edn, ed. Th. Mommsen and P. Meyer (Berlin, 1954). |
| ELF | J. Bidez, ed., *Imp. Caesaris Flavii Claudii Iuliani: epistulae, leges, poematia, fragmenta varia* (Paris, 1922). |
| *ILS* | H. Dessau, ed., *Inscriptiones Latinae Selectae* (Zurich, 1974). |
| *PLRE* 1 and 2 | *The Prosopography of the Later Roman Empire*, vols. 1 and 2, ed. J. R. Martindale et al. (Cambridge, 1971 & 1980). |
| *PWRE* | *Real-Encyklopädie der klassischen Altertumswissenschaft*, ed. A. Pauly et al. (Berlin, 1893–). |
| *RIC* 8 | *The Roman Imperial Coinage*, ed. C. H. V. Sutherland and R. A. G. Carson, vol. 8, J. P. C. Kent, *The Family of Constantine 337–364* (London, 1981). |
| *VS* | H. Diels, *Die Fragmente der Vorsokratiker*, rev. edn W. Kranz (Berlin, 1956). |

# PREFACE

Around the year 350, a young orator and philosopher by the name of Themistius delivered a speech to the Emperor Constantius II in Ancyra (modern Ankara). Although Constantius was a Christian and Themistius a non-Christian educated in traditional Hellenic *paideia*, imperial favour quickly followed. Themistius first graduated to an officially funded teaching post in Constantinople, the new capital of the eastern half of the empire. Then, much more dramatically, Constantius catapulted Themistius into the city's senate in 355. Constantius continued to show Themistius great favour until his death in November 361, as did three subsequent Christian emperors. Themistius pronounced keynote speeches for the Emperors Jovian (363–4), Valens (364–78), and Theodosius (379–95), before he eventually disappeared from public life, probably through retirement, in around 384/5.[1]

This project, designed to make accessible a selection of the public speeches Themistius delivered in the course of his lengthy career, has itself been a long time in the making. Mooted as long ago as 1983, it has been through several stages of evolution, even if basic methods have remained constant, with David Moncur being responsible in the first instance for translating and literary comment, and Peter Heather for historical introductions and annotation.[2] The original plan was to translate three of Themistius' best-known speeches – Orations 5, 10, 16 – together with Orations 3 and 6 as examples of Themistius' art under the Emperors Constantius and Valens. Oration 10 eventually became part of an earlier volume in the Translated Texts for Historians series, paired there with a large part of Oration 8 to explore the Gothic policy of the Emperor Valens in the late 360s.[3] At the same time, the project steadily expanded to investigate Themistius' career in much more comprehensive fashion. In the end, we have grouped the speeches into chapters, each of

---

1 On the circumstances of his retirement, see Chapter 5. Libanius, *Ep.* 18, implies that Themistius was still alive in 388, but he delivered no speeches after 384/5.
2 We have, however, commented robustly and fully in the intervening years on each other's efforts and take an entirely cabinet responsibility towards our final text.
3 Heather and Matthews, 1991, ch. 2.

which deals with either a key period in the evolution of Themistius' career, or with a sequence of events of particular historical significance. Chapter 2 explores Themistius' initial rise to prominence under the Emperor Constantius II, Oration 1 and *The Letter of Constantius to the Senate* having been added to Oration 3, which was part of the original design. Oration 1 has been translated once before, by Glanville Downey, but from an inferior text prior to the appearance of Downey's own Teubner edition. As the first speech Themistius ever gave before an emperor, it is of considerable interest, both for the early appearance of many of the themes which would become the orator's trademark, and also for its relative lack of politically pointed comment in comparison with later efforts. *The Letter of Constantius* not only marked the orator's rise to an entirely new level of prominence, but beautifully illustrates what it was about his work which attracted imperial attention. Oration 3 was delivered at the apogee of this initial period of success, when Themistius led a delegation from the Senate of Constantinople to its Roman counterpart to deliver a gift of Crown Gold.

The orator's early prominence was directly threatened, however, by the death of the patron upon whose favour it was based, Constantius II, in November 361. There then followed, in quick succession, three different imperial regimes in just over three years, those of Julian, Jovian, and, finally, in spring 364, Valentinian I and his brother Valens. Despite this instability, and despite the fact that his relationship with the Emperor Julian, a former pupil, was not as warm as one might expect, Themistius came through this testing time with flying colours. The prominence he had achieved under Constantius was eventually re-established under Valens, who ruled the eastern half of the Roman Empire from Constantinople, alongside his brother Valentinian who presided over the west. The death of Constantius, who had moved the Empire more firmly in a Christian direction than had even his father, the Emperor Constantine, also unleashed a period of great religious instability, as first Julian the Apostate turned back to traditional cultic practice, and then Jovian and Valentinian and Valens sought to defuse the conflict engendered by these changes of policy. Chapter 3, comprising Orations 5 and 6, explores both of these themes: Themistius' ability to jump between regimes, a process highly revealing of his position within them, and the religious controversies of the early 360s.

With Chapter 4 (Orations 14–16), the story leaps forward a decade and a half to the turbulent early years of Theodosius I (379–95). Theodosius' predecessor in the east, Valens, was killed by the Goths at the battle of Hadrianople in August 378, and Theodosius was eventually appointed to clean up the mess (January 379). The three speeches of this chapter, dating from early summer 379 to 1 January 383, chart the evolution of Theodosius' policies as he struggled to constrain the Goths, and provide another case study – to go alongside Orations 5 and 6 – of the means employed by Themistius to make a successful transition from one imperial regime to another. They also provide fascinating insight into Theodosius' developing relationship with the western colleague who had appointed him: the Emperor Gratian, elder son of Valentinian I.

Chapter 5, finally, brings us to the twilight of Themistius' career, and a controversy which erupted when the orator consented to become urban prefect of Constantinople for a brief period sometime between late 383 and the autumn of 384. Orations 17 and 34 not only illustrate the nature of this controversy, but were also used by Themistius to survey his entire career, as he developed his self-justification for taking office upon this basis. These speeches provide, therefore, a logical climax to the book, allowing us privileged access to how the orator himself wished his lifetime's achievement to be viewed.[4]

That wish has not, however, been granted, or at least not straight-forwardly so. For the best part of forty years, and in the midst of considerable political and religious turbulence, Themistius kept himself centre stage in the political and cultural life of the capital city of the eastern half of the Roman Empire, successfully negotiating his way through four changes of imperial regime. The fourth century, in both east and west, throws up other examples of intellectuals carving out careers for themselves around imperial courts. Ausonius, tutor to the future Emperor Gratian, comes immediately to mind, whose extraordinary nepotism inserted a host of unlikely relatives into various posts in the mid-370s. The authors of the Gallic corpus of Latin prose panegyrics represent other examples of less extravagant success, and, in the eastern Empire, men such as Libanius and Himerius had their moments of glory.[5] Compared to Themistius, such men were briefly flickering

4 *Orr.* 17 and 34 are also translated in Penella, 2000, together with *Or.* 31 which belongs to the same period. Penella's interests are much less historically focussed than our own, however, so that it is far from redundant to have included them in our study as well.

5 Ausonius: Matthews, 1975, ch. 3; Gallic panegyrists: Nixon and Rogers, 1994, 8–10. Libanius gave only one imperial panegyric: *Or.* 59. On Himerius, see Barnes, 1987.

candles indeed. No other fourth-century orator even comes close to his tally of eighteen surviving major speeches, all delivered on important state occasions, the vast majority before ruling emperors.[6] The pagan servant of Christian emperors, Themistius was the great political survivor of the fourth century: the Talleyrand of his time.

It is hardly surprising, given this extraordinary survival act, that Themistius was, in his own lifetime, and continues to be, a figure of some controversy. Some of the controversy, indeed, he deliberately stirred up himself. As professor of philosophy in Constantinople in the early to mid-350s, for instance, Themistius aggressively advocated the virtues of his own approach to the subject, in part by explicitly criticising other intellectuals in highly public forums. At other times in his life, the controversy was much less under his control. First of all, Themistius' promotion to the Senate of Constantinople in 355 and other associated successes generated the persistent accusation that he had shown himself a sophist rather than the true philosopher he pretended to be. After Plato's canonical definition of these terms, a sophist was an individual who claimed to be a philosopher, interested in true wisdom, but who really used this only to cover an underlying interest in immediate worldly gain. As we shall see, Themistius seems eventually to have weathered this storm, but the controversy did not die easily.[7] A further major moment of controversy then engulfed the tail end of his career, when Themistius accepted the urban prefecture of Constantinople. Here again, the charge was similar to that raised in the 350s, namely that Themistius' acceptance of such a high state office showed that had not acted with the worldly disinterest expected of a proper philosopher.

Modern views of Themistius have been heavily influenced by the ancient debates. Older scholarly opinion sided with Themistius' critics,

6 The speeches are numbered 1 to 19 because of the presence in the Themistian corpus of Oration 12, a speech in Latin purporting to be the translation of an oration addressed to Valens. Such a speech was seemingly delivered at Antioch in 376 (Socrates, *Ecclesiastical History* 4.32), but the extant Latin version is a Renaissance forgery. It is therefore omitted from all modern editions where it nevertheless maintains a ghostly presence in the lacuna between *Orr.* 11 and 13. Other speeches have also not survived. Themistius gave a now lost speech to Julian, probably on 1 January 363 (see Chapter 3), and another perhaps argued in favour of allowing Goths across the Danube in 376: see the introduction to Chapter 4.

7 On these quarrels, see Chapter 2. Gleason, 1995, chs 2 and 6, is an excellent guide to these archetypes of Hellenic intellectual identification, and to the problems, in practice, of separating them.

characterising him as an individual who, despite his own assertions to the contrary, flattered emperors to achieve worldly success.[8] More recently, a consensus of opinion has emerged which is somewhat more favourable. Downey began the trend, with Dagron, Daly, and, most recently, Vanderspoel all rallying at least partly to the cause. These scholars entirely accept that Themistius used flattery; the evidence of the speeches is anyway overwhelming. They argue, however, that the flattery was employed for worthwhile ends, not primarily for self-advancement. Themistius, it is asserted, had strong ideals in public life – derived, as he himself claimed, from his study of Aristotle and Plato – towards which he consistently worked.[9]

In our view, neither of these characterisations is sufficient. To call Themistius a flatterer fails to do justice to the importance of the political role he played out in Constantinople over close to forty years. The more recent consensus, on the other hand, has, we would argue, fallen into the trap of taking Themistius' own account of himself – the philosopher commenting independently upon major events of the day – at face value. This was a cultivated image, self-consciously created and sustained in speeches composed explicitly for public consumption. In our view, this image was designed to hide as much as it revealed about the true nature of Themistius' career.

On one level, swallowing whole Themistius' self-portrait makes him appear much more disengaged from the tough, messy, and profitable business of getting and staying ahead in political life than was actually the case. Equally important, the pose of philosophical independence camouflaged Themistius' real role in mid-fourth-century Constantinople. To understand this role, we would argue, it is methodologically vital to do two things: read the speeches in chronological order, then set their individual contents as fully as possible in their *particular* contexts.[10] Such a process might seem obvious, but it has not been done with sufficient thoroughness. In Themistius' case, the task is greatly facilitated by the relatively extensive narrative and other sources avail-

8 Surveyed by Vanderspoel, 1995, 2–3, quoting Reiske from the preface to Dindorf's edition of Themistius (xii); Geffcken, 1978, 167–8; Alföldi, 1952, 109; Piganiol, 1972, 234.

9 There are differences, but their works (see the Bibliography) all take a similar line. In our view, they represent the current consensus, although Vanderspoel, 1995, 3, considers otherwise.

10 A method adopted with great success by Alan Cameron in the case of the poetry of Claudian; see the introduction to Cameron, A. D. E., 1970.

able from the period of his heyday, which largely coincides with the detailed political narrative of imperial events provided by the *Res Gestae* of Ammianus Marcellinus. When this method is followed, it becomes in our view entirely clear that Themistius was very much closer to the imperial regimes he served than this own public pronouncements indicated. There are recurrent themes within the speeches, but his treatment of individuals and events changed over time in ways which demonstrate that Themistius deliberately altered his professed opinions to suit the needs of the regime for which he was currently working. He was, in short, an imperial propagandist – of a highly sophisticated kind – looking both to justify the specific actions of his current employer, and disseminate a general vision of imperial affairs which suited that employer's needs.

So different is this from either of the established characterisations of Themistius' career, and such is the disparity we are alleging between the image he peddled of himself and the reality of his position, that it is necessary to justify these views in detail. As a result, we have stretched the established genre of the Liverpool Translated Texts for Historians series in the amount of historical comment that we have chosen to include. Readers will find that not only do the speeches have in some cases very substantial annotation, but that there are also introductions to the individual speeches, and more general introductions to the chapters in which we have grouped them. We have also dedicated the first chapter, in what is otherwise a book of translations, to a general historical study of Themistius' career and modes of operation. The ratio of historical comment to translated speech is thus relatively high, and the book as a whole has a fairly complicated structure, comprising three interlocking layers of introduction. The introductions to the speeches deal with matters specific to the individual speech, the introductions to the chapters deal with matters common to the speeches translated in that chapter, and Chapter 1 is designed to pull everything together into a general account of Themistius' career and its transformation over time.

What has emerged, in short, from this long process of gestation is a fully argued interpretative account of the importance of Themistius within the political structures of the eastern Empire, rather than a simple set of translations and introductions. We are entirely confident, however, in the ability of our readers to develop their own views in reaction to the arguments presented here, and have no real qualms, therefore, about having stretched the genre of translation in this way. We are also highly conscious that there are at least two other strands of analysis, which would need fuller development to produce a genuinely complete picture of Themistius' life and work: philosophy and rhetoric. In the introductions and notes we have attempted to pick out some key aspects of Themistius' philosophical and rhetorical training, and how these influenced the development of his political role. We are well aware, however, that both these subject areas have their own highly developed scholarly traditions, and that we have done no more here than scratch the surface. Arguments about Themistius' knowledge of Neoplatonism continue apace, and it is very obvious to us that his literary and rhetorical education awaits definitive treatment. The Liverpool series, however, is aimed primarily at historians, and we hope that readers will be understanding of our central purposes, if, in laying out the case for a particular understanding of Themistius' historical significance, we seem relatively to have neglected other areas of importance.

Before bringing this Preface to a close, it is important briefly to introduce the textual tradition of Themistius' speeches and the style of translation we have adopted in this volume. The Petavius–Harduin edition of 1684 was the first to place the thirty-three surviving speeches of Themistius in the currently standard arrangement, which is not based upon the chronological order of their composition and delivery. Rather, it divided them into two groups: the so-called 'political' orations, arranged chronologically and numbered 1 to 19, which addressed a ruling emperor or a member of his house and were delivered on official occasions; and the 'private' orations, often impossible to date with precision and numbered 20 to 34, in which Themistius was not speaking in an official capacity. The latter included a funeral oration for his father (*Or.* 20), various epideictic pieces such as 'On Friendship' (*Or.* 22) and 'Should One Engage in Farming?' (*Or.* 30), as well as more polemical works engaging his critics such as 'The Sophist' (*Or.* 23), 'Reply to Those who Interpreted The Sophist Incorrectly' (*Or.* 29), 'Concerning His Presidency' (*Or.* 31), and 'Reply to Those Who Found Fault with Him for Accepting Public Office' (*Or.* 34).[11] However, as this volume seeks to explore, the division between the political and the private in

11 Penella, 2000, provides complete translations, short commentaries and full notes on all the private orations as well as a discussion of the 'political/private' issue at pp. 6–9. *Or.* 34 appeared in print for the first time in Mai's edition of 1816.

Themistius' life and career was not as clear-cut as has sometimes been assumed.[12]

The speeches are preserved in numerous manuscripts of which the Ambrosianus (*A*) of the fifteenth century contains all the political orations, *The Letter of Constantius*, and all but two of the private orations (as well as the speeches of Aeschines). *The Letter of Constantius* is also preserved in another manuscript of the fifteenth century, the Coslianus (Π). Since *A* and Π include some of the same orations in the same order, and also share several significant readings, they are both thought to derive from a lost exemplar of the previous century which is itself almost certainly related to a surviving fourteenth-century manuscript, the Salamanticus (ψ). Of the orations translated in this volume, all appear in *A*, *Orr*. 3, 5, 6, 14, 15, 16 and *The Letter of Constantius* appear in Π, and *Orr*. 5, 6, 14 and *The Letter* in *A*, Π, and ψ. Oration 5 appears most frequently in the tradition, being included in 26 manuscripts, possibly as a result of its edifying subject matter, and Oration 34 survives in *A* alone. Oration 6 also appears in one manuscript of the fourteenth century, the Parisinus (Θ) under the name of Synesius.[13]

Themistius' oratorical style was much admired by his contemporaries, but an author's style is often the first casualty of any translation. The translator is faced with a difficult choice in this respect. One can either attempt to reproduce the effect of the original, giving the sense of what was said without necessarily always using the same words or phrases, or follow the grammatical and sentence structure of the text as closely as possible. The latter course inevitably generates a loss of fluency from time to time, to allow the reader closer access to its detail. In keeping with the well-established traditions of the Translated Texts for Historians series, we have chosen the latter option, but hope that the individuality of Themistius' oratorical style has not been entirely sacrificed in the process.

It is, finally, our very pleasurable task to thank all those who have

12 Photius, *Bibliotheca* 74, mentioned described 36 orations described as 'political speeches', among them panegyrics of the Emperors Constantius, Valens, Valentinian Galates, and Theodosius. If Photius used 'political' to refer only to panegyric-type speeches, then we now possess only half of the Themistian corpus extant in the 8th century (cf. note 6 above). On the other hand, Photius may simply have used the term 'political' as a contrast to Themistius' philosophical works, which he then went on to discuss.

13 For a survey of the manuscripts and editions, see the preface to the Teubner edition. A full discussion the textual tradition can be found in Schenkl, 1898, 1899, 1919.

assisted us in our labours, in such a wide variety of ways. Much of the energy and enthusiasm which originally got the project properly underway in the late 1980s and early 1990s was supplied by the late Margaret Gibson. Like so many TTH authors, our debt to this great scholar is beyond accurate calculation. Similar if not even greater in scale is the amount we owe Mary Whitby. All the remaining errors are resolutely our own, but Mary has not only provided great encouragement and wise advice, but also waded through the entire manuscript, more than once, with huge care and diligence. The project would probably have never been brought to completion at all, and certainly have had a much inferior outcome, had we not so benefited from her intelligence and scholarship. Equally fundamental, Neil McLynn generously devoted part of a precious leave to reading the entire text, saving us from many errors and stimulating much fruitful reconsideration. Different parts of the manuscript have been read by many scholars, from all of whose advice we have benefited substantially. Particular thanks go to Michael Crawford, Carlotta Dionisotti, Rebecca Lyman, John Matthews, Stefan Rebenich, Bryan Ward-Perkins, and Michael Whitby. Some of the ideas aired in what follows have benefited from outings at a number of seminar and conference venues, not least University College London, together with Nottingham, Mannheim, Berkeley, and Yale universities. We are very grateful for these invitations to speak and the opportunities provided for tapping the knowledge of such a wide variety of audiences. Robert Penella and Hartmut Leppin took time out from their own work on Themistius to offer encouragement, advice, and, in the latter case, an advance copy of the item concerned. Much technical assistance, finally, has been provided at different points in the book's gestation, from Rachel Aucott, Regine May, and Andrew Kirk. We are extremely grateful for all this assistance and have done our best to ensure that the end result is worthy of the effort put into it by so many people.

Surbiton & Horton cum Studley
January 2001

# CHAPTER 1
# ORATOR, EMPEROR, AND SENATE

## PHILOSOPHY AND ORATORY

Themistius was born c.317, probably in Paphlagonia, but seems to have spent his childhood in Constantinople, a city with whose fortunes his career was to be inextricably linked.[1] After a standard grounding in Greek literature, he graduated to philosophical studies under his father, Eugenius, himself a teacher in Constantinople. Until the age of thirty, Themistius' career followed well-established patterns. He taught for a period in the city of Nicomedia, and possibly too in other cities of Asia Minor, attempting to establish his reputation as a major philosopher.[2] Hellenic intellectuals, especially in their early years, often functioned as peripatetic, self-employed teachers, until their fame was sufficient for a city to appoint them to a salaried position.

As this *curriculum vitae* indicates, Themistius was in origin an authentic exponent of Greek philosophy. From his philosophical writings, there survive five paraphrases of works of Aristotle. These were not designed as major contributions to advanced scholarship. Because of existing commentaries on Aristotle (especially, it seems, those of Alexander of Aphrodisias, although he does not explicitly mention them), Themistius considered that further interpretative work on such a large scale was unnecessary. It was his more modest intention, he declared, to produce works designed to clarify Aristotle's meaning and aid memorisation: a series of teaching aids.[3] From these texts, his intellectual

1 Paphlagonian: *Or.* 2.28d. Born c.317: *Or.* 1.18a (roughly a contemporary of Constantius II). Constantinopolitan childhood: *Orr.* 17.214c, 34.xii, xvi. Commentators have taken different views over whether he was born in Constantinople or Paphlagonia, and whether part of his education took place outside the capital; see further, Vanderspoel, 1995, 31–42; Penella, 2000, 1–2.

2 *Or.* 24 inaugurated a series of lectures at Nicomedia sometime before 344. He may also have been teaching at Ancyra before the delivery of *Or.* 1 (so Vanderspoel, 1995, 42–9), but see further the introduction to this speech in Chapter 2.

3 Themistius expounds the rationale behind his paraphrases at *On the Posterior Analytics* 1.2–12; cf. *Or.* 23. 294d–295a: Blumenthal, 1979, 176–7. Cf. Todd, 1996, 2–6. Some of his

allegiance is hard to classify. He has sometimes been described as a late peripatetic, who stood outside the mainstream intellectual developments of his day, since his clarifications of Aristotle's meaning do not tend to draw on the Neoplatonic tradition which was gathering momentum in the later third and fourth centuries. After Alexander of Aphrodisias, the next full-scale commentaries upon Aristotle's works were produced by Neoplatonist scholars in fifth- and sixth-century Alexandria.[4]

For the most part, however, Themistius' paraphrases aimed solely to bring out the literal meaning of Aristotle's words with a minimum of scholarly cross-reference and argument. By their very nature, therefore, they would be unlikely to show off the full range of Themistius' reading. The one exception to this highly economical approach is, indeed, rather revealing. In response to *De Anima* 3.5 – Aristotle's famously difficult and compressed treatment of the intellect – Themistius produced a much larger-scale exegesis. This demonstrates that he actually had a very considerable knowledge of Neoplatonic writing, a knowledge which the textbook approach of his other paraphrases largely hides. More than that, his interpretation of the passage also shows Themistius' acceptance of a number of basic Neoplatonic ideas: a strong sense of metaphysical hierarchy, with higher order entities generating lower ones, and spiritual development taking the form of self-realisation within the individual soul.[5] This would suggest that Themistius was probably much more au fait with recent Neoplatonic philosophy than the bulk of his paraphrases might initially suggest. Such a conclusion is entirely in line with the evidence of the orations. As we shall see, these tended to cite Plato quite as much as Aristotle, and important, if argu- ably commonplace, Neoplatonic ideas figured regularly within them. In Oration 5, Themistius compared the relationship between the Divinity and the emperor to that between the One and the Intellect in Neoplatonic cosmology (64b). He also expounded there a syncretising vision of tradi- tional non-Christian religion, common to fourth-century Neoplatonists, that all the cults were paths to the same end (69a). Oration 6, likewise,

---

paraphrases – especially that of *De Anima* (see note 5) – were more ambitious in scale. Of the paraphrases, three survive in Greek, two in Hebrew.

4  Blumenthal, 1990.

5  Schroeder and Todd, 1990, 34–9, with the notes to their translation at 90ff.; cf. Todd, 1996. Todd places more emphasis on Themistius' knowledge of Neoplatonism than does Blumenthal, 1990. For a still more Platonist reading, see Mahoney, 1982.

emphasised unchangingness as the essential characteristic of Divinity (73b), and used Neoplatonic explanations of the existence of imperfection among men in the sublunary world (79c-d). Examples could be multiplied,[6] but there is more than enough here to confirm the picture suggested by Themistius' interpretation of *De Anima* 3.5. As a philosopher, he had a deep knowledge of Plato, based not only on the original texts, which he often cited in his speeches, but also upon subsequent commentators.

In assessing himself, Themistius claimed to be a philosopher of some originality, an originality based on two ideas inherited from his father Eugenius. First, philosophy should be turned to practical uses, and, second, rhetoric, the art of persuasive speaking, was highly important if properly subjugated to philosophical ends.[7] It is hard to tell how distinctive these ideas really made him. As we shall see, his polemics make it clear that there were other Aristotelian philosophers active in mid-fourth-century Constantinople. Themistius, however, was dismissive of their abilities. His speeches also castigated some other rival teachers of philosophy in Constantinople as too otherworldly, overly focussed on individual spiritual development among a small body of devotees, and hence neglectful of general questions of social morality. Yet even Iamblichus, the great Neoplatonic sage himself, took students who were more interested in oratorical technique and arcane elements of their Hellenic intellectual heritage as a preparation for careers in public life than they were in leading their souls back to the One. Neoplatonist philosophers from the time of Porphyry onwards were, in fact, highly interested in rhetoric, reorganising its study as an introduction to dialectic. An interest in the practical uses of philosophy and in oratory could be found to some extent, therefore, even among Neoplatonist philosophers.[8] In the main areas where Themistius claimed to stand apart from contemporary philosophical developments, any difference, therefore, would seem to have been only one of degree.

It was nonetheless important. From the speeches, Themistius emerges as entirely committed to the ideas that the Roman state was a

6 See *Or.* 1.1a, 3a, 8b with footnotes in Chapter 2.

7 The points were made most explicitly in *Or.* 20, the funeral oration for his father, but recur at various points in his work; cf. Vanderspoel, 1995, 39–40, 43–8; Penella, 2000, 4–5.

8 For Themistius' discussion of rival teachers, see the introduction to *The Letter of Constantius* in Chapter 2. The practical side of Iamblichus is commented upon by J.M. Dillon after Brown, 1980, 23–4. Neoplatonists and rhetoric: Kennedy, 1983, 52–3, 73–86.

divinely ordained institution, figuring centrally in God's plan for humankind, and hence that Roman emperors were chosen by the Divinity and stood in a special relationship to Him.[9] This represented an acceptance of one of the ancient claims of Roman imperialist ideology: the Divine Power had given the Romans world dominion for its own purposes. Such a vision of world order had deeper roots in Greek, not least Aristotelian, ideas that public political participation was the key means of bringing human beings to their proper evolutionary state. It did so by allowing them to develop their rational minds properly to control the conflicting desires inflicted upon them by their physical senses, and thus distinguish themselves fully from members of the animal kingdom, with whom they shared these elements of sensual physicality.[10] This belief in the importance of political participation, manifested in its fourthcentury context in a belief in the divine legitimacy of the Roman state, distinguished Themistius from contemporary Neoplatonists. The latter, by contrast, sought to bring individuals to their 'proper' state through inner spiritual development, which would provide a 'born again' quality to their lives.[11] Themistius' emphasis upon political participation probably reflects, therefore, the general legacy of Aristotelian ideas upon his own thinking.

Given these intellectual roots, it is hardly surprising that when the chance came to become something more than a teacher of philosophy, Themistius seized it enthusiastically. Speaking in front of the Emperor Constantius II, probably in 347, he deployed a public persona – the impartial and objective philosopher commenting truthfully on contemporary politics – which would serve him for the rest of his career. This persona was composed of a number of key elements. In Hellenic cultural tradition, philosophers were expected to show a total disinterest in worldly concerns. They could thus tell the truth without fear or favour, since they would never be seeking worldly preferment. Free – in the sense of absolutely honest and frank – speech was their especial characteristic, a quality designated by the Greek term *parrhesia*. Within this

9 Although Themistius would admit that lines of communication were not always perfect. The Emperor Jovian's early death, for instance, he later took as a sign that Jovian had not actually been divinely chosen, despite what he had said in *Or.* 5 during the emperor's lifetime. See Chapter 3.

10 For an introduction to such ideas, see Dauge, 1981; Heather 1993a; 1993b with further refs. Themistius' subscription to them is too pervasive to require specific reference.

11 See, e.g., Fowden, 1982.

cultural construct, rulers were supposed to be more tolerant of a philosopher's frankness than they would be of other individuals. Nonetheless,
philosophers were expected to cultivate *karteria*, the strength of character necessary to confront an autocratic ruler in public and tell him a
few home truths. A further central element of the image was the philosopher's ability, based upon his training in true wisdom, to spot underlying
virtue and vice with much greater accuracy than ordinary mortals.[12]
Themistius drew upon all of these elements at different points in his first
oration to Constantius; overall, he combined them to sustain the claim
that his was an entirely unique oratorical offering.

Themistius' public presentation of himself varied little in subsequent
years. Most of his speeches contained some reference to the central equation between philosophy and insightful truth-telling.[13] Over time, he
merely added experience to his original qualifications for speaking (e.g.
*Or.*34.xiii); by the 380s, after more than thirty years' service under four
emperors, this was hardly unreasonable. The creation of the Senate of
Constantinople, and his role within it, also enabled him to exploit
another traditional behavioural trait of the politically active philosopher. Although generally independent of worldly concerns, Hellenic
philosophers had always been allowed to undertake tasks on behalf of
their home cities. This was considered patriotic and true-spirited rather
than self-serving. Themistius was thus able to portray anything that he
did for the Senate of Constantinople, even though the institution had a
far wider political role within the eastern half of the Roman Empire, as
a service for his city and hence entirely legitimate for a philosopher such
as himself.[14] These, however, were relatively minor amplifications.
Throughout his speeches, Themistius presented himself as a philosopher,
and, in later speeches, often used the abstract noun 'philosophy' to designate himself.[15]

As well as a serious philosopher, Themistius was also a consummate
rhetorician. For Gregory Nazianzen he was 'the king of words', and for
Libanius the leading orator of his day. In Libanius' case, this was no

12 On the image, see Brown, 1980; 1992, chs 1–2. Extremely insightful is Gleason, 1995,
esp. ch. 6, stressing the importance of verbal conflict as providing a key opportunity for self-
definition.
13 In just the speeches translated in this volume, passages to this effect are found in *Orr.*
1, 3, 5, 15, 16, and 34.
14 See esp. *Or.* 34.xi–xiii in Chapter 5.
15 E.g. *Or.* 5.63c–d; *Or.* 6.73b–c; cf. *Or.* 34.vii.

hastily formed judgement. One of his letters describes the care with which he and another mutual friend, Celsus, read through one of Themistius' speeches, examining in detail its play of ideas and language.[16] This skill with words was carefully tied into his philosophical image. As we have seen, Themistius' father had taught him that oratorical skill was important, so long as it was utilised for serious philosophical ends. In the controversy which erupted over his adlection to the Senate of Constantinople in the mid-350s, Themistius developed this idea further. A series of speeches made a pointed contrast between the philosopher using rhetoric to present a serious argument as effectively as possible, and, after Plato's famous caricature, the sophist using rhetorical skill for self-advancement: impressing an audience in order to win personal applause, pupils, fame, and fortune.[17] In Themistius' view, rhetoric was a morally neutral force that could deployed either for worthwhile or inferior ends.

When speaking to emperors, Themistius further bolstered his claim to be deploying rhetoric to worthwhile ends by deliberately adopting an unusual speech form. In c.350, there was no single accepted structure for a speech in praise of a ruling emperor: the panegyric or encomium. The second of the introductory rhetorical treatises on the subject attributed to Menander Rhetor, dating from c.300, advocated a mixed chronological-cum-thematic structure for what he labelled the *basilikos logos*. The introduction, its author advised, should point out the grandeur of the subject and the speaker's own insufficiency for the task, before moving on to consider the emperor's country and city of origin, his birth, the accomplishments of his character, and his deeds first in war, and then in peacetime. Quintillian, in an earlier Latin manual, saw this as one of two possible ways of structuring an imperial speech, also describing a speech organised thematically under headings provided by the four cardinal virtues: courage, justice, continence, and wisdom. In Menander's scheme, the first of these virtues would be covered under deeds in war, and the rest under deeds of peace.[18] None of this advice was prescriptive. Of eleven third- and fourth-century speeches in the Gallic corpus of Latin prose panegyrics, three adopted structures which

16 General judgements: Gregory Nazianzen, *Epp.* 24, 48; Libanius, *Ep.* 241. For the reading, Libanius, *Ep.* 1430, trans. Norman, 1992, as *Ep.* 116.

17 Esp. *Or.* 23 commenting on Plato, *The Sophist* 231d, 235a–c, 266b. See further the introduction to *The Letter to Constantius* in Chapter 2.

18 For the *basilikos logos* of Menander Rhetor, see Russell and Wilson, 1981, 76–94; Quintilian, *Institutio oratoria* 3.7.15–16.

were entirely *sui generis*. Nonetheless, the more or less biographical structure described by Menander was highly influential. Six of the Gallic panegyrics broadly adopted this approach (one adopted Quintillian's alternative format by virtue, and the remaining one combined the two), and a similar approach to that of Menander was advocated by most of the surviving manuals dealing with this kind of oratory.[19]

Themistius rejected the standard conventions of this kind of approach, but did so deliberately, carefully signalling to his audience – especially in the earlier speeches – that he knew precisely what he was doing.[20] This does suggest, incidentally, that they would probably have been expecting something along the lines of Menander's *basilikos logos*. In Oration 1, Themistius refused point blank to open up with a reference to his own inadequacy. On the contrary, he gave the speech a remarkably bold beginning, which told the emperor that he was about to hear something quite new. And in the main body of the speech, instead of organising his material by biographical progression or thematic virtue, Themistius adopted an approach much more suitable for a self-proclaimed philosopher. Starting from philosophic first principles – usually derived from Plato and/or Aristotle – to define the qualities that an ideal king should possess, he then examined the actions of Constantius to establish the fact that his practices matched up to Hellenic ideals.[21] Overall, this structure was obviously closer to Quintillian than Menander, but nonetheless quite distinct.

As far as we can tell, Themistius' approach was, in a fourth-century context at least, innovative. He claimed as much in Orations 1 and 3, and the imperial court did have to listen to many official speeches in the course of the average ceremonial year.[22] To claim originality and then fail to deliver it would, of course, have been to risk ridicule. On the other hand, his approach was not absolutely new. It had been adopted by Dio Chrysostom two centuries before, and both structural similarities and many verbal echoes make clear the extent of Dio's influence, especially

19  Gallic panegyrics: Nixon and Rodgers, 1994, 10–14; Greek manuals (Theon, 'Hermogenes', Aphthonius, and Dionysius of Halicarnassus): Russell and Wilson, 1981, xxvi–xxxi. On the general survival of the latter, see the comments of Russell, 1998, 24–5.

20  E.g. *Or.* 1.2aff., 11c–d, 16b–c; *Or.* 3.44d–45b.

21  Compare Menander's advice on how to begin (Russell and Wilson, 1981, 76) with Themistius *Or.* 1.1a translated in Chapter 2.

22  *Orr.* 1.1a, 3.44d claim that no one had previously spoken to Constantius in this fashion.

on the younger Themistius. Dio had also used Plato's famous caricature of the wordsmith entirely interested in self-advancement – the sophist – to develop a similar public persona to that adopted by Themistius: the philosopher who used words to make more substantive points than the display orator interested only in worldly success. In his orations on kingship to Trajan, especially Oration 3, Dio had likewise started from philosophical first principles to identify the characteristics of an ideal king, before turning to measure Trajan against that standard.[23] No other surviving fourth-century speeches, apart from those of Themistius, echo Dio's approach so directly, and no surviving manual recommended it as a model form. In the course of his education, Themistius had obviously come across Dio's speeches, and clearly saw their suitability for his own purposes.[24]

While his debt to Dio was thus strong, it should not be overestimated. It is clearest in Oration 1, Themistius' most immature work. At that point, Themistius was the outsider trying to attract imperial attention. It was a moment of great opportunity but also carried a high risk of failure. This made it natural, perhaps, to find a good, if unusual, model and stick to it quite closely. Later speeches were much less wedded to Dio's example. Verbal echoes become much less frequent after Oration 1, and the contents of the later speeches also maintained a substantially different balance between discussions of the philosophical principles of good kingship, and specific illustrations of their application by the current emperor. The needs of the moment led him to include in subsequent speeches more biographical material, discursive argument, and cross-reference to current affairs. The rhetorical structure of these later speeches, therefore, could not retain the simplicity of Oration 1, where first a given element of ideal kingship was discussed and then an example of its implementation sought in the emperor's actions. Despite this, Themistius' basic approach remained broadly constant.[25]

In speech structure, then, Themistius was very much his own man.

23  On Dio's speeches and his philosophical conversion, see, e.g., Jones, 1978; Moles, 1978; Sidebottom, 1990.

24  Passing citations of Dio in the works of Fronto, Marcus Aurelius, Philostratus, and Menander Rhetor show that his writings were read quite widely between his own lifetime and that of Themistius (Brancacci, 1985, 1–3), but no intervening author made such an extensive use of both Dio's writings and his self-presentation.

25  The one exception to this was *Or.* 34, where, not inappropriately, Themistius adopted the recommended structure for a speech in court (see Chapter 5).

Ancient rhetoric studied not just the generic structure of speeches, however, but words themselves, and how to use them in different combinations to achieve desired effects. In verbal construction and the interplay of sentences, Themistius' skill as a speaker had clearly been developed by standard forms of rhetorical training. Wide reading was the main method prescribed for learning how to manipulate words with power. As one might expect, a host of incidental allusions in the speeches demonstrate that Themistius was indeed widely read in most areas of Greek literature. The rhetor Libanius considered a shared love of Hellenic literature to be the foundation of the two men's relationship.[26] Sometimes, the speeches show more specific borrowings. Orations 5 and 6 drew recognisably on three speeches to emperors of the second-century orator Aelius Aristides,[27] and most of Themistius' allusions to Demosthenes and Isocrates are from respectively Orations 2 (*To Nicocles*) and 18 (*On the Crown*).[28] These were textbook examples of how to speak to rulers, which had also greatly influenced Dio.

Themistius' rhetorical training also shows up in numerous specific features of his writing. Ancient manuals emphasised that it was important for the orator to help his audience by signalling clearly what he was about to do, and by providing brief summaries of the argument at appropriate moments (no doubt the ultimate source of the old advice about writing essays). Themistius consistently followed this practice, often giving a clear, single-sentence summary of the central point that a lengthy line of argument was endeavouring to make.[29] On a quite different level, Menander Rhetor recommended that speeches associated with ceremonial presentations of Crown Gold to an emperor should, while adopting a similar structure to the imperial speech, be considerably shorter. In this collection, we translate two such speeches given by Themistius: Orations 3 and 14. In neither speech did Themistius follow Menander's recommendations as to structure. He did, however, adopt his advice on length. Oration 3 is almost exactly the length recommended by Menander (two hundred lines of modern printed text, more or less

---

26  Libanius, e.g., *Ep.* 376 (cf. Dagron, 1968, 38–9). On Themistius' general knowledge of literature, see the summary at Colpi, 1988, 193–5.
27  See further Chapter 3.
28  They are listed at Colpi, 1988, 194.
29  On the manuals, Russell, 1998, 18. Some signposts: *Or.* 1.16b–c; *Or.* 5.67b–c; *Or.* 16.211a.

equivalent to Menander's three hundred *stichoi*), and Oration 14 is even shorter.[30]

Themistius was also a master of the rhetorical techniques designed to sustain an audience's interest and comprehension. Syntax and accentual rhythm were important both for inserting variety into a performance, and for providing the audience with clues as to punctuation. Themistius carefully employed accentual rhythm to both these ends in his speeches.[31] There is a good chance, as we shall see, that an interesting rubric to Oration 1 preserves Themistius' own judgement, from hindsight, on the word power of his earliest speech. If so, the nature of the comment underlines that, as an orator, he was au fait with contemporary oratorical theory.[32] And while a translation cannot effectively render accentual rhythm, it can preserve some of the other rhetorical features of Themistius' work. As the manuals recommended, and exercises in his youth caused him to practice, Themistius' speeches carefully contrasted moments of more relaxed discourse with passages of heightened tension or emotional climax, sometimes employing particular techniques. In the middle of a sustained argument in favour of religious toleration in Oration 5, for instance, Themistius relaxed the mood by introducing Theramenes, a famous turncoat of ancient Greek history. Or again, he brought Oration 6 to a climactic ending by deliberately not using the particles which were normally a standard feature of sentence structure, but whose omission (asyndeton) was a recognised means of achieving greater verbal excitement.[33] His speeches also followed the standard practice of developing arguments by the use of historical parallels drawn from the common body of Graeco-Roman knowledge of the past. These again could be employed for a variety of purposes, to make the argument more accessible or provide variety and amusement, but perhaps above all to provide a historical perspective which emphasised the overwhelming grandeur or virtue of the current emperor.[34]

Other features could be picked out, but there is enough here to establish the point. Themistius was, as the judgements of Gregory Nazianzen and Libanius imply, as much a technically accomplished orator as he

---

30  Russell, 1998, 29. On *Or.* 14, see the introduction to this speech in Chapter 4.

31  On accentual rhythm in general and in Themistius' prose, see Russell, 1998, 33–5.

32  See the introduction to *Or.* 1 in Chapter 2.

33  Theramenes: *Or.* 5.67a–68a. Asyndeton: *Or.* 6.84a; cf. Russell, 1998, 37–8.

34  Cf. Russell, 1998, 30–1, commenting on the advice of Menander to use historical parallels throughout an imperial speech.

was a trained philosopher. Speeches of the kind he delivered required lengthy preparation. Syntax and accentual rhythm, rhetorical special effects, historical parallels: all had to be combined in a satisfying whole, which both made any substantive points that might be necessary, and satisfied the audience's twin expectations of intellectual stimulation and amusement. For while Themistius, like other speakers, might be the expert, most of his audience had been through a similar education, and could be expected to have a critical appreciation of the rhetorical art. On occasion, Themistius referred to the amount of preparation he put into his work. In part, this was a further element in his self-contradistinction from sophists, some of whom prided themselves on their ability to improvise. It can probably also be taken seriously. In a revealing comment, the Gallic panegyrist of 310 declared that anyone who extemporised before an emperor had completely failed to understand the greatness of the Roman Empire.[35] Speaker and audience were united in their expectations of sophisticated rhetoric, and, if all the nuances and effects could not be appreciated at a first hearing, there was always the possibility of reading it subsequently.[36]

Themistius was far more, however, than a clever orator. He claimed as much about himself, of course, portraying himself as a serious philosopher with great truths to proclaim. The detailed evidence of the speeches, however, indicates that his claim was really true in a quite different sense. In the course of his forty-year career, Themistius went well beyond the parameters established by his predecessors for a socially active philosopher. The particular cultural and political conditions of mid-fourth-century Constantinople allowed him to carve a role in public life which had been entirely unavailable to Dio some two hundred and fifty years earlier, or even to his father just a generation before.

35 Themistius: e.g., *Orr.* 16.199c–200c, 25 (the latter speech consisting entirely of an explanation of why he was unable to extemporise at Valens' request). *Panegyrici Latini* 7.1.2; cf. Russell, 1998, 34–9.

36 Libanius seemingly often received copies of Themistius' speeches to read at leisure: *Epp.* 434 (*Or.* 2), 1430 (the lost panegyric of Julian). In 357, Themistius presented the library of Constantinople with a collection for students to peruse, and some speeches were repeated: e.g. *Or.* 5 for Jovian's consulship was delivered both in Ancyra and Constantinople.

## PHILOSOPHY AND POLITICS

To get at the reality behind Themistius' self-portrait, it is important first of all to recognise that he played the game of politics for substantial rewards. His public persona denied this, but the denials are worth careful scrutiny. After entering the senate in 355, Themistius had to defend himself against charges of worldliness, which focussed, among other matters, on the official salary in grain and other foodstuffs which his position as salaried teacher in Constantinople afforded him. He defended himself by arguing that he had taken only some of the perqui-sites of his position, and these he had used legitimately. He had also, he claimed, refused most of the many other gifts offered to him by Constan-tius II. In addition, he said, he had been very careful not to vaunt himself in public. When having dinner with the emperor, he had worn the plain cloak of a philosopher – the *tribonion* – rather than the highly decorated clothes normal to imperial grandees.[37] He maintained a similar stance in subsequent reigns. Under Valens, an imperial letter to the senate recorded that, although pressed on the matter, Themistius had refused the urban prefecture of Constantinople, probably because accepting such an office was incompatible with maintaining proper philosophical independence.[38]

These public statements have been broadly accepted by one impor-tant recent study as proof of Themistius' worldly disinterest.[39] Wearing the plain garb of a philosopher amidst the gorgeous robes of court was, of course, in one sense modest. In another, it was a deliberate act of self-publicity, signalling that he had risen quite above all such worldly vanities. Every office and status had its appropriate dress in the late Roman world, so that clinging determinedly to the *tribonion* itself pressed Themistius' claims to be a philosopher. As we have seen, it was absolutely required, moreover, of the true philosopher to reject worldly rewards, or else run the risk of being caricatured, after Plato, as a sophist. Given these expectations, Themistius simply had to be able to present himself, and do it plausibly, as someone who had entirely rejected worldly advancement or he would have lost his philosophical credibility. It is not enough, therefore, just to take his own denials at face value.

37 For fuller discussion and refs., see the introduction to *The Letter of Constantius* in Chapter 2.
38  *Or.* 34.xiii with notes, see Chapter 5.
39  Vanderspoel, 1995, 87–8.

Was Themistius really as disinterested in worldly advancement as a true philosopher should have been?

In 383/4, Themistius finally accepted the urban prefecture from the Emperor Theodosius, an office he had conspicuously refused under Valens. His acceptance of this high office with all its privileges gave new life to old claims that Themistius was not a true philosopher.[40] Nor was prefectural office an isolated blemish on an otherwise untarnished record of unworldliness. Themistius' carefully worded denials of the 350s make it clear that he had accepted *some* gifts from Constantius II, together with part of his professorial salary.[41] He also carefully pointed out that Constantius had offered to give him *anything* he might want: thus emphasising the extent of the emperor's regard for him. Nor was Themistius averse to dwelling – in letters and speeches – on other marks of imperial favour, particularly invitations to travel and dine with the Emperors Constantius and Valens.[42] In a court-dominated political world, access to the emperor was jealously sought and guarded as the route to preferment. Themistius' less formal rewards were thus nonetheless real and recognised as such by his contemporaries. On hearing of his friend's presence at Constantius' dining table, Libanius wrote,

> your presence at table denotes a greater intimacy, that your pro-
> fessions arise from concern for your friends, that anyone you
> mention is immediately better off, and that his pleasure in grant-
> ing such favours exceeds yours in receiving them (*Ep.* 66.2 trans.
> Norman, 1992, as *Ep.* 52).

The equation between access and power could not be more clearly stated.

Other successes were still more tangible. Themistius entered the Senate of Constantinople as a direct result of imperial favour. This was something of which he was obviously proud. The survival of Constantius' letter of adlection among manuscripts of Themistius' speeches suggests that he placed it among them himself, and we also know that he sent copies of the letter to Libanius and other friends in

40  On this tenure of office, its benefits, and the quarrels it provoked, see further Chapter 5.

41  Themistius' wording esp. in *Or.* 23 was so evasive that it has been thought that he turned down all the perquisites of his professorship, but the speech does eventually make clear that this was not the case. See the introduction to *The Letter of Constantius* in Chapter 2.

42  Constantius: Chapter 2. Valens: *Or.* 34.xiii with attendant notes: Chapter 5.

Antioch.[43] Such imperial letters were themselves marks of favour, and
Themistius went on to receive more. The refused prefecture under
Valens was clearly the occasion of another such missive (*Or.* 34.xiii),
and a law of Constantius II on admissions to the Senate of Constantinople, likewise singled out Themistius for special mention (*C. Th.*
6.4.12). In similar vein, Constantius also raised a statue to Themistius.
Both the fact of the statue, and the verses which adorned it, were again
mentioned by Themistius to Libanius, and no doubt to other acquaintances as well. Libanius duly asked to see a copy of the verses,
mentioning in the same letter that Themistius had dropped hints as to
their nature in a letter to another Antiochene rhetor, Eudaemon.[44]

Equally public and equally grand was the political profile he developed under Constantius II, once he had become a member of the Senate
of Constantinople.[45] Themistius not only led embassies to various
emperors on its behalf (see below), but also played a prominent role in
what was clearly a major senatorial expansion. In 358/9, Themistius
toured some of the leading cities of the eastern Mediterranean looking
for suitable recruits. After this expansion, Themistius became a standing
member of the committee to vet further candidates for admission. He
would later claim to have been personally responsible for expanding
membership of the senate from three hundred to two thousand. This
probably represents the total expansion of the senatorial order in his lifetime, rather than those he personally recruited in 358/9, but many
Constantinopolitan senators clearly owed their elevation at least in part
to Themistius' support,[46] and the whole enterprise made him a man to
cultivate. A letter of Libanius from this period pictured Themistius
sleeping gently on the riverbank, while senatorial fish landed themselves
(*Ep.* 86 trans. Norman, 1992, as *Ep.* 44).

Themistius was also, of course, a teacher of philosophy, running his
own school in Constantinople. How should we envisage this establish-

43  Libanius, *Ep.* 434 (trans. Norman, 1992, as *Ep.* 12). The fact that the letter has a rubric
may suggest that it was included in the early collection of his own speeches that Themistius
presented to the library of Constantinople: see the introduction to *Or.* 1.
44  *Ep.* 66.5–6. Themistius eventually enjoyed two honorific statues: *Or.* 34.xiii.
45  Vanderspoel, 1995, 68–9, 105–6, suggests that he also became *princeps senatus* at this
point, but we would argue for a different interpretation of *Or.* 34.xiii, the passage in question. See Chapter 5.
46  The claim is made at *Or.* 34.xiii. Themistius recruited 6 out of 30 new senators who
appeared in the letters of Libanius c.359/61: Petit, 1957, 349–54. See further Chapter 2.

ment? From the pseudo-Julianic letters to Iamblichus, and Iamblichus' own letters to his more worldly pupils, it clearly remained customary in the fourth century for rich young men of the Greek east, while preparing themselves for a career in public service, to pursue at least a little philosophy. Philosophy was seen as a standard part of the preparation for such a career, and was not studied merely by Neoplatonic devotees.[47] The point can be illustrated, perhaps, by some recent archaeological discoveries at Aphrodisias. Within the ruins of the late Roman city have been found the remains of what would appear to have been the school of a teacher of philosophy. Its physical layout is very striking. The establishment was designed around a central apse in which were set two pairs of shield-portraits representing famous political leaders and the philosophical tutors with whom they were associated: Socrates and Alcibiades, Aristotle and Alexander. Other evidence suggests that this was a school dedicated to mystical Neoplatonism, but, even here, more than mere lip service was being paid to the importance of philosophy in the training of young men for a career in public life. A greater number of the fee-paying pupils who supported the establishment, one imagines, came for lessons in practical philosophy than for unworldly speculation, so that even a dedicated Neoplatonist needed to uphold the more general educational purposes of Hellenic philosophy.[48]

This would have been still more true of the school of Themistius, who, after Aristotle, consistently asserted the importance of philosophy as a practical discipline. Leading philosophers, paired with their most famous pupils, the direct verbal echo of the portrait pairs from Aphrodisias, formed a recurrent image in Themistius' speeches.[49] As Themistius' personal prominence grew, so must have his attractiveness as a teacher for young men with an eye to their futures. Again, however, the demands of his public image meant that Themistius had to be careful.

47 Cf. the comments of Dillon after Brown, 1980, 23–4.

48 On this school, see Smith, 1990 (with extensive illustrations and plans); among other shield portraits were two of the main Neoplatonic saints, Pythagoras and Apollonius of Tyana.

49 *Or.* 5.63d: Augustus and Arius; Tiberius and Thrasylus; Trajan and Dio; the 2 Antonines and Epictetus. *Or.* 11.145b: Philip and Aristotle; Alexander and Xenocrates; Augustus and Arius; Trajan and Dio; Tiberius and Thrasylus; Marcus Aurelius and Sextus; Diocletian and a Byzantine philosopher (the 2 Antonines and Epictetus are omitted). *Or.* 34.viii (in the context of a different argument): Alexander and Aristotle; Augustus and Arius; Scipio and Panaetius; Tiberius and Thrasylus.

Another traditional attribute of the sophist was a desire to profit from
rich students. Hence, in defending himself in the mid-350s, Themistius
took care to point out that he did not press his students for fees.[50] It was
in this era too that a philosopher of Sicyon, possibly a student of Iamblichus, transferred his entire school to Constantinople. Questioning the
oracle of Apollo, he had received the answer that Themistius was the
wisest man of his day, and promptly acted on the information. In 359,
likewise, Celsus, a former student of the same philosopher, moved to
Constantinople to enrol in its senate and study with Themistius.
Throughout this time, the Aristotelian *Paraphrases* had been circulating
in Hellenic educational circles; it was their arrival in Sicyon which
prompted the philosopher's transfer.[51] As the case of Celsus makes
clear, Themistius certainly continued to teach philosophy after he
became a senator of Constantinople in 355, when his increasing prominence attracted a host of pupils.

Themistius' own letters, unfortunately, have not survived. The ghost
of one of them was written into the margin beside its appropriate counterpart among Libanius' letters in the *Codex Berolinensis*.[52] From
Themistius' pen, therefore, we do not have the extensive collection of
approaches to possible patrons for favours, and endless letters of recommendation for pupils and other acquaintances, such as form the back-
bone of other contemporary books of letters, especially those of
Symmachus and Libanius himself. That Themistius played such roles,
and hence would have written such letters, is entirely clear, however,
from the forty or so surviving letters written to him by Libanius, and
two from Gregory Nazianzen. These demonstrate that Themistius used
his increasing prominence in Constantinople to function as a patronage
broker of considerable influence. Not surprisingly, the earlier letters –
from the first half of the 350s – show a marked tendency to enlist Themistius' aid for men with similar cultural interests to himself: rhetors and
other Hellenic intellectuals who wanted to move their teaching interests

50 *Or.* 23.288c–294c. See further the introduction to *The Letter of Constantius* in
Chapter 2.
51 *Paraphrases* and philosopher: Themistius *Or.* 23.294d–296b. Celsus: Libanius, *Ep.*
86. See Vanderspoel, 1987a, 1995, 84, for the suggestion that the philosopher was Hierius,
a former student of Iamblichus.
52 Libanius, *Ep.* 241 (both trans. Norman, 1992, as *Ep.* 42): that it survives alongside the
appropriate letter of Libanius perhaps indicates that it was preserved only among the latter's correspondence.

to Constantinople, or try alternative careers as imperial civil servants.[53] In the later 350s, Libanius started to write to him on matters to do with the Senate of Constantinople. Their precise nature is worth a little comment. Libanius clearly perceived Themistius as able and willing to use his influence to fix the election expenses of friends and acquaintances, so that they could enter the senate at reduced cost. Themistius was thus worldly enough to engage in a little manipulative corruption.[54] Beyond such specific matters, we also find Libanius approaching Themistius more generally as a patron: to arrange introductions, or provide help with legal matters of one kind or another.[55]

By the later fourth century, emperors were fulminating against abuses of normal practices of recommendation (*suffragium*), whereby patrons charged fees for effecting introductions.[56] We cannot know whether Themistius charged fees for his introductions, or even if he made much money from students' fees. These possibilities should not be discarded out of hand, however, and, in general terms, the imprint of his power as a social fixer could hardly be clearer. Privileged access to a series of emperors attracted a host of requests and suitors. Indeed, to have been surrounded by a flock of young men who were themselves going places would have further enhanced Themistius' personal prestige. Even before he finally accepted the urban prefecture from the Emperor Theodosius in 383/4, therefore, Themistius was the recipient of very real rewards. A leading senator of Constantinople, he undertook important public embassies on this institution's behalf, enjoyed access to the persons of various emperors, who granted him major marks of public distinction, and was given jobs which brought in their wake extensive powers of patronage. His carefully crafted public image – the independent philosopher – meant that Themistius could not be seen to enjoy public office or a state salary. These limitations did not act as a real barrier to the acquisition of power and influence, however, nor, probably, to wealth either, although there is no very substantial documentary evidence to work with on this point.

53  Gregory Nazianzen, *Ep.* 48; Libanius, *Epp.* 77, 301, 364, 368, 483, 575, 1452.

54  *Epp.* 70 (cf. 99 and 252) for Olympius; 86 for Celsus; 40 for Julianus. The repetitive pattern of Libanius' requests surely indicates that Themistius did indeed organise favours of this kind.

55  Introductions: Libanius, *Epp.* 291, 62, 55, 1186. Legal matters: *Epp.* 68/91, 117, 664, 1495.

56  On *suffragium* and its abuses, see Jones, 1964, 391–9.

If the rewards of Themistius' chosen path were thus enormous, so were its potential dangers. Political influence was a highly valued commodity, which could not but attract jealousy. Eunapius recounts the career of another philosopher, Sopater. Coming to the court of the Emperor Constantine in the 320s, Sopater achieved great prominence and influence for a time, but was eventually brought low by a hostile clique of jealous courtiers led by the Praetorian Prefect Ablabius. He was eventually executed (*Lives of the Sophists* 462–3). Themistius faced at least the danger of a similar fate. Late Roman politics was played for high stakes, with death a not unusual consequence of failure.[57] Another type of failure is represented by the rhetor Himerius. Briefly prominent under the Emperor Julian, he then faded into obscurity.[58] Maintaining pre-eminence for over thirty years under a variety of regimes, without generating either sufficient hatred or boredom to cause one's downfall, was an extraordinary feat.

In part, this was surely due to a range of important friends, whose assistance, at appropriate moments, Themistius readily acknowledged. In Oration 16, he recalled that Saturninus, consul for 383, had for thirty years been his friend and supporter.[59] More generally, the speeches throw up echoes of the determination with which Themistius had to fight his corner over his many years in the limelight. As we shall see in more detail later, Themistius' career faced one moment of particular crisis: its relative eclipse under Julian. In this reign, a different group of Hellenic intellectuals – Neoplatonist theurgists, especially Maximus of Ephesus – usurped Themistius' position close to the reigning emperor.[60] Once Julian was dead, Themistius took the opportunity to signal forcefully in his first speeches for both Jovian and Valens that, thanks to these emperors' actions, 'proper' philosophy (i.e. himself) was now re-established at court. An upstart, indeed fraudulent opposition had been routed.[61] Over time, Themistius' speeches displayed an increasing tendency to self-assertion. Many of his later offerings contained some reminder to their audience of Themistius' high standing with the reigning

---

57 Cf. the Chalcedon trials under Julian which saw the purge of many of the chief administrators of Constantius, or the destruction, after Valentinian's death, of the Pannonian faction who had dominated his later years: respectively Matthews, 1989, ch. 6; 1975, ch. 3.

58 Barnes, 1987.

59 *Or.* 16.200b (Chapter 4); cf. *Or.* 1.17b–18b (Chapter 2).

60 See Chapter 3.

61 *Or.* 5.63c–d; *Or.* 6.73b–c; see further Chapter 3.

emperor. Oration 8, for instance, referred obliquely to criticism aimed in his direction, and went on to stress how much the Emperor Valens, who was under no obligation to do so, valued Themistius' advice. It finished by referring to the tutorship over Valens' son which Themistius now exercised.[62] In later years, Themistius was careful to mention that he was playing a similar role for Theodosius' son Arcadius (*Or.* 16.213a–b). While friends such as Saturninus were no doubt important, the speeches show that Themistius had, throughout his career, firmly nailed his flag to the imperial mast. Anyone attacking him knew that they might also be considered to have attacked the emperor(s) who valued him so highly.[63] Proximity to a succession of emperors was the underlying basis of Themistius' prolonged success, and he was not afraid to flaunt it.

Set in context, Themistius' speeches and Libanius' letters allow us to penetrate some way beyond the bland façade of the truth-telling, independent philosopher which their author so carefully erected. A little gentle probing reveals the determined careerist with an interesting rhetorical angle to exploit in the fact that, as a philosopher, he had to tell the truth. On the basis of his philosophical credentials, Themistius strove most successfully to stay atop the greasy pole for over thirty years. Unable, because of the need to live up to his image, to take formal office, his success depended entirely on close personal ties to a series of emperors. But this does not yet get us to the heart of Themistius' extraordinary success. Rather, it merely redefines the question. Why did a whole sequence of emperors find him such an attractive addition to their regimes?

## THE USEFULNESS OF PHILOSOPHY

The adoption of a rhetorical format which departed from Menander Rhetor's *basilikos logos* did not prevent Themistius from flattering his imperial subjects. While discussing the philosophical virtues which would make for an ideal ruler in Oration 1, for instance, Themistius nevertheless exploited most of the usual encomiastic photo opportunities: Constantius' ancestry, his looks, his personal physical accomplishments in martial arts and so on (e.g. *Or.* 1.1b, 8b etc.). More

62  *Or.* 8. esp. 119d–120b: trans. at Heather and Matthews, 1991, 35–6.
63  See esp. but not uniquely *Or.* 34.i and Themistius' defence of his urban prefecture in Chapter 5.

generally, Themistius' stress on philosophical principle was in practice an alternative encomiastic strategy, not an entirely different enterprise. Viewed through Themistius' lens, every emperor, at least while alive, turned out, coincidentally, to conform to the successive images of the ideal ruler which our hero constructed from the works of Plato and Aristotle. Constantius II was such an ideal ruler in Orations 1 to 4, Jovian and Valens both proved to be, as we shall see, in Orations 5 and 6, and Theodosius was even more ideal, especially in Oration 34.[64]

No doubt this was all very pleasing to the emperors concerned. But the appeal of being praised in a new fashion must quickly have lost its novelty. Nor, one imagines, can Themistius' tenaciously maintained claim to truth-telling have been sufficient guarantee, after a while, that the current emperor really was a philosophical ideal incarnate. Credibility was a major problem facing imperial speechwriters. Justifications of imperial policy in set-piece speeches, delivered on ceremonial occasions, were a constant feature of court life, and some contemporaries were aware that they were not straightforwardly truthful. Cassius Dio, senator and *assessor* of the Emperor Severus, in a passage specifically referring to foreign affairs, was already pointing up the problem in the third century:

> After [the establishment of the Empire], most things that happened began to be kept secret . . . and even though some things are made public, they are distrusted because they cannot be verified; it is suspected that everything is said and done with reference to the wishes of the men in power at the time and their associates.

In the later fourth century, Augustine made the same point in a retrospective account of the occasion on which he had been invited to deliver a panegyric while teaching in Milan.[65] Themistius' pose as truth-teller *extraordinaire* might initially have done something to allay such doubts, and was certainly meant to, but its effectiveness can only have diminished over time. He was already facing challenges to his self-proclaimed honesty, for instance, by the mid-350s. An important passage of Julian's *Letter to Themistius* can only be read as a sarcastic, or at least teasing, response to Themistius' claims to particular truthfulness:

---

64  *Or.* 13 argued that the same was also true of the young Emperor Gratian.
65  Dio, *Roman History* 59.19.3 (quoted in Millar, 1982, 2); Augustine, *Confessions* 6.6.9.

> You say that God has placed me in the same position as Heracles
> and Dionysus of old who, being at once philosophers and kings,
> purged almost the whole earth and sea of the evils that infested
> them . . . .When I read these words I was almost dumbfounded;
> for on the one hand I was sure that it was unlawful for you as a
> philosopher to flatter or deceive; on the other hand I am fully con-
> scious that by nature there is nothing remarkable about me –
> there never was from the first nor has there to be now . . . (*Letter
> to Themistius* 253c–254b, trans. Wright, Loeb)

At precisely the same moment, considerable doubt was also being raised
over the other important claim Themistius derived from his philosophical pose, namely that he was detached and uninterested in worldly
self-advancement.[66] By themselves, therefore, neither rhetorical novelty
nor an inherently greater credibility will explain Themistius' long-term
success. The potential of both was draining away by the mid-350s.

In Hellenic cultural tradition, the philosopher was the defender *par
excellence* of the correct values imparted by a traditional education
(*paideia*). He was the ultimate intellectual, called in at moments of high
political drama to identify and defeat the forces of evil: very much the
territory of Zola and *J'accuse*. In particular, cities had long employed
philosophers for difficult embassies to Roman emperors, when some
unwelcome truth had to be spelled out, exploiting their traditional right
to freedom of speech (*parrhesia*), their own personal bravery (*karteria*),
and the greater tolerance that an emperor was expected to show them
(see above). These traditions had not yet lost their force in Themistius'
day. Eunapius could plausibly present the philosopher Sopater as
improving, by influence and argument, the character of the Emperor
Constantine, and Himerius likewise claimed that Hermogenes moder-
ated the faults of Gallus Caesar some thirty years later. In the 370s, likewise, the cities of Epirus chose the philosopher Iphicles to brave the
legendary anger of the Emperor Valentinian I, and expose the corrupt
mismanagement of Illyricum by its Praetorian Prefect, Petronius
Probus.[67]

Themistius' self-presentation exploited these traditions in a variety of
ways. *Parrhesia* figures in the speeches, on occasion, as a technical term,

---

66 See Chapter 2.
67 Sopater: *Lives of the Sophists* 462. Hermogenes: Barnes, 1987. Iphicles: Ammianus
30.5.8–10; cf. Brown, 1980; 1992, chs 1–2.

and it was precisely in a further dimension of this image that much of
Themistius' usefulness for his imperial employers lay. All of the
emperors to whom Themistius was close – Constantius, Jovian, Valens,
and Theodosius I – were Christians, even if some pursued more aggressively Christianising policies than others.[68] Many of the local landowning elites who ran the eastern Empire for them, however, remained
Hellenic pagans. The pace of religious conversion is difficult to judge,
but it is probably significant that only in the later 380s did Christians in
the Theodosian regime feel strong enough to start destroying pagan
temples in substantial numbers. This is particularly associated with the
praetorian prefecture of Maternus Cynegius, who seems to have been
acting at least in part on personal initiative in encouraging bands of
monks to destroy pagan shrines.[69] Likewise, it was only from the 390s
that aggressively anti-pagan legislation started excluding non-Christians
from imperial service.[70] Before this date, the experience of Julian's reign
had led first Jovian, and then Valentinian and Valens towards policies of
religious toleration in the 360s and 370s. Even as late as 384, the pagan
senator Symmachus and Bishop Ambrose of Milan could both plausibly
claim that their co-religionists represented majority opinion in the
Roman senate.[71]

The essential pattern of Themistius' career can be characterised,
therefore, as one where a self-styled Hellenic philosopher served a
succession of Christian emperors, who ruled their empire via substantially non-Christian local landowning elites. The active participation in
local government of these elites, it must be stressed, was critical to the
accomplishment of such vital state functions as taxation and law and
order. The late Roman state was in some ways highly centralised, but,
equally important, covered vast areas of territory on the basis of pre-
industrial communications. In emergencies, messages could be transmitted at speeds of over two hundred kilometres per day via relays of
galloping horsemen. Any large-scale response to such messages, in
terms, say, of troops in the case of frontier problems, was limited to

68  Themistius spoke with much greater freedom about religious toleration before Jovian
than he did before Valens, even though both regimes pursued policies of legal toleration: see
Chapter 3.
69  Matthews, 1975, 140–2; cf. Matthews, 1967.
70  For a survey, Fowden, 1978.
71  Symmachus, *Relatio* 3; Ambrose, *Ep.* 18; cf. Matthews, 1975, 203ff. For further discussion of the pace of conversion, see the introduction to Chapter 2.

steady walking pace (both of men and of the oxen used to draw wagons), and more routine governmental business was generally conducted by officials who moved around at about forty kilometres per day.[72] In an Empire stretching from Hadrian's Wall to the Euphrates, such speeds of communication could not but hamper the exercise of central control, and some areas were even out of reach for large parts of the year. North Africa (admittedly a special case) was routinely cut off from Italy between November and March when sailing conditions were adverse. In such circumstances, much power had to be devolved to men of local influence, who, in cooperation with local imperial officials (often recruited from the same peer group), allocated and raised taxes in their cities, and assisted provincial governors in the administration of justice.[73]

Building a partnership with such men was crucial to the enduring success of any regime, for they were often insulated by distance from immediate central control. If something was perceived to have gone wrong at the local level, the imperial centre could mobilise an apparatus of enquiry, but this was a lengthy procedure, and chains of political connection might still protect local and regional powerbrokers. A worst-case scenario is provided by the troubles of Lepcis in North Africa. Here, a dispute between local and regional authorities over the financing of a military campaign which had begun in 363 was only finally resolved after 375, despite a number of intervening and brutal enquiries ordered by the Emperor Valentinian, whose ability to get at the truth was effectively blocked (Ammianus 28.6). In such circumstances, the opinion of local landowners, allied to their willing participation in imperial administrative structures did matter, and much effort was deployed by emperors to establish good relations with them.[74]

Against this backdrop, Themistius' participation in a Christian-led regime carried something of a talismanic quality. For a whole series of Christian emperors, employing Themistius affirmed a commitment to continuity – vital for attracting elite support – in the midst of cultural transformation. As a philosopher, he was the guardian of traditional

72 Important messages: Ramsay, 1925. Routine business: the Theophanes Archive in Roberts and Turner, 1952, esp. 105–7.

73 For a general introduction to these matters, see Jones, 1964, chs 13–14.

74 The works of John Matthews have been devoted to the functioning of the late Roman Empire through networks of personal connection. Further aspects of government are discussed in Wickham, 1984; Heather, 1994. On Theodosius and these elites at the start of his reign, see Chapter 4.

*paideia*. If he could speak in favour of a particular Christian emperor, and if that emperor was happy to favour him, this sent an important signal to Hellenic elites. Whatever worrying cultural novelties that Christian ruler might have introduced, he nevertheless continued to support traditional values to the extent that an old-fashioned philosopher, the guarantor of *paideia*, could both find him praiseworthy and be treated respectfully by him in turn.

This imparting of cultural reassurance shows up very clearly in the speeches. Rather than simply avoiding religion and other potentially contentious cultural matters, Themistius took a much bolder line. Christianity may have had non-Hellenic origins, but, by the fourth century, a long dialogue with Mediterranean culture had led to considerable syncretism. Platonism had fundamentally shaped both Christianity's theological doctrines and the language in which they were expressed, and, over the centuries, commentators had established and extended the common ground, in moral and other teachings, between Christianity and traditional Hellenic *paideia*. Throughout his career, Themistius rooted himself firmly in this middle ground, stressing what was shared by both the new and the old. Even *philanthropia* – for Themistius the imperial virtue *par excellence* – had, by the mid-fourth century, become a term common both to Christians and non-Christians. Stressing the importance of imperial *philanthropia* was the equivalent of modern politicians saying that they believe in low inflation, low interest rates, and full employment: bland, reassuring generality.[75] Beyond his immediate impact as a speaker with greater personal credibility, a pose which was already being challenged by the mid-350s, Themistius the pagan philosopher was thus generally useful to Christian emperors as a cultural symbol. The detailed contents of the speeches indicate that Themistius also performed a highly useful function on a further, and much more specific level of political operation.

In their own lifetimes, each of Themistius' imperial patrons was compared, in turn, to a set of ideal virtues derived in some way from Plato and Aristotle, and each was found to be the personification of those virtues. Less often noticed is the fact that, after their deaths, Themistius was entirely ruthless, whatever favours he may previously

75 Glanville Downey believed, on the contrary, that *philanthropia* was Themistius' pointed counter to the claims of Christian tradition, but this is unsustainable: see the introduction to Chapter 2.

have received from them, in pointing out, explicitly or implicitly, the same emperors' faults. Constantius II was primarily responsible for Themistius' rise to prominence, and, while he lived, Themistius professed to see in him the ideal philosopher king. After the emperor's death, however, Orations 5 and 6 identified a number of Constantian deficiencies. The fact that taxes had risen under his rule, his involvement in the dynastic bloodbath which had followed the death of his father Constantine in 337 (*Or.* 6.74b–c), and his paranoiac inability to share power on a reasonable basis (76a–b) all received considerable attention. During his lifetime, Valens was likewise an epitome of virtue. When Themistius reconsidered Valens in the time of Theodosius, however, his lack of proper experience in public office prior to his imperial promotion was now portrayed, despite previous explicit remarks to the contrary, as the major hindrance to the success of his rule.[76] Examples can be multiplied. Although Themistius was not so closely associated with the Emperor Julian, he did compose a panegyric to him, probably in honour of his consulship on 1 January 363. It has unfortunately not survived.[77] Orations 5 and 6 were at points heavily critical of Julian and his policies, especially on the religious front (Chapter 3). Gratian too, the ideal ruler of Oration 13 given in 376/7, came in for rather more dismissive treatment between 379 and 383 in Orations 14, 15, and 16 (Chapter 4). Undiluted praise of emperors in their own lifetimes, therefore, was matched by equally pointed critiques after their deaths.

On the most basic level, this readiness to be economical with his loyalties was absolutely necessary to Themistius' developing career. It allowed him to navigate from one regime to another, as different emperors came and went. Savaging dead friends also added some credibility to his stance as a truth-teller. Themistius claimed to tell the unvarnished truth at all times, but truth-tellers in autocracies do not have a great life expectancy. Standing up in front of Constantius II in all his pomp, and telling him to his face that he was a fratricide comparable to the sons of Oedipus, or Valens that he was an overpromoted nobody, would have generated an exciting, but brief, political career. In such contexts, telling the truth after the event is about the best that anyone

76  Valens alive: e.g., *Or.* 8.112d–113c. Posthumous criticism: *Or.* 15. esp. 196–197a; *Or.* 16. esp. 205d–206c (both trans. in Chapter 4).

77  Not, at least, in its original form; an Arabic translation perhaps survives: see Chapter 3.

could be expected to do, and probably went some way, in his audience's minds, to substantiating the claims Themistius made about his credibility. The parallel comes to mind of Khrushchev's famous denunciation of Stalin at the Twentieth Congress of the Communist Party of the Soviet Union in February 1956, nearly three years after the latter's death. Such a performance was quite impossible in an autocrat's own lifetime, and, even if one had previously served him and had indeed been as protege (as Khrushchev indeed was, having risen to the Politburo under Stalin's rule), some personal credit might still be gained for even a posthumous condemnation.

Turning on former patrons had more, however, than a personal significance. None of the regimes Themistius served was the product of a smooth transfer of power. Jovian had not been designated by Julian before the latter's death. The succession of Valentinian – and hence Valens – was improvised after Jovian's early and mysterious demise. Theodosius, another non-dynastic successor, was promoted only because Valens was killed by the Goths at Hadrianople. In such circumstances, these new regimes had to establish themselves in part by justifying the political discontinuity they represented. For these emperors, it was extremely useful for a known adherent of the previous regime, who was also a self-styled teller of the unvarnished truth, to damn in public some central aspect of the previous political order. Again a parallel with Khrushchev might be helpful. His 'secret' speech to the Congress was the most dramatic break with the past, but more or less explicit attacks on Stalin – under the code of attacking the misuse of a cult of personality – were made by all the main contenders for power after Stalin's death. These began within a month of the dictator's death in March 1953, and were mounted even by Beria, Stalin's chief executioner, in the months before his own fall in July 1953. All of these figures were aiming to sell themselves as candidates for supreme power by identifying a major problem in the old order which they would rectify. Placed in context, Themistius' posthumous critiques of dead imperial patrons can be seen to have served the same function. Indeed, the closer one looks at the speeches, the harder it becomes to avoid the conclusion that all their substantive contents were dictated by the immediate needs of current rulers. The most notorious example of this phenomenon is Themistius' treatment, in Oration 5, of Jovian's peace with the Persians in 363. This was a total disaster for the Roman state, yet, in a speech celebrating Jovian's consulship on 1 January 364, Themistius stood up and claimed it as a Roman victory, as Jovian's regime was itself trying to do. No other ancient commentator saw the peace as anything other than a calamity. The correspondence between the argument of Themistius' speech and the immediate demands of the current regime could not be clearer. Themistius himself, indeed, once Jovian was safely dead, characterised the peace as a defeat that needed reversing.[78]

The speeches translated in this volume offer many similar examples. The difference between Themistius' characterisations of the Emperor Theodosius in Orations 14 and 15, for instance, is very striking. In the first (early summer 379), Themistius portrayed the emperor as a military hard man elevated to the purple to win the Gothic war. By the second (January 381), leadership in war had been demoted to an ancillary imperial virtue, the emperor's main job having now become sound civilian government. The likeliest explanation of this switch of emphasis is a major military reverse, which Theodosius' army had suffered at the hands of the Goths in the summer of 380. This had caused the emperor to surrender control of the war to Gratian (see Chapter 4). In Orations 6 and 8, likewise, Themistius made the best of a bad job when faced with the Emperor Valens' relative lack of experience in high public office. Valens' deep understanding of home economics was wheeled out as evidence of his suitability for the purple.[79] But once Valens was dead and his successor had contradictory requirements, then, as we have seen, Themistius portrayed this inexperience as the root cause of Valens' mistakes. Orations 14 to 16 also show that Themistius quickly became enmeshed in the complexities of Theodosius' dynastic ambitions. Gratian moved in and out of focus in these speeches, according to the extent of Theodosius' current need of his military support, while Oration 16 was brought to a close with a eulogy of Theodosius' son Arcadius. This speech was given less than three weeks before the latter's promotion to Augustus, a promotion which Gratian never sanctioned. It is extremely hard to see Oration 16's combination of emphasis on Arcadius and downplaying of Gratian as mere coincidence (see further Chapter 4).

Between the different orations, then, there are blatant inconsistencies in Themistius' treatment of the same persons, issues, and events. Since

---

78 For the details, see Chapter 3, and compare the account in *Or.* 5 with Themistius' throwaway reference at *Or.* 16.213a (Chapter 4) to a possible rescue of 'all the territory of Mesopotamia that others abandoned . . .'

79 *Or.* 6.81b–c; *Or.* 8.112d–113c.

these differences correlate with the immediate needs of current emperors, the simplest explanation is that Themistius, far from being an independent commentator on events, knew precisely what particular end(s) any given speech was required to serve. How Themistius was briefed must have changed over time. In Oration 1, he was still an outsider. Nonetheless, the points of overlap between his speech and others of Julian and Libanius to the same emperor indicate that he was praising Constantius in terms which the Constantian regime had itself defined.[80] Someone close to the emperor, therefore, had presumably given him a clear indication of at least some of the general points that should be made. This probably also applied to the speech's accounts of the latest round of warfare with the Persians and a judicial amnesty: the two specific matters which it mentioned.[81] This need not mean that the speech followed an agreed script. At the very least, however, key points must have been discussed beforehand, even if their rhetorical formulation – one might guess – was left entirely in Themistius' hands.

From the mid-350s, the procedure must have been different. As the close confidant of a sequence of emperors following his appointment to the Senate of Constantinople, Themistius presumably had some input into policy-making. As remains the case in the modern day, the need to make a policy publicly acceptable can have a substantial effect upon its content. Even if Themistius was primarily a publicist, mainly concerned with 'how' matters should be presented, this was a considerable vantage point from which to exert influence. In reflecting upon his own career, he claimed in particular to have guided some of Valens' decisions. This claim was made in the time of Theodosius, rather after the fact, so that one is initially tempted to treat it with caution.[82] There is, however, some convincing supporting evidence. Themistius spent much time with Valens in the late 360s, for instance, when the emperor was fighting a difficult Gothic campaign,[83] and was again with him at Antioch in c.375. Even more striking is Themistius' sudden dash westwards from

---

80  E.g. *Or.* 1.1b, 5b, 7c–d with footnotes in Chapter 2; cf. Vanderspoel, 1995, 79.

81  *Or.* 1.12a–c, 14c–15d. Libanius, similarly, was in communication with imperial representatives before he gave his speech to Constantius (*Or.* 59 pref.), a speech which worked hard to explain away potentially embarrassing episodes in Roman–Persian relations. Someone presumably indicated to him, therefore, which areas needed careful handling. We owe this point to Michael Whitby (pers. com.).

82  *Or.* 31.354d; cf. Vanderspoel, 1995, ch. 7.

83  See Heather and Matthews, 1991, ch. 2.

Mesopotamia to Gaul, probably in 376, as part of a vital diplomatic mission looking to negotiate military assistance from the western Emperor Gratian for dealing with the Gothic problem which had suddenly unleashed itself upon the Danube.[84] By this stage of his career, Themistius' prominence had come to place him apart from the normal run of orators giving imperial panegyrics. His uniqueness is also firmly reflected both in the large number of keynote speeches Themistius gave, and in the frequency with which he handled sensitive issues: dynastic transitions under Jovian, Valens, and Theodosius, Jovian's humiliating peace with the Persians, religious policies in the aftermath of Julian's reign, Theodosius' non-defeat of the Goths, and so on.[85]

When the orations are looked at more closely, therefore, Themistius' pose of philosophical independence quickly collapses. Apart from acting as a generally reassuring cultural talisman, he also became fully involved, over time, in the gritty matter of policy-making and its justification. Placed in context, all of his speeches can be seen to have been framed to justify current regimes and their immediate policies, often by damning predecessors who had acted differently, even if Themistius had served and praised those predecessors in their own lifetimes. The further question raised by all this, of course, is why did Themistius and his imperial employers go to so much trouble? The Late Roman Empire was an autocracy. Emperors did not have to win elections. Why was so much effort expended on justification in this kind of political system? The answer to this question lies, we would suggest, in the audience before whom Themistius performed.

## ORATOR AND AUDIENCE

Themistius' ostensible audience was usually the emperor himself. Sometimes this really was the case. The principal target for Oration 1 was Constantius II whose favour Themistius was then keen to attract (Chapter 2). It has recently been argued that this was also true of

84  For further discussion with full refs, see Chapter 4.

85  Nixon and Rodgers, 1994, 26–31, suggest that the authors of the Gallic corpus of panegyrics exercised rather more independent control over the contents of their orations than we would argue is generally the case with Themistius. This is not necessarily a contradiction. For the most part, the Gauls were speaking as political outsiders, like Themistius in Oration 1, and that speech is likewise much less politically pregnant than the later orations. The speaker's own position, therefore, may have been an important variable.

Oration 14, his first speech to the Emperor Theodosius, and, a priori, it is possible that his first speech to every new emperor had this same purpose. Apart from Oration 1, however, the contents of all of the other first speeches under new regimes – Oration 14 together with Orations 5 and 6 to Jovian and Valens respectively – suggest, as we shall see in the chapters which follow, that they were formulated at a point when Themistius was already a political insider. All three concentrated on central issues of the moment, and dealt with them in ways which suited the reigning emperor.[86] Strikingly, these speeches were never given right at the beginning of the new reigns. Themistius did not travel with the first senatorial embassy from Constantinople to Antioch, where the Emperor Jovian was residing in the summer of 363. Their first rhetorical encounter came on 1 January 364. Likewise, Themistius did not address Valens in the spring of 364, when the new emperor was appointed, but only early the following winter. Theodosius, too, was not greeted by our orator immediately upon his promotion to the purple in early 379. Oration 14 tells of an illness, which had prevented Themistius from travelling to Thessalonica before the early summer. The illness may have been genuine, but this repetitive pattern of delay is of some importance. At the start of Jovian's reign, Libanius described Themistius being courted by 'all the powerful men'.[87] Like the actual contents of the orations, this pattern of delay suggests that Themistius unfolded his philosophy to new imperial patrons only *after* negotiations had already established the basic parameters of their relationship. Although personally addressed, the relevant emperors were thus apparently not the prime audience for Orations 5, 6, and 14. Only in Oration 1 does there seem any real chance that we are seeing the young Themistius baiting his rhetorical hook in the hope of reeling in an emperor.[88]

86 Themistius' outsider status at the moment of delivery of *Or.* 14 has been argued by Errington, 1996b. Both the martial presentation of Theodosius and its guarded remarks about Gratian indicate to us, however, that it was the speech of an insider: see the introduction to *Or.* 14 in Chapter 4. *Or.* 5 concentrated on Jovian's elevation, his 'successful' peace with Persia and the importance of a tolerant religious policy. *Or.* 6 was in large measure a sustained attempt to show that the splitting of the empire between Valentinian and Valens would not, as so often in the past, generate civil war. On these two speeches and the relevance of their themes to Jovian and Valens, see Chapter 3.

87 Libanius *Ep.* 1455; see further Chapter 3.

88 It is also far from impossible, of course, that *Or.* 1 had been preceded by some form of direct or indirect contact between emperor and orator. Our knowledge of Themistius' biography is too sketchy to be certain that he ambushed the emperor cold.

If Themistius' audience was not primarily the emperor in these and his other speeches, who was it? After 355, when he became a member, many of his speeches were either given before the Senate of Constantinople, or in the course of embassies conducted on its behalf. As such, the contents of these speeches, even when given away from the city, would have been made known to its senate. Oration 5, addressed to Jovian at Ancyra, was given a second reading in Constantinople (Socrates, *Ecclesiastical History* 3.26), and this may well have been true of the others not originally delivered in the capital. To understand the nature and importance of the orations, therefore, it is necessary to understand the distinctive character of this body. In its mid-fourth-century form, it was a relatively new foundation, the old curia of Byzantium having been re-established by the Emperor Constantine, when he refounded the city as Constantinople. It was perhaps only in the reign of Constantius that its members were all given the same status – *clarissimi* – as their counterparts in Rome; originally many had been somewhat less distinguished *clari*. In the mid to late 350s, as we have seen, Constantius greatly expanded its numbers, recruiting from richer curials of the east, and continuing his father's policies of granting senatorial status to increasing numbers of high-level civilian and military functionaries. He also brought to a conclusion the processes by which senators of Rome resident in the east relocated to Constantinople. By c.360, the senate had thus come to be composed of senior and retired imperial functionaries, civilian and military, and a substantial cross-section of the richer landowners of the eastern Mediterranean. A considerable overlap already existed between these two groups, in any case, because local landowners (former curials or decurions) had been moving out of their town councils and into imperial service for the past generation or two, attracted by the increasing advantages of the many new careers which were opening up in the bureaucracy. Between c.250 and 400 AD, the number of attractive jobs in the imperial bureaucracy increased from about two hundred and fifty overall to at least three thousand per generation in each half of the Empire, a twenty-fold increase. Most of this massive recruitment had been made from among the curial classes. As the fourth century progressed, most of these careers in imperial administration brought either senior equestrian status (the *perfectissimate*) or, increasingly, senatorial rank, at the very latest upon retirement.[89]

89 See further Dagron, 1974; Chastagnol, 1982; Heather, 1994 and below Chapter 2.

The new senators did not lose contact with the home provinces from which they had come. After the riot of the statues in 387, for instance, and again when advancing the claims of his friend Thalassius, Libanius mobilised support among Constantinopolitan senators of Antiochene origin.[90] The letters of the Cappadocian fathers, likewise, are full of requests for help to great imperial functionaries, several of whom had Cappadocian origins. Here, common origin provided the starting point of the relationship which the requests exploited.[91] More local imperial officials might also have links to provincial society. It also seems to have been not uncommon for men to govern their home province, a career pattern which transformed but did not break off the operation of linkages in local landowning societies.[92] Such interconnections – based on travel, letter writing, marriage, and peripatetic study – provided the wiring through which the 'conductivity' (as Peter Brown once labelled it) of the landowning classes of the eastern Mediterranean flowed: their ability to act over vast distances as a surprisingly homogeneous group of opinion.[93] The body assembled in Constantinople by the Emperor Constantius thus represented a fair cross-section of the upper echelons of the landowning, tax-paying, tax-gathering, and locally dominant opinion by whom and for whom the Empire was run, a cross-section which maintained strong ties to the local political communities from which they had, at this point, only recently emerged.

In his speeches, Themistius often portrayed himself as championing senatorial opinion to the emperor. In Oration 16, for instance, he stated that the senate only kept him at its head for his speeches (200a–c). On many occasions, however, the contents and contexts of the speeches demonstrate that Themistius was in practice doing quite the opposite:

90  387: Libanius *Or.* 20.37 (cf. 22.33). For Thalassius, Libanius mobilised twelve senators of Antiochene origin: Petit, 1957, 350–1.

91  Basil of Caesarea's main court contacts were both natives of Caesarea: Sophronius (*Magister Officiorum* and Urban Prefect of Constantinople: *Epp.* 32, 75, 96, 177, 192, 273) and Aburgius (Praetorian Prefect of the Orient: *Epp.* 33, 75, 147, 178, 196). After his time as bishop in Constantinople, Gregory Nazianzen had a wider range of contacts: *Epp.* 93–7 (to different friends after his return home); cf. 128–30, 132–4, 136–7, 168–70.

92  Inscriptions from Aphrodisias record the local roots of numerous late antique governors of Caria: Roueché, 1989, nos. 7, 24, 32, 38–40, 53–4, 66 (the latter honouring Aphrodisias as his father's homeland).

93  The interconnections of eastern elites still await the kind of treatment provided for the west by Matthews, 1975. For some introductory thoughts, see Heather, 1994; or, from a different angle, Brown, 1976.

advocating the virtues of established imperial policy to the senate. It was, of course, not other senators, but the Emperor Constantius II, who had appointed Themistius to the senate in the first place, and it was the favour of subsequent emperors which maintained his pre-eminence. Such a conclusion should not, therefore, in general terms, provoke too much surprise. To cite some specific examples: it was not Jovian who needed to be convinced of the virtues of the – in fact humiliating – peace agreement of 363 in Oration 5, but the tax-payers of the cities of the east, among whom there had already been open dissent (Zosimus 3.34.3). Or again, in the case of Oration 16, it was not Theodosius, but elite opinion, which needed reassuring that the Gothic peace of 382, a marked departure from normal Roman expectations of victory over 'barbarians', was a 'good thing'.[94]

These are perhaps the most blatant instances where Themistius was clearly attempting to sell an item of imperial policy to the senate, rather than representing senatorial opinion to the emperor. The number of documentable instances, however, where Themistius was advocating either established imperial policy, or placing an interpretation on past events which suited the needs of the current regime, is, as we have seen, very large. In doing so, he was ready to play rhetorical tricks. From the time of Jovian onwards, Themistius often cast elements of his speeches as pleas to the emperor in support of the case he was making. In speeches translated for this volume, he made pleas for religious toleration in Oration 5, for good relations between Valens and his brother in Oration 6, and for more senators for Constantinople in Oration 14. On the face of it, such pleas were apparently designed to convince somebody to do something that they were not already doing. Hence it has recently been argued that they should be understood as direct attempts on Themistius' part to influence imperial policy-making. This is the point, it is claimed, where the orator stuck his head above the parapet to make the points that really mattered to him.[95]

But some of these pleas, at least, cannot be taken at face value. By the time Themistius addressed Jovian on the subject, the emperor had

94 On these cases, see further Chapters 3 and 4.
95 The view of Vanderspoel, 1995, esp. 148–53 (on Jovian and religious toleration). Similar too is Dagron, 1968, 95–112, and Daly, 1972 on *Orr.* 8 and 10. These speeches refer to a senatorial embassy led by Themistius to Valens which attempted to persuade him to halt the war of 367–9 with the Goths.

already passed a measure of religious toleration which encompassed non-Christians (see Chapter 3). It was not Jovian, therefore, who needed to be persuaded of the virtues of religious toleration. Likewise, there is not the slightest sign that any substantial tension ever hampered relations between Valens and his brother (Chapter 3). The main text of Oration 14 also shows that Theodosius had already been appointing new senators for Constantinople, even before Themistius opened his mouth with the same request (Chapter 4). If emperors were already doing what Themistius wanted, what was the purpose of all this pleading?

As a rhetorical device, its main effect was to attract the audience's attention away from the emperor as the source of a given policy. If, in a formal speech delivered to an emperor, someone began to plead with him to continue what he was already doing, this planted the idea that he might not. Such a strategy might serve a variety of functions. The likeliest potential hindrance to a Christian emperor such as Jovian pursuing a policy of religious toleration was, in fact, other Christians. It was always possible that particular bishops or extreme Christian ascetics might demand that their religion's claims to uniqueness be followed through by a Christian emperor to their logical end. A case in point is Ambrose of Milan in the early 380s, who successfully deployed such arguments to prevent the Emperor Valentinian III from restoring the Altar of Victory to the Senate House in Rome.[96] Pleading for religious toleration, therefore, might have been an attempt to protect the emperor, making it easier for him to claim that, in upholding it, he was merely responding to the demands of a large body of public opinion, represented by Themistius the guardian of *paideia*. This kind of interpretation also works for the Gothic peace of 382. Once Themistius had dwelt at length on the reasons why it was such a good idea, the emperor was afforded a further defence against possible critics. The main reason for Themistius adopting a pleading tone, we would argue, was probably not to change imperial policy, but to help deflect potential criticism. Themistius' pretended independence, of course, was critical to the strategy. If he looked too much like an insider, it would have failed to have any effect.[97]

---

96 Ambrose, *Epp.* 17 and 18; cf. Matthews, 1975, 203–11; McLynn, 1994, 151–5.

97 A similar interpretation also works well in the case of Valens' first Gothic war: Heather and Matthews, 1991, ch. 2 on *Orr.* 8 and 10.

Such an interpretation of Themistius' pleas is much more plausible than envisaging him as making overt attempts, on ceremonial occasions, to change imperial policy. Policy-making in any autocracy is for most of the time carried out behind closed doors, not in the open by the casting of votes. On the face of it, the 383 round in the on-going Altar of Victory dispute was conducted in public by formal letters: one from Symmachus and two from Ambrose. In practice, however, even this dispute was mostly run by controlling access to the emperor and hence shaping the outcome of relevant imperial decision-making.[98] This was indeed generally true of the later Roman Empire where overt consensus was a prime requirement of public life, underlined both ceremonially and in communications between members of the elite.[99] As we have seen, at least under Valens, and probably earlier too, Themistius probably did become involved in formulating policy as well as justifying it. In all likelihood, however, this participation was not conducted primarily via the public speeches, but in other moments of more private consultation, which, by their nature, are hidden from us. Themistius' orations were about publicising and justifying policy, not formulating it, and, in particular, about using the Senate of Constantinople as a conduit to manipulate elite opinion across the eastern Mediterranean.

In many ways, then, the Senate of Constantinople was the key to Themistius' career as a spin doctor, the reason he put so much effort into rhetorical pyrotechnics over thirty years. Constantius II created an assembly of imperial bureaucrats and leading landowners, few of whom, at this stage in the institution's evolution, were so bound into life at Constantinople that they had lost their local roots. The existence of this body, in a general context of primitive communications, provided

98 In the earlier round under Gratian, Symmachus had been prevented by Christian courtiers from presenting the pagan viewpoint to the emperor (*Relatio* 3.1; cf. Cameron, A. D. E., 1968; McLynn, 1994, 151–2). The contents of Ambrose's first letter (*Ep.* 17, esp. 15–17: its closing appeal to Valentinian's father and brother) suggest that the same courtiers had reported the contents of Symmachus' *relatio* to the bishop, so that this was hardly an open debate. See further McLynn, 1994, 166–8, on the entirely academic nature of Ambrose, *Ep.* 18, supposedly the bishop's formal reply to Symmachus.

99 Ceremony: MacCormack, 1981; cf. Symmachus' refusal in his letters to do more than allude in an evasive manner to disputes or great events: Matthews, 1974. On policy-making in the later empire, see Brown, 1992, chs 1–2. There could be moments of dramatic public confrontation, but these were exceptional, being conducted by figures outside the body politic, whether philosophers, such as Iphicles (above note 67), or Holy Men, such as Daniel (*Life of Daniel the Stylite* 70–85) and Martin (Sulpicius Severus, *Life of Martin* 20)

emperors with the means of reaching a large percentage of the greater and lesser landowners (respectively the nobility and gentry in medieval historical terms) by and for whom the Empire was run: the former by direct communication with the senate, the wider audience via indirect diffusion from senators to their home cities.

Selling such an audience the emperor's side of the story – both in terms of the overall conduct of his regime and in the handling of particular, usually sensitive, issues – was a highly worthwhile activity. Even though the Empire was an autocracy, the political consent of these local elites mattered both for general and specific reasons. In general terms, as we have seen, there was so much inertia in a centralised governmental system operating over such distances with such (in modern terms) extremely primitive communications that local elites in practice had great autonomy. On occasion, they might be constrained into raising and paying taxes, as in the riot of statues in Antioch in 387, but using force was both inefficient and unsustainable in the longer term, its employment a sign that normal systems had broken down. Hence the Emperor Theodosius' response to the riot was reasonably conciliatory, and, generally speaking, emperors sought to get local elites to raise taxes voluntarily.[100] More specifically, discontent, especially at the top end of the elite, among men who were also involved in the bureaucratic structures of the state, could be a source of usurpation. To be successful, any usurper obviously required military forces, but non-military elites could suborn troops, and any usurping regime required the kind of funds that only the bureaucracy could raise to sustain itself beyond anything but the shortest term. One leading bureaucrat, the *Secundicerius Notariorum* Theodorus, was executed under Valens in 371/2 when a round of séances started to develop political overtones (Ammianus 29.1.8-9), and the rise to power of the Emperor Jovian involved disposing of another leading notary, the *Primicerius Notariorum* Jovian, whom some were clearly favouring for the throne (26.6.3). More generally, for all Themistius' efforts on his behalf, the Emperor Valens never successfully won over hearts and minds in Constantinople. Early in his reign, the city and

---

100  On rebuilding communication in the aftermath of the riot, see Heather 1994, 30–1. Brown, 1995, ch. 2, argues persuasively that the need to bring in the taxes was one reason why Christian emperors hesitated to constrain pagan landowners into changing religion. The need to defend divinely ordained Graeco-Roman civilisation against the threat of barbarians was the major ideological justification for the existence of taxation: Heather, 1993a; 1993b.

its senate were potent sources of support for the rebellion of Procopius, and opinion remained hostile to him down to 378, when, shortly before his death in battle at Hadrianople, his handling of the Gothic war led to open protests. Procopius was linked by marriage to the house of Constantine, and the senate, as we have seen, contained large numbers of Constantian appointees. These men would presumably have preferred some kind of dynastic continuity.[101] Emperors needed to win general support among local elites, therefore, both to make government function, and to minimise the risk of rebellion. From the late 350s, the Senate of Constantinople provided a perfect channel of communication for both of these tasks.

No doubt this audience was exploited not only by Themistius, but by other speakers as well, whose speeches do not happen to have survived. It is unlikely, however, that any of the possible rivals could have matched Themistius' remarkable range of qualifications for the job. In his case, philosophy reacted with rhetoric to produce a uniquely powerful impression upon this particular audience. He was a master of the language common to the senatorial class, and could draw on the traditional kinds of arguments and illustrations which they might find convincing. Oration 10 is a beautifully worked example. Here Themistius established the complete red herring that Valens' success in his first Gothic war (367–9) should be judged by the ending of annual payments to the Goths, identifying them as 'tribute', the paying of which was traditionally anathema to Roman opinion. The payments were in fact annual gifts, designed to help keep a subservient Gothic regime in power, and their ending signalled a greater degree of Gothic independence. The argument, however, was extremely well done, and has deceived many modern commentators. No doubt it was equally effective at the time.[102] Sometimes, of course, his efforts were less successful. No one, it seems, was taken in by claims that Jovian had in some way won the war against Persia, and Theodosius' peace with the Goths was clearly not accepted

101 Themistius gave *Or.* 6, which predated Procopius' revolt, as part of a rhetorical double act designed to win over opinion in the Constantinopolitan senate: see the introduction to this speech in Chapter 3. On Procopius' revolt and its sources of support, see Ammianus 26.6ff. with commentary in Matthews, 1989, 191–203, esp. 199–201 on Constantinian propaganda and dislike of Valens' financial policies as the main issues on which Procopius could generate support. Protests in 378: Ammianus 31.11.1; Socrates, *Ecclesiastical History* 4.38.

102 Analysis and translation: Heather and Matthews, 1991, ch. 2.

by everyone as a good conclusion to the preceding six years of warfare.[103] Such outright and relative failures were hardly Themistius' fault. Even the greatest of propagandists can do little to sell disaster as success, and for the most part, presumably, Themistius was successful, or he would not have continued to be used for speech-making. This, of course, is the underlying point. Propaganda without an audience serves no useful function. The Senate of Constantinople, with its web of wider connections across the eastern Mediterranean, provided emperors with an audience that was worth manipulating, and Themistius' potent mixture of philosophy, rhetoric, and politics was an ideal intermediary between the two.

## CONCLUSION: SPIN DOCTOR AND FACTION LEADER

Over the course of his adult lifetime, an initial impact based on rhetorical innovation was deepened and sustained by the more enduring pillars of Themistius' career: adding Hellenic cultural credibility to Christian imperial regimes, and disseminating a sophisticated brand of propaganda before a discerning and politically worthwhile audience. Themistius was much more, therefore, than either a flatterer, or a philosopher who used flattery as a means to particular ends. Rather, his career was based on manipulating opinion on behalf of the emperors he served, within a body which rapidly became a central focus of political life in the eastern Mediterranean: the Senate of Constantinople.

This was done partly through rhetoric: his handling in set-piece speeches of the great issues and events of the day on formal ceremonial occasions. The contents of the speeches themselves, when set fully in historical context, well illustrate this aspect of his career. Less obviously, Themistius must also have exercised influence on quite another level, through the chains of connection which his role in recruiting for the senate had allowed him to establish. Themistius knew many, or perhaps even all, of the senators of Constantinople personally. Some he had recruited himself in the late 350s, but, even in subsequent years, he remained part of the panel approving membership, and hence came into contact with newer recruits too.[104] Others in their student days would

---

103 The range of reaction to the Gothic peace of 382 is surveyed by Pavan, 1964, who failed to recognise that Themistius was not an independent commentator.

104 *C.Th.* 6.4.12. This stayed on the books despite Themistius' relative eclipse under Julian, so that he presumably had some contact with all subsequent promotees.

have attended the lectures he gave on the importance of applied philosophy, and courted him both then and subsequently for jobs and other favours. No one was better placed, therefore, to deliver the backing of a substantial block of senatorial opinion when imperial policy needed support. We strongly suspect, in other words, that the formal speeches were preceded by extensive lobbying to prepare the ground for their favourable reception.

Policy in the autocratic later Roman Empire was substantially made by the interaction of factions and interests. With established influence over a substantial body of senatorial opinion after the late 350s, it is not too much in our view to see Themistius as one of these faction leaders, the head of one of a series of interest groups whose haphazard interaction shaped imperial destiny. This faction was composed of a number of different but probably overlapping elements: those recruited by him especially in the late 350s, former pupils, and those who had sought him out for favours. To judge by parallel examples, there are likely to have been more and less loyal individuals within each category, as well as many individuals with ties to more than one faction leader. A possible analogy to the kind of faction-management such an assembly of individuals required might be the desperate list-keeping of that eighteenth-century English parliamentary grandee, the Duke of Newcastle, whose efforts to garner support were famously explored in the works of Namier. Newcastle had various types of influence over a wide range of individuals, but this never translated into an automatic number of votes. Neither Themistius nor his emperors needed to win votes, but, as we have seen, all imperial regimes required a broad base of support. Control of such a faction would help explain, of course, why Themistius was courted so earnestly by Jovian, Valens, and Theodosius, and why even Julian, already sarcastic about Themistius' truthfulness in the mid-350s, could not afford to reject him entirely. Themistius had, to use Newcastle's terms, his own substantial 'interest', which, following his role in its recruitment, would naturally have viewed him as its leader, and would have been alienated from any regime which had not included him in some way in its distribution of power and patronage.[105]

It may be, too, that, following on from this, a final point can be made about Themistius' historical importance. As we have seen, his claims to philosophical independence cannot be taken at face value; he was an

105  See esp. Namier, 1968.

insider performing rhetorical tasks for a sequence of imperial masters. Looked at more closely his ostensible pleas were no more than a clever rhetorical strategy, and rather than challenging ruling regimes, the speeches were concerned to expound and justify their policies. That said, Themistius' very presence in a regime imposed certain limitations upon it. Above all, the fact that his participation was used to signal cultural continuity placed boundaries on the extent to which any such regime might adopt more radical Christianising agendas. To keep him on board, some kind of lip service had to be paid to the Hellenic cultural traditions he claimed to personify. The point can perhaps be illustrated from events of the 380s. Themistius disappeared from active public life in c.384. It was at exactly this point, under the praetorian prefecture of Maternus Cynegius from 384 to 388, that the first radical round of pagan temple destruction by Christians was unleashed.[106] This might be pure coincidence. But Themistius' retirement removed from Theodosius' regime one of the power blocs which would have set itself precisely against this kind of more radical Christianisation. Themistius had set out his stall throughout his career, as we have seen, in favour of the idea that Christianity and traditional Hellenism could coexist, and it must be doubtful that Cynegius could have have let loose his campaign had Themistius still been active: or not, at least, without provoking a major dispute. Fundamentally, cultural coexistence was the one policy Themistius consistently advocated. Most of the other views he expressed in the speeches are much too closely correlated to the needs of his current imperial employer for us to have any idea of whether he really believed in them himself. Not only did his speeches advocate tolerant coexistence both explicitly on occasion and implicitly throughout, but his whole career, as we have seen, was based on the idea that such an accommodation was possible. In private as well as public, he must surely have acted as a brake upon overly vigorous Christianisation.[107]

Other, longer-term processes, apart from Themistius' retirement, also underlay Cynegius' freedom to act: not least the progressive Christianisation of eastern landowning elites. It may even be, indeed, that

106 See above note 69.

107 Like the Duke of Newcastle, Themistius had a longer term aim, beyond the manipulation of patronage to immediate advantage, which guided his public life. This aspect of Newcastle (his devotion to the Whig party and the Protestant succession) was famously missed by Namier: Butterfield, 1957.

Themistius' retirement was part of a more general moment of that elusive political phenomenon: generational shift. The generation recruited with him and by him into the senate in the mid-350s would, like Themistius himself, have been passing out of active public life by the mid-380s. Their places were taken by individuals among whom processes of Christianisation were further advanced. Themistius' retirement is thus emblematic of the changes which made possible Cynegius' career of destruction. This also helps explain why Themistius had no successor. Christian emperors needed pagan apologists only when much of the audience to which they were playing was itself pagan. Once a critical mass of the landowning elite became Christian, the image of the political philosopher lost its potency.

Themistius' career thus operated, with equal effectiveness, on a number of different planes, which, between them, explain his extraordinary political longevity. On one level, he was a talisman, a symbol that the importance of traditional Hellenic values was being recognised by Christian emperors in a period of huge cultural change. He was also a spin doctor, selling imperial policies to the Senate of Constantinople. Using speeches of about an hour before an audience that was both trained to appreciate his rhetoric and important enough to respond constructively to the political message, he sought to build consent for a whole sequence of imperial regimes and policies. At the same time, although this must be more shadowy, being implicit in the development of his career rather than explicitly illustrated in his speeches, he was probably also a senatorial faction leader in his own right, at least from the late 350s. His role in Constantius' expansion of the senate provided him with a secure political foundation which saw him through even the bad times of Julian's reign, and led Jovian, Valens, and Theodosius subsequently to court his support. In return, he received huge rewards: numerous marks of personal distinction, great political influence, quite probably considerable personal wealth, and, when the time was ripe, he cashed in his chips as a philosopher to accept a brief tenure as urban prefect and a secure retirement. In Plato's terms, therefore, it would be hard not to see him as more of a sophist than a philosopher, but this does not do him anything like full justice. His influence – on all levels – must always have been deployed in favour of religious toleration, and his commitment to this one big idea goes some way towards balancing out his otherwise pretty shameless willingness to trim his political sails according to the current breeze. Themistius' was an improvised career of bold invention, and, as a pagan philosopher serving a series of mutually hostile Christian imperial regimes, he must surely rank as one of the most skilful navigators ever to brave the treacherous waters of dynastic politics.

# CHAPTER 2

# THEMISTIUS AND CONSTANTIUS:
## THEMISTIUS ORATIONS 1 AND 3, CONSTANTIUS' LETTER TO THE SENATE

### HONOURS AND OFFICES

In either c.347 or c.350, Themistius gave the first of his formal political orations before the Emperor Constantius at Ancyra in Asia Minor. It was the start of a beautiful friendship. At about this time, Themistius was already teaching philosophy in Constantinople, the city in which he had spent much of his childhood. In 348/9, for instance, the future Emperor Julian seems to have studied the text of Plato's *Laws* under his direction there.[1] A letter of Libanius from 362 confirms the point. In this, he commented that Themistius and himself had by then been acquainted for 12 years (*Ep.* 793), so that they originally met in c.350, and it is more than likely that they encountered one another as teachers in Constantinople. By the mid-350s at the latest, Themistius held a publicly funded teaching post there. Publicly funded teachers received an annual stipend from the city in which they taught, where the less fortunate had to rely solely upon student fees: a much more precarious existence. Whether Themistius already held a funded post when he taught Julian is unclear.[2]

A state-funded chair in the imperial capital was itself a mark of some favour, of course, but the unusual intimacy of the developing relation-

---

1 Julian, *Letter to Themistius* 257d, 258a–d, quoting *Laws* 713–714a; Smith, 1995, 26–9.

2 *Or.* 33 has sometimes been seen as Themistius' inaugural speech as public professor of philosophy in Constantinople, and refers to a new bronze coin which was thought to have been issued in 348/9: Seeck, 1906, 295 n. 1; cf. Vanderspoel, 1995, 49. The coin was really introduced in 354, however, and the speech's contents better fit the circumstances of 359/60: Callu, 1978; cf. Penella, 2000, 44–5. Themistius certainly held a funded chair by the late 350s when controversy erupted around him, and the Emperor Constantius' language implies that he was doing so by 355 when he was adlected to the senate (on both matters, see *The Letter of Constantius* below). It is likely enough that Themistius had been holding the post for some time at that point, but there is no explicit evidence as to exactly how long.

ship between emperor and philosopher became fully apparent in 355. In that year, Themistius was adlected by letter of the emperor to the Senate of Constantinople, a text translated below. He responded with Oration 2 as a thank offering, and Constantius returned the compliment by setting up a bronze statue to celebrate the philosopher's achievements.[3] More and less formal honours continued to emphasise Themistius' increasing prominence in subsequent years. On 1 January 357, Themistius gave a further speech to the senate celebrating the start of the joint consulship of Constantius and his cousin, the Caesar Julian (Oration 4). Although given in Constantinople, a copy of the speech went west to the emperor, who had been detained there by civil and foreign wars since the early 350s (see below). Themistius himself soon followed. In May 357 he led an embassy from the Constantinopolitan senate to Rome, where Constantius was making a rare imperial visit to the Empire's capital city, an event designed, among other things, to celebrate the emperor's military successes against a pair of western usurpers. Oration 3, delivered on that occasion, is translated below.[4]

Even more impressive in some ways than these great moments in the imperial limelight were the less formal marks of Themistius' influence and power which followed. In the late 350s, Constantius decided to expand the membership of the Senate of Constantinople. Among his chosen methods was the despatch of Themistius on a recruiting campaign in the eastern Mediterranean in 358/9. Should anyone have been left in any doubt of the standing that Themistius had by this stage achieved within the regime, a formal imperial pronouncement, partly preserved in the *Theodosian Code*, underlined the point in May 361 (*C. Th.* 6.4.12). Constantius there declared that the presence of 'Themistius the Philosopher, whose learning enhances his rank' was specifically required, along with that of other men of the highest rank, to be involved in the process of admitting any further new members to the senate.[5]

The overall fact that Themistius rose to great prominence under Constantius could hardly be clearer, but one issue has generated much controversy. Did the emperor promote his philosopher to the post of

---

3  The statue is mentioned at *Or.* 4.54b.

4  The case for dating *Or.* 3 after *Or.* 4 was established by Seeck, 1906, 296–7, and Gladiis, 1907, 9–10; cf. Vanderspoel, 1995, 96. Scholze, 1911, 13–20, unconvincingly argues the reverse.

5  General accounts of Themistius' rise: Stegemann, 1934; Dagron, 1968, 5–27; Vanderspoel, 1995, esp. ch. 2.

proconsul of Constantinople in the late 350s? Before the formal institution of an urban prefecture, on either 11 September or 11 December 359, the proconsul acted essentially as the city's governor with legal, financial, and logistic as well as ceremonial responsibilities.[6] The main evidence in favour of a Themistian proconsulship is provided by some letters of Libanius from the late 350s. In particular, in letter 40 of 358/9, to a certain Julianus, Libanius wrote that Themistius was now 'leading the City' and held its 'reins' in his hands. These comments have been enough to convince many scholars that Themistius had governed the city as its proconsul, and certainly show that contemporaries were conscious that Themistius had achieved a new pre-eminence at this time.[7] But, as Gilbert Dagron pointed out, Themistius' own writings contain no explicit mention of such an honour. In particular, Oration 34, which retrospectively reviewed Themistius' entire career, is entirely silent on the matter. As we shall see in Chapter 5, this speech was framed to defend Themistius' later assumption of the urban prefecture of Constantinople in 383/4, and, in doing so, mentioned in passing all the honours previously granted to him by different emperors. If there had really been such a promotion, therefore, a proconsulship under Constantius would surely have been included.[8] It is also noticeable that in *C. Th.* 6.4.12, of May 361, Constantius listed Themistius apart from other individuals designated as ex-office holders. This seems to indicate that he was not then one of their number, as an ex-proconsul would again have been.[9] While Themistius clearly did occupy some position of extra prominence in the late 350s, therefore, it was not the proconsulship.

6 Proconsuls and Prefects: Dagron, 1974, 215–39. The institution of the urban prefecture is dated 11 September by the *Chronicon Paschale* and 11 December by the *Cons. Const.* Themistius is known to have rejected an offer of the post of urban prefect on one occasion before he accepted it from Theodosius, but this probably took place under Valens: see Chapter 5.

7 First argued by Sievers, 1868, 211–15; reaffirmed by Seeck, 1906, 298–301, and then generally accepted; cf. Daly, 1983, 164–7.

8 Penella, 2000, 219 n. 19, argues that there were rhetorical reasons why Themistius would not have mentioned an earlier proconsulship in Oration 34, namely that he wanted to avoid seeming to have chased after office throughout his career. This is unconvincing. If Themistius had held the proconsulship under Constantius, it would have represented the previous high point of his career, and his entire – Constantinopolitan – audience would have been well aware of it. To omit the most important post of his life from an account of his past which was designed to justify his present behaviour would have vitiated the whole exercise.

9 Dagron, 1968, note ii, 213–17; cf. Vanderspoel, 1995, 106–8, and our further discussion of *Or.* 34. xiii–xiv in Chapter 5. A second element in Dagron's argument is ill-founded. In his

What, then, should we make of Libanius' references to Themistius' extra dignity. Chastagnol suggested that he might have been made vice-proconsul, an office whose existence is not actually attested. More recently, Vanderspoel has argued, on the basis of section 13 of Oration 34, that Themistius exercised a continuous *prostasia* ('presidency') within the Senate of Constantinople from 357 down to the point at which he was speaking in the early 380s. An administrative office could not have been held for such a period, and Vanderspoel suggested that it might be identified with the post of leading senator – *princeps senatus* – which was not an office with administrative responsibilities, but a position of great dignity with certain formal rights and duties, and which was held continuously.[10] But Vanderspoel's reading of Oration 34 seems to us too literal. At that point in the speech, Themistius was trying to claim that being urban prefect in the 380s was no more than a natural extension of all his previous activities on behalf of the Senate of Constantinople. Elsewhere in the speech, *prostasia* is the term he used for the urban prefecture itself. What Themistius would appear to have been arguing, therefore, was that all his efforts on behalf of the city had in

---

view, three speeches of the late 350s – *Orr.* 23, 26, 29 (esp. *Or.* 23.291d–292d) – confirmed that Themistius had refused the proconsulship under Constantius (a refusal Dagron equated with the incident referred to at *Or.* 34.xiii). Daly, 1983, esp. 171–5, successfully demonstrated, on the contrary, that these speeches show Themistius refusing the perquisites of some salaried position, not the position itself, so that the refusal of office mentioned in *Or.* 34 must refer to a separate incident (although we would disagree with Daly on precisely which one: see the introduction to *Or.* 34 in Chapter 5). Daly went on argue that the perquisites referred to were those of the proconsulship, and thus attempted to revive the traditional consensus against Dagron that Themistius had indeed held this office under Constantius (Daly, 1983, 178–89). This part of the argument is less convincing. As Daly himself recognised (181–2) Libanius' language is highly ambiguous; neither his letters nor any of Themistius' speeches of the 350s refer to the philosopher holding an administrative office in the imperial bureaucracy. Daly also failed to explain why *Or.* 34 should have omitted to mention the supposed proconsulship. As we shall see, there is good reason to suppose, rather, that the controversy of the late 350s focussed upon Themistius' general prominence in public life and the perquisites were probably those attached to a publicly funded teaching post (see the introduction to *The Letter of Constantius*). Daly's arguments about the proconsulship have been followed by Brauch, 1993a, 41; Penella, 2000, 2.

10  Vice-proconsul: Chastagnol, 1976, 350. *Princeps Senatus*: Vanderspoel, 1995, 104–8. In 4th-century Rome, the post of *princeps senatus* was held by, among others, the elder and younger Symmachi (Chastagnol, 1960, 69–72). No *princeps* is known from Constantinople, but parallels between old and new imperial senates, at least from the late 350s, suggest that the post probably existed: Dagron, 1974, 143–4.

reality made him its prefect long before the actual title was conferred upon him.[11] Indeed, a more general explanation of the change in tone of Libanius' letters from the late 350s can be offered along similar lines. By that date, Themistius had led an embassy to Rome, received a statue and other marks of imperial favour, and was busily engaged in recruiting new members for the Senate of Constantinople. In our view, Libanius' respectful tone can be satisfactorily explained as a reflection of this highly impressive public profile, rather than as the result of any specific office or dignity.

The benefits to Themistius from his friendship with Constantius are only too obvious. Distinctions aplenty came Themistius' way, and in their wake enormous powers of patronage. The only real limitation upon him was that the nature of his philosophical vocation meant that he had to be extremely careful about holding administrative office or in being seen to enjoy too many financial benefits. As we shall see, the late 350s saw a series of attacks upon him, all, in different ways, zeroing in upon the question of whether he had in fact betrayed his philosophical vocation for material gain.[12] Themistius could not afford to be seen to profit too obviously from his relationship with Constantius, or he would lose the philosophical status on which his public persona and entire career were based. For similar reasons, in Oration 2, when thanking Constantius for his adlection to the senate, Themistius noted that the emperor had offered him any gifts that he might choose, and that, although heavily pressed, he had turned most of them down (i.e., not all).[13] At one and the same time, this allowed him both to emphasise the regard in which he was held by the emperor, and make the point that he had never acted out of worldly ambition. If the benefits from all this for Themistius are very clear, the advantages to Constantius from such a close accord with a non-Christian, Hellenic philosopher are not, at first sight, so straightforward. For Constantius, like his father Constantine, was a Christian emperor, deeply committed to the cause of the new imperial religion.

---

11 For *prostasia* as the prefecture, see *Or.* 34.xiii–xvi in Chapter 5.

12 See the introduction to *The Letter of Constantius* below.

13 *Or.* 2.25d–26a: 'I did not allow my house to be inundated with greater blessings than are appropriate for philosophy.'

## THE RELIGIOUS POLICIES OF CONSTANTIUS

The reign of Constantius is infamous for the extent to which the emperor involved himself in the developing doctrinal disputes of Christianity, above all the so-called Arian dispute on the nature of Christ. The emperor threw his imperial weight behind moderate opponents of the Creed established at Nicaea in 325, who wanted definitions of faith to convey a greater sense of separation and hierarchy within the Godhead. This involved him in conflict both with convinced proponents of the Nicene creed, above all Athanasius of Alexandria, and more radical subordinationist theologians such as Aetius. Complete consensus was never achieved in Constantius' reign, but it is important to realise that, at the time, his position seems to have gathered a working majority of eastern bishops to its flag.[14] The emperor's adherence to Christianity was declared equally strongly in his public attitude to non-Christian religious cult: 'paganism'. For Constantius maintained, and probably also extended, the anti-pagan initiatives of his father.[15] This is a controversial subject, not least because some important pieces of imperial legislation have either not survived at all, or else only in fragmentary form, making it difficult to be certain of their precise significance. In addition, as we shall see, contemporary commentators on this legislative sequence sometimes provide conflicting characterisations of its effects.

Aside from such evidential problems, it is also important, when seeking to understand Constantius' policies, to take full account of problems of enforcement. Enacting a piece of legislation was only the first step in a lengthy process. Because of huge distances, primitive communications, and bureaucratic structures which were cumbersome and inherently limited in their ability to interfere in the running of local communities, enforcement in the Roman Empire required a positive response from the representatives of either local or central government. Without this, nothing would happen. This is nicely illustrated, in the case of legislation designed to deal with the problem of fleeing city councillors, by Libanius' forty-eighth oration. A general law existed which allowed city councils to press into service local landowners who should have been counted among their number, but had used imperial service or some other excuse to claim an exemption. Libanius' speech makes

---

14 Outside of Egypt, perhaps, where Athanasius recruited busily. See, e.g., Hanson, 1988, on the theology, and Barnes, 1993, on the Church politics.

15 For a general account, see most recently Beard et al., 1998, 369–75.

clear that there were three potential barriers between the issuing of this law by the emperor and its local enforcement. First, its existence had to be known of in general terms. Second, you had to know precisely where – i.e. in which governmental office – to find a copy of it. Third, someone had to take the initiative to have the law applied in any particular case. Sheer distance, more generally, added a fourth. Even when there was more than one imperial centre, as was the case for much most of the fourth century, it was still extremely difficult for legislators to have any confidence that localities really were following imperial instructions. Even when there was no political opposition to a measure, sheer inertia on the part of enforcing agents was a substantial problem. On the other hand, if a local vested interest was under threat, there were many obstacles which could be placed in the path of an imperial order.[16] All this raises a serious methodological question. It becomes difficult to know, especially in the case of religious measures that have not survived in their original form, whether particular aspects of pagan cult, known to have continued after a given law was issued, were legally licensed by it, or had merely proved impossible to eradicate in practice.

Constantine started to favour the Christian Church immediately after his defeat of Maxentius in 312. The *Liber Pontificalis* lists a string of early endowments and the emperor's letters on the Donatist dispute in North Africa give equally clear evidence of the emperor's attitude.[17] After his defeat of Licinius in 324, Constantine became more aggressively pro-Christian. Eusebius of Caesarea's *Life of Constantine* records a series of measures taken at that point, including the claim that the emperor banned pagan sacrifice. This has occasioned much debate. Most of the other measures mentioned by Eusebius are detailed within the texts of the imperial letters and other official documents which the historian ostensibly transcribed, and whose authenticity is now generally accepted.[18] The ban on sacrifice, on the other hand, is reported only in Eusebius' own words, with no transcription of the relevant decree.

16 Libanius, *Or.* 48.15; cf. Bradbury, 1994, 131–3, for a similar argument using the example of continuing sacrifice at the temple of Mamre which came to Constantine's attention only after some time: Eusebius, *Life of Constantine* 3.52–3. For an introduction to law enforcement, see Harries, 1999, ch. 4; Jones, 1964, ch. 14. Fowden, 1978, suggests that the anti-pagan legislation in the 4th century foundered on the fact that many imperial officials were themselves still pagan.

17 See, e.g., Lane Fox, 1986, 622–3.

18 See now Cameron and Hall, 1999, 16–21, 239; cf. Lane Fox, 1986, 627; Hall, 1998.

There is also no such surviving decree in the *Theodosian Code*, and Libanius, looking back from the 380s, reports that it was Constantius who banned pagan sacrifice, not Constantine, who, he claimed, made no substantial change in religious matters.[19]

That Eusebius either told an outright lie or else was completely misinformed is not, however, likely. For one thing, the relevant chapter of the *Code* (16.10: *de paganis, sacrificiis et templis*) provides only a fragmentary record of relevant imperial legislation for the period down to the start of the reign of Theodosius I (c.380 onwards). Relevant laws of the Emperors Jovian, and Valentinian and Valens, known to have existed from other sources, have not survived. The most likely explanation here is that the progressively more aggressive anti-pagan legislation of the time of Theodosius I onwards rendered much of the earlier legislation on the topic redundant. Hence, by the time the *Code*'s commissioners came to do their work in the 430s, these laws had been out of date for forty or more years, and copies of them had probably not been kept.[20] There is also more positive evidence that Constantine's reported edict did once exist. A further law against sacrifice from his son and western successor, Constans, refers back to a similar prohibition enacted by his father (*C.Th.* 16.10.2). There seems little doubt, therefore, that Constantine did indeed legislate against pagan sacrifice as Eusebius maintains.[21]

19 Eusebius, *Life of Constantine* 2.24–60 with the ban on sacrifice at 2.44–45; Libanius *Or.* 30.6–7. For surveys of recent debate, see Cameron and Hall, 1999, 243–4; Bradbury, 1994, 122–5; Barnes, 1989, 322–5; Errington, 1988, 311–12. Relatively recent studies such as MacMullen, 1984, 50, and Lane Fox, 1986, 635ff., 667, have either denied the existence of the law or disputed its effects. There is no such dispute over Eusebius' reports that Constantine later both shut certain temples and confiscated temple treasures: *Life of Constantine* 3.54–8.

20 Lost religious legislation: see the introduction to *Or.* 5 in Chapter 3. On the processes for collecting materials, see the debate between Matthews and Sirks in Harries and Wood, 1993. The commissioners were required to include even redundant legislation, but they had to find it first.

21 Cf. Bradbury, 1994, 125–7, who refutes the argument of Errington, 1988, that the ban on sacrifice was quickly lifted, and convincingly introduces Libanius *Or.* 1.27 into the argument, where the uncle of Libanius' friend Crispinus is found sacrificing despite a prohibition which must pre-date *C.Th.* 16.10.2. Thus far we also follow Barnes, 1989, 322–5, who is surely correct to reject the supposition of Jones, 1964, 91–2, that the ban on sacrifice should be dated later than the mid-320s. Jones saw it as incompatible with the so-called 'Edict of Toleration' issued at the same time, but see below. We also see no reason to suppose that the law did not apply in the west as well as the east (*contra* Barnes, 1989, 331).

Without the original text, however, its precise historical significance is hard to reconstruct. According to Eusebius, Constantine legislated against blood sacrifice, the killing of victims on the altars of the gods. If the report is precise, this ban was quite specific, in that, by implication, it allowed many other traditional pagan cultic practices to continue: the lighting of lamps and candles, the singing of hymns, and the burning of incense. This was the pattern under later 'tolerant' Christian emperors, when blood sacrifice was banned, but these other forms of piety allowed. And no contemporary source, at least, maintains that Constantine shut down pagan cultic practice in its entirety.[22] We strongly suspect, therefore, that Constantine did issue a law, but that it was quite precisely worded. Indeed, not only did much other pagan practice continue through most of the fourth century, but a new type of blood sacrifice – the *taurobolium* associated with the cult of Magna Mater – gained in popularity among elite pagans of the city of Rome, who even advertised their participation in the rite on inscriptions. This suggests that the *taurobolium* was not covered by the old law on blood sacrifice, again indicating that it must have been quite specific.[23]

Therefore, although Constantine's anti-pagan legislation has not survived, its central thrust can probably be reconstructed. Paradoxically, almost the opposite is true of his son. *C.Th.* 16.10.4 is a law of Constantius, probably from the mid-350s, which on the face of it ordered all pagan temples to be closed forthwith:

> It is Our pleasure that the temples shall be immediately closed in all places and in all cities, and access to them forbidden, so as to deny to all abandoned men the opportunity to commit sin (trans. Pharr).

---

Cf. Beard et al., 1998, 223–6, 372, such measures could be seen within an existing tradition of emperors seeking to eliminate *superstitio*.

22 Different forms of pagan piety: e.g., Lane Fox, 1986, 69–72, 218–22. Later pattern: Libanius *Or.* 30.7 on Valentinian and Valens, and, indeed, the early reign of Theodosius I. Cf. generally Bradbury, 1994, 129–30; Brown, 1995, 11–18; Beard et al., 1998, 239–42, 371–2, on Christians' general need to avoid the ritual pollution of blood sacrifice, which could nonetheless be combined with more ambiguous attitudes towards other acts of pagan piety.

23 On the *taurobolium*, see McLynn, 1996: analysing the very public corpus of inscriptions from the Phrygianum on the Vatican, close to St Peter's. The lack of a quoted text thus seems to us more important than Barnes, 1989, 323, would allow.

It has often – quite reasonably – been interpreted as a general law to this effect.[24] The matter is worth, however, closer investigation. For one thing, the surviving text is only an extract from an originally much longer law, made in the 430s by the *Theodosian Code* commissioners. They were charged with including laws of general significance (*generalitas*), and were allowed to extract statements of general principle from much longer laws which, in their entirety, had often originally addressed only a specific case. The developing line of thought evident in the surviving extract suggests that this may be true of *C.Th.* 16.10.4, in that the closing of temples *per se* was seemingly not the law's central purpose. Although it opens with the order quoted above, the rest of the text makes clear that Constantius' primary legislative purpose was to prevent the sin of sacrifice. All of the law's specific penalties were directed against those who continued to sacrifice, not against those who kept their temples open. In other words, it represented an extension of the policies of Constantine – banning blood sacrifice – rather than the opening of an entirely new strand of attack. The chances are, therefore, that the law did originate in a specific instance of continuing sacrifice being brought to the emperor's attention.[25] That said, once a law exists, lawyers can attempt to apply it to a variety of problems, not necessarily identical to that addressed in the original case. Did this generally worded response to a specific problem have the effect of closing the pagan temples in Constantius' Empire?

Some temples were evidently not only closed, but dismantled as well. Texts dating from the reign of Constantius' pagan successor, Julian, mention six specific instances. We know that some temples had already been closed by Constantine, however, and two of the six seem to fall into this category.[26] The sources do not report, however, a total closure

---

24 E.g., Jones, 1964, 116.

25 On the working principles of the commissioners, see Matthews, 1993. For a similar interpretation of the equally general-sounding anti-pagan strictures of *C.Th.* 16.10.10, see McLynn, 1994, 331–2.

26 Temples were ordered to be rebuilt under Julian at Cyzicus, Aegeae, Arethusa, Heliopolis, Gaza, and Alexandria; see Barnes, 1989, 325–8. Sozomen, *Ecclesiastical History* 5.4.1–5, reports that the Christian majority of the population of Caesarea in Cappadocia also destroyed temples of Zeus and Apollo, leading Barnes (*loc. cit.*) to suppose that temple destruction under Constantius was a widespread phenomenon. Barnes does not, however, discuss *C.Th.* 16.10.4, or consider general problems of enforcement. Temple closures under Constantine: Eusebius, *Life of Constantine* 3.55, 56, 58 (cf. Cameron and Hall, 1999, 301–5), the latter two being Aegae and Heliopolis, where rebuilding took place

of pagan temples during Constantius' time and their re-opening under Julian, which is what we might expect had *C. Th.* 16.10.4 really come into general effect. While the mid-fifth-century Church historians do report the opening of temples under Julian, they suppose that it was Constantine who had shut them. One possibility is that they have confused Constantine with Constantius, and that their reports of a general temple closure are otherwise sound. It seems more likely, however, that they have here imported into the fourth century fifth-century assumptions that no Christian emperor could have tolerated open temples. For they also claim that Jovian shut the temples again after Julian's death, and we know that this was not the case.[27] Among more contemporary sources, both Julian and Libanius agree that Constantius' reign saw the passing of further important anti-pagan legislation.[28] The former's writings are nowhere very precise, but, in one key passage of his seventh oration *Against Heraclius*, the now Emperor Julian wrote, in general, of the Constantinian dynasty's actions against traditional cult that 'the sons demolished the temples which their father had profaned' (*Or.* 7.228b–d). This is clear testimony that Constantine's sons pushed the anti-pagan effort onto a new level. A consequent need to restore the temples was also reflected in Julian's policies. One of his first measures as emperor, on 4 February 362, was to order the general repair of temples and rebuilding of any that had been destroyed. Thus inscriptions generally heralded him as the 'Restorer of the temples'.[29]

The point seems to be confirmed by Libanius. Born in 314, he was already an adult at the time of Constantine's death in 337, and really ought to have known which emperor did what during his adult lifetime. As we have seen, later in life in the 380s, Libanius claimed not that Constantius had shut the temples, but that he did effectively prevent sacrifice (*Or.* 30.7). As the first Christian emperor, Constantine was

---

under Julian. In the latter case, it seems better to accept with the majority of the MSS that dismantling took place under Constantine: Theodoret, *Ecclesiastical History* 3.7.3 against Barnes, 1989, 326, n. 119, who would read Constantius.

27 Socrates, *Ecclesiastical History* 1.2, 3.1, 3.24; cf. Sozomen, *Ecclesiastical History* 1.8, 2.5, 5.3. On the realities of Jovian's reign, see the introduction to *Or.* 5 in Chapter 3.

28 In his summation of Constantius' virtues and vices, Ammianus records only the emperors' meddling in Christian affairs: 21.16.18.

29 *ELF* 42; cf. *AE* 1969/70, 631 (Jordan), *ILS* 946 (Mursa), *ILS* 752 (Numidia), Arce, 1984, no. 106 (Baalbeck). For secondary commentary, see now Smith, 1995, 211–12.

obviously a powerful behavioural model for the pagan Libanius to want to hold up before Theodosius as an example of toleration. He might, therefore, have been inclined to stretch a point.[30] On the other hand, many people who had been adults under Constantine and Constantius were still alive when Libanius wrote to Theodosius in the 380s, so it would have destroyed his credibility to base his case on a palpable falsehood. Overall, then, even if Constantine surely did enact some kind of ban on blood sacrifice, it does nevertheless seem likely that Libanius is correct in reporting that Constantius greatly strengthened it.

If problems of law enforcement are added into the equation, then the testimonies of Julian and Libanius are, in fact, quite compatible with the rest of the evidence. The direction of Constantius' legislative intention in *C. Th.* 16.10.4 was, as we have seen, to prevent sacrifice, if necessary by shutting the temples. Thus Libanius' report, the law itself, and the general tendency of Julian's writings could all be taken as mutually confirmatory indications that Constantius' reign, by making it possible to shut temples, reinforced the effectiveness of the ban on sacrifice initiated by his father. That is still not to say, however, that all the temples were shut. The available evidence indicates that the model of enforcement outlined above in the case of fleeing councillors applied equally vigorously in religious affairs too. When visiting the city of Ilium in the winter of 354, for instance, Julian had to have the temple of Athene opened, and was surprised to find all the other shrines there in very good order. Reports of damage to them turned out to be deliberate camouflage on the part of local pagans, and the local Christian bishop had also been piously tending the pagan shrines and altars (*Ep.* 19). There clearly had been an order which the local community had to be seen to have complied with, but clearly no enforcement agency had come to check that the reported damage had actually been imparted. As this incident suggests, and Julian's other writings confirm, the attitude of local city councils was a crucial variable in determining the outcome of any religious initiative. The non-response of the substantially Christian council of Antioch famously blocked Julian's hopes of a pagan revival within that city's territory in 362/3, and it is notable that he likewise blamed non-Christian Antiochenes and their lack of pagan religious enthusiasm, rather than any imperial law, for their failure to prevent the dismantling of the temple of Apollo at Daphne. Other cities were more

---

30  As argued, for instance, by Bradbury, 1994, 127–9.

guarded than the Antiochenes in their response to Julian – greeting the emperor politely but not actually doing anything – while still others, like Batnae and Emesa, were positively enthusiastic.[31] In specific circumstances, individuals of particular standing could take less consensually based initiatives. This would appear to have been the case in Alexandria where late in the reign of Constantius, the local bishop, Julian's former teacher George of Cappadocia, and the regional Roman army commander, the *dux Aegytpi* Artemius, between them organised the seizure of the temple of Serapis in 360 in the face of popular opposition. Such cases seem to have been rare, however, and were certainly risky. After Constantius' death and the succession of Julian in the following year, George was lynched by an angry Alexandrian mob, and Artemius tried and executed. In the face of such restrictions upon enforcement, any idea of 'general' – in the sense of universally and automatically applicable – law is a chimera. Emperors could pass generally worded legislation, but enforcement always involved a process of negotiation with intermediate powers. Partial or even notional compliance was always a possible outcome.

In sum, the evidence of Julian and Libanius makes it clear that Constantius' legislation provided Christian-dominated city councils and Christian high officials with greater legal opportunity to take hostile initiatives in the case of particular pagan temples, and, at the same time, made it that much more important to avoid being seen to sacrifice. It probably generated a climate of opportunity, however, rather than a total crackdown. This could well have been at least semi-deliberate. Reliance upon local initiative meant that, unless imperial officials took a lead (as in Alexandria), positive action was dependent upon generating a consensus among the local landowners gathered in their city councils. Emperors presumably understood this as well as anyone else, and may well have tacitly accepted the situation. In the fourth century, Christian emperors had to govern through a landowning class which was still substantially pagan (see below). At the same time, they faced pressure from Christian religious lobbies pushing them vigorously to advance the cause of the new religion. The practicalities of enforce-

31 Antioch: Julian, *Misopogon* 346b (on Daphne); cf. 361d–363c. Different attitudes elsewhere: *Misopogon* 357c (Emesa), 360d–361b (a general characterisation); *Ep.* 58: Beroea and Batnae. For general discussion of the response to Julian's paganism, see Bidez, 1930, 228–35 with refs; cf. Browning, 1975, 136–40; Bowersock, 1978, 91–3.

ment allowed emperors, at least in part, to square this seemingly vicious circle. Strongly anti-pagan, pro-Christian noises could be made at the imperial centre, even enacted into formal legislation, safe in the knowledge that events on the ground would not tend to move faster than was consensually acceptable to individual local communities. Hence the pattern observable in the evidence – whereby some communities dismantled their temples, while others preserved them, either openly or more covertly – was probably perfectly acceptable even to a Christian emperor in general terms. Constantius could thus enact pro-Christian laws with the assurance that inherent limitations upon enforcement meant that pagan landowning opinion need not become generally alienated from his regime.[32]

Indeed, while the writings of Julian and the later Church historians naturally emphasise pagan–Christian conflict, there are strong hints elsewhere that a de facto religious consensus prevailed. The pagan Libanius was willing, for instance, to write letters on behalf of a Christian friend, Orion, who had benefited from selling off bits of dismantled pagan temple, while, as we have seen, a single individual, Pegasius, was willing to act as bishop of Ilium and yet keep its temples in good order. As bishop, Pegasius had presumably also submitted the reports which had led Julian to expect, contrary to what he actually found, that the temples of the city had suffered damage.[33] From these few surviving illustrations, it seems rash to assume that local communities in the time of Constantius tended to follow any general path, whether towards vigorous Christianisation or away from it. We are thus not convinced that the six surviving examples of temple destruction provide a general guide to norms of religious behaviour under Constantius across the eastern Mediterranean. There is obviously no way to be sure, but instinct suggests the opposite, namely that these were exceptions – which is why they were mentioned – rather than illustrations of the general rule. It is

32  Cf. Bradbury, 1994, 132–9, for a similar argument applied to the religious legislation of Constantine.

33  Libanius, *Epp.* 763, 819. Pegasius: Julian, *Ep.* 19. Cf. Fowden, 1978, 60, Pegasius has often been seen as 'really' a pagan, since he later applied for a job in Julian's pagan priestly hierarchy. We are much less sure that he should not be seen as a convinced inhabitant of the middle ground which existed between Christianity and paganism (see below). For a similar argument from a different direction, stressing the moral limits to acceptable intimidation imposed by shared concepts of *paideia* among the Roman ruling class, see Brown, 1995, esp. ch. 2.

equally striking that, outside of Constantinople, Rome, and the Holy Land there is no substantial evidence of Church-building before the last third of the fourth century, i.e. well after Constantius' death.[34] It was in this broad context of only patchy religious change that the relationship grew up between the positively Christian Constantius and his pet pagan philosopher, Themistius.

## EMPEROR AND PHILOSOPHER

The advantages to Constantius of this relationship in such circumstances emerge clearly from the three texts translated in this chapter. First and foremost, all three texts emphasise Themistius' claim that, as a philosopher, he could not but tell the truth. As we have seen, this stance had obvious importance in addressing the credibility gap faced by imperial spokesmen. Oration 1, probably of 347, begins with the bold claim that, because Themistius was a philosopher, the emperor was about to hear the truth for the first time. He reinforced it by adopting an unusual speech form which departed from the established norms of panegyric. Oration 3 replayed the claim, about a decade later, before a different audience, the Senate of Rome, the theme having also figured in the meantime in Constantius' letter of 355 which adlected Themistius to the Senate of Constantinople.[35] But novelty is, by definition, an easily exhausted commodity. The logical conceit of the truth-telling philosopher could not retain its power to convince forever. Indeed, given that the audiences he addressed certainly understood their own autocratic political system, one wonders if his claim to veracity (as opposed to his demonstrated rhetorical prowess) was ever wholly believed.[36] Right from the beginning, therefore, and certainly as time progressed, Themistius' second and deeper value to his Christian imperial employers lay in his general cultural kudos: the recognised Hellenistic philosopher who was ready to express approval of their regimes.

As we have seen, Constantius was an avowedly Christian ruler who identified himself closely with his religion, both in settling its internal disputes and in furthering its interests against the competition provided by pagan temples. At the same time, he had to govern an Empire where

34 *Contra* Barnes as above note 26; Church-building: Mitchell, 1998, 66–7.
35 Dates, contexts and speech form: see the introductions to the individual texts below.
36 On Themistius and the credibility gap, see Chapter 1.

Christians formed far from a majority of the population. The speed and extent of Christian conversion is controversial and will probably remain so, because no precise figures exist for numbers of pagan and Christian adherents at different moments in time. There is reason to think, however, that Christian numbers have tended to be underestimated. Recent arguments in favour of a degree of conversion among even the Empire's landowning elite prior to Constantine's declaration of a Christian allegiance do seem generally convincing.[37] At least one distinguished Christian Roman senator has been identified in the consul for 317, for instance, to stand alongside the handful of Christian senatorial ladies whose existence has been recognised for longer.[38] The idea, set out by von Haehling, that it was only in the reign of the Emperor Gratian (375–383) that Christians first numbered a majority among holders of the highest-ranking imperial offices must also be revised in the light of Barnes' more recent studies. Barnes suggests the following figures for the three offices for which we have more or less complete listings of office-holders for the reign of Constantius:

i)   Non-imperial Consuls: 13 Christians, 6 pagans, 12 of unknown affiliation
i)   Praetorian Prefects: 8 Christians, 3 pagans, 3 of unknown affiliation,
iii) Urban Prefects of Rome 352–61 (after the defeat of Magnentius): 3 Christian and 2 pagan.

The result is a substantial upward revision in both absolute and relative terms of the numbers of Christians in high office, and a corresponding adjustment to established views of the extent to which Christianity penetrated Roman senatorial circles in the first half of the fourth century.[39]

37  For a polemical review, see Barnes, 1989, 307–11 with full refs, arguing against some minimising competitors, esp. Lane Fox, 1986; MacMullen, 1984.

38  The consul was Ovinius Gallicanus: Champlin, 1982. Senatorial ladies: Eck, 1971; cf. Barnes, 1973.

39  Von Haehling, 1978, esp. 614–18, whose work was framed as the continuation of Eck, 1971. Reworking: Barnes 1989; 1995. Barnes had in his sights the influential study of Brown, 1961, which saw Petronius Probus, who came to prominence in the 360s, as the first Christian Roman senatorial male of real distinction, and those implicitly or explicitly developing Brown's account on the basis of Von Haehling: e.g., Salzman, 1990.

These upward revisions, however, must be placed fully in context. Outside, arguably, of Egypt and Syria, Christians comprised only a relatively small percentage of the total rural population of the Empire. The conversion of the countryside was a process which would require centuries rather than decades to complete.[40] More specifically, the imperial offices which can be subjected to full prosopographical study are a highly unrepresentative and statistically insignificant sample of the total number of imperial offices and dignities. By the year 400, there existed 6,000 jobs, Empire-wide, in the imperial bureaucracy which led to senatorial status, and around 23,000 altogether, counting all officials and their various staffs. Their number had grown steadily through the century, and, while the total was smaller under Constantius, his reign did see an important phase of bureaucratic expansion.[41] Studies of the occupants of just three posts out of 23,000 (6,000, if we limit consideration just to senatorial posts) obviously cannot hope to give a general picture of the religious affiliations of the broader Empire-wide landowning elite. The three posts studied by Barnes include, in fact, some of the most prominent civil positions within the whole governmental structure. Appointments to them, one may presume, are likely to have been governed by quite different criteria – not least the political dependability of and need to reward specific individuals – than those to much more mundane bureaucratic positions, which nonetheless still placed the holder among the Empire's elite. Constantius may indeed have preferred Christians for the very top jobs within his gift, but this would hardly be surprising, and does not necessarily tell us much about the imperial civil service in general.

For the religious affiliations of these less exceptional men, no detailed figures are available. What one can say, however, is that, a few prominent exceptions notwithstanding, the vast majority of the new posts in the bureaucracy were filled from among the local landowning elites, who had previously dominated their city councils (*curiae*). As the balance of opportunities shifted, they exploited every chance to expand the focus of their political activity into the burgeoning and increasingly rewarding

40 For introductions, see generally Fletcher, 1997, chs 1–2; cf. the studies assembled in Settimane, 1982 (on the west), and Trombley, 1993 (on the east).

41 On numbers, see Heather, 1994, 19; cf. more generally Vögler, 1979.

sphere of imperial service.[42] Given the nature of this recruitment pool, the likelihood remains strong that, in the middle years of the fourth century, the majority of these men were not Christian, or, at the very least, that their Christianity coexisted with a traditional education in Hellenic culture. The educational bedrock of this class remained the intensive study of language and literature under the care of the grammarian and rhetor, with the highly traditional moral and cultural education that this curriculum entailed. Even for those who were avowedly Christian, this education was the badge of status to which all members of the landowning elite aspired, and, in the reign of Constantius, no sustained assaults had yet been launched upon the importance of traditional Hellenic *paideia*. It was this traditionally educated class, both in the imperial bureaucracy and at home in their native cities, who ran the basic life support systems by which the Empire functioned: raising taxes, maintaining local law and order, providing political support and stability. Indeed, given the huge size of the Empire and its relatively primitive communications, a very substantial amount of local autonomy was, as we have seen, a structural feature of its organisation.[43]

In religious and cultural terms, this generated a finely balanced situation. While himself a convinced and vigorous Christian, Constantius had to run his Empire through a landowning class which held firmly to traditional cultural values and was probably still largely pagan.[44] The same had been true, only more so, for his father Constantine, the first Christian emperor, so that both father and son had to tread carefully. Constantius, as we have seen, may have made strongly Christian noises in his legislation, but did not engage in heavy-handed enforcement. His father, similarly, had banned blood sacrifice, but otherwise insisted that he would not use force to change religious allegiance. An important part of Constantine's legislative sequence of the mid-320s was a famous letter,

---

42 On this process, see Heather, 1994 with further refs. MacMullen, 1984, 29, 32–3, guessed that Christians amounted to 5/60 million, or one twelfth of the population, in the early 4th century. While accepting with Barnes, 1989, esp. 308, that MacMullen failed to realise that toleration had allowed Christianity to prosper from c.260, one twelfth still seems to us a large proportion. Barnes considers it a substantial underestimate. This is all guesswork.

43 On this education, see Kaster, 1988; Marrou, 1948. Cf. more generally Fowden, 1978, on pagans in the administration and Brown, 1995, esp. ch. 2, on shared *paideia* as imposing clear limits on potential Christian intolerance.

44 Cf. the discussion and similar conclusion of Trombley, 1993, 168–88.

quoted by Eusebius, which, while proclaiming the superiority of Christianity with extreme vigour, nonetheless twice emphasised that no one was to be constrained to convert. This emphasis, significantly, provided its closing note.[45] Whether out of a sense of realism, or because they thought it inappropriate, these early Christian emperors did not push so hard in favour of their new religion that they alienated culturally conservative landowning opinion.[46] This general situation provided Themistius with the opportunity to deploy a public persona that was tailor-made to service a fundamental imperial need.

Within the structure of Hellenic thought and society, the philosopher was the guardian of correct social and ideological values. It was the philosopher's job, among other things, to declare what was compatible with Hellenism, and indicate what should be rejected.[47] This tradition, combined with the necessity faced by Christian emperors of not alienating the class by and for whom the Empire was run, allowed Themistius to create his own niche in public life, positioning himself precisely between Christian emperor and Hellenic landowners. Essentially, Themistius used his philosophical credibility to minimise the potential for cultural alienation between emperor and landowning classes that was inherent in the former's Christian allegiance. Right from the beginning, in Oration 1, his first speech to Constantius, this approach was deployed with daring, and to judge by the favour which followed, to great effect. He neither rejected the emperor's Christianity as incompatible with Hellenism, an impossible option for one wanting imperial preferment, nor merely passed over this potentially difficult subject in silence, a defensive strategy which would have been in tune with the kind of advice generally given in rhetorical handbooks.[48] On the contrary, Themistius faced up to religion head on, developing his own

45  Eusebius, *Life of Constantine* 2.47–71. In our view (and that of Cameron and Hall, 1999, 247–8), Barnes, 1989, 323, understates the importance of this document, focussing on its anti-pagan rhetoric rather than its specific order, carefully repeated, in favour of toleration.

46  The emperors might have chosen not to push enforcement hard, despite their occasionally rigorous rhetoric, because they respected the values of traditional *paideia* (Brown, 1995, ch. 2), or because they saw only voluntary conversion as virtuous: as suggested by Themistius in January 364: *Or.* 5.67b–68c (see Chapter 3).

47  See Chapter 1 with full refs.

48  E.g., the advice given by Menander Rhetor simply to omit the subject whenever something in the emperor's background (region or city of birth, family etc.) was insufficiently honourable: ed. Russell and Wilson, 1981, 80.

rather bolder strategy. In Oration 1, and subsequent speeches, Themistius presented himself as an answer – or part of an answer – to the problem of potential ideological alienation, by consistently identifying areas where common ground existed between traditional Hellenic values and the new Christian religion of his imperial master(s). His authority for doing so lay in his philosophical status, and his whole career was built upon using that status to make the claim that Hellenic values and his emperors' Christian religion were not fundamentally incompatible.

This was possible because Christian doctrine had evolved in a Mediterranean intellectual context where platonising philosophical assumptions were generally accepted without question. Many of them, indeed, were quite easily reconciled, on certain levels, with Judaeo-Christian visions of Creation and a single God who actively sought to foster the divine spark inherent in the human beings He had created. In spite of dissenting voices, a process of accommodation had begun as early as the Gospel of St John, with its *logos* theology, and continued in the work of the Christian apologists. In particular, in the third century Clement of Alexandria and Origen had developed coherent theological systems which accepted with some adaptation many basic premises of platonising Greek philosophy. Essentially, Greek thought was used by Christian thinkers to fill in the gaps, as it were, in the Old and New Testament evidence, and to turn Christian teachings in separate areas (about God, Humanity, Creation etc.) into an intellectually coherent system. Among the influential ideas accepted by most Christians was the Platonic division of the cosmos into two parts – the sensible and intelligible – distinguished by the manner in which human beings could approach an understanding of them. Knowledge of the sensible world was provided by the physical senses (sight, smell etc.); the intelligible world could be known by intellectual activity alone. Many Christians could also accept the basic Platonic vision of progression in the cosmos, with an all-powerful God at the centre, and a progression outwards to inferior created beings of various kinds, all of whom as far as man, a transitional figure between the sensible and intelligible worlds, contained a spark of the divine essence. Inferiority here was expressed not only by being on the wrong side of the sensible/intelligible divide, but also by being multiple rather than single. A great defining characteristic of the all-powerful Divinity in Greek thought was singleness as opposed to multiplicity. The Divinity was the one force or power which had ever existed simply by itself, and by and from whom, in some sense, all other creatures had their being. Increasingly in the third and fourth centuries, the total superiority of the Divinity was likewise agreed to be so far beyond all other creatures that it could in many ways be best described in the negative terms of apophatic theology: Unchanging, Uncreated, Indivisible etc.[49]

The fit was, of course, far from perfect. In particular, the idea of the Incarnation, mixing the Divinity in some way with the sensible matter out of which human bodies were created, contravened fundamental ideas about differing substances, and was total anathema to non-Christian Platonists.[50] Even here, however, Platonic ideas were highly influential. Some of the competing visions of the Christian Trinity which filled out the New Testament evidence where Jesus talked about Himself as being sent by the Father and doing His will adopted the Platonic imagery of agency. The Son was thus envisaged as having proceeded from, and hence as necessarily being secondary to, the Father, sponsoring the subordinationist types of Trinitarian doctrine to which Constantius II subscribed. Since the Son had in some way proceeded from the Father, then the Son had necessarily to be subordinate, and there is a fascinating passage in Oration 1, given of course to Constantius, where Themistius referred to the care that was necessary when defining the Divine in philosophical terms.[51] And, in more general terms, the cultural overlaps were more than sufficient to allow Themistius to draw upon common ideas and language whenever he wanted to talk about religious matters. Themistius never needed to lay out in his speeches an entire theological system, where the incompatibilities

49 Some introductory literature in English: Wiles, 1967; Chadwick, 1967, chs 8–11; Armstrong, 1979; 1990; Lyman, 1993. This process depended largely upon transformations in Platonism itself: Armstrong, 1967, 15–30, pts. 3–4; Wallis, 1972, esp. chs 1–2. Cameron, A. M., 1991, esp. ch. 4, explores the importance of this overlap in explaining long-term Christian success.

50 Ando, 1996, explores the progressive victory of Christian intellectual intolerance. On the limits of tolerance from the pagan side, see Athanassiadi, 1992, esp. ch. 5 on the emperor Julian. More generally, Ando, 1996, 171–6, argues that the middle existed only as a rhetorical conceit; too much in Christian belief was philosophically incompatible to pagans. In strict terms, this is surely correct, but the argument underestimates the capacity of individuals to 'pick and mix' their own religion out of seemingly incompatible elements. The classic case is Pegasius of Ilium. Ando, 1996, 201, considers him a 'false' convert; we suspect he saw no need to choose: note 33.

51 Trinitarian debates: e.g. Kopecek, 1979; Hanson, 1988; cf. *Or.* 1.8b below.

between Christian and pagan thought would necessarily be exposed. All he did was draw from time to time, in isolated fashion, upon particular philosophical ideas which were appropriate to the intellectual progression of his current speech. This made it much easier to stick to areas of religious consensus.

Themistius used, for instance, the traditional names for the old gods and goddesses (Zeus etc.), where the context – implicit or explicit citation of Homer and other ancient authors – demanded it. In more abstract passages, however, he consistently adopted the usage *Theos*, which can only really be rendered 'God' with a capital G. Over the previous centuries, indeed, intellectual Graeco-Roman religious thinking had moved firmly in monotheistic directions. Behind the plethora of minor celestial powers, fourth-century Neoplatonists and other pagan intellectuals detected a single overarching Divine Power.[52] This transformation of belief conveniently provided the non-Christian Themistius with a monotheistic religious language which was far from out of place when addressing a Christian emperor. Themistius could talk about 'God', and his audience could gloss the term as it chose. He could also do the same with religious epithets and metaphorical imagery, much of which was common to both pagans and Christians in the fourth century. In Oration 1, for instance, Themistius played on the image of the emperor imitating God as the Good Shepherd. This could evoke both traditional Graeco-Roman conceptions of kingship and the Gospel parable.[53] At a slightly more profound level, he also used such shared premises as the sensible/intelligible divide, singularity versus multiplicity, and – another highly influential Platonic idea – the division of any perceived phenomenon into its exterior accidents and fundamental substance.[54]

Hellenistic concepts of kingship had also, by the late Roman period, long since added a religious dimension to state theory. Emperors were chosen by God, because the Empire was God's chosen agent in the world. From Eusebius of Caesarea onwards, certain Christians, at least, were ready to accept this basic picture of the relationship between heavenly and earthly power, and merely re-identified the God concerned:

52  See, e.g., Armstrong, 1967, chs 12–16; Liebescheutz, 1969; Wallis, 1972; Athanassiadi, 1992.

53  *Or.* 1.10a; cf. e.g. Markus, 1974, 54–5, for identical statues of Hermes and Christ as the Good Shepherd. Epithets: *Or.* 1.4d, 9a–b. See more generally Cameron, A. M., 1991, 126–32.

54  See the notes below to *Or.* 1.1a, 2b, 3a, 4b etc.

not the Neoplatonic One, but the biblical Creator providentially engaged in arranging earthly affairs. Imperially involved Christians and non-Christians were thus both saying the same things about the relationship of God and the emperor, and, once again, Themistius was able to discuss such matters in an entirely inclusive fashion. His characterisation of the emperor as 'Law Incarnate', put in place by God properly to moderate, where appropriate, the harshness of the letter of the law fully exploited this readily available middle ground.[55]

In later years, Themistius was even ready, on occasion, directly to cite Judaeo-Christian texts. Proverbs 21.1 on divine guidance for rulers was used by him in three different speeches, once even to correct Homer's vision of Zeus giving human beings sometimes good fortune, and sometimes bad. Likewise, the biblical language of weapons being turned into ploughshares is strongly echoed in Themistius' comments on Theodosius' peace with the Goths in 382.[56] Apart from the Good Shepherd image from John 10, there are no further explicit allusions to scripture in Oration 1. There is one other passage, however, which deserves comment. At Or. 1.12, Themistius developed a picture of the luxuries and evil acts that characterise a tyrannous ruler. A lengthy list was built up, but Themistius' final image referred to tyrants off-handedly as individuals who exchange their good name for silver. Certainty is impossible, but the Christian tradition includes one figure who famously exchanged his good name for silver. It would be entirely in line with Themistius' exploitation of the religious middle ground for him to have wanted Christian listeners to recall Judas Iscariot.

The last example is obviously debatable. It is important to recognise, however, that it fits a very general pattern in Themistius' work whereby the different orations tend to pluck out, from among the vast range of possible ideas available in the texts of Hellenic *paideia*, those which had significant Christian counterparts. Humanity's need for forgiveness and likeness to God, reflecting the fact that man was made in God's image, are central Themistian ideas, drawn from classical authorities. But they also had important resonance, of course, within Christian thought.[57]

---

55  State theory: see esp. Dvornik, 1966. Law incarnate: *Or.* 1.15a–b; cf. 9b–c with notes.

56  Proverbs: *Orr.* 7.89d, 11.147b–c, 19.228d–229a (following Plato's treatment of *Iliad* 24.527ff. at *Republic* 379c–7); cf. Downey, 1962. Swords into ploughshares: *Or.* 16.211a–b; cf. Vanderspoel, 1995, 207, and below Chapter 4.

57  Dagron, 1968, 152–3 with refs.

More isolated instances are dotted throughout the later speeches. Oration 4 referred to man's weakness in only believing in things that can be seen or touched, recalling the Gospel story of Thomas. Oration 6 celebrated God, as we shall see, as the Father of all mankind, making all mankind brothers. Oration 7 declared that the sum of the moral teaching of Socrates and Plato amounted to the idea that one should love one's neighbour and even one's enemy. Oration 19 claimed that, according to Lycurgus, it was important to return good for evil.[58] In all these cases, Themistius cited Hellenic authorities for ideas which had great significance for the Christian religion.

What are we to make of Themistius' treatment of religious and moral issues? According to Glanville Downey, Themistius was constructing an alternative vision of virtue in statecraft from that championed by fourth-century Christians. In his view, Themistius echoed scripture to show that traditional Graeco-Roman *paideia* already contained everything that was good about Christianity. Likewise, Downey argued, Themistius championed throughout his career the use of *philanthropia* – 'love of mankind' – as a term for the single quality which made an emperor God-like, because it had Stoic roots, and thus by-passed any claims to pre-eminence in the Christian tradition. More specifically, Downey also argued that Themistius was being supercilious about the Emperor Constantius' involvement in doctrinal controversies in Oration 1, when he referred to the care with which philosophical terms have to be used when describing the Divinity.[59]

It is unlikely, however, that a man seeking favour via a public speech before an absolute monarch would have left himself open to the possibility of being perceived as 'supercilious'. It is noticeable too that Themistius never entered the debate over the priority of Greek versus Judaeo-Christian moral teaching. The correspondences between the two had long been noticed, and arguments over whether Moses had preceded Plato, or vice versa, had become a standard part of Christian–pagan polemic.[60] Themistius never once mentioned this debate, being content with the common ideas and making no claims about priority. Even in

58  *Orr.* 4.50d; 6.76b–78b; 19.226d–227b; cf. Dagron, 1968, 158–9.

59  *Or.* 1.8b; cf. Downey, 1962, 484. See also Downey, 1955; 1957. Downey's interpretation has been accepted by Ando, 1996, 178–9.

60  The idea that Greek philosophers had studied the Old Testament was already aired by the 2nd-century apologist Justin, the Platonist Numenius, and taken further by Clement of Alexandria: Chadwick, 1967, chs 9–10; Dillon, 1977, 361ff.

the case of *philanthropia,* Downey's own footnotes indicate a rather different conclusion from the aggressively pagan interpretation he ascribed to it. By the fourth century, *philanthropia,* far from being a uniquely Hellenic term, was another concept generally in use by both Christians and pagans. Already in the third century, writers such as Origen and Clement of Alexandria had used it to describe the particular kind of love towards men shown by God, their Creator. In the fourth century, likewise, Christian writers on both sides of the debate over the Nicene definition of faith regarded *philanthropia* as the special characteristic of God which stimulated the Incarnation, and hence made salvation possible. So general, indeed, was its use in Christian circles that the term appears in a number of early liturgies, although these are notoriously difficult to date precisely.[61] Eusebius of Caesarea had even said that the Emperor Constantine (Constantius' father) was imitating the *philanthropia* of God.[62] *Philanthropia* would thus have been a very odd term to adopt if one were attempting to counter the influence of Christianity in state circles. On the contrary, the championing of *philanthropia* confirms that Themistius aimed deliberately to occupy the by now extensive middle ground between Hellenic *paideia* and the Christian imperial religion.

Themistius' acquaintance with Christianity should not be overstated. It may well be that his knowledge of Christian scripture was second-hand.[63] As Dagron argued, however, that is not really the point. Other contemporary Hellenes were either actively hostile to Christianity – men such as Porphyry or the Emperor Julian – or else refused to have anything to do with it. Even though it became such an influential force in his lifetime, for instance, the writings of Libanius display no specific knowledge of any Christian text. In this context, a willingness even to pretend to knowledge of Christianity and to celebrate ideas common to Hellenic and Christian tradition (especially when this involved some manipulation of the literal truth) transmitted an important signal. In Oration 1, like all his works, Themistius indicated to the emperor that he would champion the view that a substantial middle ground existed

---

61  Origen, *Contra Celsus* 4.17; Clement, *Stromateis* 7, 3, 19, 1; cf. Pseudo Clem., *Homilies* 12, 25–33. Fourth century: Eusebius, *On the Theology of the Church* 2.18; Athanasius, *On the Incarnation* 1.3, 12, 6. Liturgical uses: *Apostolic Constitutions,* Liturgies of St James and St Mark. Cf. Downey, 1955 with further refs.

62  Eusebius, *Tricennial Oration* 2.2.

63  Dagron, 1968, 153.

between the old and the new (as, in some ways, it did).[64] This strategy was well conceived to be attractive to the emperor. Although himself a Christian, Constantius ruled an Empire in which there was not yet a Christian majority population, either in the countryside or among the landowning elites of the old Greek cities of the eastern Mediterranean. A philosopher of impeccable Hellenic credentials, who was willing to state that the emperor's new religion was perfectly compatible with traditional cultural norms, was thus a very useful weapon in helping Constantius' regime attract support from the landowning classes essential to the governing of the Empire. Don't be put off by the Christianity, Themistius was implicitly stating, the emperor is really (in Mrs Thatcher's inimitable words) 'one of us'. For Constantius, this pagan support had further importance because other contemporary strands of Hellenistic philosophical opinion were very overtly hostile to Christianity, and Themistius, as we shall see, deliberately confronted them.[65] Themistius, then, won great renown, and Constantius got in return the stamp of Hellenic approval.

The three texts translated in this chapter between them illustrate the evolving relationship of philosopher and emperor. Oration 1, from the later 340s or very early 350s, represents a bid for imperial favour on the part of an outsider, offering little informed comment on the policies and issues of its day. *The Letter of Constantius* which adlected Themistius to the senate in September 355 demonstrates the longer term success of Themistius' strategy of cultural rapprochement. In its text, as we shall see, Constantius allied himself with Themistius on the terms that Themistius himself had originally proposed in their first public encounter, and reaffirmed in years of public teaching and debate. In Oration 3, of May 357, the greater maturity and closeness in the relationship of emperor and philosopher are very much apparent. The speech focussed not – as had Oration 1 – on the speaker's strategies for self-promotion, but discussed important and highly sensitive political issues. The man bidding for preferment at Ancyra had won through triumphantly, and could now deploy his talents in the service of his imperial master, both in generally selling the regime as pro-Hellenic, and in justifying its policies in detail.

---

64  Cf. Dagron, 1968, ch. 4, esp. 149–54.
65  See the introduction to *The Letter of Constantius* below.

## ORATION 1
## ON THE LOVE OF MANKIND OR CONSTANTIUS:
## INTRODUCTION

**Date**

The date and circumstances of Themistius' first speech before a reigning emperor are far from straightforward. According to the rubric prefacing the speech in the manuscript tradition, it was given at Ancyra. The subscription to one law preserved in the *Theodosian Code* places Constantius II there in March 347 (*C. Th.* 11.36.8), and, in older scholarship, this was taken to be the moment of delivery. As Seeck pointed out, however, even if only one Ancyran subscription survives in the Code, Constantius must often have been there. Ancyra lay on the main road from Constantinople to Antioch, and the latter was the main military base for the Persian front, which was often disturbed in the later 340s and 350s. For Seeck, a much better indication of date was to be found in the fact that the speech entirely failed to mention Constantius' brother Constans, emperor of the west. Seeck argued that, had Constans been alive, it would surely have done so, and hence chose to date the speech to 350, after Constans had been murdered by the usurper Magnentius. Working on the same premise, a recent study has slightly modified Seeck's argument. This suggests that the date was in fact 351, arguing that Constantius' amnesty mentioned in the speech should be equated with the first amnesty offered by him to supporters of the usurper Magnentius in that year. In this more precise form, however, the argument fails to convince. If the speech really belonged to 351, we would expect its focus to have been the western usurper, who was now a much more pressing threat to the security of Constantius' world than the Persians on whom Themistius concentrated. Themistius' characterisation of the amnesty (*Or.* 1.14b–15a) likewise suggests something on a much smaller scale than a general offer designed to win political support away from a dangerous enemy.[66] The year 351 is unconvincing, therefore, and, in our view, the dating indications available in the text of the speech leave open the possibilities that it was delivered in either c.347 or late 350.

The most explicit indication of the speech's possible date is provided

---

66  Seeck, 1906, 293–4; modified by Portmann, 1992. Seeck's arguments largely ousted the older preference for 347: refs. and counterargument as Vanderspoel, 1995, 73 n. 9.

by its discussion of an incident in Constantius II's continuing wars with
the Persians, when the emperor's nearby presence forced the Persian
ruler Shapur to withdraw his forces from an action they were undertaking on Roman soil. Themistius' words – emphasising the Persians'
manoeuvrability – make it clear that this recent action had involved a
Persian retreat rather than a major battle (11b–c). There are two main
possibilities for the action being referred to, namely the sieges of Nisibis
in 346 and 350, where the intervention of Roman forces caused Persian
retreats without set-piece battles being fought. Vanderspoel has recently
argued that this sequence of events best fits the known action of the 346
campaigning season, when the Persians were forced to withdraw by the
arrival of Constantius and his troops. For Vanderspoel, the fact that
Constantius himself remained in Antioch in 350 is enough to rule out
this year's action as that being referred to, since Constantius was not
'nearby' in that year, as the speech records. The speech would thus fall
between the campaigning seasons of 346 and 348: i.e. c.347 (in 348, a
major battle was fought with the Persians at Singara; if the speech had
followed this action, it would surely have mentioned it).[67] While
accepting the significance he ascribes to Persian 'manoeuvrability', we
would read Constantius' 'proximity' as having a rather less specific
meaning, referring generally to the placement of the Persian Empire
next to that of the Romans. This interpretation has the effect of salvaging
the year 350 as a possible date for the speech based on the Persian war
passage.

The other possible indication of date is provided by a veiled reference
to inter-dynastic rivalry between Constantius and his brothers, where
Themistius commented that God made prosper the regimes of those
who imitated Him, but took power away from inferior individuals (*Or.*
1.9c). By itself, the hint is too obscure to know whether Themistius had
in mind the distant past or something more recent. On the death of
Constantine, his three sons and Dalmatius, the son of his half-brother,
divided the Empire: Constantine II gained Gaul, Spain, and Britain;
Constans inherited Africa, Italy and Illyricum; Dalmatius received
Macedonia and Thrace; Constantius came to rule Asia and Egypt
(*Anon. Val.* 35). Dalmatius was killed in 337, when Constantius gained

---

67  Vanderspoel, 1995, 74–6. Downey, 1958, 63 n. 15 (following Dindorf's commentary,
499), equated the Persian's destruction with one of the two battles of Singara, but Vanderspoel is entirely convincing that a major battle had not occurred.

Thrace and Constantine Macedonia. Constantine was killed in 340 while interfering in Constans' territory in Italy. Relations between Constantius and his one surviving brother Constans remained tense throughout most of the 340s, before the latter's murder at the hands of Magnentius in January 350.[68] Following Constans' death, there followed a period of negotiation before Constantius declared his implacable hostility to Magnentius and launched the campaigns which led to the latter's destruction. Themistius' dynastic comment would thus fit both the political context of the later 340s, and that of c.350. In the former case, it would have been a moralising judgement on the likely fate of the still-living Constans, based on that of his dead brother Constantine II, should his hostility continue towards Constantius. It would also have been appropriate, however, to the period of negotiation in 350, after Constans had fallen, but before Constantius had declared his hand against the usurper. At this point, a panegyricist would have to be evasive, since Constantius' regime had not yet decided whether to accept Magnentius (a policy which would have demanded much justificatory condemnation of Constans) or attack him (requiring a very different approach to the dead Augustus).

The action described on the Persian front and the veiled dynastic comment thus leave open two possibilities: c.347 (after the first siege of Nisibis in 346, but before the battle of Singara in 348) and late 350 (after the breaking of the second siege of Nisibis, but before Constantius declared war on Magnentius). The second possibility offers a much narrower window than the first, making c.347 perhaps preferable. It may even be, as used commonly to be held, that Oration 1 was indeed delivered during Constantius' visit to Ancyra in March 347.

### Circumstances

Quite what Themistius was doing at Ancyra is also uncertain. Vanderspoel has recently suggested that he was temporarily holding a teaching post there. There is no explicit evidence for this, but we know that Themistius did some teaching at Nicomedia early in his career, and, if analogy is appropriate, his contemporary the rhetor Libanius held a series of teaching posts in different cities during the early part of his

---

68 Most recently, Barnes, 1993, esp. ch. 7, and, with specific reference to the date of *Or.* 1, 313 n. 21.

career. After c.340, Libanius taught at Athens, Constantinople, Nicaea, Nicomedia, and Constantinople again, before settling in his native Antioch in 353. Themistius' early career could well have followed a similar pattern, and, if the earlier of the possible dates for the speech is preferred, he might well have been teaching at Ancyra.[69] If the later date is chosen, however, Themistius would by then have already been established at Constantinople,[70] in which case he presumably went to Ancyra specifically to address the emperor: another young orator getting his big chance to frame an imperial panegryric.

Such an opportunity could have come about in a number of ways. Indications in some of the roughly contemporary Latin prose panegyrics suggest that the speakers had put themselves forward: professional teachers in search of renown (to attract better or richer students) or imperial preferment. There were many formal ceremonial occasions in the late Empire when such speeches were given.[71] Nonetheless, to win such an opportunity was a major coup for a young man, and influential friends and contacts at court were no doubt very helpful in this, as in so many other areas of life. Against this background, it is noticeable how much attention Themistius paid in Oration 1 to the emperor's 'friends'. With a treatment of the subject by Dio Chrysostom in mind, which itself may have drawn on Plato's vision of ruler and auxiliaries working in perfect harmony in the *Republic*, Themistius noted that the emperor's virtue transmits itself to his friends who serve him willingly. He also emphasised later on in the speech that nothing was more crucial to the success of a reign than the high quality of those who serve the ruler.[72] Themistius was certainly making a perfectly valid point here about how much any Roman emperor – ruler of a vast territory possessing pathetically inadequate communications – required trustworthy subordinates to enforce his rule. At the same time, he may also have been working into the speech a graceful compliment to the man or men who had helped him obtain the opportunity to speak.

69  Vanderspoel, 1995, ch. 2.

70  Julian was taught by him in Constantinople in 348/9.

71  Occasions: Mattingly, 1950; 1951; Nixon and Rogers, 1994, 26–9; cf. MacCormack, 1981, esp. 1–14. Selection: Nixon and Rogers, 1994, 30–3, stressing self-selection on the part of schoolmen and others who were not imperial employees, and the initiative of city senates in choosing their own ambassadors, *contra* Pichon, 1906. For further discussion of this point, see Chapter 1.

72  *Or.* 1.10c–d; 17b–c with notes below.

Friends, indeed, remained important to his career. In Oration 16 of 1 January 383, celebrating the consulship of Fl. Saturninus, Themistius noted his own thirty-year relationship with the consul, including the remark that Saturninus had 'helped correct me once I had established a reputation' (200b). Saturninus is known to have been *cura palatii* sometime before c.360. The duties of this functionary are a little obscure, but it was certainly a court administrative post close to the emperor,[73] so that Saturninus would have made an excellent patron for Themistius to cultivate. That is not to say, of course, that it was Saturninus who arranged Themistius' opportunity to speak at Ancyra. Saturninus was a political survivor, a man, like Themistius, who negotiated his way across a number of changes of regime, not to mention the Gothic war, in order still to be active in 383. Themistius may well have cultivated a series of court officials in the late 340s, not all of whom survived to be celebrated subsequently. What is clear is that access to the emperor in a highly centralised palace system was crucial to individual success, and that Themistius was well aware of it.[74]

## The Speech

Having once been given the opportunity, Themistius grabbed it in both hands, as the text of Oration 1 itself shows. In its opening lines, he deployed the public persona which would sustain him, as we have seen, for the rest of his public career.

> Now, for the first time, your majesty, there comes on the scene for you both an independent speech and a truthful praise giver, and there is no word, however insignificant, that he would utter of his own free will for which he shall not render account to philosophy (*Or.* 1.1a).

Straightaway, the audience was introduced to the idea that as an impartial and objective philosopher, Themistius could not but tell the truth. This status also enabled him to claim that, because he was drawing on traditional repositories of Hellenic wisdom – particularly Plato and Aristotle – he could, moreover, see more clearly than other commentators

---

73  Jones, 1964, 375.

74  Cf. the *amicitia* networks around the court crucial to individual promotion which show up in the more or less contemporary letter collections of Ausonius and Symmachus. On the latter, see esp. Matthews, 1974.

where the emperor's true political virtue might lie. Where other speakers praised emperors merely for the external trappings of their power and status, Themistius, because he was a philosopher, could discern the true moral worth of Constantius and the real foundations of his regime (*Or.* 1.1a–2b).

The audacity of Themistius is worth underlining. Standing up in front of a highly autocratic ruler and his court, used to hearing many speeches in the course of the average ceremonial year, and claiming to have something new to offer is the sign of a great risk-taker. With knowledge, from hindsight, of Themistius' subsequent success, it is easy to underestimate the risk he took. Nor was his boldness limited to the speech's opening lines. As we have seen, Themistius, although a non-Christian, then went on to root Constantius' virtuous rule in proximity to God, and used Plato and Aristotle – the key repositories of *paideia* – to 'prove' that this was the case. Constantius' Christian religion was thus no barrier to his coming up to scratch even when viewed through the lens of traditional Hellenism. A middle ground between Christianity and *paideia* was thus identified and occupied; the old wisdom and old cultural values could still be of service to a Christian emperor. The speech concluded with an equally daring bid for imperial favour. As we have seen, the emphasis Themistius placed in the speech on the importance to the emperor of his 'friends' – his eyes and ears – in creating good government was in part, probably, a graceful compliment to the patrons who might advance his career. The speech closed, however, with the thought that there could be no better comrade for an emperor than philosophy, which must tell the truth (18a–b). This reinforced a rhetorical conceit adopted earlier in the speech, where Themistius presented his words as doing no more than reporting and ordering what everybody was already saying (3d–4b). In other words, Themistius presented himself in the middle of the speech as having already acted as the emperor's eyes and ears – his friend – and offered at its end to continue the same service. Like the speech's opening, this was a bold bid for favour.

As was only appropriate in one claiming to be telling the truth 'for the first time', Themistius also adopted, as we have seen, an unusual form of speech structure. The speech carefully signalled that its author was familiar with the norms of the *basilikos logos* (speech to an emperor) as described in rhetorical handbooks such as that of Menander Rhetor (e.g., *Or.* 1.2b, 16c), but departed from them radically. Taking Plato and Aristotle as his starting point, Themistius set out to establish from first principles what the character and actions of the ideal ruler should be like. He then compared the specific actions of his imperial subject to these ideals established a priori, 'demonstrating' thereby that Constantius did indeed conform to the profile of an ideal ruler.[75] In both his self-presentation as truth-teller and his rhetorical emphasis upon philosophical principles of ruling derived from Plato and Aristotle, Themistius was greatly influenced by the four speeches *On Kingship* of Dio Chrysostom. The influence of Dio's third, moreover, is particularly marked in this, Themistius' maiden offering. Not only is their basic approach similar, but Themistius also borrowed from Dio many of the signs, deriving originally from Plato, of how the 'true king' might actually be recognised.[76] It would appear, then, that faced with the potentially major but also rather stressful opportunity of speaking for the first time to an emperor, Themistius adopted a sensible strategy. He found a good but perhaps not too well-worn exemplar and exploited it fully. Like the boldness of his initial remarks, Themistius' avoidance of a more usual rhetorical strategy was clearly designed to attract attention, and, like his truth-telling philosophical persona, the form of speech he adopted was destined for a long career.[77]

In all respects – word choice, generic form, and thematic treatment – Themistius' first Oration was, then, a carefully crafted and sustained play for imperial favour. It is not certain that it bore immediate fruit. As we have seen, it is uncertain when Themistius was appointed to a publicly funded chair in philosophy in Constantinople. The contribution of the speech to his longer term success, however, is not in doubt. The boldness of Oration 1 was part of an overall strategy of self-advancement which saw Themistius thrust himself into the public eye in elite circles of the eastern Mediterranean.[78]

Although certainly successful in promoting his career, a very interesting rubric, added later as an introductory comment to the speech, suggests that a subsequent editor considered Oration 1 not absolutely successful as a piece of rhetoric:

75  For the *basilikos logos*, see Menander Rhetor in Russell and Wilson, 1981, 76–95. Themistius' departure from this norm is discussed in more detail in Chapter 1.

76  *Or.* 1.5c–d (courage); 6aff. (self-control); 8a–b and 14bff. (justice).

77  On Themistius' general use of Dio, much less marked in other speeches, see Chapter 1.

78  On the details of Themistius' rise to prominence, see the introduction to this chapter.

> This was delivered at Ancyra in Galatia when he first met the king, while still a young man; as a result it does not altogether master the *Idea*.

This is of interest for two reasons. First, it may well represent Themistius' retrospective appraisal of his own salad days. Only a few of Themistius' speeches have such rubrics (Orations 1, 2, 4, 20, and *The Letter of Constantius*), none of them later in date than 1 January 357. In Oration 4, of 356, Themistius mentioned the fact that, thanks to funds made available by the Emperor Constantius for the copying of manuscripts, the library of Constantinople was now able to expand, and that Themistius was going to donate to it a collection of his own speeches. It is possible, therefore, that the rubrics mark out these speeches.[79] This being so, the most likely identity for the author of the comments would be Themistius himself, although others have been suggested.[80]

Second, and this point is unaffected by the identity of the author, the comment draws attention once again to the rhetorical tradition within which Themistius' speeches had to be framed. *Idea* was a technical collective term in late antique Greek rhetorical theory, developed from older concepts of stylistic 'virtue'. It covered the different responses an orator might seek to extract from his audience, and how to generate them. In Themistius' day, Hermogenes' book on *Idea*-theory was rapidly becoming the canonical text on the subject, although its dominance in this field did not become fully established until the later fourth and fifth centuries. This text made a primary distinction between *Ideas* appropriate for 'political' language, and those more suited to the 'panegyrical'. Assuming that it was the former that the commentator (whether Themistius himself or another) would have had in mind, Hermogenes identified the most important political *Idea* as 'force' (*deinotes*): the correct combination of rhetorical effects to achieve an

---

79  Themistius *Or*. 4.61c–d; cf. Vanderspoel, 1995, 77 n. 29.

80  Seeck and Schenkl, 1906, argued persuasively that the brief comments must all have been written by one man. Noting the parallels between the introduction to *Or*. 2 and the *Philopolis*, and the fact that one MS marginal note identified their author as Libanius, they suggested that it was indeed the latter who was asked to write brief notes for the Themistian collection. This is possible, but not conclusive. Libanius had already been established in Antioch for about three years by 356.

overall persuasiveness of argument.[81] The likelihood that this is a correct interpretation is increased by *The Letter of Constantius* which picks out 'forcefulness in words' (*logon deinotes*) as a potential reason for promoting someone to the senate (19c: translated below). It was presumably in this respect, therefore, that Themistius (if he was, indeed, the author of the rubric) found the speech less than perfect. To the modern eye, indeed, it does seem less effective than some of his subsequent efforts. The most obvious difference between Oration 1 and Oration 2, whose rubric is without negative comment or evaluation, is the former's relative lack of specific examples adduced to justify the overall case being made, namely that Constantius had shown himself to be Plato's ideal philosopher king. There is sometimes also a lack of rhetorical clarity at the moments when the speech moves from the plane of general philosophical argument to discuss specific aspects of Constantius' character, and the transition from a general characterisation of the failings of the Persians to specific recent events also seems rather sudden. All these features suggest a lack of complete structural control on the part of the author.[82]

Whether the ancient commentator had these features in mind, or different ones, is unknowable, since he chose not to elaborate further. Either way, the speech's failings should not be overstated. The criticism is, after all, only a relative one. It strongly implies that the other speeches with rubrics did indeed master the necessary *Idea*. This is perhaps another reason for seeing a successful Themistius, looking back from the safe vantage point of the senate a decade later, as the author of the comment, grandly able to concede that he hadn't always been perfect. Moreover, as we have seen, there is every reason to think that the speech served its immediate purpose. Bold in its claims, unusual in its structure, it said to Constantius that Themistius could identify the common cultural ground which would enable a Christian Roman emperor to govern a state which was still run for him, in large part, by a traditionally minded Hellenic landowning elite.

---

81 Hermogenes can be read in the translation of Wootten, 1987. For discussion, see Rutherford, 1992; 1997; and, on the evolution of the canon, Kennedy, 1983, 96–101; Heath, 1995.

82 E.g., *Or.* 1.8c–d initially moves to a particular aspect of Constantius' virtue, but then slips back to the more general discussion of anger and self-control begun at 6a. Persian transition: *Or.* 1.12a.

## ORATION 1
## ON LOVE OF MANKIND OR CONSTANTIUS:
## TRANSLATION

(This was delivered at Ancyra in Galatia when he first met the king, while still a young man; as a result it does not altogether master the *Idea*).[83]

[1a] Now, for the first time, your majesty, there comes on the scene for you both an independent speech and a truthful praise-giver, and there is no word, however insignificant, that he would utter of his own free will for which he shall not render account to philosophy.[84] For this reason it is necessary for him to praise only those things which he has admired. And in you he has admired a single spiritual quality above all your possessions together.[85] [2a] It is these things, rather, that the average praise-givers see, and celebrate in their speeches: the size of the empire and the number of its subjects, invincible phalanxes of infantry, troops of horse and a great wealth of armament, impregnable screens of weapons, finely woven dragon standards aloft on their gilded shafts, billowing and flapping in the wind.[86] The more polished of them approach a little closer to you and touch upon your crown, your cloak, your inviolate belt and your glittering robe.[87] Yet others consider that in some way they apprehend you more closely still [b] who recount in detail the armed dance, nimble leapings in full armour and manoeuvres

83  For discussion of this comment, see the introduction to *Or*. 1.

84  The first sentence of his first speech established the stance Themistius would maintain for the rest of his life. The sense of εἰσέρχεσθαι ('to come on stage') as a technical dramatic term is retained. Themistius often describes the scene of his orations as a metaphorical theatre (e.g., *Orr*. 4.54b; 3.44b; 15.185a), although he was at pains to dissociate his activities from the practice of display oratory (see the introduction to *The Letter of Constantius*).

85  An example of Themistius' Platonising discourse, which bridged the gap between pagan and Christian. By definition, a single quality must be greater than multiple qualities derived from it, and a spiritual quality greater than any material possession: see the introduction to Chapter 2.

86  This approach – accusing others of noticing external trappings, while he sees the emperor's true essence – is modelled on Dio Chrysostom, *Or*. 3.91–5; cf. the introduction to *Or*. 1.

87  An allusion to the custom of *adoratio*, whereby high-ranking functionaries were offered the imperial purple cloak to kiss. Supposedly introduced by Diocletian, it could also be used as a public mark of favour, and its withdrawal as a symbol of hostility: Matthews, 1989, 244–9. See also *Or*. 11.142a for a comparison between the outer richness of imperial state robes and the true *kosmos* ('order' and 'ornament') of the soul.

on horseback, and they naturally sing praises of a body which from the third generation of royalty is so disposed to labours.[88]

But these men equally fail to understand that every king has but small power to maintain his rule by his hands or even his entire body in comparison with the force of his mind; whoever is able to see that, he is the one who can distinguish the true king and admires you, not what is yours.[89] [c] And indeed, the others also experience what one might expect. For the soul is quite simply something which is more difficult to perceive than the body. The eyes of most men see the latter in an instant but are unable to apprehend the former. The surface attributes which surround the king, being intricate and pleasing to the eyes, cheat the sight of what is within, just as I think, the outer gates of some holy temple constructed out of costly and painted masonry, by turning the onlookers towards themselves and engaging them, robs the shrines of their gaze. [d] But even there the sensible and pious man, I think, proceeds straight to the inner sanctum while most men stay outside and are beguiled like cattle by the ornament around the temple.[90] If what I am saying is still not clear, we shall shed more light on the meaning from what is, I think, a yet more illustrious example. In the case of God, whose works and progeny all these things are, is it equally easy to perceive both Him and His creations? [3a] Or is it not the case that nature has fashioned eyes for the latter right from the start, and it is possible when they are open to see the sun, the moon, all the other stars and the whole of heaven, while to catch sight of Him who is beloved [is possible] for whoever might eventually come to Him through them.[91]

88  Constantius II was son of Constantine I, and grandson of the tetrarch Constantius Chlorus. It was a standard pattern in praise speeches to move through the subject's origins, birth, education, and accomplishments: Russell and Wilson, 1981, 76–95. Themistius here signalled that he would deliberately not follow this approach. Constantius was skilled at the pyrrhic dance (performed in full armour) and was an accomplished horseman (see Ammianus 21.16.9; Julian, *Or*. 1.11a–b). Themistius thus managed to work in some standard forms of praise while stating that he would not be doing so. Themistius later used Constantius' lineage in a disparaging context: *Or*. 8.115c.

89  I.e., again in Platonising terms, Themistius will be admiring the substance not the accidents of Constantius' kingship.

90  A favourite Themistian image, see *Orr*. 3.45c–d, 34.vi

91  Themistius makes the distinction between those elements of the universe which can be perceived using the physical senses, and the higher order beings, especially God, who have to be approached by intellect alone. This was another Platonising commonplace: see the introduction to Chapter 2.

But since my speech has successfully come to anchor at an image that is both entirely appropriate and quite beautiful, come, let us ride at it and draw the conclusion that remains.[92] And so, just as, I think, His creations reveal God's nature so his [the king's] actions demonstrate royal virtue to those who can progress from the deeds to the doer. **[b]** To where, then, do the deeds lead us, and what kind of path do they reveal? It is not one that is hard to travel and overshadowed, the kind along which most tyrants slink as if to the dens of beasts, but one which is broad and maintains clearly visible tracks, nor does it lead on to some savage and dangerous animal – a bear, boar, or lion clothed in a king's name – but to a heavenly creature which is the most easy-going and gentle of all, 'sharing in its nature some truly divine and modest element', and bestowed from there to those here, for their care.[93] Before we begin to track him down, let us agree what message concerning him we shall proclaim in our speech. **[c]** All you men who are steered by the same helm, if you discover it [i.e. the speech] to be cheating even in the smallest degree, insult and reject it and cast it from philosophy for doing things which are neither righteous nor in accordance with her laws. But, if in all that it praises, it tells the truth, then do not be angry with it, nor think it a flatterer instead of a praisegiver. For nothing is more inimical to truth than flattery, but praise is virtue's witness.[94] **[d]** Each man bears witness to what he knows. And so, as he who understands one particular thing among everything else is a good witness to it, so too those who recognise it are good witnesses to virtue.

You[95] understand then what my discourse has established: only philosophers are witnesses to virtue. But let this too be added to our proclamation. My fellow men, be aware of this too, that every word you utter about the king, time and again in the market places, in the theatres, in your houses, **[4a]** in the baths, while voyaging or travelling by land, while at leisure or at work, my speech has collected them all and put

92  The first of many nautical references in this oration.

93  This vision of two paths, one broad and easy leading to royalty, the other narrow and dangerous leading to tyranny, is based on Dio Chrysostom, *Or.* 1.67ff., where Hermes shows them to Hercules. The concept of kingship being sent down from heaven for the care of mankind is repeated at *Or.* 6.73a–b, and echoes late Roman state propaganda which held that the earthly order maintained by the Empire was divinely ordained and echoed that of heaven; see generally Dvornik, 1966, chs 8, 10–12. The quotation is from Plato, *Phaedrus* 230a.

94  The same thought is developed at greater length at Dio Chrysostom, *Or.* 3.17–24.

95  Plural = whole audience.

them together as our shared offering. And you shall hear from us in ordered form what you say casually to each other. And so if it is lies you speak, then it is lies you shall hear; but if it is the truth, we shall give you back what is yours. But it *is* the truth you speak; for, had you been lying, you would not have spoken these things. Listen then to this voice, to see if you recognise it as your own.[96]

You recite, do you not, and sing to each other of one special virtue of the king. Shall I speak the name of that virtue? [b] But I know well that those present will shout it out and snatch the name from my lips before it is finished. Yet I did tell you that I gathered this together from you, and I am not making out that it is my own discovery. Your word is really quite short and not polysyllabic but I shall give it back like a coin, adding the power of the name like interest [upon it]. I consider that it is the king who loves mankind[97] who is quite perfect in the virtue in question and there is nothing that he lacks for his good name to be complete. [c] Follow my words in this way. Does it seem to you the characteristic of one who loves mankind to wrong and injure men, and to plan and effect this very thing as if he hated them? Or is it ridiculous to think so? Surely it is necessary in such circumstances that he be just. What else? Would the man who loves mankind wish to act intemperately towards men or indeed commit outrages against them? Or least of all? For how would the name prove true? Surely this at least bears witness to his self control. [d] But does he who loves something and values it highly, hand it over to an enemy who is trying to destroy it, or does he fight with all his strength to ward off the outrage? And so whom is it fitting to call the brave man? The one who fends off the rages of others but himself destroys his darlings through his own rage?[98] Or is it the especial mark of love of mankind not to be over-

96 Themistius claims to present the common view of Constantius in more analytical form. Since he was going on to say nothing bad, the only way a listener could have unmasked him as not telling the truth was by arguing that Constantius was not as good as Themistius said.

97 τὸν φιλάνθρωπον βασιλέα: the first mention of this great Themistian theme, which again bridged the gap between classical culture and Christianity: see the introduction to Chapter 2. φιλανθρωπία and φιλάνθρωπος are translated literally ('love of mankind' etc.) throughout to retain the effect Themistius aimed to achieve in his comparisons with other qualities described by *phil-* compounds. The basic approach is again Platonising. *Philanthropia* is the single – hence superior – virtue of God and kings, from which multiple – hence inferior – other virtues derive: cf. note 49.

98 This would have brought to mind a comparison with Hercules, the great archetype of human bravery, who destroyed his wife and children on being driven mad by Hera.

come by anger? What else, indeed, can mildness, reasonableness and gentleness with justice be called?[99] **[5a]** So you see that when I knock on this small word,[100] the whole swarm of virtues speaks out in response, and rather my speech goes its own way, and is not dependent upon the king in proceeding with greater certainty. For whenever [someone][101] possesses the soul of a king and reveals all good things gathered together in one place, then he is revealing such love of mankind. Is he not as far removed from greed as from cruelty, or as far from arrogance as from savagery? Let us not grieve [him] by speaking even the very name of intemperance. For he does not consider happiness to lie in a life of luxury, **[b]** but in doing what is most noble, guarding his soul by reason rather than his person by bodyguards, so that it is assailed by no passion. For he understands well, I think, that it is necessary for him who wishes to rule others first of all to rule himself.[102] And it is indeed shameful to suppose that athletes at Olympia take very good care of themselves with both diet and exercise, but that the world's champion is at the mercy of pleasures. **[c]** However, I find that his innate love of mankind is a provider of all these things for him. You may learn the reason from me.

Just as we say there is one virtue for men, another for dogs, another for horses, so there is, I think, one which is peculiar to a king and is royal beyond all others – to which the rest are linked as if leading to a single peak. For if we were to examine each one carefully by itself, as if turning over a coin, we shall not find one which so displays the mark of royalty as the one called courage. **[d]** For a king must certainly possess this, and indeed all the other virtues as well. And yet, if you take hold of this alone, it does not bear the stamp of royalty but rather you will see that it has

99 τόδε δὴ πρᾷον καὶ τὸ ἐπεικὲς και τὸ ἥμερον: cf. Downey, 1962. This recalls the New Testament 2 Cor. 10.1: διὰ τῆς πρᾳότητος καὶ ἐπιεικειας τού χριστού ('by the meekness and gentleness of Christ'), and was perhaps meant to; see the introduction to Chapter 2. But it also recalls Aristotle, *Nicomachean Ethics* 112, so that Themistius firmly located himself on religious common ground.

100 See Plato, *Theaetetus* 179d. Downey's translation misprints 'word' as 'wood' here.

101 We suggest τις to supply sense to the Teubner text.

102 A central topos of Graeco-Roman civilisation, which claimed that it enabled the individual to become more rational by learning to control bodily passions by developing the mind. See, e.g., Heather, 1993a; 1993b, or Eusebius, *Life of Constantine* 2.13–14 on Constantine's mastery of himself and his emotions. On Constantius' ceremonial presentation of his superhuman qualities in his entry to Rome in 357, see the introduction to *Or.* 3. Constantius' temperance was a well-publicised feature of his character: Ammianus 21.16.4–6; Julian, *Or.* 1.10c, 16a–c, etc.

imprinted on it that of the soldier or general, since the great glory of a commander and a captain is to be brave beyond most ordinary people.[103] But what about endurance? Self-control? Are these not spiritual qualities for private citizens? **[6a]** I for my part say that much-celebrated justice is a king's most precious possession. For what is more divine than a just man who has the power to do many wrongs [but does not]? Self-control indeed comes near this. For what use is a ruler who is not free?[104] This is the tyrant who at one and the same time rules other men and gives himself up as a slave to his passions. All in all, this is how it is with all these virtues, it seems to me. For each of them, when one examines them for oneself, is a distinction shared by all mankind **[b]** but becomes that of a king precisely at the moment when love of mankind sets its seal on it. Just as I think the stamp of God transforms plain gold, which before shows only gold's beauty, into a divine image when it has appeared on it.

Let Homer come to my speech and let him tell of love of mankind as a beautiful thing:

'Never did I see with my eyes one so excellent
nor yet noble – for he is like a king'.[105]

**[c]** For in each man's nature there is, I think a personal stamp of virtue which is of advantage when it is present; and, conversely, great harm results if it does not possess it. What is there noble in a farmer or a cobbler being mild? How will his mildness benefit the majority if his neighbours hardly recognise him? How ridiculous it is to attest to love of mankind in a weaver or a carpenter who has a mean dwelling, and who scarcely leaves his house through weariness and lack of leisure. Such a man will regret it if he is not very circumspect and gentle. **[d]** But whenever that 'eye' is serene 'to which the people are entrusted and which has so many cares',[106] this is the good fortune which is shared by all. The shipowner and the merchant do not pray that the straits at

103 Courage is also placed first at Dio Chrysostom, *Or.* 2.54ff. (a long list of royal virtues). This passage likewise highlighted justice to which Themistius also devoted particular comment. But Themistius' overall message – that none of these is royal without 'love of mankind' – owed nothing to Dio.

104 Free, that is, from bodily passions: see note 102.

105 Homer, *Iliad* 3.169–70: Priam's observation on Agamemnon, pointed out by Helen from the walls of Troy.

106 Homer, *Iliad* 2.25, 62. As the eye is the most important of the body's vital organs, so the emperor is the Empire's.

Chalcis are calm – how many either sail on it or see them? – but rather the Hellespont, the Aegean, and the Ionian, **[7a]** which all merchant ships cross.[107] And so if the king's spirit does not run high, and savage blasts of wrath or anger which are easily fanned by small cause, do not stir it up and disturb it, then it is possible not only for merchants and sailors but also for all men to sail through their lives in safety, whether one has embarked on a large vessel or a tiny skiff, the one taking hold a rudder, as it were, the other making do with a rower's cushion. And even if someone wants to come on board as a non-paying passenger, for this man too the voyage is favourable, **[b]** being windless, calm, and still.

It is dangerous enough for a private citizen to be easily seized by anger, but much more dangerous for one who could do anything once enraged. For I consider anger to be a short-lived madness but the man who rages in weakness is less capable of harming those close to him than one who has power and strength. The first may cause problems only for himself, but others too enjoy the other man's sickness. How many would Polydamas or Glaucus strike or kill when in black rage? Whole tribes and races, on the other hand, **[c]** felt the madness of Cambyses.[108]

So while admiring many things in the king, I admire most of all that he has softened all the passionate element of the soul as if it were iron and rendered it useful instead of useless,[109] and beneficial instead of harmful. For he does not allow it to rush ahead of reason, nor permit it, like a horse champing on its bit, to ignore the charioteer, who alone is the preserver of virtue in the soul and dwells in the man who possesses it throughout his life.[110] I hold anger to be a more dangerous passion than

107  The narrow straits at Chalcis separate Attica from Euboea, a crossing which many fewer ships made than the more important ones that follow (Hellespont, etc.).

108  Cambyses was the son of Cyrus and king of Persia 529–521 BC; described by Herodotus as a mad and savage tyrant (3.30–38). Polydamas and Glaucus both appear in Homer as mild and cautious characters. The Trojan Polydamas invariably counselled discretion, much to Hector's annoyance (he ignored him once too often when going out to meet Achilles: *Iliad* 18.249ff.), and Glaucus agreed to exchange armour with Diomedes the Greek rather than fight him, accepting thereby the worst of the bargain since his was of gold but Diomedes' of bronze (*Iliad* 6.119–236). Themistius' point is that even if they had not been so mild, it would not have affected large numbers of people.

109  Cf. Vanderspoel, 1995, 78: an almost direct quotation from Plato, *Republic* 411a–b. Plato, however, continued by warning that this process, if allowed to progress unchecked, would cause feebleness.

110  Cf. Vanderspoel, 1995, 78: this would have brought to the audience's mind Plato's famous image at *Phaedrus* 246a. On the ancient idea that reason's control of physical desire underpinned civilisation, see note 102.

pleasure. For everyone who is not completely dissolute shuns the latter vigorously **[d]** because it is entirely base and obviously enslaving. And because of this, even quite insignificant and run of the mill people often appear superior to this passion, but very few are completely above anger. For this motion of the soul which is commended as virile and noble, slips into many quite easily under the mask of virtue.[111]

**[8a]** Furthermore, that love of mankind is a yet more royal virtue than all the rest of the company, you may learn from this. The king of the entire universe is not called by men wise or patient or brave. For what is fearsome to him against which he should need courage, or burdensome that he should overcome it with endurance? What kind of physical pleasures are there which he does not conquer through self control? And if justice [lies] in contracts and partnerships between those who have entered into agreements,[112] **[b]** even this might defile in some way the life which is superior to all contract.[113] But, as I said, while we consider these names to be unworthy of God as too trifling or inferior for Him, we are not ashamed to call Him a lover of mankind. And this is why. Man's intelligence naturally considers everything inferior to Him which it is able to find in any of the things which derive from Him.[114] Thus intelligence ascribes to the source of all things being beyond being, and power beyond power, and goodness beyond goodness, hesitating, however, and moreover being cautious in the association of the terms.[115] **[c]** But even though [intelligence] is like this, it does not

---

111  In his discussion of different types of self-restraint, Themistius slipped from general principle to Constantius himself. Constantius prided himself on his self-control, and was famous for it: refs. as above note 102. Ammianus also notes that Constantius went to great lengths to be considered just and merciful, although his anger was fierce: 21.16.9–11. As Vanderspoel, 1995, 79, rightly comments, Themistius was clearly praising Constantius here in terms favoured by the emperor himself. For the suggestion that a lack of control in this transition might have been behind the perception of the speech as lacking rhetorical 'force', see the introduction to *Or.* 1.

112  As it is said to be for the sake of argument by Socrates at Plato, *Republic* 331eff.

113  On this basic vision of the Divinity, compare Aristotle, *Politics* 7.1.10 (1323b).

114  A fundamental principle of Neoplatonic cosmology. Everything proceeds from, and is therefore inferior to, the one universal principle in the hierarchically ordered universe: e.g., Wallis, 1972, 61ff. This was a formulation which Platonising Christians would have found unobjectionable.

115  Downey, 1958, 59 n. 11 (elaborated at Downey, 1962, 484–5), suggests that this might be a reference to the Christological debates raging in Constantius' reign. This may well be so, since Themistius is ostensibly underlining their importance, and, in the preceding sentence, implying that Christ would have to be subordinate to God the Father, which was

despise love of mankind, but exults in the term as if it had discovered
something peculiarly appropriate. How therefore is that man not truly
blessed who alone is able to share a virtue with God? How is this ornament not especially fitting above all the rest for a king, when not even
the Father of all things will disdain it? How is it not right to hate and
scorn tyrants who are able to emulate God but do not wish to?

[d]I laugh when I call to mind one of the kings of the past because he
set such great store by thinking he shared in a certain divine power and
a superior nature, and compelled men to dedicate temples and statues to
him as to a god, but in no way whatsoever chose to love men as God
does.[116] Indeed men render the former things [i.e. temples and statues]
to God, and He renders the latter [i.e. love] to men. It is not the man
who pursues His honours but the man who pursues His virtue who
imitates Him, [9a] nor is he who deems himself worthy [of those
things][117] His devotee, but he, who being His devotee, shares them out.
And so the one who is not worthy forces such an honour, and the one
who is worthy, does not wish to have it. The former because he is in this
respect impious, the latter because in this he would recognise those who
are better. Hence it is natural that a king who is dear to God is one who
loves mankind. Mutual friends are those who take delight in the same
things. And he alone truly knows that it is necessary to serve God by
likening one's mind to His with all one's power. For this is what it is to
admire Him, this the great hymn, this the true reward, this a fitting dedi-
cation for a king: to fashion not bronze, silver or gold, [b] but his own
soul into an image of God. The philosopher desires this too but, falling
short in his power, seems altogether imperfect in the form [of that
image]. But the man who, above all other men, is both able to and does
choose the good, this man is a perfect and complete image of God and
the former is on earth as the latter is in heaven, guiding some portion of
the whole realm and trying to imitate in turn the director of the

---

indeed Constantius' broad view: see most recently Barnes, 1993, ch. 18. Downey is surely
mistaken in seeing the reference as sarcastic: see the introduction to Chapter 2.

116  Reading εἴσασθαι after Harduin and Dindorf. Probably a reference to Domitian
who decreed for himself the title *dominus et deus* and demanded that statues to him be
made of gold. Although a great builder of temples, he did not dedicate one to himself, but
Themistius' knowledge of the past was often sketchy.

117  There is a six-letter lacuna in the text which we fill with τούτων 'those things' (i.e.
honours).

whole.[118] [c] The good master welcomes this service and promotes his rule and entrusts him with a greater share while removing it from those who are inferior.[119]

But although this speech, having discovered a quite beautiful image in a superlative example, is keen to linger at the spectacle, let us return it albeit against its will from the divine to the mortal sphere, gently encouraging it back and showing that in no way shall it be false to itself, but it will perform a less dignified but yet more notable service. And so, speaking generally, it should be considered that no one, [d] neither ruler nor craftsman, will achieve success in carrying out his proper task if he does it hating and begrudging it. A groom cannot look after horses who does not love them, nor the herdsman cattle who is not familiar with the herd. That flock is ripe for the wolves whose shepherd dislikes it, and the goats reap misfortune if they are pastured by one who hates them. [10a] So too whoever pastures the flocks of mankind must love this creature.[120] For such a man would care for it with pleasure, loving it like a child and not suspicious of it like an enemy, just as I think a bad cowherd only knows how to do a great deal of milking and to fill his pails with milk, to cheat the expectant herd of its feed, taking no heed of good pasture, and, if it should come upon it itself, removing it, making himself fat and stout while letting the cattle waste away and weakening them.[121] [b] Such a man however shall enjoy his indulgence for a short time, his herd swiftly perishing and he will become a hireling instead of a herdsman, a porter perhaps or a charcoalburner, supporting himself painfully and with difficulty. But the good shepherd gains much from his work and is

118 Downey, 1958, 60 n. 12, comments that these phrases describing the good king as the 'image of God' are so common in pagan literature that Themistius did not necessarily have Christian usages of the same phrase, such as 2 Cor. 4.4, in mind. Cf. note 93; this echoed standard late Roman imperial ideology on the relationship of the emperor and God. Constantine was similarly described by Eusebius at *Life of Constantine* 2.11–12: 'emulating in his royal actions the love of mankind of the Greater Being [i.e. God]'. Themistius thus again located himself on ground common to Christians and non-Christians alike.

119 This would have brought to the audience's minds recent dynastic events, either those of 337–40 if the speech was given in c.347, or the death of Constans if the speech were given in late 350 (see the introduction to this oration).

120 Again Themistius chose an image to find common ground between pagans and Christians. Compare the parable of the Good Shepherd at John 10 (cf. Downey, 1958, 60 n. 14) with, e.g., the frequent references to good and bad shepherds in the speeches on kingship of Dio Chrysostom: *Or.* 1.13, 17–20, 28; *Or.* 3.41; *Or.* 4.43–4.

121 Themistius obviously had overtaxation in mind.

able to offer more in return, warding off wild beasts and looking out for healthy grass. And indeed cattle greatly love the loving herdsman in return, [c] as dogs the huntsman, horses their horse-loving master, and the flock of mankind the king who loves mankind. For no creature is deceived[122] in this way and is bitten by friendship, nor can a lover be loved in return by any other such person except a lover in this way,[123] but just as he especially hates the man who wrongs him, so he particularly welcomes the man who does him good. If it is a fortunate and blessed state to look on the friends you have, how much more blessed is it for those on whom you look to be your friends? So whoever shows clearly that he has the title of kingship sees as many friends as there are men – [d] his subjects who fear for him rather than fearing him[124] – and he alone does not play false to the nature of kingship. He leads those who are willing not those who are in fear, his rule is voluntary not enforced. The evidence for this? Men seek it naturally like those who are unable to lead their lives without it. Nobody seeks out what he will fear but what he will love. Indeed, he who is mighty through fear is superior to those who cower, and so is not mighty; [11a] he, however, who rules through love of mankind rules over men who all stand erect and are exalted. The former adds nothing to his own stature but cuts it away from his subjects, the latter by making all great is still greater than them all. Moreover, neither is that man elevated who, even if he does not cast down his neighbours, does not rise above them, nor is a king truly so-named whom no free man obeys. For what difference is there between such a man and a rich nobody who has many slaves and who exalts himself and puffs himself up because he is better than all his servants? [b] It is the task, I think, of a true king not to humble the upright, but to lift up those who are laid low, so that as far as it is in his power he is more fortunate than the fortunate. The true tyrant does not want to be more blessed than the blessed, but

122  We adopt Reiske's suggestion of σαίνεται for the Teubner αἰσθάνεται σαίνειν: 'to wag the tail' of dogs welcoming their master (*Odyssey* 10.217, 16.6) became 'to fawn on/ flatter' (Aristophanes, *Knights* 1031) and so 'to appear deceptively friendly'. This reading is encouraged by *Or.* 22.273b – *On Friendship* – which uses similar terms to express the idea that humans, like animals, respond to kind treatment. See also Aeschylus, *Ag.* 795–8, and Sophocles fr. 885.
123  Cf. *Or.* 24.304d where Themistius related the myth whereby Eros only began to flourish when his counterpart Anteros was conceived by Aphrodite.
124  A favourite Themistian phrase, used also of Valens at *Or.* 6.80d. The importance of friends to a king is a theme on which Dio also waxed lyrical: *Or.* 3.86–115; cf. *Or.* 1.30–2.

more blessed than the wretched. Just as, I think, some prison warder who has many prisoners under him is happy and rejoices that he is more fortunate than those in the stocks. And because of this, I believe, the Persian is a ruler who is far removed from the title of king. For not only does he consider that all his subjects are mere slaves, and makes them so, **[c]** but even his own relatives, his brother and his son, including him to whom he intends to hand over the kingship. He is really quite ridiculous who considers his brother a slave but thinks himself a freeman.[125]

And so there is no benefit in keeping an upright diadem, but a twisted character, and to have a golden sceptre but a soul more worthless than lead, to clothe one's body in fine and intricately worked garments **[d]** while exhibiting a mind naked of virtue; to hit the mark when shooting birds but miss good sense in one's deliberations, to be accustomed to ride easily on horseback, but to fall more easily from justice. For he who desires what is in no way fitting, but destroys more than he will gain,[126] that man is deceived. He is unjust in his zeal, foolish in his opinion and senseless in his hope. We consider the happiness of such a man to be more polluted than the fate of Oedipus, to whom they say his mother bore children who were also at the same time his siblings.[127] What wonder is it, then, that he who stood outside nature itself stood apart from reason? How does it not follow that the man who looks straight at the king's whole life is looking straight at his weapons?[128] **[12a]** For it was surely not possible for the undisciplined man to admire the self-controlled one, and for one who desires to possess more [to admire] the just man, for the cruel man to admire the mild one, and the one who lives his life closer to wild beasts the gentle one. For nothing is more completely inimical to virtue than wickedness, nor is there anything which hates or despises it more. For I think every bad man considers the

125 Shapur II, king of Persia 309/10–379. Persia was the great enemy, and hence was crucial to the Romans' self-definition to establish their superiority. Vanderspoel, 1995, 80 n. 40, suggests that Themistius may in particular have had in mind Shapur's brother Hormisdas who had fled to the Roman Empire in c.324 and served Constantius faithfully. By 347, he was hardly hot news, but still made a good living symbol of the superiority of the Roman way.

126 Following Dindorf's reading ἢ λήψεται.

127 Oedipus killed his father and married his mother, with eventually dire consequences for all concerned. Themistius later used the mutual destruction of the sons of Oedipus as a parallel for the fate of the Constantinian dynasty at *Or.* 6.74b–c (see Chapter 3).

128 I.e., Constantius' virtues – self-control, justice, mildness, and gentleness – are self-evident to those who examine his life, and are weapons against which Shapur cannot prevail (see what follows).

better man a refutation, and deformity is even more manifest, I suppose, when it is seen close to beauty.

This then is what brings about the ruin of that man: not Mesopotamia, but the virtue of the king shining out next to him. **[b]** And he [Shapur] does not understand what is the only advantage of proximity, which is to entrust the steering oar of his mind to one who is near by and knows how to steer,[129] and to lash his ship [the Persian state] to the great vessel [the Roman Empire]. For, in my opinion, this is better than to put to sea on a small pinnace without steering gear or other equipment, and to fight to the finish with a great and strong trireme carrying many solders, and many oarsmen and marines, and a helmsman reared at the tiller from his infant clothes. Such a man [Shapur] is terribly at sea when it comes to a naval battle,[130] **[c]** even if for some little time he might escape ramming through his manoeuverability.[131]

But we must recall our speech which is turning away from the track on which it set out at the beginning: that the king who loves mankind also has the highest degree of reverence for mankind. For he has especial respect for all those for whom he has especial love. This is the very reason for his not easily doing wrong to man. Indeed such a man places the highest value on the praise he receives from men. For every lover it is good above all else to be praised by his darlings. Whoever desires to be praised wishes to be good. **[d]** For thus he might win love. But how much more appropriate, by the Graces, to name a king as loving

129 An image borrowed from Plato, *Cleitophon* 408b, which may provide the key to understanding the reference to Constantius' 'proximity'. This has been interpreted literally as dating the speech to a moment when the emperor was close to, but not actually on the Persian frontier (Vanderspoel, 1995, 74–6). At *Cleitophon* 407eff., however, Plato puts forward the argument that unless you are able to make proper use of your attributes, you might as well not have them at all. Whoever does not know how to use his own possessions will necessarily not be able to use other people's, and someone who cannot play his own lyre will clearly be unable to play his neighbour's (408a). The only answer, therefore, for those who cannot make proper use of their souls is to resign control to one who is experienced in 'the steering of men' (τὴν τῶν ἀνθρώπων κυβερνητικήν), which is described as justice and its administration. In similar vein, Themistius seems to be suggesting here that Shapur, whose 'soul is more worthless than lead' (11c), and who is entirely unfit to manage his own empire, should abandon his designs upon Roman territory (11d), and hand over control of his own affairs to Constantius, the steersman *par excellence*. If so, πλησίον should be interpreted metaphorically. Since the Roman and Persian empires are contiguous, Shapur's and Constantius' qualities can be directly compared as if they were neighbours.

130 A rather contrived adaptation of Plato, *Republic* 551c.

131 An important paragraph for dating the speech: see the introduction to *Or.* 1.

mankind, than as loving wine or loving pleasure or loving gold or loving silver. The majority [of kings], while ruling men, love gold and desire to be rich and think themselves so, but they are more miserably poor than those who have not even small wealth. For while the latter often sell their clothes because of need, the former exchange a good name for silver.[132] **[13a]** If it is shameful for a champion to yield the Olympic olive crown for a fee, it is even more shameful for a king to relinquish the crown of virtue for money. All government requires both praise and punishment together as its tools, the one increasing virtue, the other curtailing wickedness. The guilty and inhuman tyrant, however, exceeds the errors in his punishments [of them], while he fails to do justice to deeds well done in his honour. For what reward from such a man do we hear of that is equal in magnitude to the punishment of removing a man's skin?[133] But the rewards bestowed by our own gentle king **[b]** are far above the good deeds [that inspired them], and his punishments are fairer than the crimes. For is it characteristic of love of mankind to do good or harm? Philosophy better understands the reason for this.[134] And he seems to be king of reward not punishment. Hence, because of this, the law has from the beginning put rewards into the hands of the king and punishments into the hands of executioners, allotting the actual task to the latter, but merely the issuing of orders to the former, as proper in the one case, and necessary in the other.

**[c]** A successful general does not reward the hero and punish the deserter for the same reason, nor does a charioteer goad an intractable horse as he encourages and urges on one that is well-schooled. One could say that the dignity of a king derives more from honouring than punishing. For such is the imperial purple and the crown that, in honouring, he gives a share of what belongs to himself, but in punishing, he gives what he in no way possesses. Just as honour turns men to good and punishment deflects them from what is base, it is more appropriate for a king to bring about what is good than what is base. For the one only removes from the worse, **[d]** while the other gives a share of the

132 It is striking that, of the different forms of wealth bad kings (tyrants) might love, Themistius finishes with silver and picks it up again here. Avaricious kings were universally held to be a bad thing, but the emphasis on silver suggests that Themistius perhaps meant to bring to mind Judas Iscariot (cf. esp. Matt. 26.15). See further the introduction to *Or.* 1.

133 The last humiliation inflicted upon the 3rd-century Roman Emperor Valerian captured by Shapur I.

134 We delete ξυνή following Harduin and Dindorf.

good as well. For nothing so sharpens or increases virtue as a sure hope of prizes. For there is in us, as Plato says,[135] something which is not a child but, as it were, a youth of good breeding, mettlesome and a lover of excellence in whom, though indeed often asleep in many people, an expectation of honour awakes and arouses and [14a] applies the goad to virtue more sharply than any gadfly. It is perhaps still more beneficial to take thought of useful rather than useless men for each task. For example, in a ship the helmsman does not have equal care for the sailor and the passenger, nor in the body does a doctor have the same care for the hair as for the eye. For because of its less important nature, the one does not cause manifest harm to the whole, but it is necessary that the whole has an interest in the good health or otherwise of the other.

So if it is better to pay attention to good things than to bad, [b] and good men require honour and bad men punishment, then it is better for the king to incline towards honour rather than vengeance. Most punishments do not exist for the sake of benefiting wrongdoers; for they take away life and do not benefit it, even if they appear to be of advantage to everybody else. And surely this is why, most wise king, you removed death from the list of punishments, thinking it a ridiculous remedy, which professes not to benefit the sick man but to assist the healthy. [c] Or is this the wisdom of this ingenious remedy: that it does not cure those to whom it is applied but is of advantage to those to whom it is not? But in my opinion every cure should be of help to the person who encounters it rather than to others. And it will be of help by not destroying but rather by improving. The more skilful doctor is one who does not cut off the ailing leg but tries to set it straight and restore it.[136]

Now shall I tell you the reason for this opinion? The old law, I think, [d]

---

135  Plato, *Phaedrus* 77e (cf. *Republic* 549e–550c); the first passage is cited in Downey's edition but not in his translation: Downey, 1958, 64 n. 16.

136  Portmann, 1988, 133, 261 n. 3, is surely correct in supposing that Themistius had some specific, and presumably recent act of Constantius in mind. Vanderspoel, 1995, 81 n. 43, is not convinced because no specific measure can be identified in the surviving Roman law codes. But the legal sources for the 4th century are very incomplete (see, for instance, the introductions to Chapters 2 and 3 on 'missing' religious legislation), and Themistius' general method is to find an appropriate general principle to heighten the praise due to some specific act. 15d–16a suggests that Constantius made some kind of legal distinction, which removed a death sentence from one whole category of crimes or from one individual in a particular *cause célèbre*. At *Orr.* 16.212d, 34.xviii, Themistius made great play of what was seemingly a particular case of Galatian youths of senatorial family: see Chapters 4 and 5.

in trying to be fearsome stretches out its hand and cries out for the sword, threatening the same death for wrongs in cases when these were not comparable. The reason was that the law would not be able to stand firm if it attempted to adopt a subtle approach to wrongdoings. Dissimilarities in human affairs, in admitting no categorisation, lead the man who attempts to follow them into uncertainty. [15a] Hence, I believe, it seemed best to make a single and harsh declaration for everyone and for every occasion, so that it would be possible to achieve a successful outcome in respect of matters which had not yet occurred.[137] And so this alone was left in the lawgiver's control. And because of this, the law, like some disagreeable and headstrong man, often gives the same answer to people asking different questions. Since this was the case, and since the law, because of this constraint, was making similar utterances on dissimilar matters, the severe punisher was able to lay hold of its actual words and to hold fast to what it said. [b] And because of this, the law often condemns to death one whom it would have released had it been able to give out another voice, committing an unlawful act in some sort of legal way. The king who loves mankind acknowledges the deficiency of inexactitude in the written law, and himself adds what is impossible for it, since, he is, I think, himself the law and is above the laws.[138] For him to make this addition is to remove the harshness of the law. Just as by stroking it its master calms and relaxes the anger of a pedigree dog [c] which is aroused and barking, so the king who loves mankind often soothes the anger of the law and, if it is prescribing execution, for instance, persuades it to punish with exile. And if it is banishing another, he thinks it sufficient to remove some of that man's goods. Equally, it is for justice, which is perhaps gentle and sympathetic towards what is of like nature to itself, henceforth to take a position on wrongdoing in general, and distinguish

---

137  Reading τὰ μηδέπω γεγονότα following Schenkl's conjecture.

138  This is Themistius' consistent characterisation of the emperor's position with regard to the law; i.e., one of total sovereignty: he is the νόμος ἔμψυχος lit. the living law: see further *Orr.* 5.64b (Chapter 3), 16.212d (Chapter 4), 19.227d; cf. Vanderspoel, 1995, 151. Themistius thus takes a particular stance in a debate, going back into antiquity, as to whether a legitimate ruler was bound by written law or not. For Themistius, a king is bound only by his own written laws: *Or.* 6.73 (Chapter 3). The other side of the argument, that a legitimate emperor should bind himself to obey existing written law, was sometimes aired by 4th-century writers (Dagron, 1968, 127–34, citing Libanius, *Or.* 59.12–13). This view could not survive the brute fact, already well established by the 4th century, that the emperor had become the only active source of new Roman law, and hence could hardly be bound absolutely by previous written pronouncements. See, among many others, Honore, 1981, ch. 1.

between error, wrongdoing, and misfortune.[139] For wrongdoing is the transgression of the man who has planned and made a calculated choice; **[d]** error is, I think, a more violent movement of emotion, when some desire or anger suddenly leaps out, with the spirit not giving way entirely to the motion. But misfortune is complete disaster itself and a fault which attaches itself to someone from somewhere outside. For example, let us cast some clarity on the argument from real events. It is possible to kill a man either by planning to do so, or when in the grip of anger, or by accident, **[16a]** such as when exercising or hunting, just as the story has it that Adrastus, a Phrygian exile, who had fled to the court of the king of the Lydians, shot at a beast while out hunting, but missed it, and hit instead the son of the man who had received him.[140]

It is the characteristic of love of mankind to examine carefully these things, and not to punish what has happened at random, but to seek out an excuse for fair dealing. And if anyone thinks that though gentleness is such a fine thing, wickedness grows greater because of it, let this man here and now show the damage, **[b]** how much it was sustained and flourished, and what momentous acts it wrought, or rather [let him show] what great[141] tragic events were once played out, when it [justice] received the other kind of treatment [i.e. indiscriminate harshness], when fire and iron were a source of terror to it.[142]

The king has amply demonstrated that [wickedness] is not watered by love of mankind,[143] but rather it dries up, yields, and submits when justice passes its hand more gently over it. And it is possible to see rather than merely hear about these things. But my speech proclaims something unusual and extraordinary. For it undertakes to double this great praise, **[c]** which it has gone through up to this point, and not

---

139 On this distinction, see Aristotle, *Nicomachean Ethics* 5.8.1. Themistius returned to it again at *Or.* 9.123d; cf. Downey, 1958, 66 n. 17 (with further refs.). On the importance to Themistius of the emperor tempering harsh written law, see Dagron, 1968, 129–32.

140 Herodotus 1.35–45.

141 Reading ἡλίκα for ἡνίκα after Cobet.

142 In this complex and possibly corrupt passage, Themistius compared the present state of affairs, where justice was being exercised with mercy and discrimination, to the harshness of the previous judicial regime in which threats and torture ('fire and iron': standard Roman judicial tortures) were applied as a matter of course. As part of this, he challenged an imaginary critic to give examples to support a case that the latter was preferable.

143 The phrase derives from Plato, *Republic* 550b.

interweave it with another equally great theme, as is customary.[144] But see how great the addition is. For to accomplish these things at this man's time of life deserves not only just twice as much amazement, but rather many times over.[145] Can anyone say that one should be equally amazed at an old man who displays prudence and a young one? Or at a mild and gentle man full of years and at one who is in his full prime? No wisdom is required to make this distinction. [d] And among private citizens too, the longer the time that worthy and good men [live], this shows them to deserve less honour, and the shorter time reveals them worthy of more. For it is not as admirable for virtue to follow age, as for it to bypass and outrun time, especially that portion of it [virtue] which is inherent in old age but is at odds with youth. I did not think that steadiness, calm and gentleness could occur at the time which most disturbs and stirs up the spirit, nor is it easy for me discover it happening. [17a] But men of such an age are generally quick to sudden anger and, darting off, are borne by their emotions like ships without ballast.[146] But the king, being steered by intelligence, forces the billows of youth to grow calm, and to him alone does the phrase 'gentle as a father' apply, because of his virtue but not because of his years.[147] Consider, by the God of Friendship (Zeus), how difficult it is to preserve fairness in circumstances such as these. [b] For most men, through weakness, cannot bear good fortune as if it were a burden, but how much more difficult [is it] at such an age at which men least suffer regulation and then only under duress?

But come, placing a fitting crown on our speech, let us offer this to the king as a perfect gift. Is the king who loves mankind not also, most of all, a lover of his friends. Indeed, if he has taken great thought for mankind, does he not take the greatest thought for his friends? And if he loves those who live under him, he shall especially love those who live with him, [c] and if he can bear least of all to harm his subjects, in no way would he cause pain to those who share his life.[148] For he understands

144 A further reference to the standard thematic progression of subjects normal to a panegyric which Themistius deliberately ignored in this speech. See note 75.

145 Constantius was born in 317 (*PLRE* 1, 226), and was hence about 30 when *Or.* 1 was delivered. We omit χρῆσιμον after Harduin.

146 Cf. Plato, *Theaetetus* 144a.

147 The quotation is from Homer, *Iliad* 24.770, *Odyssey* 2.47, 234. On this general conception that reason is required to control emotion in the civilised man, see note 75.

148 I.e., the imperial courtiers, on whom see further Matthews, 1989, 269ff. On their importance to Themistius' career, see the introduction to *Or.* 1.

that neither wealth of gold, nor of silver nor or precious stones is of such great benefit to a king as a wealth of true friendship. For the man who must see many things and hear many things and have a care for many things at one and the same time, for him two ears and two eyes are too few and one single body and its one soul within. But if he is rich in friends, he will both see afar and will hear things that are not close to him and he will know what is far off, like the seers, and he will be present to many at the same time like God.[149] [d] And so knowing this, he behaves towards each of his friends as to his own body and to his own soul, and friendship with this man is the only thing that is both exalted and at the same time totally secure. To be exalted in tyrants' affairs is dangerous. For whenever one thinks that one walks closely in step with them, then they thrust you away and throw you over a steep cliff or into a deep chasm. [18a] They raise men up not to keep them aloft but so that they can cast them down from above. And yet many of those who fall catch hold of those who push them and carry them down with them. But those who take hold of the king's right hand know that they are held by a safe cable and will be held to the end.[150]

This, then, is the true and honest and pure offering to you from philosophy your contemporary,[151] and it does not flow from the tip of the tongue, while the spirit sounds the opposite from within, but whatever dwells within, this also comes forth from the lips. [b] Philosophy is free from those reasons why man feigns his praises. For her, money is of no consideration at all, nor does she require honour, keeping what is of value within her.[152]

149 This passage was repeated almost word for word by Themistius at *Or.* 23.267a (Penella, 2000, 91 n. 4). By implication, this definition already numbered Themistius among Constantius' friends, since he had already claimed that what he offered in Oration 1 was no more than what ordinary people were saying (*Or.* 1.4a). In other words, he was already acting as Constantius' eyes and ears. See also *Or.* 6.75b (Chapter 3).

150 Reading προσεχόμενοι after Harduin, Dindorf and Iacob. The discussion of the importance of friends to an emperor is based on Dio Chrysostom, *Or.* 3.104–7; cf. Vanderspoel, 1995, 81.

151 ἡλικιώτιδος is ambiguous, and can mean 'comrade' or 'contemporary'. Downey, 1958, 69, chose 'comrade', but the rest of our knowledge would accord with Themistius having been born in c.317, like Constantius (Chapter 1, note 1), so 'contemporary' may be correct: Vanderspoel, 1995, 31ff. Cf. too *Or.* 4.58b where Constantinople is described as ἡ τῆς βασιλείας ἡλικιῶτις since it was founded in 324, the year Constantius was raised to the purple.

152 Philosophy – i.e. Themistius – always tells the truth and is not interested in money, so cannot be bought: see further Chapter 1. Themistius closed *Or.* 1 by emphasising the ele-

# THE LETTER OF THE EMPEROR CONSTANTIUS TO THE SENATE CONCERNING THEMISTIUS: INTRODUCTION

After graduating to a publicly funded chair in philosophy at Constantinople, the next major advance in Themistius' career came in 355, when Constantius promoted him to the Senate of Constantinople by formal letter of adlection.[153] A Greek translation of the letter, which was originally written in Latin, survives in manuscripts of Themistius' speeches. It would appear, from the fact that a brief rubric is attached to it, that the letter was included among the collection of his early speeches which Themistius presented to the library of Constantinople in 357.[154] Such imperial letters were in themselves public marks of high favour, which, along with the grant of statues, marked an individual's rise in status. Grants of both kinds were carefully noted by contemporaries, and not least by Themistius himself.[155]

## Themistius and Constantius

Constantius' letter made it clear that he had advanced Themistius to senatorial rank because of his *paideia*: his cultural and educational achievements as a philosopher. In particular, the letter noted that Themistius had consistently advocated an active philosophy of engagement with the practical problems involved in the right ordering of society. The letter referred to such matters as the correct roles of the population and senate, familial relations, and the general teaching of virtue. All of these subjects, Constantius reported, Themistius had

---

ments of his public persona which would make him a valuable imperial tool: the culmination of his bid for favour.

153 *adlectio* allowed a man of non-senatorial background to be promoted by imperial order to the senate. Individuals of senatorial descent proceeded to full membership by election to various formal posts and by giving the requisite games: Jones, 1964, 530–42.

154 Libanius read the emperor's letter in a Greek translation – probably the version surviving with the speeches – sent to him by Themistius along with a copy of *Or.* 2: Libanius, *Ep.* 434. Themistius perhaps had a hand in this translation which might explain some striking reminiscences of his own style. Given his self-professed ignorance of Latin (*Or.* 6.72e), a translation could not have been his own unaided work, but the Latin might have been based upon a Greek draft that he prepared. On the rubrics, see the introduction to *Or.* 1.

155 See *Or.* 34.xiii–xiv trans. in Chapter 5.

expounded to large numbers of people: 'companies of young philosophers' as the letter puts it.

The so-called 'private' orations confirm the substance of the emperor's remarks. These speeches range in date from Themistius' early days as a teacher to the period in Constantinople. All bear the imprint of the three programmatic ideas which characterised Themistius' version of the Hellenic *paideia* appropriate to a philosopher:

a)   A philosopher should be involved in public life.
b)   A philosopher should speak about correct behaviour to large numbers of people, not just a select few.
c)   As a consequence, it is reasonable for a philosopher to use rhetorical skill when presenting his ideas, to make it easier for large numbers of people to listen to them.

These ideas were already present in what would appear to be his earliest surviving speech, given at Nicomedia at the outset, perhaps, of a teaching stint there. In this speech, Themistius portrayed philosophy and rhetoric as Eros and Anteros; neither could flourish without the other. This speech probably dates from the 340s, possibly even the early 340s. The same ideas featured equally strongly in the funeral oration Themistius gave for his father in the mid-350s. In addition to programmatic or self-justificatory speeches, there also survive some examples of the kinds of speech Themistius gave when presenting philosophy to the masses. Oration 22 on friendship, Oration 32 on love of family, and the incompletely preserved Oration 33 are all examples of this kind of speech.[156]

Set in the context of contemporary cultural evolution, Themistius' particular brand of Hellenic *paideia* was carefully designed to attract the attention of a Christian emperor. Since Plotinus in the third century, an important strand within Hellenism had seen the emergence of the Neoplatonic sage: the philosopher mystic. The central concern of such

---

156   Nicomedia: *Or.* 24; an early dating in the 340s is based on the negative argument that Libanius taught there between 344 and 349 but came to know Themistius only later in Constantinople (Libanius, *Ep.* 793.1 of 362 notes that they had been acquainted for 12 years). Themistius might have taught in Nicomedia in c.349/50, but before Libanius' arrival seems more likely: Penella, 2000, 23–4 with n. 84 for full refs. Funeral speech: *Or.* 20, dated to winter 355: see Vanderspoel, 1995, 89–90 with refs. Themistius signals the importance of these ideas to his work clearly, hence they have been picked up in the full range of modern scholarship; see, e.g., Meridier, 1906, 9–14; Dagron, 1968, 42ff.; Vanderspoel, 1995, 20–3; Penella, 2000, 4–5, with further discussion in Chapter 1.

figures was the spiritual awakening of the individual in order to re-achieve unity with the One – the original divine essence – by contemplation and/or mystic rites. Ethics were by no means completely ignored, and such men continued to undertake the philosopher's traditional services for their cities – particularly the handling of embassies. Nevertheless, both for themselves and for their relatively small groups of followers, the central point of existence was personal spiritual development. One important strand in this developing tradition – Plotinus, Porphyry, and Iamblichus in successive generations together with their disciples and associates – is illustrated in *The Lives of the Sophists* of Eunapius of Sardis.[157] As this and other texts confirm, the developing Neoplatonic tradition recast the philosopher, after the example of Plotinus and his disciples, as an ascetic, withdrawn Holy Man, as much given to mysticism and miracle-working as to the study of ancient texts and the definition of political virtue. Equally important, such figures could not but be hostile to the new Christian religion. Its claims to unique religious authority were totally incompatible with the patterns of spirituality advocated by the Neoplatonists, who sought to defend the rites of traditional non-Christian cult as one of the main paths to spiritual awakening.[158]

Themistius' philosophical programme both implicitly and explicitly set itself up in direct opposition to the Neoplatonic Holy Man. Among the extant fragments of his philosophical speeches are attacks on those who called themselves philosophers, but had no interest in practical matters, hiding themselves away with just a few devotees, particularly young men whom they sought to attract away from their normal social duties and ties. Such specific critiques point up the more general critique of Neoplatonist traditions inherent in Themistius' overall vision of Hellenic *paideia*.[159] Where the Neoplatonists drew on the metaphysical strand in Plato's teaching, Themistius drew more on the political philosophy of Aristotle to emphasise the philosopher's role in maintaining

157 For an introduction to Plotinus, see Armstrong, 1967, chs 12–16; more generally, Wallis, 1972, ch. 1; Gerson, 1996. For an introduction to Eunapius, see Penella, 1990.

158 Fowden, 1982; Lim, 1995, ch. 2. Cf. the fierce hostility to Christianity of Porphyry and the Emperor Julian, who attached himself to this tradition: Athanassiadi, 1992; Smith 1995, ch. 7.

159 *Or.* 21.254b–257c, *Or.* 22.265b–c, and *Or.* 28.341c attack secluded or solitary philosophers. *Or.* 29.347b–c (and *Or.* 22.265b–c) berate those who drag young men away from normal society. See further Meridier, 1906, esp. 40–2 with refs.

proper social order through teaching moral virtue to the individual, seen as part of a working community of human beings. In practical as well as metaphysical teaching, Themistius thus advocated a brand of Hellenism which minimised the possibility of conflict with the Christian religion. His theological comments, as we have seen, were carefully restricted to those Platonic commonplaces which, by the fourth century, underpinned both Christian and non-Christian cult.[160] In philosophy, likewise, his teaching of social values both to individuals and larger crowds was broadly compatible with the emperor's Christian religion, and certainly encompassed nothing as hostile to it as the sages' emphasis on spiritual mysticism. His teachings in Oration 22 on true friendship or Oration 32 on family values, for instance, were both compatible with Christianity.

Not only is Themistius' strategy as a Hellenic intellectual interesting in itself, but of equal if not greater historical importance is the fact that it was successful in attracting the attention of the Emperor Constantius. As we have seen, the latter was committed to advancing the Christian cause, but had, nevertheless, to govern an Empire whose political structures, especially on a local level, were still dominated by landowners educated in Hellenic traditions.[161] In this context, Themistius' intellectual strategy offered Constantius a version of Hellenic *paideia* emasculated of elements hostile to the emperor's Christianity. Constantius responded enthusiastically. What is really striking about *The Letter of Constantius* is its complete acceptance of Themistius on the latter's own intellectual terms.[162] At different points, Constantius praised Hellenic philosophy – at least as refracted through Themistius' prism – as the path to sound thought and right opinion, and hence virtue in the individual (19c–d, 20b–c). Philosophy was held up in the letter, likewise, as an example to all (22a), and Themistius' practice of it, emphasising his combination of philosophy and rhetoric directed towards practical ends, would add greatly – so the letter claimed – to the moral virtue of the senate (21b, 22b). As the letter concluded, philosophy was the 'chief of the sciences' and it was entirely in line with the aspirations of his

---

160 See the introduction to *Or.* 1.

161 See the introduction to Chapter 2.

162 It is so literally striking that one wonders if Themistius himself drafted it (cf. note 154). This is not impossible. Cassiodorus seems to have written his own letter of appointment to the praetorian prefecture in early 6th-century Italy (*Variae* 6.3).

father, the Emperor Constantine, for the new senate, for Constantius to have appointed to it 'the best man' in the person of Themistius (23b–d).

For all his Christianising agenda, therefore, Constantius was ready to recognise in a highly public context – namely a formal, open letter to the Senate of Constantinople – the great if not indeed overriding social importance of one vision of traditional Greek *paideia*. The letter contained no explicit ideological adjustments to Themistius' expressed views which might be attributed to the emperor's Christianity. It didn't have to, of course, because Themistius' intellectual programme had already made them itself. Themistius had defined a version of *paideia* which the Christian Constantius could enthusiastically endorse. Given its broader significance in allowing the emperor to make soothing cultural noises towards the Hellenic landowners who ran his Empire, this was a service well worth the promotion to the senate celebrated in the *Letter*.

## Themistius and the Opposition

Not everyone was so impressed with Themistius' intellectual achievements as the Emperor Constantius. From programmatic and self-justificatory material he produced in the 350s, there emerge fascinating glimpses of the highly competitive intellectual life of mid-fourth-century Constantinople. It was presumably his success in this world, added to the cultural alliance which he offered the Christian Constantius, that in the long term generated Themistius' senatorial promotion.

The public nature of this competition emerges with particular clarity. Teachers were accustomed to be escorted through the streets of the city by corteges of their students, their size providing a highly visible measure of a teacher's popularity.[163] In addition, apart from his presumably private teaching of advanced philosophical matters,[164] Themistius was also accustomed to make set-piece speeches before large crowds. Two venues are referred to in the orations. One was the so-called Theatre of the Muses. This has not been identified, but was clearly a theatre or theatre-like space where large crowds could be gathered. Indeed, on occasion he would announce speeches in advance and summon the crowd to come to listen to him. The emperor himself, it

163 *Or.* 23.293c–294a; cf. Meridier, 1906, 22.
164 Cf. *Or.* 33.366b–c.

seems, sometimes even attended, but the space was large enough to accommodate people from every quarter of the city, including Galata. The crowd there was accustomed to express its approval by shouting and clapping.[165] There was, in addition, a smaller venue with a more select audience, about which Themistius is entirely unspecific, but which may have been the Senate of Constantinople itself.[166]

The competition fought out before this audience sometimes went beyond implicit attacks upon Neoplatonism in general into direct *ad hominem* assaults. Oration 21, for instance, was devoted to a definition of the actions of the true philosopher, which, it eventually emerges, was directed personally against a specific rival who had evidently been attacking Themistius' own credentials. In the speech, Themistius adopted the tactic of citing passages from Plato and Socrates to establish the characteristics of a true philosopher. The resulting list appears at first abstract, but eventually slips into a personal incident from Themistius' life and the present tense. The *ad hominem* nature of the diatribe is then confirmed by the use of the second person singular in addressing the unnamed opponent. The opponent's identity would presumably have been obvious to the speech's original audience.[167]

---

165 Theatre of the Muses: *Orr.* 21.243a; 26.311b–d; 33.364c–d. Crowds: *Orr.* 21.245d; 22.265a–c; 23.282b–83b, 299a–b; 26.311, 324b–c. Summoning: *Orr.* 21.243a; 26.312b–c, 313d–314b (noting that Themistius had gathered the crowd on three successive days). Applause: *Orr.* 23.282d–83b; 26.311c. At *Or.* 23.292b–c Themistius noted that the emperor had often heard him speak; in the speeches there are occasional references to the presence of an *archon*, who may or may not be Constantius, or occasionally other reasons to think him present, at *Orr.* 22.266c (cf. Penella, 2000, 17–18); 25.310b (note too the title; cf. Penella, 2000, 25–6); 28.343a–c (cf. Penella, 2000, 30–1); 33.367d (cf. Penella, 2000, 44 and 208 n. 9).

166 Referred to at *Or.* 26.311b–c (cf. 313c and 326d–327a) which distinguished the 'senate' and the 'assembly' as the two audiences to which Themistius had access. The former thus provided his more select audience, perhaps; the reference certainly dates the speech after his adlection to the senate.

167 Personal incident: *Or.* 21.255d–256a (see further below). Themistius switched to the 2nd-person singular at 262d. Some have thought that the speech was an attack on several rivals: e.g., Meridier, 1906, 1–8; Penella, 2000, 15. In response to different characteristics of the true philosopher, Themistius did ridicule various imposters: the low-born man with a little learning (246c–249c: see Fowden, 1982, 48–51, on how poverty was considered to generate an unavoidable tendency to greed), the charlatan, who pretended to study Aristotle (247c), the plagiarist with no interest in practical matters (251a, 253b), and, more generally, on those whose greed pushed them to harass their pupils for fees or take up legal advocacy (260a–b, 261b). Themistius' closing emphasis on one individual – 'you' singular – leads us to suspect, however, that these were all characteristics of the same person.

Such a world offered many opportunities for public acclaim. Themistius himself referred to the vocal applause with which his public speeches were customarily greeted. One of the speeches also described how a certain philosopher, originally from Sicyon, came to Constantinople, together with all his pupils, just to study with Themistius. The philosopher had consulted the oracle at Delphi as to who was the wisest of living philosophers.[168] The crowd could be volatile, however, and rivalry intense, as Themistius' own *ad hominem* remarks demonstrate, so that these successes were by nature transitory. At one point, Themistius was denounced to the city authorities in Constantinople and arrested for having a guest in his house whose presence had not been licensed by them.[169] Themistius' acquaintance Libanius had also found the intellectual competition within the city ruthless and hard to handle. Because of his success as a self-employed, unsalaried teacher, two salaried competitors at one point enlisted the assistance of Limenius, proconsul of Constantinople, to trump up charges of magic and sorcery against him. They succeeded in having Libanius expelled (Libanius, *Or.* 1.46–8).[170]

This world of momentous but fragile victories in intensely public competition goes a long way towards explaining the attraction, for Themistius, of the Senate of Constantinople. This was a much more secure anchor for personal prestige than the shifting perceptions of the crowd. Even a seat in the senate was not enough by itself, however, to protect him from the hostile attentions of jealous rivals. Indeed, his own highly personal attacks on opponents, made in front of the baying crowd, would only have stimulated, one imagines, further opposition, especially if they were well aimed. Altogether, the sources record at least two and possibly as many as four moments in the second half of the 350s when Themistius' public reputation was challenged. Two letters of Libanius, datable to 355, mention that Themistius had recently been facing some kind of opposition or difficulty.[171] These may or may not refer to the incident when he was denounced to the city authorities for harbouring an unlicensed foreigner (*Or.* 21.255d–256a). In the late 350s, moreover, after his return from an embassy to Rome (see below),

168 Applause: note 165. Philosopher: *Or.* 23.295b, 296a–b; see also Chapter 1 note 51.

169 Loss of support: *Or.* 26.314a–b. Guest: *Or.* 21.255d–256a: probably the philosopher from Sicyon: see previous note.

170 Such ferocity was not limited to Constantinople. See now Gleason, 1995, esp. xxiii, on the winner-take-all zero-sum-game played by public speakers; cf. Lim, 1995, ch. 2.

171 *Epp.* 402 and 7; cf. Penella, 2000, 14–15.

Themistius responded publicly with Orations 23 and 29 to further attacks upon his good name, in the course of which dispute some of Themistius' philosophical colleagues even turned against him.[172] Finally, the *ad hominem* attack Themistius made on an unnamed accuser in Oration 26 may also have belonged to this context, or might have been stimulated by yet a further moment of controversy. This speech certainly belonged to the period after Themistius entered the senate in 355, and possibly again to the late 350s.[173]

Aside from the obviously malicious denunciation of Themistius' hospitality mentioned in Oration 21, the charges levelled at him in the controversies of the later 350s all shared the same starting point. The basic thrust of their attack, using a distinction which went back to Plato's Socratic dialogues, was that Themistius had shown himself to be not a real philosopher, but a sophist. In this context, the distinction implied that Themistius was not a true seeker after wisdom but someone who used philosophy as a cloak for personal ambition, whether in the form of fame or wealth. Against an opponent who styled himself a philosopher, this was an obvious line of attack within the norms of Hellenic discourse. The distinction between the true seeker after wisdom and the sophist went back to Plato's own efforts to define the particular virtues of his own intellectual endeavours, above all in *The Sophist* and the *Greater* and *Lesser Hippias*. The thoughts expressed in these works rapidly became a standard benchmark for establishing one's own virtue, or the lack of it in an opponent. Themistius himself made use of these works in Oration 23, when he extracted from them six characteristics of the sophist, and showed that his own behaviour did not at all fit their collective description. Once again, he turned self-defence into an *ad hominem* attack against a figure whose behaviour, by contrast, did fit Plato's criteria. At least, a fellow Constantinopolitan intellectual perceived it as such an attack, and Themistius' further comment on the matter in Oration 29 was highly unapologetic. The bottom line of the second speech was that he had not intended an attack, but if the cap should happen to fit someone in particular, then that was not Themistius' fault. In Oration 21, likewise an obviously personal attack, Themistius adopted the related strategy of pretending

---

172  *Or.* 23.298a–99a referred to the Roman embassy (357) as 'recent'; Seeck, 1906, 300; cf. Vanderspoel, 1995, 108–10; Penella, 2000, 21–2. Philosophical colleagues: *Or.* 26.314a–b.
173  See note 166.

that he himself was not a philosopher in order to expose the limitations of another. Being perceived to stand on the right or wrong side of the dividing line between philosopher and sophist was thus a deciding factor in one's public reputation.[174]

Aside from the general charge of sophistry, these speeches also show that two more specific accusations had been levelled against him. One centred on his summoning of the crowd to the Theatre of the Muses. This, it was alleged, was classic sophistry, both in that Themistius had acted in a manner previously unknown to philosophers, and, more important, that he had clearly been seeking public adulation. It was this charge that Oration 26 was framed to refute.[175] More doubt surrounds the charge Themistius was defending himself against in Oration 23 (and, by extension, Oration 29 which quickly followed). Gilbert Dagron thought that he could identify within Oration 23 a cross-reference to an incident mentioned in Oration 34 where Themistius turned down the offer of an official post from an anonymous emperor. It has since been shown, however, that in Oration 23, Themistius made no claim to have declined the position itself, but merely the material perquisites attached to it, so that these are quite separate incidents.[176] What was the post whose perquisites Themistius refused in the 350s?

As a preliminary point, it is important to recognise that he did not claim to have turned down all the perquisites attached to the post, merely those which might be perceived as dishonourable. In Oration 23, Themistius eventually admitted, indeed, that he had in fact done precisely what was alleged, namely that he had used grain and oil issued to him by the state as the perquisites of office to feed and hence attract students. As with most late Roman offices, the position in question clearly came with a number of ration entitlements (called *annonae* in

174 The criteria of the sophist in *Or.* 23 were taken from Plato, *The Sophist* 231d–e, 233b–41b, 268c–d: Penella, 2000, 114 n. 9. Our reading of *Or.* 29 is similar to that of Penella, 2000, 21–2, and somewhat less conciliatory than that of Vanderspoel, 1995, 109, 239–40. For *Or.* 21, note Themistius' reference to the fact that Socrates would sometimes pretend not to be a philosopher to discomfort sophists (259a–d). On public debate as a critical moment in intellectual self-definition, and the general importance of the philosopher/sophist distinction, see Gleason, 1995, chs 2 and 6.

175 *Or.* 26. esp. 313d–314a.

176 The passage in question is *Or.* 23.292b–c. We follow the response of Daly, 1983, 174–5, to Dagron, 1968, note ii, 213–7. In the introduction to Chapter 2, however, we argue against Daly's further suggestion that the post in question was the pro-consulship of Constantinople.

Latin), which amounted to a daily right to so much food. What Themistius denied was that this recycling of his salary showed him to be a mercenary sophist. Two arguments were framed to sustain this denial. First, he had not taken any of the luxuries that should also have been his by right of office. Second, he had never attempted to commute any of the food rations into a cash payment. Both these points, he claimed, showed that he possessed the disinterest in material goods proper to a philosopher.[177] In the course of this extended exercise in self-justification, Themistius mentioned the figure of thirty *choinixai*, seemingly the sum total of the income that was currently the bone of contention. The original meaning of the word *choinix* was a specific dry measure of grain, but it also quickly acquired the metaphoric meaning of the minimum amount of grain required to keep an individual alive for a day. Among other things, therefore, it seems to have been used as a Greek equivalent for the Latin *annona*. If that is its meaning here, then Themistius' office would appear to have attracted thirty ration allowances. By chance, a law preserved in the *Theodosian Code* records that thirty *annonae* was the level of reward granted public professors of rhetoric in the western imperial capital of Trier in 376. The level of reward mentioned by Themistius would be of the correct order of magnitude, therefore, if it was his professorial salary that Themistius had been being using his to support his students. We think it probable, therefore, that the public professorship in Constantinople was the office in question.[178]

Themistius' various speeches in self-defence attempted to counter these specific accusations, as well as the general charge of sophistry. In

177 Admission: *Or.* 23.292a: an important point since Themistius has generally been taken to have turned down all the perquisites of the office: see, e.g., Daly, 1983, 174–5, or Vanderspoel, 1995, 87, with further refs. Refusal of luxuries and no commutation: *Or.* 23.292b–293b. The luxuries were probably the so-called *cellaria* which also came with official posts; they might consist of anything from clothes, to baggage animals, to cash: Jones, 1964, 396–7. It seems to have been reasonably common for food rations to be commuted on occasion into cash payments, and soldiers were notorious for enforcing commutation on tax-payers at punitive rates.

178 30 *choinixai*: *Or.* 23.293c. As a dry measure, 1 *choinix* was the equivalent of 3 or 4 *kotulai* or 1.5 to 2 pints. On its metaphoric meaning, see, e.g., Bonner, 1965, 128 n. 59, after texts such as Diogenes Laertius 8.18 where it meant 'daily food'. Law of Trier: *C.Th.* 13.3.11 with Bonner, 1965. Penella, 2000, 120 n. 21, likewise suggests that the perquisites of professorial office were meant here, but does also think that Themistius simultaneously held the proconsulship of Constantinople.

Oration 26, he admitted that his speeches to large crowds were in recent terms an innovation, but argued that Socrates had acted similarly. He also argued that he was not a sophist in search of applause and fame, but a serious philosopher transmitting a serious message. It was indeed the quality of the message which demanded that large numbers of people hear it; any rhetoric was merely to make it more palatable.[179] In Oration 23, as we have seen, he did in the end admit to having used his food allowances to feed students. Again, however, he denied the charge of sophistry. By no means, he argued, had he been mercenary – one of the main charges Plato had made against sophists – since he had taken only the food, and not vast amounts of that. He had, in addition, accepted no fees from his students, and urged that he be judged by the moral qualities they displayed. If, under his teaching, they displayed suitable moral virtue, as he argued they did, then his support of them was entirely justified.[180]

His defence emphasised above all that, in both teaching his students and speaking more generally about moral virtue to the crowd, he had been serving the city of Constantinople, and that this was entirely in line with the behaviour expected of a Hellenic philosopher. He had not, in other words, compromised his philosophical independence in the hope of material gain. Whether Themistius' counterarguments were convincing to his contemporaries is impossible to say. Some modern commentators have not found them so, but perhaps he did not have to be more than plausible. He was a member of the senate, had the emperor's ear, and, as he stressed in Oration 2 (his speech of thanks to Constantius for the adlection), the emperor had offered to give him every kind of gift that he might need.[181] To continue to press the attack against him was potentially dangerous, therefore, for Themistius was never slow in asserting his imperial connections.

179  Precedent: *Or.* 26.315d–321d. Importance of message: *Or.* 26. esp. 325c–d.
180  Fees: *Or.* 23.288c–d. Qualities of his students: *Or.* 23.289a, 290c–291c.
181  *Or.* 2.25d–26a: see note 13 above.

## LETTER OF THE EMPEROR CONSTANTIUS TO THE
## SENATE CONCERNING THEMISTIUS:
## TRANSLATION

[The letter concerning the *clarissimus* philosopher Themistius was conveyed and read in the senate on the Kalends of September in the consulship of Arbetio and Lollianus [355]. The *clarissimus* Justinus, Proconsul [of Constantinople] read it.][182]

[18c] If you and yours are in good health, it is well; I and the army are in good health.[183] It is natural, conscript fathers, for you to rejoice both in taking pleasure in the multitude of victory trophies as well as in enjoying the present peace in safety. And with this in mind, I am always making the attempt at one moment to add some realm to the Roman imperium through force of arms and at another to discover some benefit for the subject nations through the rule of law.[184] Indeed it is no doubt out of habit in expectation of one of these things that you have now convened, [d] either an announcement of martial successes or some largesse of peacetime bounty. But I think it right that I not only bring you pleasure through common benefits, but also, as far as is possible, keep in mind and give the appropriate consideration to these things as far as the individual is concerned, since the appreciation of common advantage is greatest when its enjoyment reaches each individual. [19a] And so, if the purpose of state policy is its effect on the individual, one should pay the closest attention to this before all else: but even more so, if truth is to be told, it is also when I deem an individual worthy of an appropriate honour, that I bestow a common gift. For no favour bestowed with reason and judgement belongs only to the man

182  On the origin of this and similar rubrics, see the introduction to *Or.* 1. The MSS read the corrupt Arepio for Arbetio.

183  This sentence is only found in some MSS, so the Dindorf and the Teubner editions consign it to the apparatus. It looks like a genuinely formulaic expression, however, which we have chosen therefore to include; so too Penella, 2000, 237 n. 2.

184  Victory – the practical expression of Roman superiority over outsiders ('barbarians') – was the prime virtue expected of emperors: McCormick, 1986. In the Roman view, the rule of law was what particularly made their society superior to that of any outsiders ('barbarians'): e.g. Heather, 1993a; 1993b. It may well have been standard diplomatic practice, therefore, for communications between emperor and senate to begin by paying lip service to these twin great poles of Roman self-definition.

who receives it, but a common prize is set before every man for all similar efforts.[185]

Well then, it was his celebrated reputation that brought the philosopher Themistius to our hearing,[186] and I conceived the notion both as king and on our own part[187] to repay his virtue with an honour appropriate to it, [b] by enrolling in the assembly of the most illustrious fathers a man who takes pride in the right things.[188] For I have in mind to honour not only Themistius through the favour, but, in no less measure, the senate as well which I have considered worthy to share the gift that befits philosophy.[189] And so in giving the honour, you will receive it back and in so receiving it, give it back again. For different things enhance different people and make them notable – [c] for some it is the glory of their wealth, for others the abundance of their possessions, for a few duties to the state, and for others forcefulness in words.[190] For all men of good sense strive towards one and the same summit of repute by diverse and complex ways.[191] However, while some of the many paths are circuitous and precarious, the only one that is safe and secure is the path of virtue.[192] And whenever someone is to be enrolled in your company, you look for this before all else, [to see] if he travels this course [of virtue], [d] and you hold no other thing to be the mark of recognition of the most illustrious man

185  Cf. *Or.* 16.203d–204b of 383 (see Chapter 4). Ammianus reports that Constantius was indeed careful in making promotions: 21.16.1 and 3.

186  Themistius had previously given *Or.* 1 to Constantius, but the wording suggests that the emperor had in mind the reputation Themistius had built up subsequently as a teacher of philosophy in Constantinople.

187  We retain the Teubner text's ἡμέτερας rather than amend to ὑμέτερας as Dindorf (followed by Penella, 2000, 238 n. 3). Constantius was signalling that he chose Themistius for personal as well as official reasons.

188  Deleting δὶ ἀλλήλων after Lewy, 1886, 307.

189  We read ἣν τοῦ μετασχεῖν δωρεᾶς ἀξίαν; see the Teubner apparatus for other possible conjectures.

190  Hermogenes identified force (δεινότης) – the combination of effects to achieve an overall persuasiveness of argument – as the most important *Idea* for political language: see the introduction to *Or.* 1.

191  In the 4th century, senatorial status became a common element in previously separate career ladders in the army and the bureaucracy. This process was formalised under Valentinian and Valens in the 360s, but was already significantly advanced by Constantius. See further Heather, 1994.

192  An allusion to Hesiod, *Works and Days* 289ff.

except sound thought and right opinion, which is what philosophy pursues above all else.[193]

His system of education[194] is enough for Themistius to be considered worthy of the highest honour, both in his teaching of philosophy according to his own manner, and, all the more so, as it may happen, when he remains silent.[195] For it is not the man who merely makes a show of his virtue who is worthy of honour but the man who actually possesses it. And it is fitting for reward to follow those who are worthy, [20a] even if they themselves do not make special efforts to show themselves so. Moreover this man, whom the present speech proclaims, does not practise a solitary philosophy, but he shares out the benefit which he has painstakingly assembled with even greater pains among those who are willing [to hear], having established himself as both a mouthpiece of the sages of the past and an acolyte at philosophy's inner sanctuaries and shrines. He does not allow the ancient teachings to wither away, but [ensures] that they always flourish and are renewed. [b] He has personally been instrumental in all men living their lives by reason and cultivating learning.[196]

And you too can see, conscript fathers, that no task in human existence could be accomplished in the noblest and best fashion without virtue, neither at home nor in the city. It is in the thorough training and education of the young men for this [i.e. virtue] that those who are rightly the leading men in philosophy may be thought of as the common fathers of all men. These men instruct fathers in how they must receive honour from their own sons, and children in the kind of care they must receive from their fathers. [c] To summarise this in a few words, the truth is that the philosopher is the judge and the overseer of all. For in the matter of how one should treat the people and how one should

193 Constantius, despite his evident Christianity, could nevertheless here declare allegiance to traditional Hellenic cultural values. See further the introduction.

194 *Paideusis*: this could mean learning in a general sense (so Penella, 2000, 232), but what follows suggests that Constantius has in mind the particular educational programme Themistius had been pursuing as professor of philosophy in Constantinople.

195 I.e., both in teaching and in his life – cf. what follows – Themistius has shown himself a true philosopher, while not showing off his accomplishments (as a sophist would do).

196 Constantius seems to have had in mind here both Themistius' programmatic assault on Neoplatonic philosophers interested in individual spiritual awakening (see the introduction to this speech), and his Aristotelian paraphrases which had certainly prevented old learning from 'withering away'. On Themistius' version of *paideia* as the route to individual and civic virtue, see further Chapter 1.

honour the senate, he is quite simply the tried and true yardstick for the whole state.[197] Now if it were possible for all men to practise philosophy, baseness would be driven from the life of men, all excuse for injustice rooted out, and there would be no need for the compulsion of the laws. For those things which they now keep away from through fear, they would hate through choice.[198]

[d] I am brought enthusiastically to this present theme for other reasons. While it is my heart's desire that philosophy should shine in every part of the world, I especially wish it to flourish throughout our city. And indeed I know that this has happened in her case because of Themistius, since she takes pride in her companies of young philosophers and is a house of learning open to all, [21a] so that all men from every quarter have conceded that the city is supreme in philosophy and the teachings of virtue flow forth from her in every direction as if from some pure spring.[199] So as I said when I began, the honour I am granting is shared by you and by Themistius. [b] For in receiving from us a Roman dignity, he offers Hellenic wisdom in return, so that for this reason our city is revealed as the summit both of good fortune and of virtue. For being pre-eminent in all other good things, she now acquires the most valuable one as well. For if it is the sign of a loving emperor to fortify her with walls, to adorn her with buildings within, and to crowd her with a host of citizens, how much more so is it to augment the senate with such an addition that shall improve the souls of those who dwell in her and raise up the gymnasium of virtue along with all the other buildings? So that he who furnishes the city with the other things bestows most important advantages, but he who pays attention to intellect and learning [c] provides the sovereign boon which many desire but few achieve.[200]

197 Again Constantius here very publicly indicated his acceptance of traditional Hellenic values, which saw philosophers as the guardians of *paideia*.

198 Cf. *Or.* 1.14d–15c, where law is a blunt instrument requiring to be tempered by royal mercy.

199 See the introduction to this speech for examples of the philosophical competition Themistius had eclipsed. Constantius probably also had in mind the philosopher who came from Sicyon on the strength of Themistius' reputation: *Or.* 23.295b, 296a–b with the introduction to this Chapter.

200 Providing buildings and particularly wealthy citizens for its council was a traditional gesture of 'friendship' to a city by a ruler within traditional Graeco-Roman value systems. In emphasising that paying attention to *paideia* was even more important, Constantius again publicly indicated his assent to traditional, non-Christian cultural norms.

I know therefore that to proceed to add all the other reasons why Themistius should be worthy of the highest honour is not the action of those who understand philosophy's greatness. For where a thing is itself the most self-sufficient of all good things, if you do not promote it alone but add other elements to it, you will not make it greater by what you add, but diminish it by thinking that it requires a supplement.[201] **[d]** Let us, however, bear with the argument which shows that, philosophy aside, the man is worthy of your assembly. For if it is just to co-opt and give love in return to those who are especially loving, then Themistius by his own free choice has been our lover and through his native judgement has preferred our city to the one which bore him, and has been a citizen in his outlook before being one in name.[202] See the importance of this – to reveal to those from other places, who are fortunate in other ways, that where we live is worthy of love. **[22a]** For it was not because of domestic need that he took refuge in our city's prosperity, but, though careless of wealth, he is nevertheless not oppressed by poverty.[203] It was among us that he thought of marriage and having children, which safeguards the succession of the family line. Such things are praiseworthy in an ordinary man, but are of the highest importance when found in a philosopher. For if he whose life should be set out like a standard and goal for all other men, if that man should honour our city and look to the future of his family line and measure his desire for money according to his need, then he shall lead on many to do likewise. **[b]** For do not think that the true philosophy banishes itself completely from communal life or turns itself entirely away from the care of common affairs, but know that the man who cares most for the city is also the one who, in turning men into the best people, always makes them the best citizens as well.[204] Consider therefore the abundance of

201 An instance of the Platonic framework to Themistius' thought: multiple things flow from a single original quality to which they are necessarily inferior. See, e.g., *Or.* 1.2b–3a.

202 Themistius was born in Paphlagonia, but spent some time in Constantinople as a child. As a mature man, he seems to have established himself in the city from the late 330s. *Or.* 23.298b of 357 comments that he had been there for 20 years.

203 It was necessary for the Hellenic philosopher, while not coveting riches, to have sufficient independent means to avoid worldly temptation: cf. Brown, 1992, 62–3. On the specific accusations of worldliness levelled at Themistius, see the introduction to *The Letter of Constantius*.

204 For the significance of Themistius' programmatic emphasis on the practical importance of philosophy as opposed to Neoplatonic emphases on individual spiritual awakening, see the introduction to *The Letter of Constantius*.

good qualities which have equipped the most illustrious man for you. He is rich in words and yet is not poor in money, he chooses the city of his own free will and is not forced to live here because he has to, but would leave only if forced to do so.[205] Why should I say anything else? I have given to you as a *clarissimus*[206] the unique philosopher, **[c]** an extraordinary citizen of our city, whom one might address with good reason as a citizen of the World.

But I know well that Themistius does not listen to this whole catalogue of praises with equal pleasure but only has regard for those which relate to philosophy and wishes the rest either to be spoken of in moderation or left in silence.[207] And I have prolonged this speech not so as to indulge the man, [as it would] were I to go through every point equally, but in order to reveal to you that I leave nothing unexamined or untested in what is to be carried out by my judgement. Themistius, if truth be told, has not just recently become familiar to me, **[d]** but has been so for a long time and through his forefathers. Such is the extent of the knowledge available to me about the man that while I am able to list even the more distant of his ancestors, whom the old tales recall, I am happy to let this pass.[208] For close at hand there is his father, because of whom it is superfluous to recall the others. **[23a]** You are not unaware of this man's identity, to pronounce whose name is enough to display philosophy's topmost peak, and there is no land, race or city which has not heard of Eugenius' reputation.[209] That man, whom you would attest to have been inspired by philosophy throughout his life, that man, whom none of the ancient teachings and systems of education escaped, that

205 Senators of Constantinople and Rome were required to be resident in their cities. This was relaxed in 383 (*C.Th.* 6.1.3), not least because new grants of senatorial status were greatly increasing numbers: see further Heather, 1994.

206 λαμπρότατος. According to *Anon. Val.* 6.30, Constantine originally made the new senators of Constantinople mere *clari* as opposed to the *clarissimi* of Rome. But some Constantinopolitan *clarissimi* are known from Constantine's reign, and the distinction had disappeared by the mid-350s at the latest: Chastagnol, 1982, 229.

207 It was a necessary part of his philosophical persona for Themistius to be seen to reject the trappings of worldly success, a strategy which Constantius' words here furthered.

208 Like many elites based on landed wealth, that of the late Roman world placed a high premium on old, well-established families, traditionally ridiculing parvenus. See, e.g., the satires directed by Libanius towards some senators of Constantinople in *Or.* 42. These should not be taken at face value: Heather, 1994.

209 No work by Eugenius survives. Themistius claimed to have learned from him the importance of harnessing rhetoric to the purposes of philosophy: see further Chapter 1.

man who was his own rival in intellect and life, and who in each field was his own inferior and his superior too, that man, therefore, who was the best of all men, [b] who was the chief of all, is considered to be equalled only by his son and only Themistius is his successor both in family line and in philosophy.

On account of all that has been said, therefore, we must bind and join the best man to the assembly. For thus we might also do what is pleasing to my divine father, by making the council which takes its name from him bloom and flourish with the greatest of good things.[210] [c] For it is necessary to give to rhetoric above all else its fitting dignity and to give back to wisdom its special honour, to learning the appropriate reward and to virtue the prize that is its due, so that the chief of the sciences, I mean philosophy, shines out everywhere and in all things.[211] For thus it shall turn out that all the other arts shall get greater attention, [d] whenever the first and best receives its proper honour. And so, it is clear from what has been said that what I have given to Themistius, I have given to you. I give great honour, I am well aware, to my own father too, having consecrated to the name of the most godlike man not a temple or a gymnasium but a good man.[212]

## ORATION 3
## EMBASSY SPEECH ON BEHALF OF CONSTANTINOPLE
## DELIVERED IN ROME:
## INTRODUCTION

### Date and Circumstances

Themistius' third oration was delivered some time in May 357. The Emperor Constantius II was engaged in a state visit to the imperial capital, which lasted from 28 April to 29 May when it was cut short by trouble on the Middle Danube (Ammianus 16.10.20). Themistius met the emperor in Rome – clearly by prearrangement since imperial visits

210 Constantius' father Constantine founded the senate after his defeat of Licinius in 325: *Anon. Val.* 6.30 with secondary commentary in Jones, 1964, 525ff.; Dagron, 1974, chs 4–6. For another look at the political circumstances, Heather, 1994, 14–16.

211 Rhetoric combined with philosophy does seem to have been a particular characteristic of Themistius, learned from his father: see note 209.

212 Constantius thus had no problem in considering that a non-Christian could be a 'good man', or in supposing that his father would have similarly recognised Themistius' virtues.

to a major capital were arranged carefully in advance – and delivered his speech in front of Constantius and the Roman senate, as the official leader of an embassy from the latter's Constantinopolitan counterpart.

The backdrop to both Constantius' visit and Themistius' speech was the, by then, fairly remote suppression of two western usurpers, Vetranio and Magnentius. Magnentius is consistently labelled a 'barbarian' by the sources, but was actually a second-generation Roman, born within the Empire, possibly at Amiens, of a British father and Frankish mother.[213] Having risen through the ranks of the officer corps, he commanded, by 350, two prestigious units of the western mobile field army, the Joviani and Herculiani. Early in that year, he had secured the elimination of Constantius' brother Constans, ruler of the west, and was himself declared Augustus on 18 January. In response, Vetranio, the assassinated emperor's military commander in Illyricum, also declared himself Augustus, on 1 March, while a further pretender in the shape of Constantine's nephew Nepotianus declared himself by seizing Rome on 3 June, and obtaining an imperial acclamation. Nepotianus was quickly suppressed by supporters of Magnentius, who was trying to persuade Constantius to grant recognition of his title, despite being responsible for his brother's death. Relations between Constantius and Constans had become very strained in the second half of the 340s, so that this was not necessarily the hopeless task it might at first appear. Vetranio tried to do the same, but was eventually persuaded by Constantius to stand down. According to the sources, Constantius won over Vetranio's troops by the quality of his rhetoric, deployed from a raised platform in front of the latter's army; the outcome, Vetranio's submission, and its terms, had surely been arranged beforehand. The scene was now set for a showdown between Constantius and Magnentius. A first battle between their forces was fought at Mursa in Illyricum on 28 September 351. Constantius' army prevailed, but it was a close thing, and two further years of hard fighting were required for total victory. Magnentius' forces were eventually pushed out of Illyricum and Italy into Gaul, before the battle of Mons Seleucus in summer 353 ended the usurpation. Magnentius committed suicide shortly after his defeat.[214]

These three years of civil war had far-reaching consequences for the Empire as a whole. Even the government of the eastern Empire suffered

213  E.g., Julian, *Or.* 1.33d–34a, 34d; *Or.* 2.56b–c; cf. *PLRE* 1, 532.
214  For a fuller account, see, e.g., Stein, 1959, 138–41; Barnes, 1993, 101–8.

disruption. As part of his preparations for marching west against Magnentius, Constantius had promoted his cousin, Julian's half-brother Constantinus Gallus, Caesar in March 351 and stationed him at Antioch both to watch over the Persian front and to prevent any political unrest in the east from spilling over into open revolt. By the summer of 354, however, the Caesar's self-assertive behaviour had convinced Constantius that Gallus was becoming a threat in his own right. A series of manoeuvres first isolated him politically; then, having been summoned to Italy supposedly for an interview with Constantius, he was murdered *en route*. He was not replaced, and Constantius continued to control the east directly from Italy in the nearly three years which separated Gallus' fall and the emperor's visit to Rome.[215] In the western Empire, much of eastern Gaul, stripped of troops presumably by Magnentius for the civil war, came to be overrun by Alamannic and Frankish groups. An area 300 stades (c.60 km) wide west of the Rhine had been occupied by intruders along the entire length of the river, although settlement had avoided the actual cities, and many defensive installations had been damaged.[216] The years after 353 had to be spent campaigning against them, but the warfare proved awkward, and the western armies difficult to control. In the summer of 355, a further usurper appeared among them, the general Silvanus, who, it seems, was pushed into action because of hostile plotting against him at Constantius' court. His assassination ended the revolt, but to provide a morale-boosting figurehead and cut off the flow of revolts, Constantius made his last surviving cousin, Julian, Caesar in November 355 and sent him to Gaul. In the first instance, Julian was given no real power and Constantius was as much worried about a potential revolt on the part of his Caesar as about the inroads of the barbarians. The two rulers campaigned together in 356, if with somewhat limited success.[217] A successful, but protracted and rather bloody civil war, three other

215 A vivid account of Gallus' fall is provided by Ammianus 14.1, 7, 9, 11; cf. Matthews, 1989, ch. 3.

216 Territory and damage: Julian, *Letter to the Athenians* 279a–b; cf. Ammianus 16.2.12, 3.1–2 on Alamannic and Frankish occupation. The accounts are in broad terms mutually confirmatory.

217 354 campaign: Ammianus 14.10; 355 campaign: Ammianus 15.4; 356 campaign: Ammianus: 16.2–3. Silvanus: Ammianus: 15.5–6 (cf. Hunt, 1999). Julian: Ammianus 15.8; Julian, *Letter to the Athenians* 275c–278a. For general commentary, see most recently Matthews, 1989, ch. 6.

actual or perceived usurpations, continued difficulties on the Rhine frontier, and the promotion of the only partially trusted Julian thus provided the backdrop for Constantius' state visit to his imperial capital and Themistius' third oration.

Such visits were rare in the late Empire. In c.400 AD, the poet Claudian considered that there had only been four such visits in the whole of the preceding century. He was perhaps slightly mistaken (there may have been five), but this only emphasises the rarity of the event. Rome had long since ceased to be a centre of political power in even the western Empire; this had shifted north to Trier and Milan.[218] In making the visit, Constantius clearly had it in mind to secure the loyalty of important senatorial landowners, who had never previously been under his direct control. Even when they were ruled by his brother Constans, there had been tensions between eastern and western halves of the Empire, and little direct contact.[219] To that end, the visit combined a judicious mixture of military and civilian behaviour. Constantius entered the city, dragon standards flying, in a huge military parade, his stiff comportment emphasising the superhuman, god-like qualities customarily required of an emperor in this era. Once inside the city, his demeanour changed. Games were given for the masses, where Constantius graciously accepted shouts and acclamations. He addressed the senate, admired the temples and other monuments, filled the priestly colleges, and lavishly entertained small groups of senators. The now civilian emperor's behaviour emphasised peace, civility, and freedom.[220] Taken together, the different aspects of his behaviour made two important points. First, having survived so much turmoil, Constantius' reign was now militarily secure and hence likely to last. Second, he was an emperor who would distribute the right kinds of rewards to western senators who sought his favour through loyal service.

### Themistius and Constantius

Into this setting, Themistius led the delegation from the Senate of Constantinople. Both the occasion of the speech and its contents make

---

218  Cf. Barnes, 1975, with further refs.
219  Most recently Barnes, 1993, esp. ch. 7.
220  Matthews, 1989, 231–5; cf. Woods, 1999, for possible innovations in the circus performances.

clear the transformation of the relationship between philosopher and
emperor which had occurred since the delivery of Oration 1. No longer
a professional teacher with a perhaps once-in-a-lifetime opportunity for
preferment, Themistius came to Rome as the leader of a senatorial
embassy to present Crown Gold to Constantius. Crown Gold – *aurum
coronarium* – was an offering of gold, actually fashioned into crowns
and in theory voluntary, paid individually by cities of the Empire. The
gold was contributed by two categories of landowner: senators and
decurions.[221]

Oration 3, indeed, would appear to be the speech which accompanied
the formal presentation of the crowns to the emperor. Although it does
not follow the topical outline for such a speech laid down in the handbook of Menander Rhetor, this is not an objection of substance. In
Oration 1, Themistius had adopted an unusual speech form to mark out
the singularity of the uniquely truthful contribution he claimed to be
offering. Oration 3 maintained, as we shall see, the same claims, so that
a similar avoidance of the rhetorical norm is only to be expected. Moreover, he did at least follow Menander's advice in one respect; the speech
is a relatively short one, as the handbook suggests was proper for the
presentation of Crown Gold.[222] It is above all, however, the contents of
the speech which suggest this conclusion. Without any preliminary
remarks, it launched into a discussion of Constantinople's gift of
crowns, and the particular appropriateness of its delivery in Rome (40c–
41a). The fact that this topic required no introduction suggests very
strongly that the speech accompanied the presentation of the gift.

The formal pretext for Constantius' gold has been disputed. By the
fourth century, Crown Gold was offered to emperors on their accession, on quinquennial celebrations of that accession, and also on
major festal occasions such as triumphs. On the one hand, the *Chronicon Paschale* places the celebration of Constantius' *vicennalia* (20th
anniversary) in 357, the emperor having been declared Augustus after
his father's death in 337. Another alternative is indicated by Constantius' coinage, which suggests that he may have been celebrating the

221  Jones, 1964, 430.
222  Cf. Russell, 1998, 29: the speech is exactly the length recommended by Menander II.
In structure, he recommended the general pattern of the *basilikos logos* (origins, family,
education, deeds in war and peace): Russell and Wilson, 1981, 178–81. See further
Chapter 1.

thirty-fifth anniversary of his accession to the imperial title of Caesar a year and a half early.[223] No imperial anniversary was even mentioned, however, in the text of Oration 3. On the contrary, Themistius devoted considerable attention to Constantius' victory in the civil wars (42b–d), and strikingly heralded Rome as 'the city of triumphs' (42b). As we have seen, Constantius also made a military entry into the city. If Oration 3 did accompany the formal presentation of the gold, therefore, it would appear to have been the defeat of the usurpers Vetranio and above all Magnentius which provided the formal pretext for Constantinople's gift of gold. Whatever the case, the arrival in Rome of the Constantinopolitan embassy in the course of Constantius' visit there was no accident. The imperial visit to Rome will have been planned months ahead of time, and the arrival in the western capital of a gold-bearing embassy from its eastern counterpart was a carefully orchestrated part of the celebration. The same was true of Themistius' speech.

Certain themes familiar from Oration 1 were replayed for the Roman audience. Themistius was still the truth-telling philosopher who, by definition, was incapable of telling a lie (44c–45a, 45c–46a), Constantius remained Plato's ideal philosopher king (45a–b etc). Just as significant, however, are the differences. In particular, the balance between discussions of a priori principles of kingship and the specific actions of the emperor was weighted much more heavily in favour of the latter compared to the earlier speech. Not only did this rectify what may have been the fault Themistius himself perceived in Oration 1,[224] but it also reflected both Themistius' increased knowledge of imperial affairs and his greater confidence in knowing how even sensitive matters should be handled. In Oration 3, for instance, Themistius was quite happy to dwell at some length on the important but tricky dynastic issue of the emperor's relationship with his brothers. From the brothers' deaths and loss of power, he had no qualms in drawing the conclusion that their actions had prompted the withdrawal from them of Divine favour (48c–d). This

---

223 Coinage: Burgess, 1988, 83–4; cf. *Cons. Const.* s.a. 357 which reads xxxv (Constantius was made Caesar on 8 November 324). In his edition of the *Cons. Const.*, Mommsen altered xxxv to *vicennalia*, but it is unclear that this is correct. See further Vanderspoel, 1995, 101 n. 138. On the manipulation of anniversary dates, see Bagnall et al., 1987, 17, 23–4. A *quinquennium* could in practice mean anything between three and six years depending upon imperial convenience.

224 See the introduction to *Or.* 1.

is not a subject on which one would dare to speak without being confident of having taken an appropriate line.[225] The point is merely emphasised by the speech's silences. For one thing, there is no mention at all of Gallus and the failed experiment of his rule in the east. The subject was probably far too sensitive for a public airing, since no one else but Constantius could really be made responsible for this unhappy sequence of events.[226] Equally interesting, but rather more enigmatic, is the complete absence from the speech of Constantius' second and still, in 357, current Caesar, Gallus' half-brother Julian. Julian had been appointed in 355, so that he played no part in the defeat of the usurpers, and mentioning him in that context would have been inappropriate. On the other hand, the two emperors had waged a joint campaign on the Rhine in 356, the campaigning season immediately preceding Constantius' visit to Rome, and the speech does refer, if briefly, to the emperor's wars in the west (41d–42a). Some suitably small mention of Julian would have been appropriate there, but none was forthcoming. Perhaps Themistius was aware of growing tension between the two men, or perhaps any mention of Julian was considered likely to detract too much from Constantius' glory.[227] Either way, both the speech's contents and its omissions make clear the transformation in Themistius' status which had worked itself out since Ancyra. No longer a seeker after favour, keeping well away from dangerous waters, he could now navigate his way skilfully around the rocks and reefs of Constantian court politics.[228]

### Rome and Constantinople

A similar conclusion is suggested by the speech's treatment of its most significant additional theme: the new imperial city of Constantinople and, in particular, its relationship with Rome, where Themistius was actually speaking. Overall, the speech maintained a careful balancing act. The attractions of the new city received full coverage. Constantinople, the Romans were told, has great beauty (40c–41a), by which Constantius was entirely enthralled (42c). The two capitals were also

225  Contrast with this Themistius' very veiled comments at *Or.* 1.9c above.

226  According to Julian, *Letter to the Athenians* 270d–271a, Constantius suffered from a bad conscience over the murder, later considering his own childlessness a punishment for Gallus' death.

227  On the deterioration of relations between the two, see Matthews, 1989, 87–100.

228  A similar conclusion was reached from a different direction by Wirth, 1979.

presented as natural allies, Themistius developing a nicely conceived parallel whereby Constantine set out from Rome to free Constantinople from one tyrant, while his son, Constantius, set out from Constantinople to free Rome from another (43a–c, 44a–b). Nonetheless, his final conclusion was that Constantinople was happy to stand in a slightly subordinate position (41c–d, 42a–d). One major theme of the speech, therefore, reinforced the charm offensive which Constantius had launched in visiting Rome in the first place. The old capital should not fear the new – nor its ruler – both of which could offer valuable support.

The speech also had a more specific point. Towards its end, Themistius returned to the subject of Constantinople, this time detailing the emperor's care for the city, rather than the theme of its relationship with Rome. Constantinople, Themistius told his audience, was only half-built at the time of Constantine's death, and nobody knew at the time whether it would remain an imperial capital. Since then, Constantius had done more work in the city than his father, and greatly increased it in honours, as measured in particular by the size of its senate.[229] In Themistius' pronounced view, the city now belonged more to Constantius than to his father, and Themistius finished by expressing the hope that the emperor would continue to show it still more favour in the future (46d–48c). He reinforced this by observing that one could tell it was God's will that the city should be advanced (even though Themistius had earlier denied that he was asking for any addition: 46d) from the fact that only Constantius of his brothers had cared for the city, and it was only Constantius who had prospered (48c).

Why did Themistius talk at such length about the city of Constantinople, and particularly its senate, in front of the Senate of Rome? Vanderspoel, taking the passage essentially at face value, has recently argued that Themistius was concerned about a possible switch in the emperor's interests westwards, and was trying to coax him into granting Constantinople more favours, in particular perhaps a formal state visit such as the one he was currently engaged in at Rome.[230] This is possible, but Themistius was well aware of the difficulties which had kept Constantius in the west (*Or.* 3.41d–42a), and the emperor's overall commitment to Constantinople was hardly in doubt. His buildings in

229 *Or.* 3.48a. Themistius would use the same yardstick for measuring honour – i.e. the size of the senate – at *Or.* 14.183c–184a: see Chapter 4.
230 Vanderspoel, 1995, 103.

the city included an enormous granary, the transformation of Constantine's mausoleum into the Church of the Holy Apostles, the searching out of new water supplies (although it was to be 373 before these started flowing into the city), a great bath house, and many other public buildings.[231] Moreover, taking Themistius' own yardstick for measuring honours, Constantius had already brought many new men into the Senate of Constantinople. This was true of Themistius himself, of course, but Oration 3 is also quite explicit that that there had by that date been many other new appointments as well. These had come about because people wanted to join, not because they had been drafted in as had been the case under his father Constantine (48a).

Themistius' emphasis on the importance of senatorial honours takes on added interest in the light of subsequent developments. The delivery of Oration 3 was quickly followed by a major senatorial recruiting campaign, in which Themistius played a prominent role. In 358/9, he travelled round the eastern Mediterranean looking for likely candidates. About a dozen of the men he recruited turn up in the correspondence of Libanius, all former members of the curial classes of their respective cities. In all, Libanius' letters mention 55 senators of Constantinople, of whom more than 30 were recruited in the period 359–61. Themistius was also picked out as a special member of the committee named in May 361 as responsible for further senatorial promotions.[232] At the same time, Constantius gave total formal equality to the senates of Rome and Constantinople. Constantine's new senators at Constantinople had in origin been lesser status *clari* rather than the *clarissimi* of Rome, and Roman senators resident in the eastern Empire had remained members of their own body. By c.360, if not before, both bodies had equal status, and membership was decided on purely geographical grounds. Roman senators resident in the east were now transferred to Constantinople.[233]

231  See generally Mango, 1985, 27, 39–42. Themistius, *Or.* 4.58aff. gives a much fuller account; cf. Vanderspoel, 1995, 98–100.

232  Recruiting campaign: Petit, 1956, 154–5; 1957, 349–54; Dagron, 1974, 132–3. Committee: *C.Th.* 6.4.12. In 384, Themistius claimed that he had been responsible for an expansion of the Senate of Constantinople from about 300 members to 2,000. The figures probably give a general sense of the increase in size during his active lifetime, but may well exaggerate Themistius' personal contribution: see *Or.* 34.xiii in Chapter 5.

233  Heather, 1994, 12. Some *clarissimi* are known from Constantinople at an early date, so Constantine's body was perhaps composed of mixed ranks: Chastagnol, 1982, 229.

Themistius' third oration was thus followed by a total transformation of the entire senatorial order leading to the creation of two equal
senates – Rome and Constantinople – for leading landowners and
imperial officials in west and east respectively. In this light, it becomes
more than likely that the emphasis of Oration 3 upon past recruitment
to and hopes for further expansion of the Senate of Constantinople was
no accident. Unless we are to credit Themistius with an unlikely degree
of prescience, it is only natural to suggest that, as would be the case on
other occasions in his career, Themistius' speech was being used as part
of a campaign to prepare important bodies of opinion for a significant
evolution of policy. At least some senators of Rome might well have
been jealous of their unique status, so that the projected transformations
required sensitive handling to minimise potential opposition in the west.
Using Themistius in this task, with his self-presentation as the entirely
independent philosopher speaking for the Senate of Constantinople,
helped transfer responsibility for a potentially awkward decision away
from the emperor's person, and indeed allowed the emperor to present
himself as responsive to reasoned argument. Oration 3 thus represents
the first example of a strategy which Themistius and his employers were
to employ regularly in subsequent years.[234]

It is quite likely that the speech – which was, after all, in Greek – had
an eastern audience in mind too. Themistius' speech – the pronouncement of its formal ambassador – was no doubt also presented in some
way to the Senate of Constantinople, perhaps via a second reading as
was the case with Oration 5 (see Chapter 3). It was the east, indeed,
which was primarily affected by the expansion which quickly followed.
Why did Constantius decide to expand the eastern senate so dramatically
in the later 350s? The measure came into force at a point when the
emperor controlled the whole of the Roman world, and was himself in
the west, hovering suspiciously over his newly created Caesar, Julian, so
strikingly absent from Oration 3. The years 358/9 saw not only the senatorial recruiting campaign, but also serious treason trials aimed at
important figures resident in the two eastern political centres of consequence outside of Constantinople: Antioch and Alexandria.[235] Given
the sequence of events which had marked the brief reign of Constantius'
previous Caesar Gallus – executed for showing too much independence

---

234  On these transfers of responsibility, see Chapter 1.
235  Constantius and Julian: Matthews, 1989, ch. 6. Treason trials: Ammianus 19.12.

in gathering his own supporters at Antioch[236] – a tempting political context for senatorial expansion suggests itself. Wooing richer members of the eastern curial classes by grants of senatorial status, thus forcing them to relocate, at least in part, to Constantinople, while at the same time using treason trials to eliminate potential opponents, looks like a stick-and-carrot approach designed to keep politically significant groups in line at a point when Constantius had – or thought he had – to concentrate on the west.[237] The particularities of the argument cannot, in the absence of more specific accounts of Constantius' motives, be pressed. That the senatorial transformation was a hugely significant political manoeuvre must, however, be emphasised.

In general terms, then, it is most unlikely that the coincidence between Themistius' remarks and subsequent imperial policy was accidental. Themistius' personal role in the formulation of that policy, however, is entirely unclear. Was he close enough to Constantius to influence policy-making, or did he as yet remain merely a messenger, an expert, at most, on the presentation of policy? These superficially clear distinctions would obviously have blurred in practice, as they do in modern politics, but Constantius had been in the west since 352/3, and Themistius' embassy only arrived there in 357. It seems unlikely, therefore, that he had played as major a role in the decision to increase eastern senatorial numbers as he was to do in its implementation. What is clear, however, is that Constantius' senatorial policy helped set the pattern for the rest of Themistius' career. The emperor created a new-look Senate of Constantinople which provided Themistius with his natural forum. A body composed of a substantial cross-section of the leading landowners of the eastern Mediterranean had been created, before whom it was desirable to win consent for imperial policy. Themistius would henceforth act as go-between for emperor and senate, if not quite in the manner that his own speeches indicated. The transformation also reinforced his public image. One thing Hellenic philosophers were allowed to do was undertake tasks for their cities. Themistius was able to frame all his subsequent actions as those of a city representative in spite of his obvious imperial

236 Matthews, 1989, 33–5.
237 Cf. Heather, 1994, 14–21, setting this development in the more general political context of managing the landowning elites of the eastern Empire. Constantius was eventually forced to leave Julian to his own devices through a combination of the unexpected Middle Danubian troubles which cut short his visit to Rome (see above), and the disastrous loss of Amida in the east.

connections, and, for most of the rest of his career, would avoid further charges of having betrayed his philosophical calling.[238]

## ORATION 3
## EMBASSY SPEECH ON BEHALF OF CONSTANTINOPLE
## DELIVERED IN ROME:
## TRANSLATION

[40c] For no other city is it possible, your imperial majesty, to discover a crown that is fitting for you or another offering of thanks for your virtue, but those who attempt to give in return an honour that matches the benefits they have enjoyed inevitably fall far short of what is deserved.[239] And for her who takes her name from your father but is in reality yours rather than your father's,[240] even the attempt is quite fruitless. For indeed if we were to offer up all the wealth in her possession having fashioned it into crowns, we are not providing this honour[241] from our own resources, [d] but merely hand back a small portion of what we have received to him who has given it. Therefore, just as those who have made frequent and heavy borrowings but repay in short measure are not praised for what they pay off, but are brought to justice for what they have left unpaid, so in our case too must all the thanks we shall offer be judged a tiny fraction of the debt we owe. [41a] And it is surely not surprising that our city alone happens to be well provided but not with an offering which comes close to what is deserved. For she is herself, in her entirety, your crown and votive offering. And so what need is there to look elsewhere for some way of returning thanks to you for her beauty and size? For by being as she is, she glorifies him who made her. Even though the matter has no solution, the Fair City deserves to be loved because she

238 See also, however, the quarrel over Themistius' urban prefecture explored in Chapter 5.

239 Themistius' embassy came to Rome with 'Crown Gold': see the introduction.

240 I.e., Constantinople; Constantius' father was Constantine who refounded the city and renamed it. The city is characterised throughout the orations as a female entity. The assertion that Constantinople now really belongs to Constantius rather than Constantine was justified later in the speech.

241 The text reads τὴν ἀρετήν (lit. the virtue); we follow one of Jacobs' conjectures τὴν δε τιμὴν.

searched out her essential nature so as not to seem entirely to fall short
of the due measure.[242]

[b] For there are two ways in which men make more august and
magnify the thanks they offer; one is if they make as many as possible
witness the honour, the other if they appear not to be flattering but
acting spontaneously and of their own free will. The first of these makes
the bounty more widely known, the other frees the recompense from
suspicion, and the city has taken thought to ensure that both conditions
are fulfilled in what is now being done by her, bringing forward the
honour at the world's summit [i.e. Rome], and employing as servant a
man who must speak the truth,[243] not taking half measures in either of
these, but rather as far as possible exceeding the mark.

[c] Consider first your imperial majesty, the city in which she found
the occasion for the offering. For she does not proclaim the crown at
Olympia or Delphi nor assemble the Greeks at the Panathenaia or the
Dionysia, as the ancient Athenians once did in flattery of their Macedonian masters,[244] but it is in the city which rules cities [Rome] that she
who through you rules in second place binds the brow of him who rules
mankind, [d] and indeed makes this city, which alone is more prestigious
than the one giving it, a witness of the honour. Thus is our theatre more
glorious and equal to the crown and its proclamation. And just as
Homer's Thetis does not consider it right to intercede on her son's
behalf while Zeus is abroad at the court of Oceanus but on his return to
the heavens, even to the pinnacle of heaven, pleads her case and obtains
a hearing,[245] [42a] so the Fair City chooses not to disturb her own
Zeus while he is defending and making provision for the Oceanic territories,[246] but once he returns to Olympus and takes his seat on its
topmost pinnacle, entreats him, ministers to him and attempts to share
the festive occasion which heaven and the god celebrate through each

242  The epithet καλλίπολις – 'Fair City' – was used by Plato (*Republic* 527c) with reference to his ideal city and is frequently used of Constantinople by Themistius.
243  I.e., Themistius himself, the truth-telling philosopher: see Chapter 1.
244  Plutarch, *Life of Demetrius* xi–xiib. The Athenians were said to have hailed Demetrius IV Poliorcetes as a saviour god after his liberation of Athens from Demetrius of Pha-
lerum.
245  Homer, *Iliad* 1.423ff. Thetis had been unable to plead her son Achilles' case to Zeus
while he was feasting with the Ethiopians by Oceanus, the river which encircled the earth.
246  Constantius' wars against the Franks and Alamanni: see the introduction to this
speech.

other, the one shining out, the other reflecting the radiance. And because of the city [i.e. Rome] our celebration becomes quite complete. For she [Constantinople] who shares both its Tyche and name [i.e. New Rome] [b] takes her share and is present among the celebrants.[247] A dance is formed which in its three perfect elements is the most perfect of all. The queens join their voices in song, the coryphaeus leads off and the whole of the earth and sea add their voices of good omen.[248] Their hymn fills all the tribes in the east and all the races in the west with harmony, the victories rise up into the heavens with the sun and joining it on its bright journey to the west come down to earth with the king in the metropolis of triumphs.[249] Surely this dance seems on a par with those of Daedalus, which that man, as Homer says, wrought for Ariadne at Knossos; [c] or rather, since the creator of the dance is superior, is not what follows also so?[250]

The present circumstances offer both of you the opportunity to boast, you [Constantius] to the very heart of your empire, and the new Rome to the old; you – of the qualities of the city by which you have been enthralled, she – of the qualities of the man by whom she is courted. Moreover, both have the chance to learn from what you have seen, you – that you have gained one greater than she [Constantinople] may be; she – that she is vanquished by one of such a size [i.e. Rome]. Nor is she ashamed for the future to stand in the second rather than the front rank and is not aggrieved or distressed because it is here that you

247 As her ability to join in the dance described in the following sentence makes clear, Themistius had in mind when using Τύχη here the goddess who personified Constantinople's Fortune, rather than impersonal destiny. This personification is often illustrated upon coins.

248 The three elements are Rome, Constantinople and Constantius. In dramatic performances the *coryphaeus* led the chorus and engaged in dialogue with actors. For a similar identification of the emperor in his council, see *Orr.* 4.54b; 16.201b.

249 This suggests that military victory over the usurpers provided the pretext for Constantinople's Crown Gold; see the introduction to this speech.

250 *Iliad* 19.590ff.: on the shield which he made for Achilles, Hephaestus depicted the intricate dances of Knossian youths and maidens. The dance analogy from a few lines previously is continued, although in the Homeric passage ὁ χορός is the area where the dance takes place rather than the dance itself, and Daedalus its designer rather than its choreographer. Daedalus went on to design the labyrinth to house the Minotaur and supervised Icarus' ill-fated flight. Themistius did not want to associate Constantius with Daedalus' less auspicious or successful devices.

are holding the first celebrations of victory **[d]** for those feats of prowess and triumphs for which she sent support and mobilised.[251]

And there are other and closer ties shared by both cities. I do not refer to the longstanding alliances nor to all the assistance she gave and the combined efforts she made on behalf of this city when her dominion was but recently established, sailing with Pompey and helping in the destruction of Mithridates, **[43a]** always contributing as her share the most experienced squadrons of her fleet, for which even today she preserves trophies and victory inscriptions in common with the Romans.[252] No, I refer to all the fresh and recent tokens of goodwill shown on your and your father's account. It is better to recall only these.

When that barbarian revolt broke out and the Roman Empire hung in the balance, as if in a dangerous and swelling storm wave and when the succession of Constantine was in danger of being wrecked on an avenging and implacable barbarian,[253] it was only the benevolent genius of that city which preserved the glowing embers of the family, **[b]** and sent them forth to the ancient hearth of Aeneas' line [Rome]. And it is because of our [Constantinople's] founder[254] that the Germans and Jazygi do not luxuriate in the labours of the ancient Romans[255] and that Rome's proud and mighty name has not been utterly abused nor has been erased or falls to bastard and spurious successors but has returned once more to the legitimate and unsullied blood line of the kings and is preserved for us intact and undefiled. **[c]** It was from that city and from his father's tomb in our midst that this noble man set out and inflicted a

---

251  I.e., particularly the defeat of Magnentius, but also the overthrow of Vetranio, both of whom were overpowered through the resources of the eastern Empire. Again the emphasis here suggests that the defeat of the usurpers was the pretext for Constantinople's Crown Gold.

252  Mithridates VI Eupator Dionysus (120–63 BC), Rome's most dangerous enemy of the 1st century, ruled Pontus, most of the circuit of the Black Sea, and stretched his power at times as far as Cappadocia and Greece. He was undermined by a series of wars against the Romans, 89–85, 83–81, and, finally, 68–63 BC, Pompey presiding over his ultimate defeat. Byzantium was a close Roman ally from the time of its 2nd-century Macedonian wars.

253  Magnentius, whom the sources consistently label a barbarian (cf. the introduction to this speech).

254  Constantius, according to Themistius' argument: see below.

255  A development of the consistent slur that Magnentius was a barbarian. He employed some auxiliaries from beyond the frontier: Julian, *Or.* 1.36c (indicating that the Saxons and Franks mentioned at 34b–35c came from outside the Empire).

deserved punishment on the man who had raged drunkenly against this people, who had hacked at the senate and filled Tiber's undefiled waters with slaughterings and pollution.[256]

As men of the past once thought Camillus to be a second founder, because he preserved what had survived the Celtic invasion,[257] shall not the present generation make you a founder before even Romulus? When you had the chance to live quietly in peace after doubling the portion of your dominion,[258] **[d]** you neither ignored nor neglected the freedom of the city nor allowed it to pass away, but held your invincible hand over it, and it is because of this that we can address you as Emperor of the Romans and do not lie when we write and proclaim these august and ancient titles – Caesar, Emperor, Consul on many occasions, Father of the Senate. For all these would otherwise have been completely empty and meaningless and a source of tears for those who remembered them.[259]

If, then, it is a sign of closer ties of goodwill in personal friendships whenever people are seen to share the same friends and enemies, **[44a]** how much more necessary is it for those cities to join together with each other against which the tyrant plots above all others, and on whose behalf the king joins the struggle above all others? What's more, is it through the son that we are able to enjoy so many tokens and pledges of goodwill between the two cities, those from the father being less important and fewer, or has the order of the deeds merely been reversed, with

256 Magnentius is not known to have purged the Roman senate, an act which would surely have been mentioned by Julian in his catalogue of Magnentius' crimes at *Or.* 1.34a–b. Hence this is probably a reference to the short-lived putsch of Nepotianus, son of Constantine I's sister Eutropia, who responded to the fall of Constans (Jan. 350) by coming to Rome in imperial garb (3 June 350). Magnentius' chief supporter, his *Magister Officiorum* Marcellinus, suppressed this legitimist counter-coup by force (30 June 350): Zosimus 2.43.2–4; cf. *PLRE* 1, 624.

257 Marcus Furius Camillus was hailed as Rome's second founder after his defeat of the Gauls in 398/6 BC (Livy V.49.7). A similar idea appears at *Panegyrici Latini* 10.5 where Maximian and Diocletian are referred to as founders (*conditores*) of the Roman Empire by virtue of being its restorers (*restitores*). See *Or.* 13.179c for a similar characterisation of Gratian.

258 The overthrow of Vetranio in December 350 added Illyricum to Constantius' dominion, but hardly 'doubled' it.

259 Conflict with Magnentius in 351 was preceded by negotiation, and Themistius here claims that it was love of Rome and its senate which prevented Constantius from doing a deal. According to both Zosimus (2.46.3) and Zonaras (13.8), Constantius was willing to negotiate if Magnentius withdrew from Italy; there would thus appear to be some truth to the idea that Italy was a sticking point.

the overall result in no way different? The father first freed this city from a tyranny that was similar and all but identical in name, [b] and then progressed to the foundation of the Fair City, the son first furnished that city with what it needed, indeed with everything that his father had intended, and in this way has bestowed freedom upon this one, both men completing a single cycle of benefaction upon them.[260] One could say that the cities have exchanged gifts with each other: the city that was liberated providing the founder, the one that was founded the saviour.

The Fair City took pains that the theatre for her crown should be so illustrious, benevolent and well-disposed to her. Yet consider also, your majesty, the herald to whom she has entrusted the proclamation [c] and consider whether somehow in this way she does not show her thank offering to be even more prestigious. For seeking one in whom you might take most pleasure, she did not find a slick orator nor one of great stature and voice who has bellowed with ease and without pausing for breath, but – while it is not for me whom she preferred to speak of the particular qualities of the man she found – she preferred a philosopher and sought one out, considering him the best suited to perform this service and worthy of honouring a king who is both a good man and a philosopher.[261] Allow me to say, your imperial majesty, [d] that, for the first time, there now comes on the scene a free and impartial witness of your virtues, who cannot be convicted of false testimony nor yet brought to judgement for handing out praises where they are not due because he has succumbed to money or is aiming for power. Rather he is one whom the title with which he has been enrolled constrains from uttering any phrase, however insignificant, for which he shall not be held to account for all future time. [45a] For this reason he must attest to only those things which he admires and knows well.[262] In contrast,

260  Constantine defeated Maxentius to seize Rome (312) before moving on to the east to refound Byzantium as Constantinople (formal inauguration 11 May 330). Constantius endowed Constantinople (see below), before moving west to defeat Magnentius and liberate Rome (351–3). Themistius plays here upon the names Maxentius/Magnentius as well as parallels in the sequences of events.

261  Themistius devoted *Or.* 2 to the vision of Constantius as philosopher king.

262  These words recall the opening of *Or.* 1. This was Themistius' fourth major speech to Constantius, but it is presumably the senate rather than the emperor which is meant to realise that this was the 'first time' that a truly independent and hence impartial witness had come before them. The comment may also have been meant as a disparaging reference to the Christian Neoplatonist Prohaeresius who was much favoured by Constantius' brother Constans, and who had been sent by the latter to speak to the Roman senate in the

most people, in order to be more pleasing, render incredible even what is fact. What then does he know well and admire? Not the extent of your dominion, for indeed Nero ruled over no fewer men, nor yet your golden throne and your army – for thus one would admire Midas or Cambyses – nor that you shoot straight and true, nor your slaughter of lions and a menagerie of leopards.[263] What is it that he comes here to admire? What is the decree passed by philosophy that he brings hither? [b] It is that you are lenient in victory, that you lead your life with more self-control than the most moderate of private citizens, that you set the highest value on education, and that you pursue philosophy.[264] This is your strength, your army and your sentinels and bodyguards by which, alone of all your brothers, you have been kept free from harm and preserved, and with which you have exacted punishment upon the abusers,[265] and employing this equipment you took your stand against the old man [Vetranio] and with this won the bloodless victory.[266]

[c] I saw, your majesty, the very tribunal on which, speaking to the multitude, you took prisoner the man who had insane designs upon the imperial purple. I saw what was really your trophy of victory, which neither footsoldier nor horseman nor bowman helped to raise, of which the soldiers were witnesses but not fellow contestants.[267] Those who praise the other things have not admired you but what is yours and are

---

late 340s (i.e. within memory): Eunapius, *Lives of the Sophists* 492. On the other elements of Themistius' public image and his competitive approach to possible rivals, see Chapter 1.

263  References to an emperor's prowess in the field of war and hunting were stock elements of panegyric (cf. Menander Rhetor, ed. Russell and Wilson, 1981, 84–9). Nero, Midas and Cambyses were archetypical figures of tyranny and ridicule. Midas king of Phrygia was granted the power of turning all he touched to gold, which inconveniently included his food and loved ones. Cambyses son of Cyrus the Great was condemned as a savage tyrant by Herodotus (3.30–8), and had already been cited as such by Themistius at *Or*. 1.7c.

264  Themistius' approach here was similar to that taken in *Or*. 1. As a philosopher, Themistius could perceive the emperor's really important qualities, whereas other commentators noticed only insignificant exterior points. Again, however, Themistius was praising Constantius for qualities which the emperor himself wished to project; cf. Ammianus 21.16.4–6, which notes Constantius' self-control with approval, but reports that, despite wishing to be known as a man of letters, the emperor failed both in rhetoric and poetics.

265  Magnentius and his supporters.

266  By 357, Constantius was the last surviving son of Constantine I. Of his full brothers, Constantine II had been killed attacking Constans (340), and Constans by Magnentius (350). Themistius returned to the Divine Providence behind all this at the end of the speech.

267  The setting for Vetranio's surrender: see the introduction.

beguiled around the temple portals but are not willing to gaze upon the sacred images within. But the man whom no external feature amazes or turns aside, **[d]** he is the one who can discern the true king.[268] This is why he does not cast his vote in secret, nor has he put forward a different argument in the speech as a screen, nor does he praise the office of kingship while not having the courage to praise him who rules. Rather, he ascends this lofty tribunal and standing in the midst of men, he does not refuse to proclaim you with greater freedom of speech than Xenophon proclaimed Agesilaus, Aristotle Alexander, **[46a]** and, last of all, the devotee of Zeno the king of his own time.[269] For the philosopher is not ashamed of praise but of flattery, nor does he avoid bearing witness to true virtue but courting wickedness. The wise Plato, your majesty, proclaimed you before I did, and, so you do not suspect me of vain boasting, I will here and now repeat his words making no alteration great or small. For he says that it is then that life will achieve its best and happiest condition when the king is young, self-controlled, mindful, brave, majestic and a ready learner.[270]

Does he [Plato] really seem to you an inferior prophet to the Erythrian Sibyl, **[b]** or do we need the prophetic skill of Bacis or Amphilytus who will reveal to us the list of these fine and admirable words, according to any one of which he [Constantius] is quite clearly distinguished or stands out from the whole collection of past kings?[271] For we shall find that while each of the other emperors lays claim to perhaps one of these designations, yet by not embracing the others, he is deprived

268  Compare *Or.* 1.2c–d.
269  Xenophon's *Agesilaus* was a posthumous encomium of a 'perfectly good man' (1.1). The devotee of Zeno is Persaeus, and the king Antigonus II of Macedon, to whose son Persaeus acted as tutor after Zeno himself declined to go to Pella. On these pairs as archetypes of Themistius' political ideal where ruler cooperated with philosopher-advisor, see Chapter 1.
270  Plato, *Republic* 503c–d, *Laws* 709e, 710c. Themistius had already used Plato's definition of the ideal king with reference to Constantius at *Or.* 4.62a, and was to do so again to describe Valens at *Or.* 8.119d, and Theodosius at *Orr.* 17.215c and 34.xvi.
271  The Sibyl was originally the proper name of a single prophetic female whose name and function became generic and plural. There were at least ten Sibyls associated with various locations in the ancient world, among which was Erythrae, one of the twelve Ionian cities in Asia Minor. Bacis was a Boeotian oracle-collector 'maddened by the Nymphs' (Pausanias 4.27.4), whose oracles were known from the 5th century BC (Herodotus 8.20). Amphilytus pronounced an oracle to Peisistratus (Herodotus 1.62–3). Amphilytus, Bacis and the Sibyl are listed together as oracles at (Ps.) Plato, *Theages* 124d.

of even seeming to fit the description. But in sketching you in that speech; O divine being, like an exact image of the form, Plato has somehow managed to hit upon the perfect example.[272] [c] And even if nothing of what has been said is the case but only the enthusiasm for philosophy, which, just like Justice as the poets say,[273] you brought back as she was departing from mankind and turned her round, restoring her to favour and regard, I would not hesitate to bear witness to this. Now you accept these words from a philosopher while philosophy accepts the truth from you and return thanks to her for her praises because she does not lie.

[d] It would be possible, your majesty, to speak at greater length on the kind of city with which the contest of goodwill exists, and how she is equal to the task of seeking out a worthy offering, but the present moment does not allow it. But there are two reasons why we have now made a start. The first is to recall what we have achieved through you, the second is to ask for no addition to what has been given – for that does not follow – save safety for what you have granted.[274] So to sum up what has gone before, [47a] when almost all men thought that the city's good fortune would die along with your father,[275] you did not permit or allow this, nor have you made the city conscious of the change, but, if truth be told, have generated a great consciousness of improvement. For not only did you preserve intact the inheritance from your father, but you increased and augmented it, not resting content with what you received from him but making further additions on your own behalf, [b] and engaging in a noble rivalry with the founder as to who could surpass the other in his benefactions.[276] Thus king is matched with king,

272 Themistius adapts the Platonic concept of the ideal form, the real essence of an object which one can only come to know through use of the intellect rather than physical senses, claiming that Constantius is an exact earthly image of the spiritual ideal of kingship, rather than a lesser one, incorporating only some of the necessary qualities.

273 Hesiod, *Works and Days* 256ff.; Aratus, *Phainomena* 96ff.

274 This did not prevent Themistius from asking for more honours – i.e., more senators – for Constantinople at *Or.* 3.48c below.

275 The Tetrarchic emperors, who preceded Constantine, operated from a variety of regional capitals (Trier, Milan, Sirmium, Antioch, Thessalonica, Nicomedia and Heraclea on the Propontis), each of which was favoured with extravagant building programmes and other marks of favour. The pre-eminence of some of these (esp. Thessalonica, Nicomedia, and Heraclea) proved only temporary, so that Constantinople's continued dominance was far from automatic: see, e.g., Millar, 1992, 40–53 (with 53–7 on Constantinople); Dagron, 1974, chs 1–3.

276 For details, see the introduction to this speech.

son against father. Once the gods too pitted themselves against each other in such a rivalry as they disputed over Attica, Athena against Poseidon, he offering the sea, she displaying the olive shoot.[277] The whole city was the object of your contest and ambitious rivalry and it is now difficult to determine to whom she more justly belongs: **[c]** to him who sowed the seeds, or him who nurtured and brought them to fruition. Whoever may be the victor, the vanquished rejoices, and it is the father who rejoices. For this is the victory which is better for the city.

This indeed is how matters stand. Your city differs from your father's in more respects than his did from its predecessor and has progressed to a true and permanent beauty from an artificial and ephemeral one. She was previously, it seems, the object of desire for an impatient lover eager to satisfy the eye so that even as she glittered she grew old. But the adornment with which you have dressed her, **[d]** is designed for lasting beauty and, outstripping the ephemeral in her fresh bloom, she certainly surpasses the most ancient cities in her permanence. For when, emerging from the womb into the light of day, she was left bereft of her father and in need of infant clothes, you as a good elder brother took her up like a delicate little sister, **[48a]** and immediately considering her worthy of a proper upbringing, immediately took thought about milk and nourishment, and you showed her off to be quite beautiful and great, such as a god or king might desire. And so whereas previously, the senate received honour through constraint and the honour was thought no different from a punishment, now people flock from all sides voluntarily and on their own initiative. Before they were bribed with large tracts of land and money and considered the gifts as a lure to establish residence there, now they make offerings from their own resources and rejoice in the expense.[278]

**[b]** This is because you listened well to the wise Plato and considered enthusiasm a stronger bond than constraint.[279] Because of this

277 The contest between Athena and Poseidon over Attica was depicted on the west pediment of the Parthenon. Poseidon caused a salt stream to issue from the Acropolis and Athena countered by producing an olive shoot from the dry earth to win.

278 The hostile pagan tradition originating in Eunapius but surviving in Zosimus reports that Constantine wasted public money on useless and hurriedly built structures, some of which had to be demolished as unsafe, and that he had to bribe people to move to his new capital by spending public money on building houses for the new senators and establishing food doles: Zosimus 2.31.2–32.1. In 358/9, Themistius himself was willing to fix the election expenses of the new senators he recruited: see Chapter 1.

279 Cratylus 403c.

you have dismissed fear and bound the new inhabitants with love and desire. For from the time when she was shaped and nurtured by you to come to a full and proper flowering and flourished and grew tall, such great yearning has surged around her, such is the girdle of Aphrodite made manifest, and so many Cupids dance around, exactly as if at a festival site open to all.[280] [c] With all these good things [and those that appear so][281] flowing together into the one place from the orchestrator of human happiness, each man has the ready enjoyment of what above everything else captivates him. And the city deserves to achieve both this and still greater honour from you.[282] For it seems clear that God is guiding her course and granting deserved reward to those who understand his intention. What proof of this can I give? That you alone of all your brothers [d] exerted yourself on her behalf and out of all of them it is you who alone have fallen heir to the kingship.[283]

---

280 At Homer, *Iliad* 14.193ff., Aphrodite gives Hera her magic girdle into which Love and Desire were woven, as an irresistible charm to aid her seduction of Zeus. We read τοσοῦτοι with Ἔρωτες (Cupids) after Jacobs and Dindorf.

281 The words καὶ τῶν δοκούντων have possibly been added by a Christian commentator who sought to reduce the approving tenor of this passage, which without them would suggest that God was responsible for the captivating powers of Constantinople.

282 Themistius contradicts his earlier assertion at 46d that he would not be asking for any increase in Constantinople's honours.

283 A particular application of official late Roman state ideology, both pagan, first, and then Christian, which saw the Empire as a God-ordained and directed institution; hence God was directly responsible for the outcome of its affairs: see, e.g., Dvornik, 1966.

# CHAPTER 3

# AFTER JULIAN: THEMISTIUS ORATIONS 5 AND 6

The period of great personal success inaugurated by Themistius' adlection to the Senate of Constantinople and embassy to Constantius II in Rome was brought to an end by political events beyond his control. In November 355, Constantius had appointed his cousin Julian as Caesar: junior co-emperor in the west. Relations between the two men were never easy, and became progressively more strained when Constantius departed to the east to deal with the military crisis generated by a series of Persian offensives, which had culminated in the sack of the great fortress city of Amida and the destruction of its garrison in 359. Since 357, Julian had enjoyed great success against Alamannic and Frankish tribes on the Rhine, arousing Constantius' jealousy, and used these successes as an excuse for throwing off the control of the advisors with whom Constantius had originally surrounded him. Matters came to a head in winter 359/60 when Constantius demanded some of Julian's troops. Julian's army declared him Augustus, and he rebelled against Constantius, moving swiftly to take over most of the Empire's European territories by winter 360/1. Constantius responded by extricating himself from war with the Persians, preparing a massive counterstrike, and moving westwards. He died, however, on 5 October 361 before war could begin in earnest, leaving Julian as sole emperor.[1]

Constantius' death did not end the turmoil. Julian apostatised from Christianity, and proceeded to withdraw state support from the religion. In the course of his brief reign, his religious policies hardened, in certain areas at least, into a positive persecution of Christianity.[2] Julian was also determined to launch a major war against the Persians, but the policy misfired. After initial successes which took him as far as Ctesiphon, the Persian capital, his army was forced into a long and dangerous retreat back to Roman territory, in the course of which Julian himself was killed

---

1 On all this, see now Matthews, 1989, ch. 6.
2 See most recently Smith, 1995, ch. 7, esp. 207–18.

in a skirmish on 26 June 363.[3] After some squabbling, the army council chose Jovian as his replacement. The new emperor was forced to negotiate a humiliating peace in order to extract the remnants of the Roman army intact from Persian territory. By autumn 363 Jovian had established himself in Antioch and then, in winter 363/4, moved on towards Constantinople. He died, however, in mysterious circumstances near Nicomedia, on 17 February 364. After further lengthy discussions, a military officer by the name of Valentinian was elected Augustus and acclaimed as such by the army on 26 February. He made his way on to Constantinople, where, on 28 March, he promoted as co-Augustus his brother Valens.[4]

The twenty-four years of Constantius' reign were thus succeeded by a period of great instability: divisive religious policies, ambitious military campaigns ending in failure, and three different imperial regimes in three-and-a-half years. These years posed great challenges for the Empire as a whole, and for Themistius personally, providing the backdrop and context for his fifth and sixth orations, which are translated in this chapter. Oration 5 was given in Ancyra on 1 January 364 to celebrate the joint consulship of the Emperor Jovian and his infant son Varronianus. Oration 6 was given probably in early winter 364/5 (see below), to Valens, recently established as ruler of the eastern half of the Empire. The contents of these speeches reflect much of how both the Empire and Themistius himself reacted to Julian and his legacy: military defeat spiced with a generous measure of political and religious turmoil.

## THEMISTIUS AND JULIAN

The basic problem facing Themistius in this period was how to safeguard his own position. Closely associated with the emperor Constantius II, there was no guarantee that he would be able to replicate this preeminence under a successor. Once Julian was sole emperor, indeed, Constantius' favour itself became a potential liability, given the highly ambivalent feelings that Julian had towards his overbearing and homicidally paranoiac predecessor. Julian and his half-brother Gallus were among the few collateral male relatives of the Emperor Constantine to survive the dynastic massacre in favour of his sons (Constantine II,

3  General accounts: Bidez, 1930, 315–31; Browning, 1975, ch. 10; Bowersock, 1978, ch. 10; Matthews, 1989, chs 7–8.
4  A good introduction to these elections is Matthews, 1989, ch. 9.

Constans, and Constantius) which had followed his death in 337, and which, among others, had claimed the life of Julian's father, Constantine's half-brother Iulius Constantius. The two boys were spared: in Julian's case, reportedly, because of his age (about 5) and Gallus because he was ill and not expected to survive. After the murder of Constans in 350, Constantius appointed Gallus Caesar in 351, but relations quickly soured and Constantius had his cousin arrested and killed in 354. After a period of uncertainty, during which he wondered if he too would be killed, Julian was also made Caesar in 355, but, as we have already seen, relations again deteriorated into revolt and civil war.[5] It is thus hardly surprising that Julian harboured less than warm feelings towards Constantius, or that, as one of the former emperor's favourites, Themistius' public profile went into relative eclipse in Julian's reign.

That said, Julian had studied under Themistius, and the two seem to have exchanged letters regularly in the early 350s,[6] so that their relationship deserves careful investigation. It is first documented in Julian's *Letter to Themistius*, whose date has occasioned much debate. It seems clear, however, that the bulk, if not all of it, was written c.355, just after Julian's promotion as Caesar. It is, indeed, Julian's reply to a letter of congratulation from Themistius on that promotion, although it is just possible that the letter was recirculated again later during Julian's revolt against Constantius.[7] More important for present purposes, and less controversial, are the letter's contents. Themistius' exhortatory note – or *protrepticos* – to Julian had clearly echoed traditional Themistian themes: that the Divinity had picked out the new emperor for his superior, semi-divine nature, and what a good thing it was that Julian had now abandoned solitary philosophical studies in favour of a more active life.

5 Survival of Julian: *Letter to the Athenians* 270d. Survival of Gallus: Socrates, *Ecclesiastical History* 3.1. General accounts of relations between Julian and Constantius: Bidez, 1930, 10–26, pt. 2 chs 3–12; Browning, 1975, chs 2, 5–6; Bowersock, 1978, chs 3–5; Matthews, 1989, 87ff.

6 Julian, *Letter to Themistius* 253c, 257d, 259c, 260a, 266a; cf. Daly, 1980, 3; Bradbury, 1987, 248–9.

7 Barnes and Vanderspoel, 1981, argue that Julian added the last two paragraphs and recirculated the letter in c.360. Many of their arguments are convincingly undermined, however, by Bradbury, 1987. The only point he cannot counter, as he himself acknowledges, is the fact that the letter is allocated to the period when Julian was Augustus by MS Vossianus Graecus 77, whose attributions are largely correct. This MS is usually considered a late compilation, however, rather than a copy of a collection going back to Julian himself, so that this may simply be a mistake.

Julian, however, refused the flattery. In reply, he began by denying that he possessed a superior, divine-like nature and even poked fun at Themistius' claims to be a truth-teller *par excellence* (*Letter to Themistius* 253a–254c). The letter continued by citing Plato and Aristotle to the effect that chance – *tyche* – was the most important factor governing promotions to kingship, not the Divinity, and that the superior race set to govern men by Plato consisted not of kings but of daemons. In other words, Themistius had misread his authorities (Plato 257a–258d; Aristotle 260d–263b). The new Caesar also stressed that he had already been leading a very full and useful life, not least in the honourable activity of caring for his friends (259a–260c). Claiming that this was a life more than active enough for a philosopher, he finished the letter by disputing Themistius' claim that Aristotle had favoured an active as opposed to contemplative philosophical life and by quibbling with Themistius' use of the examples of Arius, Nicolaus, Thrasyllus, and Musonius as politically active philosophers (263c–266d). The tone of all this, it should be said, seems far from bitter: more a respectful academic disagreement.[8] Nonetheless, the disagreements are profound, and, significantly, Julian's arguments would deny the legitimacy of Themistius' whole public career. This, as we have seen, was based on the idea that a properly qualified philosopher could recognise and hence legitimately serve a divinely appointed monarch who possessed the central virtue of *philanthropia*.

It has also been argued that, if the letter was reissued in c.360, the appeal of its final paragraph that philosophers should see Julian as their leader was in part an attempt to discredit Themistius in Constantius' eyes by casting doubt on his loyalty.[9] If so, and we doubt it, the ploy failed. As late as May 361, Themistius retained Constantius' confidence, being picked out for special mention among those nominated to the panel to control future recruitment to the Senate of Constantinople (*C.Th.* 6.14.12). And this, we suspect, is the real point behind the earlier academic jousting between Julian and his former teacher. Whatever the intellectual and other bonds between them, Themistius was much too

8 Daly, 1980; Bradbury, 1987; Athanassiadi, 1992, 56, 91–3, 128; Vanderspoel, 1995, 119ff.; Smith, 1995, 27–8.

9 Barnes and Vanderspoel, 1981; cf. Vanderspoel, 1995, 122–3 who wonders if this political embarrassment forced Themistius to resign from the urban prefecture of Constantinople to which he had been nominated by Constantius. He has in mind, however, the incident in *Or.* 34.xiii (see Chapter 5), which occurred in the time of Valens rather than under Constantius.

closely associated with Constantius, whom Julian had good reason to detest and fear.

The nature of relations between Themistius and Julian after Constantius' death is subject to only fragmentary and in part contradictory reports. Themistius clearly did not disappear from public life in the manner of Constantius' highest functionaries, who were cashiered and sometimes even prosecuted by the new emperor.[10] A rather startling note in the *Suda* even claims that Themistius held the post of urban prefect of Constantinople during Julian's reign. Brauch has recently argued that this is a straightforwardly accurate report, but, in our view, it is subject to one overwhelming objection. Such a tenure of office is not mentioned in Oration 34, Themistius' retrospective account of his own career, which otherwise mentions and justifies every honour that had come his way over the years.[11] That said, Themistius certainly delivered a panegyric to Julian sometime before spring 363; it may well, indeed, have celebrated Julian's accession to the consulship on 1 January 363.[12] The speech is not extant in any Greek collection of Themistius' works, but is perhaps preserved in Arabic translation (the so-called *Risalat*). If so, then Themistius again cut his suit according to the reigning emperor's demands. The Arabic material suggests that Themistius, while retaining the rhetorical format of proceeding from general philosophical principles to the praise of the particular individual, gave an account of Julian's deeds which was cloaked in a philosophical presentation which accorded more with Julian's ideas than with Themistius' own previously stated positions on divine kingship.[13]

10 Dagron, 1968, 234 n. 26, collects the known examples: Saturninus (on whom see the introduction to Oration 1), Clearchus (perhaps prosecuted), Datianus, Florentius, and Spectatus.

11 *Suda* ed. Adler, 2, 690; cf. Brauch, 1993a; 1993b. On Oration 34, see Chapter 5. Brauch argues that the silence of Oration 34 is not conclusive since it also fails to mention Themistius' tenure of proconsular office in 359, but Themistius did not hold this position either: see the introduction to Chapter 2.

12 The plausible suggestion of Vanderspoel, 1995, 130–1. Libanius, *Ep.* 818.3 of spring 363 requested a copy of the speech; *Ep.* 1430 of November 363 praised it.

13 Cf. Brauch, 1993b, 92; Vanderspoel, 1995, 129ff., esp. his judgement on the oration at 133, which echoes that of Dvornik, 1966, 666–9. Vanderspoel also here makes the case for seeing the *Risalat* as the lost panegyric of Julian, but there are problems. Two variant Arab versions survive; hence Dagron, 1968, 223–4, doubts the attribution, while the speech's most recent editor, Shahid, argues that it is actually a panegyric presented to the Emperor Theodosius (pp. 75–80 in vol. 3 of the Teubner edition of Themistius' works).

There is good reason to think, however, that Themistius never ranked among Julian's close confidants. For one thing, Themistius himself implied as much in speeches given after Julian's death. In Oration 5 to Jovian, Themistius devoted considerable space to making the point that he was now back in imperial favour (*Or.* 5.63c–64d). This would have been otiose had he really been Julian's urban prefect. A stray piece of text, likewise, refers to a moment of philosophical debate during Julian's reign where the emperor publicly decided in favour of Themistius' opponent. This vignette does indicate that Themistius had not disappeared from public life, but equally suggests that relations between Themistius and Julian retained their intellectual difficulties.[14] More generally, Julian belonged to the mystical Neoplatonist tradition which regarded Christianity as anathema. This tradition, concerned with the inner spiritual development of the individual, was one of those roundly attacked by Themistius as professor of philosophy in Constantinople under Constantius, and in opposition to which he had framed his own more Aristotelian, socially active and religiously more neutral version of Hellenism. In Julian's eyes, therefore, Themistius can only have appeared much too willing to compromise his Hellenism to Christianity in general, and in particular to the religious policy of the Emperor Constantius.[15] Past affiliations, aggravated by intellectual differences, thus rendered Themistius a relatively unattractive figure for Julian. He had not been so closely identified with Constantius, however, as to have held a major office, and, as we shall see, his role in recruiting for the senate had probably also made him an indispensable figure in the politics of the eastern Empire.

## JOVIAN AND VALENS

Orations 5 and 6 are concerned with much else besides, but they do reflect some of the ways in which Themistius took advantage of the opportunities presented by circumstance, particularly Julian's untimely death in

14 Ammonius, *Anal. Prior.* 1.1.24b18 (= *Commentaria in Aristotelem Graeca* 4.6, p. 31.17–22), modifying the interpretation of Brauch, 1993b, 99–100, in the light of the competitive intellectual environment explored above in the introduction to *The Letter of Constantius.* The dispute was between Themistius and a certain Maximus, identified variously as Maximus of Ephesus (Dagron, 1968, 235; Blumenthal, 1990, 79), or Themistius' father-in-law, Maximus of Byzantium (Vanderspoel, 1987a).

15 See the introduction to Chapter 2 and the introduction to *The Letter of Constantius.*

Persia, to win back his lost pre-eminence. No doubt much necessary negotiation between emperors and philosopher took place in ways that the surviving source material does not describe. A letter of Libanius comments, however, on the way in which Themistius was courted by 'all the powerful' early in the reign of Jovian.[16] Thanks to his senatorial recruiting activities in the latter years of Constantius' reign, which reinforced his prominent teaching career, Themistius' opinion is likely to have carried considerable weight with many of the senators of Constantinople. This may well explain why Julian, as we have seen, maintained reasonably cordial relations with him, despite their significant intellectual differences. This, combined with his cultural credentials, also made him an attractive recruit for any new regime, not least a Christian one, and both Jovian and Valens were Christians. The dynamic underlying the relationship between Christian emperor and Hellenic philosopher which had evolved under Constantius continued to apply under subsequent Christian regimes. A public display of favour towards Themistius would prompt the philosopher's endorsement, and hence reassure a substantial portion of the traditionally educated and probably still pagan majority of the eastern landowning elite.[17]

The contents of Orations 5 and 6 also suggest some of the things Themistius received in return for his support. Strikingly, both speeches are overtly aggressive in promoting Themistius' claims on the position of chief philosophical advisor. The beginning of Oration 5 to Jovian celebrated Themistius' return to favour, and underlined the fact that his delivery of a speech celebrating Jovian's first consulship was to be recognised for what it was. Jovian was 'adopting philosophy in the sight of all' and 'publicly honouring' him. The first speech to Valens – Oration 6 – was more aggressive. Again, right at the beginning of the speech, Themistius rejoiced that Valens had recognised the merits of true philosophy imparted by himself, and managed to distinguish him from 'fraudulent practitioners', whom he compared to informers or poisoners. Valens is known to have purged Julian's philosophers, particularly the wonder-working Maximus of Ephesus, where Jovian had not, and, accordingly, Themistius made sure that everyone recognised his triumph (*Or.* 6.73b–c). Givers of panegyrics might stand in a variety of

---

16 Libanius, *Ep.* 1455; cf. Gregory Nazianzen, *Epp.* 24, 28 (of the same era); Dagron, 1968, 167.

17 On all this, see further Chapter 1.

relationships to the imperial court before whom they were speaking, and Themistius himself had given a panegyric before Julian to whom he was far from close.[18] In these orations, both of which represented the first act of a formal relationship with a new imperial regime, Themistius thus underlined the centrality of his position within the new regimes.

Both speeches also demonstrated the loyalty which Themistius had clearly promised in return. Another very striking feature they share in common is Themistius' willingness to criticise his former patrons. In Oration 5, Jovian was declared a 'very Constantine' in contrast to Constantine's son and nephew (Constantius and Julian) who, it was implied, had fallen short of their predecessor's example. The speech also contained a pointed reference to the dynastic murders which followed Constantine's death, in which Constantius was deeply involved, together with disparaging references to Julian as a false pagan prophet who, among other things, had followed the ridiculous path of trying to constrain individual conscience.[19] In Oration 6, the condemnations became more strident. Constantius' lack of familial *philanthropia* was underlined by the fact that he had started as a member of large ruling dynastic group, but killed everyone off and so exhausted his dynasty, just like the sons of Oedipus (*Or.* 6.74b). The self-presentation of Constantius' own propaganda – that he was good at javelin throwing, bows and arrows, horsemanship, and avoided the pleasures of the flesh – was also explicitly picked up, and presented as an example of what kingship should *not* be about (78c). The speech's denigration of asceticism may likewise have been aimed at Julian. In addition, Themistius made a slighting reference to the election of the recently praised Jovian as one brought about by 'force of arms' alone (73c), and strongly implied that his early death made it clear that, unlike Valentinian and Valens, Jovian had not been elected emperor by God. And all this despite the fact that Themistius had recently concluded Oration 5 by noting that God had made Jovian and his son joint consuls, and would make them joint emperors in due course (71b). Themistius had not the slightest hesitation, therefore, in publicly damning former imperial patrons at the start of a new reign. This certainly had real political significance (see below), but also reflects the total ruthlessness that he had to

18  See generally Nixon and Rodgers, 1994, 26ff.
19  Criticism of Constantius: *Or.* 5.70d , 66d. Anti-Julianic material: *Or.* 5.64a–b, 65b–c, 66d, 70b–c with notes to these passages below.

deploy to stay atop the greasy pole. The right to declare oneself especially favoured by an incoming imperial regime came at the price of a total and all-embracing public loyalty.

## BUILDING CONSENSUS

The end of the Constantinian dynasty, and the circumstances of its last few years in power, meant that the two regimes which immediately replaced it faced a number of common problems. There is thus considerable overlap between Orations 5 and 6, which gives a real sense of the general political context in which both Jovian, and Valentinian and Valens had to work. In some senses, the Constantinian dynasty had ruled some part of the Empire since 1 March 293 when Constantius Chlorus was elected Caesar as part of Diocletian's new Tetrarchy. The dynasty had entirely dominated imperial politics since Constantine's defeat and deposition of Licinius in 324. The late Roman Empire was also an aggressive autocracy, where attempts to foresee the future might be read as treasonable against the reigning emperor, since they constituted an interest in alternative political configurations.[20] The death of the dynasty's last surviving adult male in June 363 thus left a huge political vacuum. Julian had in his lifetime designated no legitimate successor, and, by its very nature, autocracy makes it difficult if not impossible for an alternative regime-in-waiting to be ready to step into the breach. A first concern of any new emperor, therefore, had to be to generate consent among the dispersed landowners of the Empire, by whom and for whom it was actually run.

In this respect, there was considerable common ground between the interests of Jovian and Valens and those of Themistius himself. Themistius had to negotiate his transition to a new imperial regime, and, as we have seen, one means of doing this was publicly to criticise the failings of previous masters. For new emperors seeking to establish themselves after Julian's death, this had considerable attractions. Denigrating the achievements of immediate predecessors left the new incumbent with much less to live up to. Saying out loud what everyone had anyway been thinking about the dynastic blood-letting of the Constantinians was also an attempt to make the new order seem attractive by comparison,

---

20 One famous incidence of this under Valens: Ammianus 29.1 with Matthews, 1989, 219–25.

and hence generate an ideological justification around which political support could be mobilised. There was also a more particular point. One reasonably prominent member of the broader Constantinian family, Julian's maternal uncle Procopius, was still at large. He did formally offer his allegiance to Jovian, but under Valens he went into hiding and eventually led a dangerous rebellion which broke out in Constantinople in September 365. Constantius also left behind him a second wife, Faustina, and a posthumously born daughter. Again, in his revolt, Procopius dragged mother and child round with him and attempted to use them to show that he was the true heir of the Constantinian order, where Valentinian and Valens were mere parvenus. He seems to have enjoyed some success with this approach.[21] Such a long-lived dynasty could not but leave various fringe figures in its wake who might attempt to mobilise pre-existing patterns of loyalty around themselves. In such a context, damning previous rulers served the needs of the new political order.

After denigrating the past, the next important move was to underline the positive credentials of the new holder(s) of the imperial office, and, again, Orations 5 and 6 undertook this task. As unrelated successors to a relatively long-lived dynasty, their acquisitions of imperial office were of particular interest, and Themistius devoted considerable attention in both speeches to celebrating the entirely different modes of accession of Jovian and Valentinian and Valens, despite the fact that (or perhaps because) that of Jovian had occurred in unusual enough circumstances to be of questionable legitimacy.[22] In addition, Jovian's early death, following that of Julian, underlined the fragility of human life, and the political consequences of that fragility when the individual concerned was an emperor. Hence the demand arose that, for the sake of political stability, Valentinian, Jovian's successor, should designate a co-emperor, who would act as some guarantee of political continuity even in the face of human mortality. The demand had probably already risen under Jovian, because in Oration 5, Themistius determinedly stressed that the new emperor would have no colleague other than, at some point in the future, his still infant son Varronianus (*Or.* 5.68a; cf. 71b on

---

21 Ammianus' account of the rebellion of Procopius is discussed in Matthews, 1989, 191–203. On Procopius' use of Constantius' widow and child, see Ammianus 26.7.10; 9.3.

22 The underlying point of Ammianus' account of Jovian (25.5–10), later adopted by Themistius himself: see the introductions to *Orr.* 5 and 6 below.

Varronianus). In discussing Valens' promotion, Themistius chose to stress the administrative expediency of two emperors, presumably since it would hardly be politic to consider the possibility of Valentinian's death (*Or.* 6 esp. 75b–d).

The two speeches also reflect a number of other ways in which Jovian and Valens attempted to establish themselves in the affections of potential supporters. Oration 5 looked to reassure political opinion by picking out the continued participation, under the new man Jovian, of four major figures who had been prominent under both Julian, and, to some extent, Constantius as well. The four were Salutius Secundus (certainly), together with (probably) Arintheus, Dagalaifus, and Victor (*Or.* 5.67b). Oration 6 stressed, likewise, that under Valens it would not be open season for informers to attempt to settle old political scores (*Or.* 6.81a). Indeed, the whole ceremonial context of Oration 6 was clearly dedicated to emphasising consensus. As the speech makes clear, Themistius and Valens engaged in a double act. The day before, Valens had spoken to the senate. Oration 6 was Themistius' reply, and, among other things, he picked up on what the emperor had had to say, commenting with enthusiastic approval upon its wisdom. Not surprisingly, overt acts of courtesy had been directed by the emperor towards the city of Constantinople. Valens thanked the senators for the statue they had erected in honour of his father, and seems to have announced that he would be building some appropriate monument in the Hebdomon, the suburb of Constantinople in which he had been elevated to the purple. Building was the ultimate means of showing favour and goodwill to any locale in the Graeco-Roman view of the world. He had also declared Constantinople to be the 'Mother of the Kingship'. Oration 6 was thus part of an extended exchange devoted to unanimity and mutual congratulation: the formal public expression of the relationships required to transform a new regime into a working political entity.

A more particular example of the same general problem raised its head in both orations: the question of religion. As we have seen, Constantius had been willing to tolerate and promote non-Christians, such as Themistius himself, but had favoured Christianity and imposed considerable restrictions on the practice of pagan cult. Julian had veered in the opposite direction. The combined legacy of these emperors, and especially that of Julian, was thus one of religious partisanship at the centre which had generated the potential for substantial local conflict, depending, of course, on how local communities reacted to the religious stimuli being imparted from the top.[23] Hardly surprisingly, both subsequent regimes, although headed by Christian emperors, chose to follow policies of religious toleration.[24] Oration 5 devoted much space to the subject, and laid out many reasons why toleration was the best policy, not just for pragmatic reasons of social peace, but because the Divinity actually wanted to be worshipped in a variety of ways. Oration 6, by contrast, was more guarded, although Themistius did stress the brotherhood of mankind, flowing from the fact that all are sons of the one divine Father, and commented that all are heading towards Him. In part, the difference of tone between the two speeches may reflect the fact that a policy of religious toleration was, by the time Oration 6 was given, already well established. The speech was probably given early in the winter of 364, whereas Valens and his brother had been in power since the spring, and we know that the laws declaring toleration were among the first they passed.[25] However, Oration 5 was extremely bullish in its advocacy of toleration, and in one extraordinary passage Themistius referred to Christianity as one among three more or less equal religions, and further pointed out how divided Christianity itself was (*Or.* 5.70a–b). In Oration 6, by contrast, Themistius emphasised that different religions, although tolerated, are not necessarily to be considered equally proficient in leading the individual to God, and made no reference at all to Christian sectarianism (*Or.* 6.77c). That idea had surfaced in Oration 5 as well (*Or.* 5.69a), but it seems clear, nonetheless, that, although both regimes espoused toleration, that of Jovian allowed public discussions of religious diversity to present the religions in a much more equal light than was acceptable under Valentinian and Valens. As we shall see, Themistius' account suggests that Jovian may even have tolerated pagan sacrifice, and it is known that he did not purge Julian's philosophers such as Maximus of Ephesus, for whom life only really became difficult under Valens.

Orations 5 and 6, as will become apparent, also addressed a variety of other, more specific issues. They had, however, the same political context: the establishment of new imperial regimes as working propositions. Perhaps more than any other in late Roman political life, this was

---

23  See further the introduction to Chapter 2.

24  On Vanderspoel's arguments to the contrary, see the introduction to *Or.* 5 below.

25  The actual laws are not preserved, but at *C.Th.* 9.16.9 Valentinian refers to them having been given at 'the beginning of my reign'.

a moment when consensus needed to be generated. Themistius' stock of political ideas, drawing on what was still the common heritage of all involved, was ideally suited to the task. This, combined with the position of influence granted to him by the expansion of the Senate of Constantinople late in Constantius' reign, gave him the opportunity, which he ably seized, of managing to leap from one regime to another, even if at the ideological cost of abandoning former patrons.

## ORATION 5
## ON THE CONSULSHIP, TO THE EMPEROR JOVIAN: INTRODUCTION

Themistius gave his fifth oration on 1 January 364 at Ancyra in the heart of Asia Minor. Its delivery formed part of the celebrations being held to mark the consulship of the Emperor Jovian.[26] Jovian had been heralded as Augustus on 27 June 363 by a Roman army still trapped on Persian territory. To extract his forces, the new emperor was forced to come to humiliating terms. In return for allowing the army to retreat to Roman territory, the Persians gained the cities of Nisibis and Singara, five provinces beyond the River Tigris, and fifteen fortified centres. Upon his return, Jovian established himself at Antioch, capital of the diocese of Oriens, for the autumn.[27] As winter drew on, the court set off for Constantinople, stopping at Ancyra to celebrate the new year and with it the emperor's first consulship. At this point Oration 5 celebrated the achievements of the regime so far and looked forward to its future prosperity, not least the eventual elevation to the purple of Jovian's son and consular colleague, the infant Varronianus. Such hopes were spectacularly misplaced. On the night of 17 February 364, in highly mysterious circumstances, Jovian died in his sleep, not far from Nicomedia, but still well short of Constantinople. With his father died any prospect that the young co-consul would ever become emperor.[28]

26  Themistius mentioned the event twice: *Or.* 5.64d–65a, 71b.

27  Persian peace: Ammianus 25.7. 9–11. Jovian was at Antioch by 22 October 363 at the latest: *C.Th.* 10.19.2.

28  The favourite explanation among our sources is that Jovian was asphyxiated by carbon monoxide from a charcoal brazier (Ammianus 25.10.12–13; cf. Sozomen, *Ecclesiastical History* 6.6), but a variety of possibilities, including poisoning, are mentioned (e.g. John Chrysostom, *Homilies* 15: poisoning). Matthews, 1989, 188, points out that Julian had nearly died of carbon monoxide poisoning in Paris (*Misopogon* 340d–342a).

### Themistius and Ammianus

The speech Themistius framed for the consular celebration addressed a number of concerns. Not least, as we have already seen, its contents reflected his own interests. He did not hesitate to emphasise that he was back in full imperial favour after a real, if relative, eclipse during the reign of Julian. For the most part, though, Oration 5 addressed itself to the three main issues of more general concern which had so far surfaced in Jovian's brief reign.

The first was Jovian's accession to power itself. A point of particular interest here is the fact that Themistius based part of his discussion upon a second-century speech *On Kingship* usually attributed to Aelius Aristides. The two speeches coincide in claiming that their respective emperors were worthy of the imperial throne before they received it, and in insisting upon the peacefulness of the elections, the constancy of the emperors' characters, and their concern with justice. The second-century speech also addressed an emperor who, like Jovian, had a very young son who could be portrayed as an eventual successor.[29] The echoes are clear enough, but show just how selective Themistius was in making use of existing rhetorical exempla. He did not copy an entire speech, but used only a few extracts to help him frame just a single passage of his own oration.

In his lengthy treatment of the subject, Themistius stressed that the choice of Jovian was entirely beneficial, whether viewed from a human perspective or – in tune with Roman state ideology which held that the Empire was the Divinity's particular instrument for ordering the affairs of men – a divine one. Because of his father's virtue, Themistius claimed, Jovian was already owed the kingship before Julian's death, and had only declined to take over upon Constantius' death in order to preserve proper decorum. The new emperor had also been elected by the unanimous vote of the entire army, it is claimed, and an important sign of the divine approval underpinning the election was visible in the fact that as soon as they saw him take control, the Persians had stopped harassing the Romans and started to retreat. Themistius also noted that, unlike succession within the Constantinian dynasty, Jovian's rise to power did not involve much bloodshed.

---

29  *Or.* 35 with Behr, 1981, 399–400; Jones, 1972, 134, on its ascription. For the parallels, see Vanderspoel, 1995, 9–10; they are noted in the footnotes below at *Or.* 5.65b, 66d–67a, 67a–b, and 71b.

The extent to which these remarks have any truth to them is difficult to say, principally because Ammianus preserves an account of Jovian's succession which almost entirely contradicts that of Themistius. According to Ammianus, the army council of four senior commanders became deadlocked – Arintheus and Victor versus Dagalaifus and Nevitta – when discussing who should succeed Julian. With deadlock still prevailing, Jovian, a rather obscure figure, took power in what amounted to a *coup d'état* organised by a group of what the historian calls 'camp attendants', and at least one other possible contender for the throne was murdered in its aftermath. Moreover, as soon as the Persians heard that Julian was dead, they attacked with renewed vigour, or so Ammianus reports.[30]

This is no place to attempt to decide between the accounts in detail, but any tendency simply to believe Ammianus, because of the greater weight of circumstantial detail in his account, does need to be resisted. At the very least, Ammianus exaggerated Jovian's obscurity, nor did he tell the full story of the army council's reaction to Jovian's candidacy. Three of the four (Arintheus, Victor and Dagalaifus) turn up in prestigious posts within Jovian's regime, while Nevitta is never heard of again, so that it is pretty clear that the deadlock was eventually broken by Dagalaifus abandoning Nevitta to back Jovian. Indeed, in what is clearly a carefully constructed piece of literature, omens and other literary tricks have been used to underline the fundamental point that Ammianus wished to make. Jovian was not, in the historian's view, a properly legitimate Roman emperor, a view substantiated both by his short life and the disastrous course of his reign, in particular the surrender of so much territory to the Persians. More particularly, it was vital for Ammianus to be able to blame someone other than his favourite Julian for the disastrous end to the Persian war which Julian had started, and his whole account of Jovian was framed with this in mind. The Persian war was lost, Ammianus tried to argue, not because Julian led the army into an impossible situation, but because Jovian was an entirely unworthy successor who negotiated a humiliating peace when he could have fought his way home. He did this, according to Ammianus, to get back to Roman territory before another, more suitable candidate could make a bid for the purple. Ammianus' interest in Jovian was diametrically opposed to that of Themistius, therefore, and just as likely

30  Compare Themistius, *Or.* 5 esp. 65b–67a with Ammianus 25.5–7.

to lead to misrepresentation. Choosing between the accounts on any particular matter of detail is far from straightforward.[31]

There is, however, a more general point. As is elsewhere the case where there is a considerable overlap between them, it is uncertain whether Ammianus was writing directly in response to the relevant speech of Themistius, in other words that he had either heard it or read it. Ammianus' Latin obviously precludes any precise verbal echoes of Themistius' Greek. On the other hand, Ammianus' account has been framed precisely to contradict the kind of picture of Jovian that Themistius constructed, and this pattern recurs sufficiently often to make one think that Ammianus may indeed have had access to a set of Themistius' orations.[32] Whatever the case, Ammianus' hostile reaction to Jovian's accession and reign underlines the significance of Themistius' presentation of the events. A fundamental point of Oration 5 was to stress that, despite its most unusual circumstances among a defeated army on foreign soil, Jovian's accession was nonetheless fully legitimate – i.e. divinely approved – and entirely beneficial to the state.[33] As we have seen, Themistius was well aware that there was a problem, and strikingly changed his tune in Oration 6. In January 364, however, he was happy to deploy every trick in the book to demonstrate that Jovian's election had been entirely valid.

**The Persian Peace**

No one was likely to challenge the new emperor immediately, perhaps, so that Themistius' account of Jovian's accession was probably not too controversial. The same was not true, however, of Themistius' second port of call: the peace treaty Jovian negotiated with the Persians. In this case, as so many others, Themistius produced an account of the topic which was entirely in line with the demands of the ruling regime. Jovian's

31 See now the discussions of Matthews, 1989, 180–8; Heather, 1999. Note too Ammianus' earlier reference to the soldiers' behaviour at Constantius' funeral suggesting that the ghost of Empire, rather than the real thing, would fall to Jovian: 21.16.20–1.

32 Cf. Sabbah, 1978, 347–66. For the detailed example of likely Themistian influence upon Ammianus' account of Gothic policy, see Heather, 1991, 128–35, with the introduction to Chapter 4 below.

33 This suggests a further reason for using the 2nd-century oration *On Kingship*. If it was known as a model, then, by using it so overtly, Themistius was perhaps trying to add to the air of normality he was seeking to weave around Jovian's accession.

coinage makes it clear that the new emperor proclaimed the peace with Persia as a victory,[34] all evidence to the contrary notwithstanding. Themistius took the same line (*Or.* 5.66a–c). In some ways, however, what is really striking about Themistius' treatment of the peace treaty is its brevity. For all its importance, the topic merited but one paragraph (66a–c), no more than two or three minutes of speaking time. This brevity no doubt reflected the topic's inherent embarrassments, for, as we have seen, the terms of the peace treaty were entirely humiliating. The other obvious possible way of tackling the topic – indeed a much more truthful one – would have been to admit that the peace was a setback, but blame Julian for the defeat, and emphasise how well Jovian had done to rescue the army at all.[35] It is uncertain, of course, why Jovian's regime did not choose to take this alternative approach to the Persian peace treaty. Victoriousness, however, was the prime virtue required of an emperor, the fundamental sign that divine favour, as Roman political theory required, attended him. Especially as an entirely new regime struggled to establish itself, this may have made the admission of defeat too dangerous politically, being tantamount to accepting that divine favour had not attended the rise to power of the new emperor. In this context, it is striking that Themistius links victory and accession to the purple in a throwaway line right at the end of the speech.[36]

More particularly, too many of Julian's supporters may have been playing too central a role in the new regime for it to be ready to label the old one a complete disaster. It is also possible that the army's collective experience made such a line dangerous, because, before Julian's death, the Roman army, although beaten strategically, had not suffered tactical military defeat. This, allied with the soldiers' seeming love of Julian, may have made it difficult for Jovian's regime to blame him for the defeat.[37] Whatever the reason, or combination of reasons, his treatment of the Persian peace makes it absolutely clear that Themistius spoke

34  *Restitutor Reipublicae, Victoria Augusti, Victoria Romanorum*: *R.I.C.* 8, 230–1, 281, 424, 438, 464–55, 533.

35  Ammianus' account of Jovian was designed to show that he had squandered a victory won by Julian. The historical details he included demonstrate the opposite, that the army was entirely defeated before Julian's death, a fact of which the historian himself seems to have been at least half aware: Smith, 1999; Heather, 1999.

36  *Or.* 5.71a; cf. McCormick, 1986.

37  Further discussion: Heather, 1999.

Oration 5 as an insider to Jovian's regime, as, indeed, his opening remarks on the degree of favour now shown to himself confirm (*Or.* 5.63a–64b). He was faced with an impossible task – presenting as a victory a peace treaty whose terms blatantly contradicted the claim – and took the best course he could: telling the big lie in as few words as possible before passing to the third great theme of his speech.

## Religious Toleration

This comprised a lengthy treatment of the many virtues of a policy of all-round religious toleration, a subject which encompassed fewer pitfalls than trying to claim that defeat was actually victory. Indeed, Themistius' words have usually been taken to imply that, by the time Themistius spoke, Jovian's regime had already officially espoused such a policy.[38] Recently, however, Vanderspoel has argued that this was not the case, and that Themistius was actually attempting to push Jovian towards enacting a measure of toleration in favour of non-Christian cult. He advances two arguments. First, no Jovianic legislation in favour of toleration is to be found in the *Theodosian Code* dated before 1 January 364, when the speech was given. Second, at certain points in the speech, Themistius cast his treatment of the subject in terms of a plea to the emperor in favour of such a policy. From Themistius' words, it is quite clear that Jovian had done something to quell the religious turmoil let loose by Julian, Vanderspoel concedes, but he suggests that this was simply in the context of religious dispute between Christians, where Jovian is known to have refused to adopt an actively partisan position.[39]

The argument raises some important questions, but is in the end unconvincing. The absence of any Jovianic legislation on toleration from the *Theodosian Code* is actually rather weaker than most arguments from silence. We know that the regime which succeeded Jovian, that of Valentinian and Valens, likewise espoused religious toleration and passed laws to that effect. Ammianus tells us as much, and a later law of Valentinian, which is preserved in the *Code*, refers to earlier legislation on the subject.[40] But Valentinian's original law on the subject

38  E.g., Jones, 1964, 150.

39  Vanderspoel, 1995, 148–53; Jovian's response to quarrelling Christians is reported at Socrates, *Ecclesiastical History* 3.25.1–21; cf. Barnes, 1993, 159–61.

40  *C.Th.* 9.16.9: of the Emperor Valentinian in 371. Cf. the introduction to Chapter 2, relevant legislation of the Emperor Constantine is also 'missing'.

does not itself survive. By the 430s, when the *Theodosian Code* was being compiled, Valentinian's law had long since ceased to apply, as the Empire became more and more aggressively Christian, and it was either omitted from the compilation, or, just as likely, could not even be found. The non-survival of Jovian's similar law on the same subject, therefore, is hardly a compelling argument.[41]

Much more important is the fact that at several points in the oration, Themistius used straightforwardly indicative active verbs which describe Jovian as having already decisively promoted a policy of religious toleration, not just between different groups of Christians, but also between Christians and pagans.[42] This is not to doubt that Jovian was a Christian, nor that, as the Church historian Socrates reports, he banned certain non-Christian cults which he considered unacceptable. So much is anyway confirmed by Themistius.[43] Between them, however, these verbal usages make it certain that, in Oration 5, Themistius was discussing a toleration of non-Christian cult which already existed in law. An important passage in the speech even provides some indication as to the nature of Jovian's laws on the subject. At *Or.* 5.70b, Themistius characterised Jovian's policy as one of

> opening up the temples but closing the haunts of imposture, allowing lawful sacrifices but giving no licence to those who practise the magic arts.

This is tantalising in its imprecision. The difference between 'lawful sacrifice' and 'magic art' lay obviously in the eye of the beholder, and may or may not have been carefully defined. There is enough here, however, to indicate that Jovian's policy was much more like that of Constantine than that prevailing in the latter years of Constantius, with the temples clearly allowed to be open for some kinds of pagan cultic practice. The real question this passage raises, indeed, is whether Jovian's legislation

41  Dagron, 1968, 175–6, suggests that Jovian's legislation took the form of documents similar to those of Constantine preserved in Eusebius, *Life of Constantine* book 2. For different views of how *C. Th.* was compiled, see the essays by Matthews and Sirks in Harries and Wood, 1993.

42  *Or.* 5.67b (Jovian's legislation on divine matters 'has become'); 68a 'you decree'; 68d (2 references to Jovian allowing religious competition); 69b (because of Jovian's law, people will live at peace with one another); 70b (the emperor has allowed certain temples to say open).

43  Socrates, *Ecclesiastical History* 3.24; cf. Themistius *Or.* 5.70b (see previous note).

allowed traditional pagan blood sacrifice. Themistius' use of 'lawful sacrifice' (*thusias ennomous*) might suggest that it did, but blood sacrifice was such an anathema to Christians that, on the face of it, this would seem unlikely. Even if, as under Valentinian and Valens, only candles, hymns, anointings, and other libations were allowed, Jovian's policy would still have represented a major gain for pagans compared to the position under Constantius. And either way, the reports of the Church historians that Jovian shut down pagan cult are optimistically anachronistic.[44]

That toleration, indeed a very open and unambiguous toleration, was already the official policy of the regime is also indicated by the extraordinary freedom Themistius employed in his discussion of religion. As we have seen, one of the central planks of Themistius' approach to this contentious issue had always been to exploit the Neoplatonic overlap between Christianity and traditional non-Christian Hellenic religion.[45] In Oration 5, however, he came much closer to implying the broad equivalence between all these cults as different approaches to the same God. On this topic, at other moments when it appeared in his speeches, Themistius was much more guarded. Indeed, given Christianity's well-entrenched view of its own superiority to all other religions, and the fact that he was talking before Christian emperors, Themistius was no doubt well-advised to be so. But in one remarkable passage of Oration 5, Christianity was designated the religion of the 'Syrians' and juxtaposed with the other two main religions of the fourth-century Roman world, those of the 'Hellenes' and the 'Egyptians'.[46] He further commented that the Syrians could not even agree among themselves, and were fragmented into a number of sects (70a). This is the only point in all his political orations where Themistius felt free to comment on Christian sectarianism. And again, his comments were entirely in line with the policy of Jovian's regime, for, after lengthy negotiations during his stay at Antioch, the new emperor refused to back the claims of any particular Christian group, thus breaking with the determined partisanship of Constantius.[47] The discussion was carefully balanced. Themistius, as we have seen,

44 Socrates, *Ecclesiastical History* 3.24; Sozomen, *Ecclesiastical History* 5.3. For changes in religious policy from Constantine to Valens, see the introduction to Chapter 2.

45 See esp. the introductions to Oration 1 and *The Letter of Constantius* in Chapter 2.

46 For an introduction to the 'Egyptian' religion in late antiquity and its relationship with Hellenic Neoplatonism, see Fowden, 1986; 1987.

47 Barnes, 1993, 159–61 commenting especially on Socrates, *Ecclesiastical History* 3.25.4.

labelled some aspects of non-Christian cult as 'magic and imposture' (70b), as indeed it was traditional for philosophers to do, and stated openly that not every route to God might be of equal value (69a). Nonetheless, the relative freedom of his language is striking, and Themistius would surely never have dared to be so free had he not been entirely confident that active toleration was already the established policy of Jovian's regime.

What, then, of the fact that Themistius at a certain point cast his discussion in the form of a plea? The speech was ostensibly to the emperor, of course, and, read literally, one would naturally conclude that the plea, like the rest of the speech, was directed at Jovian. But Themistius, as we have seen, was pleading for something that Jovian had already enacted. This suggests that the plea was either an oratorical device to make the speech more dramatically satisfying, or else that it had some function other than its ostensible one of attempting to convince the emperor of the merits of the case for toleration. At this point, it is worth recalling that, as is generally the case with Themistius' speeches, the content of Oration 5 was as much directed towards the wider audience gathered to celebrate the consular day as at the emperor himself. We know too that the speech was repeated in Constantinople (Socrates, *Ecclesiastical History* 3.26), presumably to the representatives of eastern landowning opinion gathered in its senate. This broader audience suggests another kind of purpose for the plea. Jovian was himself certainly a believing Christian. And, with a little reflection, it quickly becomes apparent that the chief obstacle in the way of any Christian emperor who wished to espouse a policy of religious toleration was actually other Christians. Christian episcopal and, increasingly, ascetic pressure groups were entirely convinced of the total superiority of their religion, according to its own ideological claims, and hence entirely unready to listen to arguments about the value of old ways and the importance of freedom of conscience and religious diversity.[48]

In this context, framing part of the argument for toleration as a plea worked on two levels to attempt to alleviate the moral blackmail to which Jovian would certainly be liable from the bishops with whom, by January 364, he had already had considerable contact. Most straightfor-

---

48 The famous altar of victory controversy illustrates nicely the kinds of pressures that could be brought to bear by bishops upon Christian emperors: see Matthews, 1975, ch. 8; McLynn, 1994, ch. 4.

wardly, the emperor and his advisors may have hoped that Themistius' arguments might simply have convinced Christian senators, all of whom had still been schooled in the old *paideia*, and perhaps even the odd bishop or two, of the value of religious toleration.[49] Such individuals would then have formed a group within Christianity that was not so committed to driving forward their religion's monopolistic claims to their logical conclusion. At the same time, employing this oratorical mode may also have been designed to help protect the emperor from the same pressure, by distancing him from the policy. Making a very public request allowed the policy of religious toleration to be presented as the response to earnest supplication from an important section of his citizenry, rather than something in which he himself had taken the initiative. Whatever the details in this particular case, Oration 5, as we have seen, is only one instance among several where ostensible Themistian requests cannot be taken at face value (see Chapter 1). Themistius was a sophisticated publicist for a succession of imperial regimes, and the periodic use of the plea was but one of the rhetorical devices he employed in practising his art.

Set in context, therefore, the contents of Oration 5 demonstrate that Themistius was already sufficient of an insider by January 364 to be entrusted with handling some very sensitive issues along the lines required by Jovian's regime. Claiming that the Persian defeat was actually a victory, advocating the virtues of religious toleration, and holding up the emperor's dubious election as a model of constitutional propriety: in all of its main areas the speech was carefully framed to answer the regime's needs. As Libanius (*Ep.* 1455) tells us, Themistius' support had been earnestly sought by the new regime from its earliest days, so this is not too surprising a conclusion. Because of his role in Constantius' senatorial recruiting drive, Themistius could speak for a considerable body of eastern landowning opinion. No longer merely an academic with a clever line to sell on cultural affairs, he had taken the opportunity to recruit his own interest group, and thus to become a more generally influential figure. The contents of Oration 5 can have left no one in any doubt that the emperor Jovian had successfully gathered his support.

---

49  Similarly Brown, 1995, ch. 2.

## ORATION 5
## ON THE CONSULSHIP, TO THE EMPEROR JOVIAN:
## TRANSLATION

[63a] To praise you, majesty, for having yielded to the enthusiasm and use the pretext of the present celebration[50] as an excuse for my speech, [b] this I leave to others whose regular practice is the indiscriminate cultivation of men in power. I, in contrast, have come forward today to contribute to the festivity, not for the sake of empty show, but shall deliver some benefit that is appropriate to the honour. For this is philosophy's law, not to undertake anything for the sake of amusement alone but everywhere to mingle the beneficial with the pleasurable, just as the more gentle physicians conceal their medicines from the taste with spices. [c] And you have, in the ceremonial accompaniments of wealth, both the one which is for display alone, and also the other which at the same time both strikes the emotions and yet has not overlooked what is beneficial.[51]

But I, your majesty, must take thought still more to giving you in return a gift of thanks which is not entirely inadequate, because you are restoring philosophy, which does not much prosper among the masses at this present moment,[52] to the palace once more, and she stands near you with a more favoured aspect, and because you make the command of words no less honoured than the leadership of soldiers.[53] [d] So too the fathers of your rule promoted my predecessors in this discipline – Augustus the famous Arius, Tiberius Thrasylus, the great Trajan, Dio the Golden-Tongued, the two Antonines Epictetus – I omit the others save him who long ago took his name from the same deity as you and

50  Jovian's accession to the consulship on 1 January 364 at Ancyra.

51  A regular Themistian theme (e.g., *Orr.* 10.129d; 15.192c; 16.199c); see further the introduction to *Or.* 1. He is not a show orator, a sophist, performing for reward, but a philosopher deploying his art for the advancement of the state. Even when speaking on such a festive occasion as the celebration of a new emperor's consulship, he will therefore mix in something educative with the speech's decorative elements. He marked the transition from the one to the other for the audience at 65d. The medical analogy may have been picked up from Dio Chrysostom, *Or.* 33.10.

52  An initial reference to Plato's vision of philosophy's sad plight, if it should be cared for by inappropriate individuals, developed in more detail below at 64c.

53  Themistius regularly equates himself with 'philosophy'; hence this is an implicit reference to his own relative political eclipse during the reign of Julian, who preferred a different set of philosophers, and subsequent restoration. See the introduction to this chapter.

the founder of my house.[54] By adopting philosophy in the sight of all, you follow in these men's footsteps. [64a] In return for being publicly honoured in this way, philosophy for her part publicly returns these offerings of thanks – words that are sufficient to escort deeds through time and attach everlasting memory to things which pass away, together with seasonable advice and free speech.[55] These are philosophy's own deeds and gifts, and this is why she has from the beginning been summoned by royalty and not considered useless, not so that she should pursue Silanion's occupation, [b] to which end long ago vulgar and common folk used to act as hired servants to the Greeks.[56]

Do you want to know what is philosophy's contribution? She declares that the king is law embodied,[57] a divine law which has come down from on high at last, an outpouring of the everlastingly Good, a providence of that nature closer to the earth,[58] who looks in every way

54 Themistius' grandfather, probably, rather than (as *PLRE* 1, 291–2) his father Euge-nius 2: Vanderspoel, 1995, 33 with refs. Diocletian took the surname Jovius, hence could be equated with Jovian. On the general significance of ruler–philosopher pairings, see Chapter 1. Arius Didymus of Alexandria taught Augustus, Thrasylus of Alexandria (d. 36) was an astrologer closely associated with Tiberius on Rhodes. On Dio, see the introduction to Chapter 2. Epictetus (c.55–125) was a former slave from Phrygia who became a leading Stoic. The two Antonines are Antoninus Pius (86–161) and Marcus Aurelius (121–80). It is improbable that the former met Epictetus, and impossible that the latter did so, but Epicte-tus' letters, collected and edited by Arrian, profoundly influenced him. Themistius later repeated this list in a speech to Valens with some additions (Philip and Aristotle, Alexander and Xenocrates, Marcus Aurelius and Sextus), while Antoninus Pius and Epictetus are omitted: *Or.* 11.145b; cf. Vanderspoel, 1995, 33.

55 *parrhesia* – the technical term for a philosopher's insouciant frankness in the face of worldly power. See Chapter 1.

56 Silanion: a sculptor of the 4th-century BC famed for his portraiture of heroes in bronze. Hence Themistius will not, like a sophist, merely turn out a standard image of im-perial heroism in the hope of reward, but will offer truthful praise and useful advice (see 64c below).

57 νόμος ἔμψυχος: see *Or.* 1.15b with notes.

58 The punctuation adopted by the Teubner text has been altered in the first part of this sentence. 'The Good' was Neoplatonising shorthand for the Divine essence or One from which all creation flowed, and Themistius produces an account of the emperor's relation-ship to the Divine in this passage which likens it to that pertaining between the One and the Logos or Intellect. The latter, through whom the rest of creation has its being, came into existence by process of emanation from the One, constantly looks to, admires, and is in-spired by Him. Helpful discussions are Armstrong, 1967, ch. 15 (Plotinus) and Wallis, 1972, 47–72, 110–23 (Plotinus and some of his successors). Many of these ideas had been transferred to Platonising descriptions of the relationship between the Father and the Son

towards Him, and strives in every way for imitation, who is absolutely divinely born and divinely nourished, as Homer says, **[c]** sharing with God these other epithets too – guardian of guests, guardian of suppliants, the kindly one, the bringer of fruits, the giver of good things, orchestrator of justice, steward of ease, overseer of good fortune.[59] These are the tributes which philosophers who are not falsely named offer to kings, and Plato did not make the bald men or the bronzesmiths who assault the orphaned mistress creators of human happiness.[60]

**[d]** And so I say, majesty, that while the presentation of appropriate offerings to you in return for your goodwill towards philosophy requires more consideration and time,[61] for the present let me, as best I can, share your desire to lend support to both as you[62] celebrate this occasion. Now the spice of this speech[63] and the celebration is to display the year's title as blessed, which enlisted the happy yoke team of a father together with a son the same age as his father's imperial purple, **[65a]** and to show that this present honour has become more dignified through you rather than contributing to your dignity. One makes it a prize of kingship, the other a prelude to it, while common to both is the suddenness of the advance to better things. For both were without prior expectations, you to be made emperor from a private citizen, and he consul, since the original impulse had been for another.[64] And what one might particu-

---

within Christian theology. As in the reign of Constantius, Themistius continued to occupy the religious middle ground of philosophical commonplace (see the introduction to Chapter 2).

59 The god with whom Jovian shared most of these epithets was Zeus, demonstrating the extent to which formal rhetorical occasions in the 4th century allowed the use of non-Christian imagery; cf. *Or.* 6.80c–d with notes below.

60 At *Republic* 495c–e, Plato imagined the plight of philosophy deserted by those who should be caring for her (i.e., true philosophers and rulers), as the forced misalliance of an orphaned girl with a bald, dwarfish bronzesmith: an individual lacking in all physical, social, and intellectual quality. This picks up the original reference to the theme at 63b–c and 64a–b above.

61 Themistius often stressed that his offerings required careful consideration, making a deliberate contrast with the rhetorical value-system which praised sophists for improvising speeches on any topic without warning. Here, the thought also acted as a disclaimer.

62 Plural: Jovian and his infant son Varronianus.

63 The consular celebration is for Themistius the 'spice': a pleasant introduction to the central, educative purpose of his speech: see 63b–c above.

64 After Julian's death, the council of leading civilian and military officers first chose Salutius Secundus, Praetorian Prefect, who declined on grounds of age and ill-health:

larly admire about your foresight is that you used for your advantage even the unavoidable adversity that occurred.[65]

Up to this point, my speech has addressed you both together, now from here on, it shall tend towards you alone [Jovian], **[b]** But the young man will allow you the greater part of those things in which he too shall take no less a share.[66] We must call to mind from the recent past that the kingship was owed to you even before now through ancestral virtue,[67] but hesitating to take up what was owed on the death of the elder of your predecessors, lest you might appear to be making an attempt upon what remained of Constantine's succession, you were preserved for the present moment to recover your ancestral due without another being wronged.[68] For when Alexander met his end in Babylon, the Macedonians did not discover his true heir, **[c]** but preferred the feeble-minded Arrhidaeus to Ptolemy son of Lagus, as if discharging a debt on behalf of the dead brother to his survivor but without giving him the kingship, to

---

Ammianus 25.5.3. This caused the political deadlock which Jovian's promotion clearly broke (see the introduction to this speech). Salutius remained an important figure in Jovian's regime, so that Themistius could admit that Jovian had not been the first choice without disparagement, since Secundus had later bowed to his claims. See further 67b with notes below. Varronianus' consular appointment was entirely dependent upon his father having become emperor.

65 I.e., Julian's unexpected death and the difficult circumstances Jovian found himself in upon his succession, with the army trapped by the Persians (see the introduction to this speech). This sentence is a clear summation, of the kind Themistius often provided, of the argument of the first section of his speech, namely that Jovian's peace with Persia was a great success.

66 I.e., Varronianus will in due course be raised to the purple. See further note 118.

67 One of the correspondences with Aristides, *Or.* 35.5; cf. the introduction to this speech.

68 Julian: the last of Constantine's close male relatives. Other sources also report that Jovian owed the throne to the popularity of his father Varronianus, who had retired before 363 with the rank of count: Ammianus 25.5.4 (though see Matthews, 1989, 184); Eutropius 10.17; John of Antioch fr. 181; Zonaras 13.14. It is unclear whether this unanimity reflects reality (so Vanderspoel, 1995, 139) or Jovian's propaganda, which sought, as here in Themistius' version, to present the new emperor as the obvious man for the job. Themistius' comment that the throne nearly came to Jovian on the death of Constantius in 361 ('the elder of your predecessors') has no direct parallel, but, as so often, Ammianus' account seems to shadow it, recording how, in the funeral procession, the troops showed their rations to Jovian, in an echo of how they would sometimes behave towards a reigning emperor: 21.16.21. On the contrasts between Themistius and Ammianus identified in subsequent notes, see the introduction to this speech.

which the only successor is the man who knows how to preserve it.[69] But our voters and soldiers preferred spiritual to physical kinship and declared as true heir to the imperial purple the true heir to his virtue, and this not at their leisure or in peacetime, when the moment offered no occasion for favouritism, denunciation or bribery, **[d]** but, one could say when Enyo [War] was at its height, giving their votes among the swords and among the spears, an unsolicited judgement, an unpremeditated election which the occasion decreed and to which necessity directed them: and what is still more incredible, in an assembly beyond our borders, outside Roman territory, for the benefit of the Roman Empire.[70]

To you alone does it fall to bring forward all men either to judge or witness your attainment of rule: **[66a]** your friends as judges, your enemies as witnesses. For the Persians showed that they were voting for you no less than the Romans by throwing aside their weapons as soon as they became aware of the proclamation, and shortly after were wary of the same men of whom before they had no fear.[71] Thus they say even the Theban Epaminondas marched among the rest of the soldiers while others were the Boiotarchs, but when the phalanx was being hard pressed by Thessalians, he was proclaimed Boiotarch from the very midst of the battleline and the enemy fled away forthwith, **[b]** afraid of a general whom as a soldier they had not feared.[72] But it was not Thebans and Thessalians who elected you, the former voting willingly, the latter casting their votes involuntarily, but both the West and the East in concert, as if it was right that he who was to rule over the whole earth should hold no portion of it that had not shared in the vote.[73] You went

69 On his death on campaign in Persia, Alexander left no designated heir. One faction supported Philip Arrhidaeus, bastard son of Philip II, another the interests of Alexander's as yet unborn son by Roxane (the future Alexander IV). Ptolemy was a close friend of Alexander and a trusted general who became satrap of Egypt (323 BC) then king (304 BC), founding the Ptolemaic line. This passage, and what follows with its emphasis on Jovian as the true heir of the purple, implicitly parallels Julian with the feeble-minded Arrhidaeus, immediate successor of Alexander.

70 Most sources state that Jovian was the unanimous choice of the army. Ammianus reports that discussions became deadlocked until a faction of the army launched Jovian in what was essentially a coup (25.5.1–4). See the introduction to this speech.

71 Another contrast with Ammianus, who reports that, upon being informed by a deserter of Jovian's election, the Persians attacked with renewed vigour: 25.6.8–9.

72 See Pausanias 9.5.

73 The preceding and subsequent sentences make it clear that by the West Themistius means the Romans and by the East the Persians – cast in the same witnessing role as the

to war a spear-bearer and returned an emperor, not because of a neighing horse, like Darius, not after pouring a libation from a helmet, as Psammaticus, no jealous woman thrusting you into power,[74] **[c]** but it was through the common judgement and sentiment of two most bitterly opposed races[75]

> who now raged in life destroying strife,
> but who in turn parted reconciled in friendship[76]

who did not exchange warrior's belt for sword, but having united the whole of this earth, made the *casus belli* the starting point for alliance.

**[d]** Now, having received by necessity the entire empire at a stroke, you kept it unstained with blood to a greater degree than those who inherited by right of birth.[77] The reason was that you neither suspected anyone of being of ill disposed towards you, nor feared anyone as more deserving, and you confirmed one of Plato's two assertions: that empires will be free from revolution when those in power are fit to rule but have the least desire to do so.[78] For having changed your station from a less than pre-eminent position to the most exalted of

---

Thessalians in the Epaminondas story – not (as Daly, 1971, 71, or Vanderspoel, 1995, 143–4) the eastern and western halves of the Roman Empire. It was a topos of Roman imperialistic ideology that emperors literally ruled the whole world.

74  Darius became king of Persia because his horse neighed at a critical moment (Herodotus 3.83–4), Psammaticus because he unwittingly fulfilled the terms of an oracle (2.151). The jealous woman is Candaules' wife who forced Gyges to murder her husband and take the throne (1.8–12).

75  I.e., the Romans and Persians.

76  Adapted from Homer, *Iliad* 7.301–2: Hector and Ajax, having agreed to break off their single combat because of fading light, exchange these items of equipment. Using this passage was perhaps an attempt to present the Persian peace as a mutually voluntary cessation of hostilities, rather than an outright Roman defeat: see further below.

77  The audience would have understood this as a pointed reference to the house of Constantine, particularly the notorious dynastic murders which followed the accession of Constantius in 337 (see the introduction to this chapter), but also the trials of some of Constantius' men at Chalcedon in 361 following Julian's successful coup: Ammianus 22.3. It is interesting that Themistius uses the comparative – μᾶλλον – on the lack of bloodshed, admitting, by implication, that there had been some. According to Ammianus, an important civil servant, a *primicerius notariorum* also called Jovian, was executed by being thrown down a well, having been proposed as an alternative candidate: 25.8.18; 26.6.3.

78  Plato, *Republic* 520d: reading δυοῖν. The other assertion is a somewhat lame statement of the opposite.

all,[79] **[67a]** you neither forgot your peers, nor were prejudiced against those who had once been your superiors, nor dismissive of those who had been passed over previously. Rather, surpassing all men in fortune to such a degree, you had remained true to your policy towards all men, and, as if having realised rightly that kingship should be thought the apogee of virtue rather than of good fortune,[80] you showed Darius son of Hydaspes to be mean in generosity of repayment.[81]

Realising that the justice of his followers is the foundation of a king's security, **[b]** you restored some of the best men from all sides to office, chose others for yourself, and dismissed others.[82] And now your rule is buttressed by Nestor's good counsel, Diomedes' free spirit, by Cyrus' Chrysantas, and Xerxes' Artabazos.[83]

79 Jovian had been *Primicerius Domesticorum*, a reasonably high-ranking figure among the palace troops, who had been given the high profile task of escorting the remains of Constantius to Constantinople: Ammianus 21.16.20, 25.5; cf. Matthews, 1989, 184.

80 Cf. the introduction to this chapter on the disagreement between Themistius and Julian over whether the Divinity or Fortune – Τύχη – decided who would be emperor.

81 Herodotus 3.138: Syloson brother of Polycrates of Samos gave his valuable cloak to Darius, then an obscure member of Cambyses' guard. When Darius came to the throne he promised to repay Syloson for the gift with gold and silver but was persuaded by him instead to help in the recovery of Samos from Oroetes. Darius also richly rewarded Democedes of Crotona for curing him of a serious foot injury (3.30). In its emphasis on Jovian's constancy of character before and after the election, and his concern with justice, this section – 66d–67b – carries several points of resemblance to Aristides, *Or.* 35.7–9.

82 A not unfair characterisation of Jovian's appointments. Of Constantius' men dismissed under Julian, Jovian restored his father-in-law Lucullianus (formerly commander in Illyricum: *PLRE* 1, 517–8), the future Emperor Valentinian, Malarichus (who refused to become *Magister Equitum* in Gaul: *PLRE* 1, 538), Seniauchus (a high-ranking soldier: *PLRE* 1, 821) and Fl. Lupicinus (*Mag. Eq.* in Gaul up to 360, reappointed *Mag. Eq.* in the east under Jovian: *PLRE* 1, 520–1). The main casualty among the leading figures of Julian's reign was Fl. Nevitta. *Mag. Eq.* on the Persian campaign: he disappeared after the succession dispute and Jovian's promotion (*PLRE* 1, 626–7; cf. the further comment in the introduction to this speech). Julian's Praetorian Prefect Salutius Secundus, and three of his main military commanders on the expedition, Fl. Arintheus, Victor and Dagalaifus all remained prominent under Jovian and beyond (respectively *PLRE* 1, 814–17, 102–3, 957–9, 239), as did Fl. Jovinus, Julian's *Mag. Eq.* in Gaul, of whom Jovian was initially suspicious (hence the offer to Malarichus), but who proved his loyalty by suppressing a revolt which took the lives of Lucullianus and Seniauchus (*PLRE* 1, 462–3).

83 Nestor (throughout the *Iliad*) was famous for his wisdom; cf. Libanius who labels Datianus, chief counsellor of Constantius, that emperor's Nestor (*Ep.* 114: Vanderspoel, 1995, 147). Diomedes King of Argos combined intelligence with heroism (*Iliad* 6), Xenophon (*Education of Cyrus* 2.3.5; 8.4.10–12) portrays Chrysantas and Herodotus (8.126–9, 9.41, 66) Artabazos as perfect advisors. Themistius was probably picking four particular

Hence your legislation on divine matters has become[84] a prelude to your care for mankind. And now my speech has arrived at the point of departure to which I have long been tending.[85] For it seems that you alone are not unaware that a king cannot compel his subjects in everything, [c] but that there are some matters which have escaped compulsion and are superior to threat and injunction, for example the whole question of virtue, and, above all, reverence for the divine, and that it is necessary for whoever intends that they should exist naturally to take the lead in these good things, having realised most wisely that the impulse of the soul is unconstrained, and is both autonomous and voluntary.[86] For if it is impossible for a man who does not make this choice within himself to be well disposed to you, your majesty, according to law, how much more impossible is it to be pious and godloving out of fear of human laws, [d] ephemeral constraints and impotent terrors of the imagination which time has so often brought in and as often carried away again?[87] Then we prove to be completely ridiculous, worshipping the imperial purple rather than God, and altering our rituals with more ease than Euripus.[88] Long ago there was one Theramenes, but now all men are

----

individuals within Jovian's assembled court. Nestor – old, wise, and (by the time of the *Iliad*) no longer warlike – presumably designates Salutius Secundus, Praetorian Prefect to both Constantius and Julian, who declined the throne on account of his age (note 64). The other three were all military figures, and might perhaps stand, therefore, for Arintheus, Victor and Dagalaifus. If so, Themistius was paying tribute to the four key figures who had eventually transferred their allegiance from Julian to Jovian.

84  By using the perfect tense, Themistius firmly situates Jovian's religious measures in the past, i.e. between his election in June 363 and 1 January 364. On the significance of this in relation to Jovian's acts of religious toleration, see the introduction to this speech.

85  Themistius thus marked the transition between the 'spice' and the properly educative matter of his speech; cf. 63b above.

86  Constantine had similarly legislated on the importance of religious toleration: Eusebius, *Life of Constantine* 2.60, but without quite making the same connection that religious virtue could only be the result of voluntary, autonomous action.

87  The successive religious policies of Constantius and Julian. Constantius seems to have extended the ban on blood sacrifice established by his father, leading to closures and even some destruction among pagan temples: see the introduction to Chapter 2. Julian officially declared religious toleration, but used all his less formal influence in favour of paganism. See, e.g., Jones, 1964, 120–3; Athanassiadi, 1992, 161ff.; Smith, 1995, ch. 7, esp. 207–18 (proposing some modification to received views).

88  The Euripus was the channel between Euboea and Boeotia, whose current was supposed to change direction seven times a day: Strabo 9.403. It became a proverbial term for those of inconstant opinion: Plato, *Phaedo* 90c.

turncoats;[89] **[68a]** just yesterday he was among the Ten but today he is among the Thirty, just as now the same people are seen at votive altars and sacrifices, at shrines of the gods and altars of God.[90] But certainly not you, O most godlike king; on the contrary, while you are sole ruler[91] in all other matters and will be so to the end, you decree[92] that the participation in ritual is for all men, in this respect emulating even God, who made the favourable disposition towards piety a common attribute of nature, but lets the manner of worship depend on individual inclination. He who applies compulsion removes the licence which God allowed. **[b]** It was for this reason that the laws of Cheops and Cambyses scarcely outlasted those who instituted them.[93] But the law of God, which is your law,[94] remains immovable for all time, that each man's soul is liberated for the path of piety that it wishes. Neither sequestration of property, nor scourges, nor burning has ever overturned this law by force. While you will persecute the body and kill it, as it may turn out, the soul however shall escape, carrying its resolve free within it, in accordance with the law, **[c]** even though it may have suffered constraint as far as the tongue is concerned.

89 Literally κόθορνοι: the loose-fitting boots worn by tragic actors which could be worn on either foot. It was the nickname of Theramenes (Xenophon, *Hellenica* 2.2.31), an Athenian statesman proverbially famous for changing sides. During full democracy, he served as one of the ten elected generals. In 411 BC, he assisted in the creation of the oligarchic council of the Four Hundred, but later the same year threw in his lot with the more moderate council of 5,000. In 404 BC, he was appointed as one of the Spartan-imposed Thirty 'Tyrants' of Athens.

90 For τράπεζα as 'altar', see Athanasius, *On the Incarnation* 229, 364d; Gregory Nazianzen, *Epp.* 416, 665, 980. Julian's letters provide us with one fine example of religious adaptability: the Christian bishop of Ilium under Constantius, who maintained nonetheless the pagan shrines, and then became part of Julian's pagan priesthood: *Ep.* 19.

91 αὐτοκράτωρ: here used literally, rather than as a title. Jovian's early death, following on quickly after that of Julian, led to demands that Valentinian appoint a co-emperor who could also act as guarantor of political continuity, should there be another untimely death: see the introduction to this Chapter. This passage, together with the comment at 65b above, made it clear that Jovian was going to take no colleague other than, at some point in the future, his own son. This suggests that there may have been some need to stifle speculation about the possible appointment of a co-Augustus.

92 Present indicative indicating that Jovian had already legislated, by 1 Jan. 364, on the matter of religious toleration. See further the introduction to this speech.

93 Kings of Egypt, Cheops and Cambyses were noted for cruelty and injustice: Herodotus 2.123–6, 3.31ff. Herodotus also condemned Cambyses for his lack of respect for the beliefs of others.

94 A further indication that a law of toleration already existed; cf. notes 84 and 92.

I am sure, your majesty, that, taking to heart the reason for this divine legislation, you follow its tracks because of this – that it is in man's nature to complete with more eagerness those tasks in whose accomplishment he will meet a challenge, but to be casual in those which present no opposition. A complete absence of competition fills us with lethargy and boredom. For the spirit is always easily galvanised by opposition to take pleasure in toil. [d] This is why you do not exclude beneficial contention from pious observance, and this is why you do not blunt the goad of zeal in religious affairs: mutual competition and rivalry.[95] It is as if all the competitors in a race are hastening towards the same Judge[96] but not all on the same course, some going by this route others by that, while the man who is defeated does not go entirely unrewarded;[97] thus you realise that, while there exists only one Judge, mighty and true, there is no one road leading to him, [69a] but one is more difficult to travel, another more direct, one steep and another level.[98] All, however, tend alike towards that one goal and our competition and our zealousness arise from no other reason than that we do not all travel by the same route.[99]

95 This sentence contains two second-person singular verbs in the present indicative, again making it very clear that allowing the described competition is Jovian's current policy.

96 αθλοθέτην: one who awards prizes in the games.

97 Following the Teubner's reading οὐ πάντη. Most MSS read ἀπάντη, but this would reverse the force of Themistius' argument that there is some virtue in all religious activity and is perhaps a later Christian emendation.

98 While proclaiming toleration, Jovian was nonetheless a Christian, and Christianity's theologians never doubted its superiority to other beliefs. Themistius' speech thus echoed here the delicate balancing act that Jovian as a religiously tolerant Christian emperor had to sustain. While allowing toleration, he still needed to make clear that his religion (Christianity) was superior to its rivals: the 'direct' and 'clear' path to God. Themistius' neutral wording would have allowed pagans to reverse the message.

99 Themistius carefully balanced here arguments in favour of religious competition with a clear statement of the syncretising vision of religion propounded by some Neoplatonists in Late Antiquity: all were working by different routes to the same end. Jovian's predecessor Julian excluded Christianity from his list of mutually compatible religious systems (also Epicureans and Sceptics: Athanassiadi, 1992, 128ff.). Others were seemingly more inclusive, from the bishop-turned-pagan-priest of Ilium (note 90) to much more intellectual figures such as Themistius himself, the sophist Hecebolius (a teacher of Julian who proclaimed himself a Christian under Constantius, a pagan under Julian, and a Christian again under Julian's successors: *PLRE* 1, 409 with refs.) or, perhaps most famously, Synesius of Cyrene; cf. Athanassiadi, 1992, 28–9. This passage is similar to part of Symmachus' famous plea to Valentinian II in favour of religious toleration in the case of the Altar of Victory (*Relatio* 3.8), leading some to posit a common source in the writings of Porphyry: Vanderspoel,

If you allow only one path, closing off the rest, you will fence off the broad
field of competition. This is man's age-old nature and the saying

one man sacrificed to one, another to another of the gods[100]

was older than Homer. **[b]** May it never be displeasing to God for such a
harmony to exist among men. In the words of Heraclitus,[101] nature is
accustomed to lie concealed, and, before nature, He who created it,
whom we especially revere and admire for this very reason, that knowledge of Him is not easy to achieve, nor is it superficial and worthless,
nor can it be grasped without sweat and with just one hand.[102] I rank
this law as no less important than the Persian friendship. Through the
latter we shall not be at war with the barbarians, because of this law we
shall live at peace with one another.[103] **[c]** We were worse towards one
another than the Persians, the legal disputes of the two religious factions
throughout the city were more damaging than their attacks,[104] O king
who is dearest to God, and past history has presented you with clear
examples. Let the scale find its own level, do not force the balance down
on one side or the other and let prayers for your rule rise to heaven from
every quarter.[105]

Your army, majesty, is not composed entirely of one and the same
type of soldier, but some serve as infantry, others as cavalry, some bear
arms, others slings, and some are assigned to your person: **[d]** some at

---

1995, 24–6 with notes. This is possible, but the thought is not so profound as necessarily to
require such an explanation of its multiple occurrence.

100  Homer, *Iliad* 2.400.

101  fr. 123 (Kirk); cf. Daly, 1971, 75.

102  Socrates, *Ecclesiastical History* 4.31 reports Themistius using a similar argument in
a speech addressed to Valens on the subject of religious toleration.

103  In the last two sentences, the use of the noun 'law' = νόμος indicates that Jovian has
already undertaken some legally valid action. Themistius also treated it as having the same
legal force as the Persian peace; cf. Daly, 1971, 73–4 and above notes 84 and 92.

104  Socrates, *Ecclesiastical History* 3.12.3 and Sozomen, *Ecclesiastical History* 5.4.8
refer to religious disturbances in the city of Constantinople (Themistius' city) between
pagans and Christians in Julian's time: Bidez, 1930, 229–30 (cf. his comments on the
impact of Julian's financial edicts at 230–1).

105  The casting of these thoughts as a plea has been taken by Vanderspoel, 1995, 148–52
to imply that Jovian had not yet (on 1 Jan. 364) committed himself to full religious toleration. Given the very direct language of what precedes it, this interpretation is very unlikely.
For an alternative, see the introduction to this speech, with Chapter 1 on Themistius'
general rhetorical use of the plea.

close quarters, while yet others are at a far remove. To some it is welcome
if they might be counted among your bodyguard but others lack the
capacity for this. Yet all alike depend upon you and your policy, not just
those in the army but all the rest of humanity too, even those of your
subjects who are not under arms: **[70a]** farmers, public speakers, those
who hold state office, and those who practise philosophy. Consider that
the Creator of the universe also takes pleasure in such diversity. He
wishes the Syrians to organise their affairs in one way, and the Greeks in
another, the Egyptians in another,[106] and does not wish there to be
uniformity among the Syrians themselves but has already fragmented
them into small sects.[107] No individual has exactly the same beliefs as
his neighbour, but one man believes this and another that. Why then do
we use force where it is ineffectual?

   While it is right then for the rest to admire the godlike emperor for the
law, **[b]** this is especially so for those to whom he has not only granted
freedom but also prescribes ordinances[108] in no worse fashion than
Empedocles did and, by Zeus, I do not mean the ancient one.[109] For he

106 Themistius used 'Syrian' as a label for Christian, based on the point of origin of the
religion (similar to, but without the same disparaging connotations of, Julian's usage of
'Galileans' for Christians). Traditional Greek culture – Hellenism – was considered a religion by some of its adepts: notably Julian, but also by Salutius Secundus, Julian's and then
Jovian's Praetorian Prefect, who was in the audience for this speech (above notes 64 and 83)
and wrote a pamphlet on the subject: Athanassiadi, 1992, 123ff., 154ff. Egypt was
acknowledged by the 4th-century Greek-speaking world to have its own non-Christian religious tradition, represented by such texts as the highly influential prophecies of Hermes
Trismegistus: e.g., des Places, 1966; Fowden, 1986. Iamblichus saw Egypt as the source of
knowledge about theurgy: cf. his *Mysteries of Egypt*: Dagron, 1968, 154–6.

107 Unlike Constantius, Jovian refused to attempt to construct a monolithic state
Church out of the so-called 'Arian Dispute': the fragmented Christian response to the
faith propounded at Nicaea: Socrates, *Ecclesiastical History* 3.25; cf. Barnes, 1993, 139–
49. In referring to Christian sectarianism, Themistius was thus still echoing his emperor's
views. He said nothing similar under Valens, who, like Constantius, attempted to create a
united Church: see the introduction to *Or.* 6.

108 The pagans. It is clear from the juxtapositions which follow – opening temples, but
closing 'haunts of imposture'; allowing lawful sacrifice, but banning the magic arts – that
Themistius can only have been talking here of paganism.

109 The original Empedocles was a philosopher and scientist from Acragas in Sicily (fl. c.
492–432 BC) who wrote two influential works, *On Nature* and *Purifications*, of which fragments survive. He was famous, according to later reports, for his power to work miracles,
including raising people from the dead, and for diving into Mt Etna in an attempt to fake his
own apotheosis, the volcano duly rejecting one of his sandals to demonstrate the fraud.
Influenced by these stories, Dagron, 1968, 159–63, argued that Themistius' 'not ancient'

knows all too well that deception and trickery batten on to each of the human virtues, and that knavery is latent in generosity and imposture in piety. For this reason he promotes the one set of qualities and restrains the other, opening up the temples but closing the haunts of imposture, allowing lawful sacrifices but giving no licence to those who practise the magic arts.[110] [c] And he lays down exactly the same laws as Plato son

---

Empedocles could only be Christ. The reference is obviously to an extent disparaging, and, for Dagron, the point was that Jovian had shown himself – by ordaining toleration – better at interpreting the pagan religion than Christ had been. Themistius was thus rejecting Christian intolerance and hinting that Christ was an imposter. But however tolerant, Jovian was certainly a Christian, and it must be very doubtful a priori that Themistius could have got away with even hinting at such an equation during a highly public consular ceremony. We suspect, therefore, that Dagron latched on to the wrong element of Empedocles' posthumous reputation. At *Or.* 13.178a–b, to Gratian, Themistius returned to Empedocles in more detail, his main criticism being the philosopher's pessimism about this world and its relationship to the divine. A central element of Themistius' discourse was support for a 'high' imperial ideology, which envisaged the Roman Empire as having a particular role in the divine plan for the cosmos, and argued that emperors were directly appointed by God, who picked out for this job individuals in His own image (cf. 64b–c). For Themistius, the point of Empedocles' teaching was thus to stress that the soul was separate from the body and argue that the physical world was a field of ills, lying outside of any divine plan. This suggests to us that the 'not ancient' Empedocles Themistius had in mind was actually the Emperor Julian. Central to the argument between Themistius and Julian manifest in the latter's *Letter to Themistius* was the relationship between the Empire and the Divinity. Julian there deliberately denied Themistius' view, arguing that, in holding it, the latter had misunderstood Plato and Aristotle (see the introduction to this chapter). During his reign, Julian also tried to reorganise paganism as well as allow it freedom of worship, so that he would again fit Themistius' description, which requires an individual who, like Jovian, had passed regulations about the pagan religion. What Themistius was saying, therefore, was that, although a Christian emperor, Jovian had passed better regulations about paganism than his immediate pagan predecessor had done. This obviates the need to suppose, with Dagron, that Themistius could have got away with publicly disparaging Christ, a supposition which has rightly worried subsequent commentators. Portmann, 1988, 181, 270, rejected the Empedocles–Christ equation for *Or.* 5, but accepted it for *Or.* 13; Vanderspoel, 1995, 25–6 and n. 94 is undecided but cautious.

110 This passage summarises Jovian's lost legislation on religious toleration. It echoed that of Constantine in closing certain categories of temple, while keeping others open, and in banning magic. The reference to 'lawful sacrifices' is harder to interpret. Given general Christian abhorrence, it is hard to believe that Jovian allowed blood sacrifice, restored by Julian, to continue. This was banned not only by Constantine and Constantius, but also by the tolerant Valentinian and Valens (see the introduction to *Or.* 5). Themistius' language does not absolutely deny it, however, and, if it did continue, this would underline the tolerance of Jovian's regime.

of Ariston, whose words I would have quoted to you if they were not too long for this occasion.[111]

But we must return to the celebration over which, although I consider it to be the most honourable of all celebrations, I am vexed in this one respect, that the Fair City [Constantinople] does not share with me now in the pleasure of these acts. No doubt at this moment, O noble city, you are celebrating with sorrowful countenance, dancing in mourning, and, having found joy in expectation, grieve more at the delay. [d] But if you could see your lover disembarked and with steps directed homewards,[112] what cries will you not utter, with what shouts fill the air once you have received, after the son and the nephew of Constantine, one who is himself the very Constantine

just so were his feet, just so were his hands and his eyes' glances.[113]

[71a] He has not taken off the bands of victory, he has not assumed the imperial purple in half measure and will preserve for you the same measure of goodwill as well. The Athenians in defeating the Persians celebrated the rites of the mysteries on board their ships,[114] and the king, following the peace, having celebrated the preliminary ceremonies of initiation outside the temple, shall perform the mystic rites inside at the inner shrine [i.e. in Constantinople]. Let us hurry, O blessed one, let us hasten our journey. See how heaven also joins in the city's enthusiasm, scattering the clouds and revealing the spring before its time.[115] [b] Pray

111  It is unclear which passage Themistius had in mind; cf. Dagron, 1968, 172 n. 140.

112  Ancyra, where Jovian celebrated his consulship, was on the main road across Asia Minor between Antioch and Constantinople. Ammianus also surrounded his account of Jovian with a sense of hurry, as in Themistius' speech, but used it to emphasise the inevitability of the emperor's early date with destiny (25.10.4–12). On this and other points of contact between the two speeches, see the introduction to Or. 5.

113  Homer, *Odyssey* 4.149–50 (Menelaus on the strong resemblance of Telemachus to his father, Odysseus). The implication is that in Jovian the true character of Constantine was reproduced, while Constantius and Julian, respectively his son and nephew, were related to him merely by accident of birth. On Themistius' disparaging, after their deaths, of emperors he had previously served, see the introduction to this chapter.

114  After the battle of Salamis: Herodotus 8.123. Cf. the introduction to this speech, the necessary equation between the imperial purple and victory echoed in this passage may well explain why Jovian's regime chose to try to present the Persian peace as a victory.

115  An observation on the weather, presumably, interesting in that it suggests that Themistius could sometimes improvise; sunny weather on 1 January can hardly have been predictable. This can be contrasted with Themistius' remarks at 64d. See also the introduction to Or. 15 for another more improvised insert, and Chapter 1 for general comment.

send to me meantime the light bearer, the consul in arms, who has already imbibed his father's qualities at the breast, to be so courageous, so imperturbable like one about to address the multitude.[116] May God, who has made him partner in this office which bears his name,[117] declare him also to be a partner in the imperial purple.[118]

## ORATION 6
## BROTHERLY LOVE, OR ON *PHILANTHROPIA*:
## INTRODUCTION

The exact date on which Themistus gave Oration 6 cannot be determined. It was clearly delivered in the Senate of Constantinople in front of the Emperor Valens. Because of the etiquette governing the functioning of the imperial college, Themistius often used 'you' in the plural referring to both Valens and his brother Valentinian. At a number of critical points in the speech, however, Themistius reverted to the singular in such a way as to make clear that only Valens was actually present. The speech was also given before the two emperors assumed their first, joint, consulship on 1 January 365, since Themistius makes no allusion to this ceremonial event of the first importance. We are still in 364, therefore, and the emperors' activities offer two points in the year when Valens was in Constantinople and the speech might have been given. The first was immediately after his elevation to the purple on 28 March. Subsequently, however, and in quick succession, the two brothers fell ill, and then went to the Danube region where they formally divided the troops, officials, and territory of the Empire between them. Valens stayed near the Danube into the autumn, and is not attested back in Constantinople until mid-December: the second possible setting for the speech.[119] Two

116 Another contrast with Ammianus who says that Varronianus ruined the ceremonies by crying and refusing to be carried in the consuls' traditional curule chair: 25.10.11.

117 The consulship; Romans reckoned years by the names of consuls.

118 Jovian died only about 6 weeks after the speech was given (17 Feb. 364), without raising his infant son to the purple, and nothing more is known of the child's fate, but, had both lived, Jovian would no doubt have made his son his colleague. On the possible significance of this, see note 91. Valentinian I made his son Gratian emperor at age 8, Theodosius' sons Arcadius and Honorius were 6 and 9 respectively. Valentinian II became Augustus aged only 4, but this was the result of court faction: McLynn, 1994, 84–5. This is another point of correspondence with Aristides, *Or.* 35.39.

119 Movements: Seeck, 1919, 216–9; cf. Vanderspoel, 1995, 156–7. On the division of the Empire, Ammianus 26.5; cf. Matthews, 1989, 189–91, with further comment below.

points indicate that December rather than spring 364 was the date of the speech. Valentinian was not present when the speech was given, and he had been in Constantinople in the spring. By December 364, however, he had moved on to the western half of the Empire. The speech also devotes much attention to the precise manner in which the brothers had divided the Empire between them (81d–82b). Again, this makes most sense if Themistius was speaking after the formal division of imperial resources in summer 364.

## The Rise of Valens

As with Oration 5 to Jovian, Oration 6 discusses the major themes which had so far marked out the new regime. Not the least important of these was Valens' accession. Themistius' main concern in discussing the rise to power of Valens and his brother was to show that their accession was entirely legitimate, and, in particular, that it had been ordained by God. It could thus be said to have happened in accordance with the demands of 'official' state ideology, which held that the Roman Empire was God's special vehicle for achieving His will in the world, and that, consequently, He intervened personally to direct its affairs.[120] This was of more than usual concern in 364, because the early and mysterious demise of Jovian after less than a year in power (June 363 to February 364) had made it pretty clear that he, at least, had *not* been chosen by God. In a couple of easily overlooked sentences of Oration 6, Themistius admitted as much. Ignoring his own extensive attempts to prove the contrary in Oration 5 (65b–67b, with its concluding reference to God at 71b), he noted early on in Oration 6 that he would seek out the sign that there was divine approval behind the events of Valens' accession. He, of course, managed to find it, but the real point is the need he felt to make his audience confident that, this time, God really was behind the new emperor. In the course of the same discussion, he also raised the possibility of an election being accomplished by the army alone, without the seal of divine approval. This could only have brought to his audience's minds the recent and highly peculiar events of Jovian's accession in the camp of the Roman army on Persian soil. Without ever saying it out loud, therefore, Themistius made it clear in Oration 6 that Jovian's was not, whatever he may have said at the time, a divinely approved and

---

120  For an introduction to this world-view, see, e.g., Dvornik, 1966; MacCormack, 1981.

hence legitimate election, and then used the comparison to point out the elements which made it clear that that of Valens was.[121]

According to Ammianus, the deeper background to Valens' election was as follows. The same council of senior military and civilian officials who had previously chosen Jovian initially elected Valentinian. When the new emperor addressed the troops, however, they demanded – not unreasonably given recent events – that he choose a colleague to guarantee greater stability in imperial affairs. Should anything happen to Valentinian, there would not then be the same kind of power vacuum that had followed the deaths of Julian and Jovian. Valentinian accepted the request in general terms, but deliberated for some time over whom to choose. On 1 March, on entering Nicomedia on his way to Constantinople, he made his brother Valens (who had earlier retired from a military career at no great rank) *tribunus stabuli*, which was probably a public declaration of intent to raise him to the purple. Later in the same month, having arrived in the capital, Valens was presented to the troops in the Hebdomon and declared Augustus.[122]

**Power Sharing**

Consideration of Valens' election naturally led Themistius into the central topic of his speech: the division of the Empire, and the nature of the relationship of the two brothers. Given recent imperial history, it is not surprising that Themistius should have devoted so much space to this topic. *Divisio imperii* was an event which could not but have made people nervous. Given the sheer size of the Empire, and the primitive nature of communications, a second source of ultimate authority within its territory was, in administrative terms, highly desirable. It helped to speed up woefully slow response times, and Themistius, in a passage based on a speech by the second-century orator Aelius Aristides about the joint rule of Marcus Aurelius and Antoninus Pius, makes this point well (*Or.* 6.75c–d).[123] It also answered concerns about political conti-

121  *Or.* 6.74a (searching for the seal of divine approval in Valens' election); 73c (the possibility of a false election by the army alone). Themistius thus eventually came to adopt a view of Jovian similar to that found in Ammianus: see the introduction to *Or.* 5 above.

122  On Valentinian's deliberations, and the reasons for his choice, see Ammianus 26.4.1– 2, with Matthews, 1989, 189–90.

123  Aristides, *Or.* 27.22–39; cf. Vanderspoel, 1995, 9, 159–60. Themistius also used some elements from another oration of Aristides when discussing Rome and Constantinople at

nuity in the face of human mortality. In practice, however, such positive considerations would have been more than outweighed by fears that a division of authority would itself generate instability and civil war.

Within recent memory, Constantius had twice attempted to share power with a family member: the Caesars Gallus (351–4) and Julian (after 355). Both had ended in disaster. Gallus was eventually kidnapped and assassinated, while only Constantius' own unexpected death had prevented full-scale civil war between himself and Julian.[124] More generally, the overall political history of the Roman Empire in the later third and fourth centuries is characterised by a series of failed attempts to find workable methods of sharing imperial power. The Tetrarchy, instituted by Diocletian in the last years of the third century, divided imperial power on a non-dynastic, non-familial basis. Constantine and his sons from the 320s, and particularly after the former's death in 337, had divided it dynastically. Both approaches generated tension and civil wars. The Tetrarchic 'system' had burnt itself out in multiple civil wars between c.305 and 325. Of Constantine's sons, Constantine II had died while invading the lands of one of his brothers, Constans, and relations between the two survivors, Constans and Constantius, had come to the brink of civil war in the 340s.[125] Not surprisingly, therefore, Themistius devoted much time in Oration 6 to emphasising the fact that good relations prevailed between the brothers, especially through the use of pointed contrasts between Valentinian and Valens and different members of the Constantinian dynasty. This was even more important, since, as we have seen, lesser members of the old ruling family, including Julian's uncle and Constantius' widow and daughter, were still at large.[126]

Once again, as with the topic of religious toleration in Oration 5, part of Themistius' treatment of *divisio imperii* was cast in the form of a plea that the good relations established between the two emperors by

---

the end of the speech: 83c–d; cf. Aristides, *Or.* 26. The degree of dependence shown at both points is similar to the use of *Or.* 35 in *Or.* 5, consisting of particular lines of thought rather than more consistent use of a formal model; see the introduction to *Or.* 5 above.

124 See the introduction to this chapter.

125 For an introduction to the Tetrarchic wars, see Stein, 1959, 82–93, 95–5, 103–5; Jones, 1964, 37–42, 77–9, 82–3. Constantinian dynasty: Stein, 1959, 131–4; Jones, 1964, 112–15; and most recently, Barnes, 1993, chs 7ff.

126 See the introduction to this chapter.

brotherly love should continue. Vanderspoel has recently suggested that this was in response to some sign of tension between the brothers having already become apparent, and contrasts the difficulties of shared imperium with the simplicity of a single Empire, noting that in the *Risalat* (if this can be taken as a translation of Themistius' panegyric to Julian: see the introduction to Chapter 3) Themistius had declared that the Roman Empire functioned best when ruled by just one emperor, a single source of authority.[127] None of our narrative sources ever refers, however, to the slightest tension between the two brothers. Valens proceeded, moreover, to consult Valentinian upon important questions such as whether to launch a punitive war against the Goths who had supported the rebellion of Julian's uncle Procopius against Valens in 365.[128] It seems most unlikely, therefore, that the 'plea' should be read literally, as though Themistius was really attempting to persuade Valens towards a point of view which he did not already share. Rather, the orator's rhetoric was surely designed to address the very real fears that division of Empire must have aroused within the landowners assembled in the Senate of Constantinople. Nor should too much weight be ascribed to Themistius' comments to Julian in the *Risalat*, if that is, indeed, what they are. As we have seen, Themistius was much too willing both to say what a given emperor desired to hear, and to damn the previously praised policies of former emperors in retrospect, for it to be at all easy to deduce his own 'true' views on any topic.

### Religious Toleration

Stressing the brotherly love of the two new emperors also allowed Themistius to introduce his second main topic – religious toleration – via the device of noting that, since all men are the creations of one God, then they are all the emperor's brothers. Valens recognised this, Themistius noted, and had therefore acted with tolerance and kindliness towards them in religious matters. As this makes clear, the regime of Valentinian and Valens, like that of Jovian, had by December 364 adopted a policy of religious toleration. Again, the actual law does not

127 Vanderspoel, 1995, 158, 160–1.
128 On this war, with translations of two of the speeches Themistius made in the course of it, see Heather and Matthews, 1991, ch. 2.

survive in the *Theodosian Code*, but it is referred to in other legislation.[129] Themistius' treatment of the topic of religious toleration in Oration 6, however, was considerably less free than it had been in Oration 5. There is no equivalent of his previous characterisation of Christianity as the religion of the Syrians operating essentially equally alongside those of the Greeks and Egyptians, and no mention of the existence of Christian sectarianism (cf. *Or.* 5.70a). Rather, Themistius put much more emphasis on the argument that, while all tend towards the same end, some religions allow the individual to see God more clearly than do others (*Or.* 6.77c). This thought had been aired in Oration 5, but was balanced by other moderating arguments. In Oration 6, by contrast, the point predominated. While certainly tolerant, therefore, it seems likely that the new regime made its Christian preferences felt more strongly than had that of Jovian. It certainly made a much more decisive break than had Jovian with Julian's philosophers. As we have seen, Maximus of Edessa in particular was soon persecuted under Valens, whereas he had been tolerated under Jovian.[130] Likewise, and again unlike that of Jovian, Valens' regime quickly chose sides in the on-going disputes among Christian Churchmen, and, like Constantius, threw imperial power and influence behind the construction of a non-Nicene doctrinal settlement, in the hope of bringing peace to the Church.[131]

### Emperor and Capital

Themistius closed Oration 6 with a series of references to a speech that the Emperor Valens had made the previous day to the senate, commenting, in particular, on the new emperor's care for the city. Valens had obviously declared in his speech an intention to build at the Hebdomon, the suburb where he had been formally acclaimed emperor by the troops, and had called Constantinople 'the Mother of his Kingship'. After noting these points, Themistius formally requested the emperor to build actually inside the city, as a thank-offering for the fact that it had witnessed his rise to power. There is every reason to suppose that this was a request which Valens was more than happy to grant. Building, in the Graeco-Roman world-view, was both the expression of

---

129  *C.Th.* 9.16.9 (of 371); cf. the introduction to *Or.* 5.
130  See *Or.* 6.72b with note 137 below.
131  Kopecek, 1979, 422ff.; Barnes, 1993, 161–3.

favour towards a city, and the fulfilment of a basic imperial duty. This was no radical request on Themistius' part, therefore, and may even have been a pre-prepared means for Valens to show his generosity to the city, and hence attract support. During his reign, a major granary was constructed, and, most important, a major hydraulic project was brought to completion which finally provided the city with sufficient water supplies for its burgeoning population. Valens was thus deeply involved in creating the infrastructure necessary to sustain the city, and there can surely never have been any real doubt about him wanting to be so.[132]

All in all, Oration 6 repeated many of the patterns observed in previous speeches. On the one hand, Themistius used the formal public occasion of delivering an imperial panegyric for his own purposes. His own credentials for speaking and standing within the regime were plainly stated. On the other, there is every sign that the contents of the speech essentially reflected the concerns of the regime, rather than any personal agenda of his own. Valens' great need, in December 364, was to attract support among the landowners of the east and to persuade them that the recent division of the Empire was viable in the long term, not just a short-term compromise which would degenerate into tension and civil war. The new regime had, above all, to be portrayed as superior to the Constantinian dynasty it replaced, some of whose lesser members still provided a potential alternative to the new order. On all these fronts, Themistius did not disappoint. One act of *philanthropia* on the part of his former great patron, Constantius, is recalled (the pardoning of Vetranio: *Or.* 6.80c), but Constantius' public image was held up as entirely insufficient for an emperor (78c–d), since it concentrated on mundane rather than heavenly virtues, and Constantius' twisted attempts to share power were thoroughly ridiculed. None of this had prevented Themistius from serving Constantius loyally while the latter was alive. Oration 6 thus makes the point very firmly that Themistius' freedom of speech (*parrhesia*) was a thoroughly *ex post facto* phenomenon.

---

132 Mango, 1985, 40–2; for a different view of Themistius' request, see Vanderspoel, 1995, 160.

## ORATION 6
## BROTHERLY LOVE, OR ON *PHILANTHROPIA:*
## TRANSLATION

[71c] Never, your majesties, did I suppose the imperial language to be essential for me, but I always thought it enough to have a sufficient grasp of my native Greek, but now, if I were able, I would exchange my tongue with those who are skilled in that way of speaking so as not to converse with you in foreign speech.[133] [d] But even though this is impossible, I shall not need a year to master the phrases you are accustomed to, as long ago Themistocles, son of Neocles did. For since he did not have honest things in mind, he naturally chose no one to be interpreter of what he was going to discuss with the king.[134] I in contrast, would beseech all men to become [72a] my aides and translators of the speech to follow. Thus I have placed more confidence in the meaning behind what will be said than in the words used. And you certainly must be the judge of speeches, scrutinising not the phrases but their intention, and especially those of men who claim to be philosophers.[135]

So be it. There is, your majesties, a goodwill and affinity between kingship and philosophy that comes from on high and God sent both down to earth for the same purpose – to care for and correct mankind, [b] the one teaching what is good, the other putting it into practice.[136] This selfsame fact, then, I hold to be the first indication of your nature,

133 Neither Valens nor Valentinian knew Greek, and Ammianus comments on the former's general lack of education (31.14.5). Although Themistius was not affected, the growth of the imperial bureaucracy in the 4th century, whose official language was Latin, forced many would-be recruits into learning the Roman tongue after an initial education with a Greek grammarian, rather than continuing with Greek rhetoric. Libanius was conscious of the change: *Orr.* 43–4, 62; cf. Liebeschuetz, 1972, 242ff. See also *Or.* 11.144d where Themistius minimises the importance of Valens' presumed inability to comprehend what he is saying.

134 Thucydides 1.137ff: Themistocles, the Athenian statesman and general, was ostracised from Athens in 471 BC. After a period in Argos he fled to the Persian king Artaxerxes I.

135 Cf. Libanius, *Ep.* 1430, trans. Norman as *Ep.* 116, for the different levels – language, ideas – on which Libanius and friends had read one of Themistius' earlier speeches. Once again, Themistius used confrontation to define and distinguish himself from other intellectuals: see further the introduction to *The Letter of Constantius.*

136 A fundamental premise of Themistius' whole career: see Chapter 1. On the emperor's supposed relationship with the Divine in Roman ideology, and the quarrel over this between Themistius and Julian, see the introduction to this chapter.

that you did not fail to recognise this affinity nor have you felt the same as the majority who, on account of fraudulent practitioners, disparage the genuine as well.[137] But not you: you do not think that poisoners have anything to do with doctors, informers[138] with orators, or in the case of any other art, those who employ methods alien to it. [c] This is why you have not driven the philosopher's cloak from the palace[139] and why it is no less esteemed in your eyes than a generalship or provincial governorship.

For Euripides, or whoever in fact it is who wrote 'Tyrants are wise through communion with wise men'[140] was not, or at least so I think, of sound judgement. For surely, he would never have considered philosophy to be well disposed to tyranny or that those most incompatible of qualities, virtue and wickedness, are alike in their nature. [d] But just as those who are exceedingly melancholic shut out those who serve them, so tyranny does not allow wisdom to approach. Dionysius sold Plato into slavery, Nero banished Musonius, and the fratricide imprisoned the man from Tyana. It was characteristic of these same men, it seems, to dishonour both brothers and philosophers, just as on the contrary, philosophy and brotherly love are necessarily kindred and equally honoured.[141] In this then tragedy fares badly, [73a] indeed worse still,

137 Almost certainly a reference to Maximus of Ephesus, pagan philosopher and wonder-worker (theurgist), who exercised great influence over and under the Emperor Julian. He survived under Jovian (see the introduction to this Chapter), but was first deported then eventually tortured and executed under Valens: Eunapius, *Lives of the Sophists* 7.4.10ff.

138 Informers were stock hate figures to the Roman upper classes.

139 Vanderspoel, 1995, 159 n. 17, wonders if Themistius has Secundus Salutius in mind. He clearly meant himself: referring to his own comparative eclipse under Julian and subsequent return to the limelight (see the introduction to this chapter). Compare the similar identifications of himself and philosophy at (among others) the start of *Orr.* 1, 5, 10, 16, 17.

140 The quotation is from a Sophoclean tragedy (fr. 13), although Plato (*Republic* 568a; *Theages* 125b) quotes it as Euripidean; Themistius was apparently aware that the matter was doubtful.

141 Plato had a long association with the court of Dionysius I and his son Dionysius II at Syracuse. His friendship with Dion, a prominent Syracusean statesman, brought about a rift between the philosopher and Dionysius II. In answer to the latter's veiled threats on Dion's life, Plato was forced to return to Syracuse, where he remained in virtual captivity until his release was engineered by Archytas of Tarentum. Musonius, the Stoic philosopher, was banished by Nero from Rome in 60, and again in 65 for possible involvement in the Pisonian conspiracy. Apollonius of Tyana, Neopythagorean sage and wonder-worker, fell foul of Domitian. Dionysius II dispossessed his half-brother Hipparinus of the throne in the

whenever it calls tyranny a god.[142] For thus it returns to the same error. For God is whatever is the absolute summit of wisdom, or rather its quintessence, and it was possible for Euripides, if he had looked up into the heavens, to discover and learn that the things there come not from tyranny but are the blessed works of a blessed rule, which does not exploit the fullness of its power for indiscriminate licence but endures for all time, according to its own laws, which it itself has laid down and preserves unchanged for the protection of creation.[143]

[b] For order is a sign not of weakness but of a nature that can neither be moved nor disturbed, and the closer that [nature] gets to the whole, the more it enjoys the highest degree of order.[144] Disorder, turmoil and confusion exist in a small part of creation but one which through its deficiencies in all these respects resulting from weakness, falls short even of the definition of existence.[145] The model of this state is not the one Minos established in Crete, or Lycurgus in Sparta, or that of the ancient Romans but the one which you two rule and which you obtained through divine consent.[146] [c] For do not think, gentlemen, that the soldiers were in charge of such an important election. It is from above that this vote descends, it is from above that the proclamation – which

---

course of an eventful career, Nero killed his brother Britannicus, and Domitian was suspected of having poisoned his brother Titus.

142  Euripides, *Phoenician Women* 506; *Trojan Women* 1169.

143  In the Greek view of Creation, divine reason took hold of formless basic matter and shaped the Universe from it, so that the same rules and principles prevailed throughout Creation and preserved its form: Sorabji, 1983, chs 13, 20; 1988, pt. 2, ch. 15.

144  In Platonic thought, the Creator was characterised by unchangingness; i.e., in contrast to human beings, the Creator did not age and die. Unchangingness – being like the Divinity – was thus a central cultural ideal, pursued on every level from that of the state to the individual. The tradition was accepted into Christianity via the 2nd-century apologists, providing Themistius with a commonplace, religiously neutral vocabulary in which to talk about God before Christian emperors. See the introduction to Chapter 2.

145  In the Greek hierarchical view of the Cosmos, sin and disorder existed only in the lowest reaches of Creation, the sublunary world of human beings on earth. In the world of the intellect above the moon (i.e. the levels of the planets, stars and sun) these things did not exist. Human beings combined both intellect (in their souls) and physical matter liable to sin via the absence of order, while beings lower than man (animals etc.) contained only physical matter.

146  Lycurgus was by tradition the founder of the Spartan state (Herodotus 1.65–6), Minos of the Cretan. On Themistius' view that the Divinity was responsible for picking legitimate emperors, see the introduction to this chapter.

Homer calls the will of Zeus – is performed through the agency of men. Hence from this it is your task to show that the soldiers were the agents of God. If you were to have confidence in might alone, you will be rightly thought to have seized power by force of arms, but if in pre-eminence through virtue, you will be seen to have been promoted from heaven.[147] [d] For this is the sign that your election is from there, not an eagle of gold, nor honorific inscriptions nor empty phrases, but a policy which looks towards it and makes every effort to emulate it. And just as someone who attempts to hold office without your warrants is intolerable to you, so someone who puts on the imperial purple without the divine token is not pleasing to God.[148] Hence it is necessary to reveal what this token might be, since in your two cases the events on the mortal plane at least were so extraordinary. Both the proclamation by the multitude [74a] and by a ruling individual carry honour; both of these have come together in you both. The one gains a triumph through the multitude, and you through the ruler; or rather, the vote of the multitude has devolved onto you. For he whom all men placed in power made you his partner, and proffered accurate proof of his having been suitably chosen in giving a share to you who are like him in every way.[149]

I take no delight in earthly events, however, but seek out the hallmark from on high and have taken pains that the election is shown to

147  The Empire's official ideology presented its political order as part of the divine plan for the universe; God upheld the Empire, and everything about a legitimate emperor, from his bedchamber to his spending department, was sacred: see further, e.g., MacCormack, 1981; Heather, 1993b. The denigrating reference to the possibility of an accession accomplished by 'force of arms' alone would surely have been interpreted by Themistius' audience as a reference to the accession of Jovian, brought about by the army alone on Persian soil. Even if in *Or.* 5 Themistius had been ready to portray it as entirely legitimate, Jovian's early death 'proved' (within the logic of Roman state theory) that it could not have been, and our orator had duly changed his mind by the time he delivered *Or.* 6.

148  Roman ideology (see previous note) was fine so long as the Empire was successful, or could be presented as such. But the recent deaths in quick succession of two emperors (Julian and Jovian) and massive defeat at the hands of Persia required an ideological explanation in terms of the Empire having departed from the divinely ordained path, and hence having lost divine favour. Thus Themistius needed to find credible reasons for thinking that the new emperors' accession was in tune with divine will.

149  Themistius succinctly summarises the course of events. Valentinian was chosen by the council of leading generals and politicians on 26 February 364. He elevated his brother on 28 March: see the introduction to *Or.* 6. The switch from 'you' singular to 'you' plural shows that Valentinian, although sometimes addressed, was not actually present when this speech was delivered, whereas Valens was.

have come from there.[150] **[b]** To begin with, then, your mutual goodwill and esteem is for me sufficient proof that your election is from a divine source.[151] For where kinship has brought to implacable enmity even those who succeeded to paternal rule and become partners in it according to law, what can one say in your case who, with no law applying constraint, followed the just qualities in your nature, and, as if it were a family inheritance, calmly and quietly divided the kingdom which others who fall heir to it have assumed through mutual bloodshed. For even though the stage of ancient dramas is sated with it, **[c]** do not more recent events surpass the stage? Who would deny this, going through in turn the youths at Thebes, the sons of Pelops, Cambyses, Nero, Domitian, the son of Severus,[152] and only yesterday or the day before, those, who though nature made them members of a group, were left solitary through their own actions, such great fecundity of lineage being wasted by itself out of a passion for sole rule.[153] Compared to you two, Xerxes matters little, Seleucus matters little, the son of Philetairus matters little. **[d]** For these men are renowned for this one thing – the moderate treatment of their brothers who disputed

150 See note 148.

151 I.e., the 'hallmark' of divine will behind the election, for which Themistius has been searching.

152 At Thebes, Eteocles and Polyneices, the sons of Oedipus, destroyed each other in their struggle for sole mastery of Thebes (Aeschylus, *Seven Against Thebes*; Sophocles, *Antigone*; Euripides, *Phoenician Women*). Atreus and Thyestes, the sons of Pelops, disputed the throne of Argos. At a banquet to mark a feigned reconciliation, Atreus served Thyestes the flesh of his sons. Cambyses murdered his brother Smerdis (Herodotus 3.31). Severus' son Caracalla killed his brother Geta, after a period of joint rule. Nero and Domitian also killed their brothers: note 141.

153 The sons of Constantine: a naturally recurring theme in Themistius' political discourse. After the initial bloodbath of 337 (see the introduction to this Chapter), Constantine's three surviving sons – Constantine II, Constans, and Constantius – first divided the Empire between themselves. Constantine II then died attacking Constans in 340, while Constans and Constantius were periodically hostile towards one another in the 340s (see most recently Barnes, 1993, chs 7–11) before the usurper Magnentius killed the former. In the 350s, Constantius promoted and then killed his cousin Gallus, and much the same pattern would probably have repeated itself had Julian not revolted. Julian, *Or.* 7.228b–c had already compared the sons of Oedipus and Constantine. Themistius shows knowledge certainly of Julian's point of view, if not his actual writings, at two other points in this speech. Cf. the introduction to this Chapter, the political point of so denigrating the Constantinian dynasty lay in the fact that members of it, particularly Julian's uncle Procopius, were still at large and a potential threat.

the kingship – and, just like other incredible stories, the Persian is celebrated for sparing Ariemenes who contested with him the ancestral
rule, while Eumenes is celebrated for conceding to Attalus after he
rebelled.[154] But you two knew that brotherly love is something more
than fairness. For you would justly be honoured not for the occasions
when you did not wrong each other [75a] but for those when you have
benefited each other. For even if the greater share of the benefaction
comes from one side,[155] in no sense is the greater share a source of pleasure to him. But, he who hands over a part of the kingdom, makes a
partner in toil of one who understands what he has taken on, which is
neither pleasure nor indolence. For he who shares out the imperial
purple for these reasons serves the empire ill, not only as regards the
one to whose wickedness he adds the means to exercise it, but also as
regards everyone else who are forced to enjoy twice the hardship.[156]

[b] Furthermore, just as the soldiers get more than they have given by
their vote,[157] so too does your brother[158] receive a bonus, and indeed[159]
one should no longer be cautious about the greater [share; i.e. Valentinian's], but that in fact is beyond reproach, because what he relin-
quished returns to him. For he has not been deprived of part of his

154 Themistius quotes three instances of fraternal conflict and reconciliation from Plutarch, *Moralia* 478aff. (*On Brotherly Love*). Xerxes did not enforce his claim against his
brother Ariemenes until the case was decided by an impartial third party. Seleucus II and
Antiochus Hierax fought over succession to Antiochus II; Seleucus is supposed to have
grieved upon hearing of his brother's death, and then been overjoyed to find him alive.
Eumenes I of Pergamum was the nephew and adopted son of Philetairos; Themistius
seems to have confused him with his son Eumenes II whose throne and wife were taken by
his brother Attalus II.

155 I.e., Valentinian who was promoted first, and then promoted his brother Valens.

156 Themistius comes to the central part of his speech: the terms on which Valentinian
and Valens have shared the Empire. In these few lines of introduction, Themistius laid stress
on the fact that Valentinian, though senior Augustus, had no desire to 'pull rank' in the
relationship, that Valens, though the junior partner, was ready and able to do his share,
and that both had a strong ethic of service to the Empire. Much of this was designed to
distinguish their partnership from the misguided attempts to share power within the Constantinian dynasty, which had previously generated conflict and civil wars: see the introduction to this chapter.

157 The choice of Valentinian as Augustus by the council was then validated by the
acclamation of the troops (Ammianus 26.1–2): the official ceremony which made him
emperor.

158 Valentinian: Themistius here switched again to addressing Valens alone.

159 Reading εἰ καὶ μὴ after *A* and *Θ*.

kingdom, but has received the status of being greater than a king. The soldiers made him a king, but you, Valens, have made him a great king.[160] By assuming the purple you have given in return another soul and another body, [c] to see and hear more, to make speeches simultaneously among those who are far dispersed and to give judgements at the same time to Syrians and Britons. The poet says that Zeus can shift his gaze from Troy to Thrace, even though it is on the other side of the sea,[161] but it is possible for him [Valentinian] to look on Italy and visit the Bosphorus at the same time, and, should he wish to take the Western Ocean and the Tigris in hand, nothing prevents him from keeping the farthest reaches of the earth in his sight at the same time. [d] Surely it seems, does it not, that you have given more than you have received?[162] Now indeed it is a fact that the dominion of the Roman Empire both to the east and to the west is defended not by soldiers, not by cavalry but by kings, two kings fit for the task, two kings who combine as one like a perfect whole.[163] For there is no retribution for the speech which honours exactly in accordance with its subject.

This too is of great importance – that the chariot pair should not fall lame, nor [76a] that the title of king be attached to both but the work fall to one only, which virtually all your predecessors endured, and so did not enjoy the partnership to a good end. Some choose their sons, others their brothers, others those nearest and dearest to them by blood, on the grounds that the honour was their due, but, by immediately claiming a larger share in the honours they were giving, they did not render them well disposed by what they gave, but provoked them by what they took away. [b] But Valentinian received a whole and divided a whole, as a brother and a father, the former by nature but the latter by

160  A crucial point. Given the recent history of the Constantinian dynasty (note 153), the audience would wish to be assured that the Empire had really been divided voluntarily, so that rivalry would not plunge the Empire into civil war. See further the introduction to this speech.

161  Cf. Homer, *Iliad* 13.3ff.

162  Themistius could not avoid the fact that, as Valentinian's appointee and younger brother, Valens was the junior partner in the purple. He balanced this, however, by arguing that it was only because Valens accepted this role that Valentinian could enjoy Zeus-like status. Compare *Panegyrici Latini* 10.3 on Diocletian's sharing of imperial rule with Maximian.

163  Themistius' account of the benefits of joint rule drew substantially on Aelius Aristides' account of the same situation under Marcus Aurelius and Lucius Verus: *Or.* 27.25–39; cf. Dio Chrysostom, *Or.* 3.104–7; Vanderspoel, 1995, 158–9.

his own making; he handed over an equal share, while keeping the whole through the compliance of his partner, and more than the chariot team which, according to Homer, Actor's two sons drive, does the Roman Empire draw breath together and feel as one. For one man does not wield the whip while the other steers, but both steer with the same reins.[164]

And so the brotherly love of the kings is in itself welcome to their subjects, and it is of greater value for most people [c] to be steered by a single policy towards ease and safety alike. For now more easily than before can we both get closer to justice, and also feel greater confidence against who are hard by their weapons.[165] But this is not the greatest of the benefits we have gained, which is that brotherly love is a sign of love of mankind, just as goodwill towards one's family and relations is the origin and principle from which goodwill to all men derives. For nature, which has placed the highest value on man and binds us together with all our fellow men, separate from all other living creatures, [d] has laid down the first principles from what is close at hand and from hearth and home; he who loves his brother will also love his family, he who loves his family will also love his native land, and he who loves his native land will also love mankind. It is impossible once caught in nature's antechamber not also to become obedient to her prompting.

[77a] Yet what need is there for me to elaborate in minute detail that those who love a brother must obviously also love mankind? Come hither, O fortunate men, come hither and recognise your true Father, the abundance of his children and the entire host of your brothers.[166]

164 This paragraph would have brought firmly to mind Constantius' failed attempts to share power with his two Caesars, Gallus and Julian. From the latter, there survives an eloquent account of what it was like to be emperor in name, but have real power exercised by 'advisors' appointed by your superior, and the resentments and jealousies any attempt to change this situation provoked: Julian, *Letter to the Athenians* with the comments of Matthews, 1989, 87ff. Hence Themistius went out of his way to stress the equality between Valentinian and Valens, which was a guarantee of no future strife. Cteatus and Eurytus, sons or descendants of Actor (also known as the Moliones) were twins (Siamese twins in later traditions) famous for their charioteering expertise: Homer, *Iliad* 11.750ff., 22.638ff.

165 As it stands, this passage is problematic. By supplying τοὺς – partially following Reiske's suggestion – the abrupt shift from the accusative is avoided.

166 The use of Father for God is typical of the carefully ambiguous religious language which Themistius employed, designed to bridge over the gap between pagans and Christians; see further Chapter 2. This whole paragraph is entirely compatible with Genesis'

They are not the mere fifty that Aegyptus sired, nor as many as the poets numbered the sons of Priam,[167] but are as many as possess the distinguishing mark of their Father: the communion of reason and the harmony of the physical and the rational. All these men spring from the same seed and are true brothers to you and to each other. [b] Look, examine the token of recognition; is it not more reliable evidence than gifts and rings?[168] For Pelops' descendants, the fact that some part of the shoulder looked like ivory was sufficient as proof of kinship, [169] but for us[170] shall not the whole body be sufficient to show our single begetter and ancestor? And yet is the spiritual kinship and likeness not much more obvious than the physical, when it is preserved as it was created? We all try to outdo each other in virtue, we are all ashamed to admit to wickedness, we cannot endure in isolation, we call for each other's help in emergencies; [c] we hasten unsummoned into dangers, a single nurse nurtures us, we hold a common ancestral property – the earth, sea, air and water, indeed all that grows and lives – some of which we have divided up between us as possessions, the rest remaining as yet undivided among us. I pass over the rest. We alone of all creatures of earth recognise our Father, either more clearly or more dimly, and even if we are set apart from one another in hierarchical order, we all lean on Him for support.[171]

---

account of Adam, and Johannine and Pauline language concerning God the Father and his children, that is humankind, as brothers.

167 Homer reckoned the sons of Priam at fifty in number (*Iliad* 24.497ff.); the story of Aegyptus and his fifty sons pursuing Danaus and his fifty daughters is told in Aeschylus *Suppliants*.

168 In Greek New Comedy and Roman Comedy, the true identity of long-lost children was often recognised by some token – a ring or another distinctive item – which had been left with them when they were abandoned as babies. See, e.g., Menander, *Perikeiromene*, *Sikyonius*; Plautus, *Cistellaria*, *Rudens*.

169 Tantalus dismembered, cooked and served up his son Pelops to the gods to test their omniscience. The trick was discovered only after Demeter had eaten part of Pelops' shoulder. On the latter's restoration to life, the missing part was replaced in ivory. Thereafter the kinship of his descendants was supposed to be revealed by the whiteness of their shoulders.

170 Reading ἡμῖν after *A* and *Θ*.

171 It is interesting to compare Themistius' treatment of religious toleration here with that at *Or.* 5.67c–70c. Some of the same points are made – such as the dependency of all men upon God, and the fact that some see Him more clearly than others – but, in comparison, the latter point is made more firmly, less space and elaboration is given to the

[d] Surely Homer, in his great wisdom, was not casually improvising in his verses when ceaselessly celebrating the Father of both men and gods as one and the same. And yet why does he not call him father of horses, or by Zeus, of dogs or lions? Because in all other beasts there is not, in my opinion, the smallest share of their creator. And so they have no understanding either of him or of each other: it is on mankind alone that the outpouring from the second bowl flows down. [78a] To share the faculty of reason is nothing other than to share the divine seed.[172] The Boeotian poet thinks the same as Homer,

> 'There is a single race of men, a single race of gods, but we are both born of one mother'[173]

neatly assimilating us to the father from the mother too. If then, all men had the same mother and the same father and spring from purer parentage, there would seem to be no difference between love of a brother and love of mankind.[174] But having now created strict and circumscribed limits to this, we are revolted by the sons of Oedipus in the tragedies, [b] as monsters and affronts to nature, yet we do not consider our plots and enmities towards each other worthy of tragedy, nor does any respect for the Father possess us if we never gladden Him by [establishing] peace with one another.[175]

---

importance of diversity, there is no equivalent of *Or.* 5.70a claiming that God wants Syrians (i.e., Christians) Hellenes and Egyptians to organise themselves differently. Christian sectarianism likewise goes unmentioned. This suggests that Valentinian and Valens adopted a markedly less tolerant form of toleration than had Jovian. See the introduction to this chapter.

172  Plato, *Timaeus* 41d, 73c–d. In a metaphor drawn from the preparation of wine at a banquet or symposium, the demiurge is pictured forming human souls in the same mixing bowl in which the universal soul was created, and in which a residue from the latter remains. Human souls are therefore a second serving being admixed with the pure celestial matter of the first, and human beings the lowest point in creation which contains any spark of the Divine. Again, much of this was philosophical commonplace, long accepted by Platonising Christian theologians.

173  Pindar, *Nemean Odes* 6.1ff.

174  While firmly basing himself on Hellenic classics, Themistius thus constructs a vision of human creation which was acceptably reminiscent for Christians of the story of Adam and Eve. On the point of this cultural strategy, see the introduction to Chapter 2.

175  The reference to Oedipus' sons, is again designed to bring to mind the fratricidal sons of Constantine: note 153. Although a superficial comparison can indeed be drawn between

By you at least, your majesties, this cannot be tolerated. But since your common ancestor promoted you as the most important and most honoured of the rest of the family,[176] may you be disposed in no other way, either towards each other or towards us, [c] than as the Father chooses; and He chooses the way of peace, gentleness and love of mankind, just as He is disposed towards His other works and offspring. Observe how lightning falls infrequently and upon few, but light everywhere and upon all. Thus it is not possible for those who despise kindness towards mankind to be likened to God. For one would not emulate him in skilful horsemanship, nor archery, nor javelin work, nor, by Zeus, in overcoming the pleasures of the flesh.[177] [d] But these virtues of the soul are entirely mundane and truly earthbound and mortal; this alone is entirely divine and heavenly: to hold easily in one's power the happiness of the human race. This is the divinity, from which we name you again and again,[178] and to which it is impious for anyone to pretend, unless love of mankind already exists in them.

Consider it in this way: there are three attributes by which God is distinguished as God: eternal life, superabundance of power, and

---

what happened to the descendants of Oedipus and Constantine, by drawing attention to the (irrelevant) circumstances of the former's parentage Themistius manages to damn the latter by association.

176 The common ancestor is God, the rest of the family humankind. According to Roman ideology, the Empire was God's particular instrument for ordering human affairs, its head – the emperor – could be considered head of the entire human family.

177 Julian praised Constantius for his horsemanship and skilled archery (*Or.* 1.11a–c; *Or.* 2.53a–54b), and Ammianus' obituary likewise stressed his skills in the areas of horsemanship, hurling javelins, and the bow (21.16.7). This unanimity suggests that these skills played a central role in imperial image that Constantius' propaganda sought to present, as, indeed, did self-control. His magisterial deportment on ceremonial occasions was famous (cf. Ammianus 16.10 on his visit to Rome), he required little sleep, did not go in for grand dinners, and was entirely chaste (21.16.5–6). Themistius thus deliberately decried here the importance in an emperor of the qualities which Constantius had stressed. Such a propaganda line clearly served the interests of Valens who was faced with the potential problem of residual loyalty to the Constantinian dynasty, which might be played upon by its minor surviving members, such as Julian's maternal uncle Procopius (see the introduction to this chapter). The passage may also have been meant to bring Julian to mind. Julian's own works stressed the importance of self-control, particularly over physical desires, and was a feature of his self-presentation which attracted considerable criticism: e.g., *Misopogon* 240b (see further Bowersock, 1978, 14–15, citing Libanius' defence of Julian's austerity at *Or.* 12.94–5).

178 Everything pertaining to the emperor and his office was customarily labelled sacred.

unceasing benefaction towards mankind. **[79a]** And it is only in the last of
these aforementioned qualities that similarity to God is attainable for a
king. For no one could think that he was close to attaining eternity in
time or competing in superabundance of power, unless he surpasses the
sons of Aloeus in madness.[179] But virtue towards mankind, gentleness
and kindness – I hesitate to say it, indeed I am very hesitant, but truth is
on my side – are these not much more accessible for him who shares in
our common nature? For this is what makes him godlike, this is what
makes him divine; it is thus a king becomes divinely nourished, **[b]** thus
divinely born, and we will not be lying when we attribute divinity to him
on these terms, rather than if he were to sever Athos from the land or fill
Asia with corpses.[180] For such deeds as these are much greater and
more extraordinary than a single earthquake or plague. And there is
not, among the marks I have listed by which God can be recognised,
any other part of His blessed nature which is more brilliant than the
Good.[181] And so it is from thence that we have considered His name as
most appropriate and worthy, since we can observe that longevity[182]
and overwhelming might are characteristic of many things that do not
possess souls.

**[c]** But Homer, it seems, was not correct in supposing that two jars
filled with the destinies of men stand in the house of Zeus, one filled
with the good the other with their opposite.[183] For there is no storehouse
of evils in heaven, but the latter jar has been compounded from the mud
and earth among us, and it is we who fill and empty it. We do not allow
the streams of good things from on high, which he furnishes ceaselessly
and with unfailing attention, to pour down unadulterated; as the philosophical poem says, he is the giver of good things, the steward of good
order, **[d]** by whose side sit Justice and Good Order, at whose side stand
the Graces, Joy, Beauty and Lovely Abundance. All these titles are his
through love of mankind: the smiling one, the friendly one, the god of

---

179  The sons of Aloeus – the gigantic Otus and Ephialtes – attempted to scale Olympus
by piling Mts Ossa and Pelion on top of one another.

180  Xerxes dug a canal through the promontory at Mt Athos to give safe passage to his
ships (Herodotus 7.22–25); it was Alexander who filled Asia with corpses.

181  Identifying the Creator with primary goodness was central to Neoplatonic thought.

182  Reading μακραίωνα Downey's text has μακαρίωνα which may be a misprint.

183  Homer, *Iliad* 24.527ff. Themistius here followed Plato's treatment of this passage at
*Republic* 379c–d.

strangers, the god of suppliants, the protector of cities and the saviour.[184]

This is the list of titles I would like to set down as yours, your majesties, as being much more divine and more appropriate than one deriving from vanquished nations. For none of the latter come from heaven: neither Persicus, nor Germanicus, nor any of those you might mention. [80a] Furthermore if the barbarians are not causing unrest at the time, those who write them must lie.[185] On the other hand, you two can use these titles inherited from your Father on high both in times of war and peace, and, moreover, as regards those who sit on thrones, they confirm this list by a mere nod and a short phrase, such as the phrase I learned a Roman emperor spoke once long ago: 'Today I was not a king, for today I did good to no man.'[186] Indeed, this very sentiment stands on an equal footing with many and mighty cavalry and infantry battles. [b] I have revered it no less than the victory trophies of Alexander. What are you saying, most godlike of kings? That today you were not a king because today you did good to no one? On what other occasion did you

184  The philosophical poem is *The Iliad*. All of these titles are used by Homer to refer to Zeus. Again, the attempt to occupy a religious middle ground is striking, especially the use of σωτήρ 'Saviour', the common Christian appellative for Christ. The Neoplatonic 'saviour' who guided men's souls towards the one was Asclepius, the Φιλάνθρωπος θεός *par excellence*: Athanassiadi, 1992, 167–8. Such common ground gave Themistus every opportunity to speak in a manner designed to appeal to pagans and Christians alike: see further Chapter 2. Again like Christianity, the Neoplatonic world-view, put forward in this paragraph by Themistius, also envisaged the Divinity as an entirely good being. In this system, evil was no more than the absence of good, or an excessive preoccupation with worldly matters; hence Themistius' 'mud and earth'. Again there was some potential overlap with Christianity in explaining sin. Augustine, for instance, found this Neoplatonic conception of evil initially powerful, even if, in the end, not totally satisfactory: see, e.g., Brown, 1967, chs 9, 10, 15.

185  The reference to the fact that, where there was no real victory to claim, people had to lie would appear to be a disparaging reference to Jovian's attempt to claim that the humiliating terms of his Persian peace amounted to a victory, even though Themistius had gone along with this in *Or.* 5 (see above). Looming generally over the Roman political establishment at this point was the recent and massive defeat at Persian hands which had caused the loss of Nisibis and other territories: see the introduction to this chapter. In this context, a disparaging reference to the victory title Persicus may also have been meant as a signal that Valens was not about to rush into attempting to reverse these losses. On victory titles in general, and victoriousness as the prime imperial attribute, see respectively Barnes, 1982; McCormick, 1986. Questioning their importance was one of Themistius' stock responses to military embarrassment: e.g., *Orr.* 8.110b; 13.174c; 18.225a.

186  Titus: Suetonius, *Lives of the Caesars* 8.1.

ever do more good to more men than when you uttered this sentiment, by
which all those who were kings after you learned what was their task, and
what they had continually to accomplish if they were to preserve the
name? And so, your majesty, it is totally just to say that not even that
day of your reign was wasted, since the deficiency you censured with
that saying, that same saying remedied.

[c] I could say much the same of yet another king, and not one from the
far distant past or from the Golden Age, but from the time of us here who
now surround you, who, after he had become master of the man who had
caused such great turmoil in the insurrection in the West, after the barbarian's flight,[187] put aside his hostility at the moment he gained the upper
hand, and repaid abuses with a superabundance of benefactions. And so
he turned the wrongdoer to repentance and punished him with his
personal pain as he realised, from the benefits he received, what sort of
man it was he had wronged.[188] [d] Hence it does not befit the true king to
injure in return, but to gain superiority over one who has caused pain by
treating him well. This is the triumph of virtue, while vengeance is the
triumph of force, and one must make oneself great not through anger but
through magnanimity.[189] For the latter greatness is divine, the former
petty and mortal, which raises one above those who cower, not those
who stand erect. I would pray that we fear not you two, but on your
behalf,[190] [81a] and that your rule be safeguarded by such fear on the
part of all your subjects as we feel for each other.

Yet now, while I am recounting to you the words of others, I do not
know how I can pass over your own, especially as I still go around with
the speech, which you delivered yesterday to the senate, ringing deep
within my ears, and which you have presented as a pledge of future
happiness.[191] Indeed, I rejoiced for humanity because it is completely
unified and everywhere in harmony. For I could distinguish clearly in

187  The usurper Magnentius: see the introduction to *Or.* 3 in Chapter 2.

188  The Emperor Constantius and his treatment of Vetranio: see the introduction to *Or.*
3 in Chapter 2.

189  A sequence of thought which again brings to mind one of the central teachings of
Christianity: loving one's enemy. Whether this was deliberate or accidental is impossible
to know, but it would fit in with Themistius' general strategy of stressing what was
common to both Christianity and the Hellenic tradition.

190  A favourite Themistian aphorism: see also *Or.* 1.10d.

191  On the rhetorical double-act between Valens and Themistius, see the introduction to
this speech.

your words, what the divinely inspired Plato prescribed concerning government, **[b]** differing only in the phraseology. For it is indeed to the advantage of their subjects that kings should first have worked themselves, that they should have been raised in an unindulged and rigorous regime, worked the land, performed public duties, lived an outdoor life, been on campaign, grown in stature through experience of the hardship of human existence, like Cyrus, Darius, Numa and the most illustrious of the Romans;[192] and it is a more grievous affliction of rule for its subjects to be exposed to informers than to barbarians;[193] just as, I think, internal afflictions are more serious for the body than those which assail it from without. **[c]** Everything I have mentioned derives from the sanctum of the Academy.[194]

I tell you, your majesty, that it is your task to hold that speech before

192 Themistius had in mind Plato, *Laws* 694ff. which contrasts the upbringing of Cyrus and Darius I with that of their sons Cambyses and Xerxes. The former were brought up as commoners; Cyrus was raised as a herdsman, Darius a member of the palace guard: Herodotus 1.107–8; 3.138. The latter were pampered as royal princes in the luxurious and female-dominated Persian court. The disasters which befell the Persian Empire during their reigns and their personal inadequacies were, in Herodotus' view, a consequence of their being overindulged as children. Numa Pompillius, the second king of Rome, was said by Livy (1.18.4–5) to have been 'trained not so much in foreign studies as in the stern and austere discipline of the ancient Sabines, a race more incorruptible than any of these times'. Themistius may, however, have been confusing Numa with Cincinnatus who was famously called from the plough to become dictator in 458 BC. The fact that, unlike Constantius and Julian, Valens and Valentinian had not been born to the purple is thus held up as an advantage and a good omen for the future. The importance of experience in household management in making Valens fit to rule is a theme to which Themistius returned some four years later in 368: *Or.* 8.113d (translated in Heather and Matthews, 1991, 28). This passage demonstrates that it originated in Valens' own speech to the senate. It was also designed to make virtue of necessity, since Valens had not held major office before his sudden elevation to the purple (as noted by both Ammianus 31.14.5 and Zosimus 4.4.1), and the ancient world was very suspicious of parvenus; see, e.g., Eunapius fr. 46. 1C. After his death, Themistius, by contrast, identified Valens' lack of experience of high office as the fundamental cause of the flaws in his rule: see the introduction to Chapter 4.

193 A change of regime was a good moment for informers to profit by questioning the loyalty of important individuals. The famous Chalcedon trials under Julian, which eventually got out of his control, led to much bloodshed, as Constantius' regime was dismantled by those seeking to benefit from the new order: Bowersock, 1978, 66ff. Valens had evidently signalled in his speech that his intention was not to rake up the past, a thought which Themistius had already echoed above at *Or.* 6.73b. Themistius did not here deny the traditional image of barbarians as enemies of the Roman order, but merely portrayed informers as worse. On Themistius and barbarians in general, see the introduction to Chapter 4.

194 The public gymnasium at Athens where Plato taught and Aristotle studied.

you, and, looking into it as if into a mirror each day with penetrating gaze, you will dispose in more becoming fashion not your hair[195] but the Roman rule. You have no need of the precepts of Marcus, nor of any other noble phrase uttered by one or other of the ancient emperors; rather, you have an inner Phoenix and an inner guide for your words and deeds.[196]

[d] Whenever I call to mind the things you said about your father, I seek no further for the cause of your brotherly love. For it is surely natural for you, who take such pleasure in his bronze likeness that you acknowledge such gratitude to those who voted for it, to place the highest value on his living likeness and love him no less than yourself, especially since you are yourself a breathing likeness from the same exemplar.[197] There was no way that you two would endure the fact that your destiny had become unequal, [82a] as soon as possible making it equal for each other, by going out to the suburbs of the city as king and commoner but returning in a short time as an imperial partnership, each glorying more in his associate than in himself, with your subjects surging around you on this side and that out of pleasure, and each of you confident that he had been duplicated. No one entered so joyfully as sole ruler as you did on dividing up the empire.[198] With how much brotherly love have you filled our homes too! Who is not ashamed for the future to dispute with his brother over slaves or a small piece of land,

195 Nero was proverbially famous among emperors for arranging his hair, and would naturally have come to mind, perhaps raising a laugh.

196 Phoenix, son of Amyntor was the young Achilles' mentor and guardian (see *Iliad* 9.430ff.). Marcus Aurelius was pre-eminent among proverbially wise emperors because of his twelve books of *Meditations*.

197 Valens' father was Gratian. From humble Pannonian origins, he rose through army service to the distinguished rank of *comes*, holding independent commands in Africa and Britain: Ammianus 30.7.1–2. The Senate of Constantinople voted him a bronze statue, for which Valens had clearly thanked them in his speech. It is unclear from Themistius' words whether the statue was raised before the elevation of Gratian's sons to the purple.

198 Ammianus (26.4.1–3) and Themistius agree on the events of Valens' elevation. The two brothers went first to the Hebdomon, about seven miles outside the original city of Byzantium and a major military base for mobilising troops: Janin, 1964, 446–7. Hence Valens' proclamation as emperor could be confirmed by the acclamation of the army, a ceremonial prerequisite for confirming legitimacy. The elevation then culminated in a triumphant ceremonial entry – *adventus* – back into Constantinople, where the new emperor was introduced to the civilian population.

**[b]** who sees that you have divided the whole earth and all races of men without a murmur?

But, just as all blood relations would not be deemed worthy of the same degree of goodwill, so you two should not give equal shares to all the rest after each other. Do you wish me to state outright who they are who should justly have a claim on the lion's share of your care? It is those whom you made the first witnesses of your sacred pact, and in whose presence you first showed off your mutual protection. Were not the Plataeans sound in their judgement, because they handed over their land to the Greeks for the contest against the barbarians?[199] **[c]** And do we not take pride, and shall we not be sound in our judgement, because we provided you with the theatre of philosophy which is not inferior, a royal city, a fortunate city, the home of fortunate emperors, a good omen for your election, not looking on but rather validating the events and no less fitting for the recipient than the donor? For it was this city, first of all the subject cities, which received the improved fortune of the one and the demonstration of the other's virtue.[200]

But I have been brought round again to the same point, and since it is necessary to remind you of what is yours, **[d]** I will attempt to say a few words about the city for myself. And yet what can I say about it that can compare with what you said the other day in the senate, calling it the Mother of your kingship?[201] For not even Constantine, had he chosen to, could have used this title for her.[202] And so, we hold these words as a pledge, by which you have set up a competition between yourself and the founder. For if that man behaved so generously towards us after increasing his dominion through our acquisition, **[83a]** what degree of enthusiasm is it just for him to contribute who has gained the rule as a result of the city's favourable destiny? For just as it is more valuable to acquire good things than to make greater one who already has them, so much more just is the basis for goodwill towards

199 Plataea was the scene of the decisive defeat of Xerxes in 479 BC which ended his attempt to conquer Greece.

200 Respectively Valens' elevation and Valentinian's love of his brother and hence of humankind.

201 In the same way that he was careful to assure senators that he would not countenance political witchhunts, Valens also expressed his admiration for their city and hence themselves.

202 Because Constantine had been raised to the purple in York in 307, not Constantinople.

the city from you. Indeed, would it not be extraordinary for you to render the outskirts, where you assumed the imperial purple, more splendid with foundations, platforms and statues,[203] but not consider that you owe the city, which you do not hesitate to call the mother of your acclamation, additional offerings of thanks? [b] Moreover, while this is your situation, if once more one were to examine the original circumstances in which Constantine took possession of the Fair City, and those in which your brother, if he acts with justice, shall have it for himself, one will discover that the election is more prestigious than the victory. For the one immediately deprived his brother-in-law of the purple while the other immediately shared it with his brother.[204] A just reward is more auspicious than a just punishment, especially if one is considering one's immediate family, and to choose someone who will be[205] an imperial partner is better than to destroy an existing one. Thus each of you is able, both individually and together, [c] to outdo the founder in just actions towards the city.[206]

So be it. Yet is the city in her own right and apart from assistance, without honour and reputation and considered of little importance by those who are going to rule over the whole of the inhabited earth? Is it not, if the whole earth is considered to be one body, its second eye, even its heart or its navel, or whatever of the parts one might say is the most important? It links the two continents, is an anchorage for maritime needs, a market for trade by land and sea, an effective adornment of

203 The Hebdomon, where Valens was elevated, did become a full-blown ceremonial centre, where many other emperors were subsequently proclaimed. Valens had presumably announced his intention to build there during his speech of the previous day. The complex eventually comprised eight churches and a suburban palace, as well as its original military camp. How much was built under Valens is unclear, but as Janin (1964, 139–40, 446–9) charmingly comments, he will have constructed 'au moins un pied-a-terre pour sa famille'.

204 Valerius Licinianus Licinius was created Augustus in 307 and married Constantine's sister Constantia in 312. He acquired the east in 313 on defeating Maximinus. Relations with Constantine subsequently deteriorated until he was deposed by him in 324.

205 Reading κοινωνήσοντα after A, Π and Ψ.

206 On the artificial nature of Themistius' 'request' here and Valens willingness to respond, see the introduction to this speech. Despite constant efforts on Valens' part to conciliate opinion in Constantinople both initially, at his accession, and subsequently, after its support for the revolt of Procopius, hostility remained. When faced with protests in the city on his way to battle and eventual death against the Goths in 378, Valens is said to have wished its destruction: Socrates, *Ecclesiastical History* 4.38.5.

Roman rule. **[d]** For it has not been built, like some sacred precinct, far from the highway nor does it keep the emperors from attending to public affairs if they are engaged in business there, but is a place through which all must pass who arrive from and set out in all directions, so that whenever it keeps them closest to home, it puts them at the very centre of the whole empire.[207] To look beyond mere utility, it is possible to have before your eyes a festival of the Graces, **[84a]** a girdle of Aphrodite, a robe woven out of earth and sea, an everlasting feast, a place where happiness is created and good fortune stored. If indeed there is anything of importance in philosophy too, it has long been the hearth of the Muses of Plato and Aristotle, and now no less, by God, preserves the kindling sparks.[208] O Zeus the king, father of men, guardian of cities, both of the eastern Rome and the western, may you protect the team of these two cities and protect the team of the kings who guard your purposes.[209]

207  A pithy and effective statement of the importance of New Rome compared with the old in the 4th-century Empire. An example of how 'far from the highway' the old Rome actually was had recently been provided by the fact that Constantius had had to cut short a visit there in 357 to deal with problems on the Middle Danube (see the introduction to *Or.* 3 in Chapter 2).

208  Among other practitioners of philosophy, Themistius certainly had himself in mind here as one preserving the sparks of the teaching of Plato and Aristotle, whom he claimed to combine. It was his usual practice in speeches to make some reference to himself: on both of these points, see Chapter 1. On intellectual life more generally in Constantinople, see the introduction to *The Letter of Constantius* in Chapter 2.

209  It is again striking testimony to the cultural climate that Themistius could use such traditional religious language in front of a Christian emperor on such a major ceremonial occasion.

# CHAPTER 4

# THEODOSIUS, GRATIAN, AND THE GOTHS: THEMISTIUS ORATIONS 14–16

Orations 14, 15 and 16 comprise the first three speeches given by Themistius to the Emperor Theodosius, who, after a five-month delay, succeeded Valens as emperor of the eastern half of the Roman Empire in January 379. They were delivered at intervals between early summer 379 and January 383. For most of this period, much of the new emperor's attention was directed towards the foreign policy problem posed by groups of Goths loose on Roman territory, who had, indeed, been responsible for the death of Valens in the battle of Hadrianople in August 378. The speeches have much to say about the Gothic war, there-fore, and the peace agreement which brought it to a close in October 382, and it is chiefly for this reason that they have been studied. They are also extremely revealing of the evolution of Theodosius' relations with his western colleague Gratian. In addition, Themistius reconsidered in all three speeches the reign of Theodosius' predecessor in the east, the Emperor Valens. To set these speeches properly in context, therefore, it is necessary to reflect upon the origins of the Gothic war, which Theodosius was called upon to fight. This also sheds further important light upon the relationship of Themistius with Valens, which had begun so promisingly in 364 (Chapter 3).

## VALENS, THEMISTIUS, AND THE GOTHS (C. 376–8)

Sometime in the mid-370s, two main Gothic groups – the Tervingi under Alavivus and Fritigern and the Greuthungi under Alatheus and Saphrax – came to the lower Danube frontier of the Roman Empire to request asylum. Previously, and for the best part of a century, they had occupied lands north of the Black Sea, but stability in that region had been destroyed by nomadic Hunnic raiders. Local Roman commanders referred the matter to their emperor. Valens, however, was in Antioch, so matters rested where they stood for at least a couple of months, perhaps longer, while Gothic embassies were sent the thousand or so kilometres to Valens, decisions reached, and subsequent arrangements made. These negotiations occupied winter 375/6 or the first part of 376.[1]

The surviving sources unanimously report that Valens welcomed the retreating Goths, because they would both provide him with extra troops, and allow him to commute recruitment taxes into cash, so that he could fill the treasury at the same time. Valens' reported joy has often been taken at face value, but it must really be doubted a priori whether he would have been pleased to see many thousands of armed Goths arrive on his borders, with all the chaos that this both generated and reflected in the Danube frontier region. The Roman Empire did have a long history of accepting immigrants, but only on its own terms. Treatment varied according to the degree of favour thought desirable in individual cases. Not surprisingly, however, emperors liked to be in total military control of the situation, and tended to break up incoming groups into smaller units, resettling them widely across the Empire to minimise the potential for future trouble. None of these conditions were satisfied in the case of the Goths in 375/6. The crisis north of the Danube was entirely out of Roman control, and Valens' main forces were heavily engaged with Persia in a struggle for Armenia (the reason the emperor was in Antioch). The policy that Valens adopted suggests that, far from being filled with happiness, he was in fact highly uneasy in the face of this situation, as indeed he ought to have been as he surveyed the collapse of stability along his northern frontier. Rather than admitting both the Tervingi and Greuthungi, which he would surely have done if truly convinced that massed Gothic manpower could solve his military problems, Valens actually accepted only the former. Subsequent events also suggest, as we shall see, that he only had enough troops available in the Balkans to exclude one Gothic group, and, because of the confrontation in Armenia, no readily available reinforcements. Valens' actual policy was constrained by circumstance, therefore, not prompted by joy: a damage limitation exercise, not the enthusiastic reception of new recruits.[2]

The reports in our sources thus reflect not the real reasoning behind

1 Best source: Ammianus 31.3–4; detailed commentary with further refs.: Heather, 1991, ch. 4.

2 Valens' joy: Ammianus 31.4.4; Eunapius fr. 42; Socrates, *Ecclesiastical History* 4.34; Sozomen, *Ecclesiastical History* 6.37. Detailed commentary, with discussion of normal Roman immigration policy: Heather, 1991, 128–35.

imperial policy, but how it was justified in public. Justifying imperial policy in public, of course, brings us very much into the territory of Themistius, and Ammianus gives the following interesting report of how matters had proceeded in Antioch:

> when . . . foreign envoys . . . begged with prayers and protesta-tions that an exiled race [i.e. the Goths] might be received on our side of the river, the affair caused more joy than fear; and learned flatterers (*eruditis adulatoribus*) immoderately praised the good fortune of the prince, which had unexpectedly brought him so many young recruits from the ends of the earth . . . (Ammianus 31.3.4)

'Learned flatterers' brings Themistius immediately to mind: an accurate, if hostile, description of him. We also know that, just before travelling west in either 376 or 377, Themistius was indeed with Valens on the Persian front.[3] The arguments used – that the arrival of new recruits would assist state finances – also recalls the kinds of cost-benefit argu-mentation that Themistius had earlier used to justify Valens' negotiated withdrawal from the Gothic war of 367–9 in Orations 8 and 10.[4] If Ammianus' jibe was directed at Themistius, it is possible that he made some now lost public pronouncement when in Antioch justifying the admission of the Goths. Another oration which Themistius is known to have delivered at more or less the same time, in which his arguments for religious toleration within the Church seem to have signalled a change in Valens' religious policy, has likewise not survived.[5] This loss could merely be an accident of transmission, but could equally be a result of deliberate suppression. Themistius certainly began the process of collect-ing his own work himself, with the collection of speeches given to the library of Constantinople in 355/6 (see the introduction to Oration 1), and both of these orations might have looked ill-judged in the light of subsequent events, after Theodosius nailed his flag firmly to the Nicene mast, and the Goths had killed Valens and destroyed his army at Hadrianople in 378.

Be that as it may, Valens allowed the Tervingi of Alavivus and Friti-gern to cross the Danube, while the Greuthungi of Alatheus and

Saphrax were excluded by force. Food quickly grew short among the former, which, combined with a Roman assault upon their leadership at a banquet in Marcianople, sparked off a revolt. This gave the Greuthungi the opportunity to cross the Danube too, since the troops who had been excluding them were now turned towards the Tervingi, a sequence of events which does indeed suggest that there were only enough Roman troops in the area to restrain at best one of the Gothic groups at a time. The situation then ran rapidly out of Roman control as Gothic raiders, probably from both groups, spread in bands across the Balkan land-scape.[6] The revolt may have occurred early in 377 as Valens could still contemplate hiring Gothic mercenaries for war with Persia over Armenia in winter 376/7 (Ammianus 30.2.6). Faced with this threat, Valens needed to organise the withdrawal of his forces from Armenia, and began also to negotiate military assistance from the western Emperor Gratian, son of his recently dead (November 375) brother, Valentinian I.

Once again, Themistius turns up in an interesting context. In 376 or 377, he visited Rome, delivering Oration 13. Its date has been much discussed, but the speech does refer to the Goths as 'tame', which would more easily fit 376, when the Goths were negotiating for and receiving admission to the Empire, than 377, when the revolt occurred.[7] The speech itself is typically Themistian in theme, celebrating the extent to which Gratian fitted the Platonic ideal of model ruler. Much more inter-esting than its contents, however, is the basic fact of Themistius' presence in the west at such an important moment. As he himself makes clear in a passage heavy with allusion to Plato's *Symposium*, his westward journey from Syria had been unusually rapid and uncomfortable:

> . . . my course was almost equal to the course of the sun, from the Tigris to Ocean [= Atlantic; i.e. the west]; it was an urgent

6 Food shortages: Ammianus 31.8.1; banquet: 31.5; cf. Heather, 1991, 132–3 with further refs.; raiding: Ammianus 31.5.3–4 with Heather, 1991, 144–5.

7 *Or.* 13.166c, 238.23; cf. Vanderspoel, 1995, 180–2 with refs. A late and notoriously un-reliable Byzantine source records Gratian visiting Rome (*Breves enarrationes chronicon* 50, ed. Bonn, 178), but Ammianus does not mention it. Scholars have been more or less scepti-cal about a possible visit (respectively Cameron, A. D. E., 1969, 262–3 n. 28; Barnes, 1976b, 327–9), but if it did take place, or was intended, it was probably linked to Gratian's decen-nalia which fell in 377 (so Seeck, 1906, 303; Scholze, 1911, 48). This could have been cele-brated, as was ceremonially and financially convenient, anywhere in the few years either side of the actual event: Bagnall et al., 1987, 24.

journey, a flight over the surface of the earth, just as you [Socrates in the *Symposium* 203d] say Eros once hurried, with sleepless days following the nights. I lived my life on the road and under the open skies, sleeping on the ground and out of doors, with no bed to lie on and no shoes to put on . . . (*Or.* 13.163c).

Even given a large measure of humorous exaggeration of the discomforts he had endured *en route*, the pace of his journey to the west was rather more hectic than might have been expected had its sole purpose been to deliver a discourse to the Roman senate on Eros and Gratian's Platonic virtues. Given this intense rush, there must have been some very substantive point to the embassy, and the chronological context suggests that the most likely matter was the organisation of a joint imperial reaction to the Gothic problem which had suddenly appeared on Valens' Danubian doorstep. Some western troops, if admittedly not a whole field army, were already available for the campaigning season of 377 (see below), which would indicate that diplomatic contact had already been made in 376. In this context, Themistius' rapid journey westward, especially if he had indeed been involved in justifying imperial policy on the admission of the Goths (see above), seems highly significant. No doubt Themistius was not the only envoy, but his participation in such a critical mission provides a further indication of just how closely involved in Valens' regime Themistius actually was.[8]

The negotiations were a partial success. Western aid was forthcoming in the subsequent two years, but suspicions and jealousies hampered military cooperation and some westerners remained unconvinced that the Goths were their problem at all.[9] In 377, Valens managed to extract a limited force from the Persian front, which he sent to the Balkans under Traianus and Profuturus. They were reinforced by western troops – the fruits perhaps of Themistius' embassy – under Frigeridus and Richomeres. Between them, they drove the Goths north of the Haemus mountains, but then made the mistake (in Ammianus' analysis at least) of fighting the Gothic main body. The conflict, near *Oppidum Salices*, was a bloody draw, after which the Romans blockaded the passes of the Haemus, keeping the Goths to the north (Map p. 204). The blockade, mounted in autumn 377, was reasonably successful until

8  The appearance of western troops against the Goths in 377 may well provide a further reason for dating *Or.* 13 and Themistius' embassy to 376, therefore, rather than 377.

9  Especially Merobaudes: Ammianus 31.7.4.

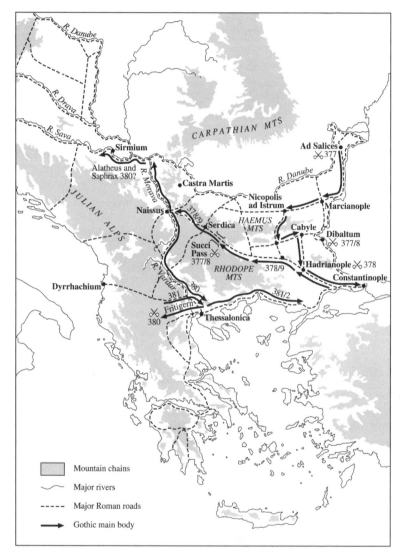

The Gothic War, 377–382

a force of Huns and Alans was recruited by promises of booty to join the Goths. In 378, the Romans tried again in larger numbers. Valens himself came to the Balkans, via Constantinople, with the bulk of his elite forces. At the same time, Gratian made ready to advance with his best troops. Unfortunately, he was held up by Alamannic raiding, which was ultimately successfully dealt with. This success, however, only made Valens both anxious and jealous, so that, when he received an intelligence report indicating that only part of the Gothic force was facing him, he decided to risk battle without Gratian's assistance. The subsequent engagement was a total disaster. All the Goths were present; Valens and two-thirds of his army fell in battle outside the city of Hadrianople on one day: 9 August 378.[10]

## THE GOTHIC WAR PART 2: ORATIONS 14–16 IN CONTEXT

Not surprisingly, a coherent Roman response to this disaster took time to emerge. Only on 19 January 379 was Theodosius, a soldier of Spanish origins with distinguished military ancestry and a successful career of his own, elevated by Gratian to the purple as emperor of the east. His appointment marked the opening of a second phase in the Gothic war, which lasted until peace was made on 3 October 382, and whose twists and turns also occasioned the three speeches translated in this chapter. Orations 14 and 15 were delivered in the course of it, and Oration 16 of January 383 devoted much space to the peace treaty which finally brought it to a close. To appreciate their full significance, Themistius' three speeches must, as always, be placed as precisely as possible in context.

Unfortunately, Ammianus' clear narrative of the Gothic war comes to an end shortly after the battle of Hadrianople. From that point on, we have to rely on Zosimus' summary of Eunapius, but rather more can be extracted from this than has usually been allowed.[11] From these sources, the following broad outline of events can be reconstructed. In the latter part of 378, after their great victory, the Goths spread across the Balkans, breaking out of Thrace, and reaching as far west even as the Julian Alps (Ammianus 31.16.7). In January 379, Theodosius was, as we

10 Ammianus 31.7–13; with commentary and further discussion in Heather, 1991, 143–7.
11 Most of the confusion has been caused by Zosimus having added a second source to the account of Eunapius at 4.34: Heather, 1991, 147ff., App. B; cf. Errington, 1996b, 15–16.

have seen, raised to the purple, and institutional arrangements, as well as the martial nature of Theodosius' previous career, make it clear that he was appointed to restore the military balance against the Goths. By this date, the latter had spilled into Illyricum, which traditionally belonged to Gratian's western Empire. On his accession, therefore, Theodosius was given control of all or part of Illyricum,[12] in addition to the eastern Balkans, Thrace, which had always formed part of the eastern Empire. The most obvious explanation of this ad hoc arrangement is that it was designed to allow him to exercise effective control of the entire war effort. At the end of 379, on 17 November, victories were formally announced over Huns, Goths, and Alans, but no further major battle had yet occurred. The Goths, it seems, abandoned Thrace entirely in 379, perhaps because of the counterattacks of a renegade Gothic general in the imperial army, Modares, which may have provided the basis for these victory announcements. The sources, such as they are, seem to indicate that the Goths wintered in Upper Moesia (Zosimus 4.25; cf. Map p. 204). Throughout 379, as we shall see, Theodosius was pre-occupied with rebuilding the eastern army that had been destroyed at Hadrianople.[13]

In 380, Theodosius committed his new army to battle. The Goths raided in two directions in this year. Alatheus and Saphrax with the Greuthungi attacked into Pannonia, while Fritigern and the Tervingi moved south into Macedonia. Much of the subsequent action is uncertain. Alatheus and Saphrax appear to have been defeated by the western forces of the Emperor Gratian, but the conventional view that he then made a separate peace treaty by which they were settled *en masse* in Pannonia seems unfounded.[14] Fritigern, on the other hand, marched south to inflict a major defeat upon Theodosius' new model army in Macedonia. Zosimus' history is too vague to provide any details, but his account of Roman military collapse (4.31.3–5) is confirmed by subsequent events. Early in September 380 Theodosius rushed to Sirmium in

12  The scholarly consensus is for East Illyricum, esp. Moesia and Macedonia (but not Pannonia and Dalmatia): Grumel, 1951, based on Sozomen, *Ecclesiastical History* 4.1–2. For the suggestion on the basis of Sidonius, *Poems* 5.107, that it was the whole diocese, see Errington, 1996b, 23–6. Gratian's forces continued to operate in Pannonia (see below), making Sozomen's account seemingly preferable, but this could have been in spite of the formal institutional arrangements.

13  For details, see the introduction to *Or.* 14.

14  Heather, 1991, App. B: this remains controversial.

Pannonia for a summit meeting, perhaps with Gratian himself, but certainly his generals.[15] The decisions taken were far-reaching. Conduct of the war now passed from Theodosius to Gratian and his generals, and Illyricum returned to western control. Theodosius himself, reportedly after a bout of illness, left his base in Thessalonica for Constantinople which he entered on 24 November 380. He arrived at his new capital, however, without having achieved either of his war aims. He had failed to remove the Goths from Illyricum (this would be achieved the next year by Gratian's troops) and the army he had put together during 379 had proved incapable of standing up to the Goths in battle.

After 380, information becomes even more sparse. In the campaigning season of 381, two of Gratian's generals, Bauto and Arbogast, drove the Goths out of Illyricum and back into Thrace (Zosimus 4.33.1–2). At that point, if not before, negotiations began. Peace was eventually declared between the Empire and the Goths on 3 October 382, after no doubt lengthy negotiations, conducted on the Roman side by Saturninus and Richomeres.

There is obviously much more that one would like to know about this second phase of the Gothic war between Theodosius' accession in 379 and its conclusion in 382. Enough is known, however, to situate the three speeches of Themistius translated in this chapter fairly precisely. Oration 14, given at the latest in early summer 379, belongs to the period when Theodosius was in Thessalonica and attempting to rebuild the shattered armies of the east. Oration 15 was given in January 381, after the major defeat which had caused Theodosius to hand control of the war back to Gratian's commanders. Oration 16 was delivered on 1 January 383, after the successful conclusion of the peace, to celebrate the consulship of one of the peacemakers, Fl. Saturninus. Changes of tone between the three speeches can thus be placed firmly against the backdrop provided by the shifting fortunes of war. Taken together, they shed significant light on the development of policy towards the Goths, on Theodosius' evolving relations with Gratian, and, indeed, upon how Themistius himself manoeuvred in these years. Valens' death had left Themistius once more adrift, bereft of yet another imperial patron; once again, he had to come to terms with a new imperial regime.

---

15 An important passage in *Or.* 15 suggests that this might have been with Gratian himself; see the introduction to this speech below.

## THEMISTIUS, THEODOSIUS, AND THE EAST

Already in his first speech for Theodosius, Oration 14, probably delivered in spring or early summer 379, Themistius deployed some of the techniques which had marked his successful transfer between regimes on earlier occasions.[16] Despite the closeness of their past association, for instance, Themistius was quick to damn Valens by implication as a man lacking in mildness and 'love of mankind' (*philanthropia*), very much as he had earlier damned Constantius II once Valens had come to the throne.[17] This, of course, had the great benefit of implying that life was now much better under the new regime. As we shall see in more detail below, Oration 14 also began the process of persuading eastern land-owning opinion that, although appointed by Gratian and hence his junior in the imperial college, Theodosius was in reality the senior of the two. Orations 15 and 16, of 19 January 381 and 1 January 383 respectively, saw these themes come to maturity. Space was devoted to the denigration of past regimes (with all of which Themistius had been closely associated) in order to celebrate the present one and assist in its establishment. What had been a victory for Jovian over the Persians in Oration 5 became an abandonment of Mesopotamia to be rectified in Oration 16 (213a). Comparison concentrated, however, upon the regime of Valens. Stress was placed in both Orations 15 and 16 on the claim that the imperial office should be the culmination of a properly progressive career in public life. This was entirely aimed at the memory of Valens, whose relative inexperience Themistius had found ways to praise at the time, not least, as we have seen, in Oration 6 (see Chapter 3), but which could now be used to point Theodosius' virtues as a much more suitable occupant of the imperial throne. As Themistius further developed the argument, it was precisely Valens' inexperience which led him into a whole series of mistakes, all of which Theodosius avoided.[18]

The public denigration of past employers signalled, of course, the

16 It has recently been suggested that Themistius was not yet an insider when he delivered *Or.* 14: Errington, 1996b, 8–9. We are unconvinced; see the introduction to *Or.* 14 below.

17 *Or.* 14.183b; cf. the introduction to Chapter 3 on Constantius, and Chapter 1 on general Themistian technique.

18 See *Or.* 15. esp. 196b–197a; *Or.* 16. esp. 205d–206c, 212c–d with the fuller discussion in the introduction to *Or.* 15. Themistius' posthumous treatment of Valens must be compared to those from the emperor's lifetime, which made virtue of the emperor's relative inexperience: e.g., Chapter 3, or *Orr.* 8 and 10 trans. in Heather and Matthews, 1991, ch. 2. Themis-

transfer of Themistius' loyalties to a new one, and, as in the past, the orator took every opportunity to underline his standing within the new regime. In Oration 15, he emphasised that he was speaking at Theodosius' personal command (192c), reminded the audience that he had kept company with a multiplicity of emperors (198a), and, in a lengthy passage, equated himself with the poet Tyrtaeus, whom the Athenians had sent to the Spartans to put fight back into them (197cff.). Oration 16, likewise, left the listener in no doubt as to Themistius' current importance. It emphasised that both the new Consul, Saturninus, and the Emperor Theodosius himself had omitted nothing that would advance his honour (200b), the same passage also happening to refer to the amount of time Themistius had spent as an insider to a succession of imperial regimes. Striking too is the end of the speech, where Themistius returned to Theodosius' son Arcadius, portraying himself as the boy's guardian and educator (213a–b).[19]

Like Orations 5 and 6, Themistius' first speeches for Jovian and Valens, these later speeches to Theodosius do not provide much insight into the more private negotiations by which the orator's transfer of allegiance to a new regime was actually effected. For Themistius, the gains were obvious. As a man without formal office – and of course, in order for Themistius to preserve his façade of philosophical independence he had to remain so – his continued influence depended entirely upon selling his services on a more informal basis to incoming regimes. The perhaps less obvious benefit to Theodosius from the relationship were alluded to in Oration 15 (185a):

> But since I am able to contribute words that are more peaceful than Homer's, or more regal than Hesiod's, why shall my voice have been shut out of the great hall [of the palace], and would ‹anyone› not permit me, according to my custom, to cull virgin blooms from the meadows of Plato and Aristotle, which no blade has touched, and to weave crowns of human happiness for the king?

As before, Themistius continued to present himself as the guardian of traditional *paideia*, and his incorporation allowed Theodosius, like

---

tius' insistence on Valens' inexperience, even during that emperor's lifetime, suggests that the ingenious attempts of Woods, 1998, to find a career for him are misplaced.

19  Similar statements about the sons of Jovian and Valens, see *Or.* 5 (above Chapter 3) and *Or.* 8 trans. in Heather and Matthews, 1991, ch. 2.

previous emperors, to claim to be operating within boundaries defined by traditional Hellenic culture. In Theodosius' case, this was of particular value, because the new emperor was at the same time publicly declaring a powerful Christian allegiance. He was the first emperor to renounce the old pagan imperial title of Pontifex Maximus, and had done so at the moment of his accession in January 379.[20] This was followed in Febuary 380 by a clear statement of how Christian orthodoxy was to be defined, and a major council of eastern bishops in Constantinople in May 381.[21] While previous emperors had also defined orthodoxy and convened councils, the rejection of the ancient pontifical robes was an act of huge symbolic importance, which represented a fundamental break with the past. No doubt it was designed to establish Theodosius' religious credentials, and win over influential Christians to his cause. It ran the risk, however, of alienating traditionally minded non-Christians among the elites of the east, of whom there were still many. An accommodation with Themistius, the symbol of traditional culture, thus allowed Theodosius to establish some kind of a balanced ideological profile for his reign.[22]

Theodosius also adopted many other energetic measures to make the east governable. Oration 14, as we shall see, sheds some light on the very widespread distribution of patronage which marked the first year of Theodosius' government, and which was crucial for the new regime in attracting support from among eastern landowners. Orations 15 and 16, by contrast, do not belong to the frantic politicking of the early days of the reign, but their on-going critique of the government of Valens did have the more particular purpose of cultivating one group of natural Theodosian supporters: all those who had lost out under Valens. Particularly in the aftermath of the attempted usurpation of Procopius in 365, and again in the magic-cum-treason trials of the early 370s, Valens had cut a considerable swathe through sections of the elite classes of the east.[23] These families formed a natural group of potential supporters for the new regime, whom Theodosius carefully cultivated by reversing some of his predecessors' policies and decisions. In particular, Theodo-

---

20 Cameron, A. D. E., 1969.
21 *C.Th.* 16.1.2 (*cunctos populos*). For the council, see Ritter, 1965 and further comment below.
22 On all this, see further Chapter 1.
23 Matthews, 1989, chs 9–10.

sius returned part of the lands of condemned individuals to their relatives, legislation which lies behind the oft-quoted *cause célèbre* of some
Galatian youths rescued from poverty.[24] Constantine had done much
the same after taking over the east from Licinius, and this general
strategy perhaps sheds some further light on Theodosius' Church
policy. As has recently been argued, Theodosius was not the totally
committed, doctrinally rigid supporter of Nicaea that later hagiography
liked to pretend. He did eventually opt for a Nicene Church settlement,
but only after much hesitation. It is far from impossible that much of
the original attraction for Theodosius of Ascholius of Thessalonica,
Meletius of Antioch and other eastern supporters of Nicaea was
precisely the fact that they had not been part of Valens 'imperial
church'. Like their secular counterparts who also received the new
emperor's patronage, they were losers who would make particularly
grateful supporters.[25]

Looked at closely, therefore, Orations 14 to 16 tell us much both
about how Theodosius set about establishing himself in the east, and
how Themistius sold his services to Theodosius. One further major
internal political theme runs through them: relations between Theodosius and his western colleague, the Emperor Gratian. Before discussing
this question, however, it is important to consider the subject common
to all three, and for which historians have usually explored them: the
Gothic war and the evolution of imperial policy towards the Goths.

## THE EVOLUTION OF IMPERIAL POLICY

For the campaign of 378 which ended so disastrously at Hadrianople, the
Roman Empire had mobilised two emperors and the elite field armies of
both east and west. The intended aim was clearly to reverse the military
imbalance which had denied Valens any real choice over whether to
admit Goths into the Empire in 376 (see above). The campaign's precise
aims are not recorded, but any subdued Goths subsequently left on
Roman territory would probably have been subject to resettlement on
Roman terms: broken up into small groups and dispersed widely over

24  *C.Th.* 9.42.8–9 with *Or.* 15.194c–d and *Or.* 16.212d; cf. Vanderspoel, 1995, 202–3.

25  Constantine: Heather, 1994. Church policy: McLynn, 1994, 108–9, offering a different
suggestion. The most recent discussion of this controversial and complex subject is Lizzi,
1996.

the Empire to minimise future risk of revolt.[26] As we have seen, Theodosius' initial remit was still, it seems, to win at least some kind of military victory; in 379 he rebuilt the eastern army, and in 380 risked it in battle. By October 382, however, the Empire was ready to make a peace treaty which, within limits, broadly recognised the Goths' right to an autonomous existence on Roman soil.[27] Policy had obviously changed in the meantime, and the tone and contents of Themistius' orations from the war years prompt some thoughts on when and how it had evolved.

Oration 15, probably delivered on 19 January 381, suggests that policy may have begun to change as early as winter 380/1. In Oration 14 of early summer 379, Themistius' tone had been entirely martial, hailing Theodosius as the man who would win the Gothic war. Oration 15 was strikingly different. For one thing, Themistius now claimed that an emperor's main job was good civilian government, and that being a good general was merely an optional extra for the job. More particularly, some eight days before the speech was delivered, Theodosius had received into Constantinople the Gothic king Athanaric who, probably old and ill (he died on 25 January), had finally been ousted by the rump of Tervingi who had not abandoned him in 376. Themistius mentions Athanaric's arrival in Oration 15, in what looks like a late insert to an already existing speech, and his commentary on this event was very striking. Themistius' overall conclusion was that Athanaric's arrival in Constantinople showed that enemies were more effectively subdued by persuasion than by force (190c–191a). This was a brief rehearsal of the line of argument which Themistius would deploy at much greater length in Oration 16 to justify the 382 peace agreement with all the Goths. Its appearance at such an important point in Oration 15 suggests very firmly that a fundamental change in Gothic policy – from outright victory to negotiated peace – was already being contemplated within Theodosius' regime by the beginning of 381.[28]

Indeed, the basic conditions which pushed Theodosius and his advisors towards a negotiated peace did already apply. Valens' army had been destroyed by the Goths at Hadrianople in 378, that of Theodosius

---

26  See further Heather, 1991, 165ff.; cf. the treatment of Farnobius' force defeated in 377: Ammianus 31.9.4.

27  See the introduction to *Or.* 16 below.

28  Insert: Errington, 1996b, 11–14, with further commentary in the introduction to *Or.* 15 below.

had just collapsed in the campaigning season of 380. It was almost certainly this second setback which made some kind of compromise necessary, and so much would already have been clear by January 381. This being so, it was necessary for the regime to begin the far from easy task of preparing opinion among the politically important landowning classes of the Empire for the idea that a negotiated peace might be the outcome to the war. Ideologically, the Graeco-Roman elite were brought up to assume their superiority over 'barbarians'. The chief virtue expected of emperors was, as we have seen, victory: the expression of this superiority. Especially given the martial fanfare with which he was greeted on ascending the throne, reflected in Oration 14, Theodosius had to prepare his public carefully for the news that, in this case, victory was going to give way to compromise. Themistius, it would seem, began the task as early as January 381. As we shall see, the contents of Oration 16 make it clear that the process of persuasion was still continuing some two years later.

## GRATIAN AND THEODOSIUS

A theme of equal importance, likewise running through all three orations, is the developing relationship of Themistius' new employer, the Emperor Theodosius, with Gratian in the west. The dynamics of this relationship were interesting from the start. Gratian was senior emperor and had been responsible, of course, for elevating Theodosius to the purple in the first place. On the other hand, Theodosius was significantly the elder of the two (about 33 to Gratian's 20 years in 379), and had behind him a successful career in the army, whereas Gratian had been made Augustus at the age of eight, simply because he was the son of the then reigning emperor, Valentinian I. Gratian had never himself held any administrative office. Themistius' comments on relations between the two emperors varied in length and tone according to the extent of Theodosius' current need of Gratian's support. Even when paying Gratian the maximum amount of respect, however, Themistius always at least hinted that, despite the legal formalities of the imperial college, his employer – Theodosius – was really the senior partner.

   Oration 14, delivered shortly after Theodosius' promotion, main-tained a careful balancing act. Themistius argued that Theodosius' over-whelming virtues made him the only possible imperial candidate: 'your virtue made you emperor . . . Gratian . . . proclaimed you' (182c–d). At the same time, Gratian was given great praise for not having picked a relation, and for having shown judgement worthy of a much older man in spotting Theodosius' qualities (182b–183a). Stressing Theodosius' virtues and fitness for office reduced, by implication, the need to praise Gratian overmuch simply for choosing the 'obvious' man for the job, and asserted Theodosius' right to act independently. Nonetheless, the speech gave Gratian a reasonable amount of credit. Oration 15 treated relations between the two men in greater detail. By and large, it presented them as equal partners in war and peace, proclaiming them rivals only in doing good, so that a single civilised order extended all the way from the Atlantic to the Tigris (198b; cf. 194dff.). The speech's emphasis on the importance to an emperor of proper experience, directed as we shall see primarily at Valens, also carried the implication that Theodosius should be seen in practice as the senior of the partners, but this was very muted.[29] By the time Oration 16 was delivered, however, some two years later, Themistius' demotion of Gratian was complete. The speech mentions him not at all in its account of the Gothic war and subsequent peace. The theme of more or less equal and active imperial partnership had disappeared. The only mention of the western emperor was a further brief reference to Theodosius' promotion, where Gratian's role was reduced to the minimum. Not even lip service was paid to Gratian's good sense in picking such an able colleague; in Oration 16, he was portrayed merely as God's herald, proclaiming a decision made in heaven (207b). By 1 January 383, therefore, no public deference was being offered to Gratian at all in a major consular ceremony in the Senate of Constantinople. This was no accident. Only 18 days after Oration 16 was delivered, Theodosius promoted his own son Arcadius to the purple, entirely without Gratian's approval. In an important sense, Themistius' account in Oration 16 of Theodosius' own promotion prepared the ground for this act. If God had chosen Theodosius directly, then clearly the future of the Empire was in his hands, and he was free to act as he thought best to secure its prosperity.[30]

The new eastern emperor was even more assertive in Church affairs. Valens' death had left an ambiguous situation in the east. For much of his reign, Valens had sponsored a non-Nicene Church settlement, which encompassed a majority of eastern churchmen, but there had been a

29  See the introduction to *Or.* 15 below.
30  For fuller discussion, see the introduction to *Or.* 16.

vocal minority opposition, and perhaps in response to the advent of the Gothic problem, Valens had, in winter 375/6, recalled exiled supporters of Nicaea. Immediately after Hadrianople, Gratian granted an edict of toleration for the east, allowing most Christian groups equality and freedom. In February 380, however, Theodosius issued his famous decree in favour of a pro-Nicene Church settlement (*cunctos populos*: *C.Th.* 16.1.2). This was a deliberate break with Gratian's policies. At Sirmium in the summer of 380, Gratian called a general council of eastern and western churchmen to meet at Aquileia the following September. Theodosius originally agreed to this, but then, in May 381, held his own council in Constantinople. Late in 381, Gratian tried again to sponsor a general Church settlement, this time at the suggestion of Ambrose of Milan. He called for a further general council in Rome for 382, but Theodosius again snubbed his senior colleague. Only three eastern observers turned up, carefully shepherded by imperial officials.[31]

On the religious front, therefore, Theodosius consistently asserted his independence, in the same way that Oration 16 shows him to have been doing in secular affairs by January 383. Indeed, as early as summer 379, Oration 14 presents Theodosius as in no sense junior to Gratian. It seems likely, therefore that the project announced in Oration 14, and carried out subsequently in both senatorial and religious spheres, of turning Constantinople into the equal of Rome was another expression of the same determination to assert independence. Against this background, it is the less aggressive Oration 15 which stands out as abnormal, with its much more respectful presentation of Gratian as Theodosius' more or less equal partner. Its context explains the anomaly. It was delivered after Theodosius' military disasters in the summer of 380 and the summit meeting either with Gratian himself or his generals. This surely explains the speech's more conciliatory mood. At that moment, when he handed back control of the war, Theodosius needed Gratian's assistance more than at any other point since January 379. This surely also explains why Theodosius was initially receptive to Gratian's idea, aired at Sirmium and quite likely in the context of the Gothic war summit meeting, for a joint Church council of east and west. Desperate for western military assistance, Theodosius had no choice but to tread carefully.

Placed in context, therefore, the three orations faithfully reflect the

31 McLynn, 1994, 123–5, 137–45.

determined assertion of independence which Theodosius is documented to have shown in other areas, particularly Church matters. Once again, Themistius' words faithfully served the interests of his current imperial master, waxing more and less lyrical upon Gratian according to Theodosius' need of his western colleague, until the end of the Gothic war removed any further need for western assistance. This prompts one final thought about the decision to end the Gothic war through a negotiated peace. As we have seen, it was a decision largely generated by the, from a Roman point of view, disappointing progress of the war. Relations between Theodosius and Gratian suggest, however, a further dimension to the decision. Theodosius was generally assertive of his independence in all fields, but was forced to restrain this for as long as he still required western military assistance. A further factor in his promotion of a negotiated peace, therefore, may have been a desire to liberate himself from military dependence upon Gratian.

## THEMISTIUS AND THE GOTHS

One last matter relevant to all three orations as a group is worth some attention. Oration 16 argues firmly that Theodosius was entirely correct to make peace with the Goths through persuasion, rather than trying to bring about their destruction by force. The argument here was very similar to that deployed earlier by Themistius in Oration 10, given in 370 for Valens, which likewise argued the case for a peaceful solution to an earlier Gothic problem. From these two speeches, it has often been concluded that Themistius had a consistent, lifelong commitment to more peaceful solutions to foreign policy problems.[32] Read as a group, however, against the changing contexts in which they were composed, Orations 14 to 16 suggest a somewhat different conclusion.

In Oration 14, for instance, delivered when Theodosius was at Thessalonica and rebuilding the eastern army in 379, there was not the slightest sign of Themistius advocating any kind of conciliatory approach to the Gothic problem. The speech celebrated Theodosius as an effective general who would put new fight into the Romans and punish the Goths. This presentation was certainly dictated by the emperor's current propaganda needs, but Themistius had no qualms about

---

32  Oration 10 is translated in Heather and Matthews, 1991, ch. 2. Themistius' devotion to peace: Dagron, 1968, 95ff.; Daly, 1972; Vanderspoel, 1995, 168–76 with n. 70, 205–7.

doing the job his employer required. The same conclusion holds true of
Orations 15 and 16. Oration 15, of January 381, was not entirely pacifist
in tone, paying lip service to hopes of defeating the Goths in the coming
campaigning season. Its central argument made the case, however, that
the real job of an emperor was not military campaigning, but ensuring
good civilian government. It combined this with a striking treatment of
the arrival in Constantinople of the former Gothic king Athanaric,
which, as we have seen, seems to indicate that imperial policy was
already contemplating a negotiated peace as the best solution to the
Gothic problem. All of this reflected Theodosius' needs, not Themistius'
opinion. Switching attention to the civilian aspects of the imperial office
diverted attention from Theodosius' embarrassing defeat at the hands
of the Goths in the summer of 380, which had led to him handing back
control of the war to Gratian. At the same time, public opinion had to
be prepared for something less than the total defeat of the Goths. The
regime required a fresh image, and Themistius duly obliged, turning
Theodosius from the general who could win the Gothic war into the
preserver of good civilian government. To suppose that Oration 15
presents more of the real Themistius than Oration 14 is thus entirely arbi-
trary. The contents of both orations were fundamentally dictated by
Theodosius' changing needs.

It is not enough, therefore, to read Oration 16 in isolation, or link it
to Oration 10, and conclude that these speeches contain personal statements from Themistius' heart. Placed in context, these two speeches
can be seen likewise to have reflected closely the current requirements
of the orator's imperial masters. Oration 10 was required to put a
cheerful gloss on a set of campaigns which had not achieved the total
military domination over the Goths contemplated at their outset.[33] By
the time Oration 16 was delivered, Theodosius had had to make a
compromise peace with the Goths, and, once again, Themistius stepped
into the breach with a ready justification. To conclude that this had
always been Themistius' preferred option is to miss the closeness with
which his speeches echoed the requirements of the moment. Indeed, in
Oration 16 Themistius, for the only time, came close to admitting that
imperial policy had been dictated by circumstances beyond immediate
control:

33 Heather and Matthews, 1991, ch. 2.

> For just suppose that this destruction [of the Goths] was an easy
> matter and that we possessed the means to accomplish it without
> suffering any consequences, although from past experience this
> was neither a foregone nor a likely conclusion . . . (211a)

Themistius may have preferred peace, but, just as imperial policy was
dictated by circumstance, so were his efforts to justify it. As it changed,
so did his justifications. That is the underlying thread of continuity, not
'a lifelong commitment to peace'.[34]

## ORATION 14
## EMBASSY TO THE EMPEROR THEODOSIUS:
## INTRODUCTION

Oration 14 cannot be dated exactly, but the general circumstances of its
delivery are clear enough. Themistius' first speech to the Emperor Theodosius, it was not delivered in the immediate aftermath of his election to
the purple on 19 January 379. As the opening of the speech reports,
Themistius had been forced to remain in Constantinople by illness,
while an initial senatorial embassy had travelled to Thessalonica to
convey the city's congratulations to the new emperor. He nonetheless
came as an ambassador, as the title of the speech makes clear, a delayed
member of the original mission. The speech's contents refer to the gift of
Crown Gold that was customary from each city on an imperial accession,
and which the original mission had brought; the speech Themistius
framed was also much shorter than his norm, in line with Menander
Rhetor's advice for oratory on such occasions.[35] In addition, the speech
also noted that Theodosius had not yet taken the field against the Goths
(181c), although he was engaged in reconstructing his army. All of this
suggests that it was delivered in late spring or early summer 379, before
the year's campaigning season had got into full swing.[36] Given this
general context, the three major themes addressed by the speech are
what one might expect: Theodosius' promotion, his relations with his
new subjects, and the progress of the war against the Goths.

---

34 The words of Vanderspoel, 1995, 176. Note too the passing denigration at *Or.* 16.213a
of the effects of Jovian's Persian peace, which in *Or.* 5 Themistius had hailed, if not without
embarrassment, as a victory (see Chapter 3).

35 See the introduction to *Or.* 3 in Chapter 2.

36 The general scholarly opinion: see Vanderspoel, 1995, 195–6 for refs.

With regard to Theodosius' promotion, neither the sequence of events, nor its political significance are fully understood – largely because Ammianus brought his narrative (deliberately, as it seems) to an end in the autumn of 378[37] – and Oration 14 does not explore them in detail. In part, this was surely deliberate. The new emperor's father, a senior general (*Magister Equitum*) also called Theodosius, had only recently been killed in mysterious circumstances, in the political shake-up which followed the death of Valentinian I in November 375. These events had also prompted the younger Theodosius to retire from the army and return to his estates in Spain. Silence on these matters on Themistius' part was only politic. Eventually, however, the Gothic crisis prompted the younger Theodosius' recall to active duty. He probably began as military commander on the Middle Danube (*dux Moesiae*), where he won further victories over the Sarmatians, to add to those he had previously achieved in 374/5. This success (duly noted by Themistius: 182c) prompted further promotions, first to *Magister Equitum*, and then to imperial power over the east. Following the account of Theodoret (*Ecclesiastical History* 5.5–6), the recall is usually dated after Hadrianople in August 378, but this leaves little time for Theodosius' victory and two subsequent promotions. As has recently been argued, therefore, it is at least as likely that the recall came earlier, in either 376 or 377.[38]

The nature of the discussions which led to Theodosius' imperial promotion is also uncertain. A second emperor already existed in the aftermath of Hadrianople in the person of Gratian's half-brother Valentinian II. This has led some scholars to argue that, since there was thus no need for a further imperial promotion, Theodosius must have been

---

37  Cf. Ammianus 31.16.9: the historian – reasonably – considered that the rule of a reigning emperor (as Theodosius still was when Ammianus wrote) could only be addressed by panegyric; the truthfulness demanded by history was likely to conflict with political expediency.

38  Traditional dating: e.g., Matthews, 1975, 91–2. Earlier date: most recently Errington 1996a, based primarily on chronological indications in Pacatus, *Panegyrici Latini* 2.10.2. An earlier date is conceivable since the court faction probably responsible for the death of Theodosius' father had itself fallen from power by summer 376 (see following note). On the other hand, the Sarmatians were long-standing imperial clients (Ammianus 17.12.15), so that Theodosius' victory over them was probably not a very hard fought one and the chronological indications in Pacatus are not conclusive. The traditional date thus remains far from impossible.

forced upon Gratian in some way.[39] Valentinian II was still only eight years old in 378/9, however, and could hardly have made an effective emperor to deal with the deep crisis left by the military disaster at Hadrianople. It is likely enough, therefore, that there was general consensus on the need to provide an effective, adult emperor for the east. The workings of factional politics – processes evidenced in the recent past in the better-documented negotiations which led to the choice in quick succession of Jovian and Valentinian – then saw Theodosius emerge as the candidate enjoying a critical mass of support in the higher reaches of civilian and military office holders. Whether the particular choice of Theodosius was more or less welcome to Gratian than any other potential choice is, given the state of the evidence, impossible to say.[40]

If Oration 14 fails to shed any light on these deep matters, Themistius was concerned to stress, in his account of Theodosius' promotion, that relations between the two emperors remained excellent. The recent history of the Empire meant that its inhabitants could not but be worried when faced by its division between more than one reigning emperor. The partnership of the brothers Valentinian and Valens was an entirely exceptional interlude of harmony in a long post-Tetrarchic history of rivalry and bloodshed.[41] And, in the longer term, as we have seen, Theodosius was indeed to be highly assertive of his political independence, and would push his own dynastic interests to the point of causing a break with Gratian over the unilateral appointment of Arcadius as Augustus in January 383. In Oration 14, however, only the merest hints of possible future tension are apparent. The speech did stress that Theodosius' virtues more or less demanded his promotion to

39 E.g., Vanderspoel, 1995, 187–95 with refs. Tension between Gratian and Theodosius has sometimes also been traced back to the assassination of the elder Theodosius. But the most likely culprits were the clique of Pannonians around Maximinus, who were all executed early in 376. It is thus unclear that Theodosius would have blamed Gratian for his father's death: Errington, 1996b, with refs. Sivan, 1993, 121, finds a further sign of resentment in the total silence about Theodosius' elevation in Ausonius' thanksgiving to Gratian for his consulship, but an argument from silence can rarely be conclusive.

40 See generally Matthews, 1971, locating the choice among senior office holders around Gratian's court. Sivan, 1993, 121, argues, against Matthews, that the key players must have been the eastern army, but this had been smashed at Hadrianople, and both military and civilian opinion will probably have been involved (as it was in the cases of Jovian and Valentinian: see Chapter 3).

41 See, in more detail, the introduction to Or. 6.

the purple, and underlined the point that the new emperor was actually older than Gratian who appointed him. For experienced consistory-watchers, this was probably a sufficient hint that Theodosius was too assertive of his rights to be willing to be seen as Gratian's junior, but, in the summer of 379, Theodosius was clearly not yet ready to give full vent to latent dynastic ambitions.[42]

Moving on to its second theme, Oration 14 also reflected at least one of the string of measures Theodosius brought into play to make the east governable: the generation of political loyalty among its constituent landowning elites. When he came to the throne, Theodosius was a distinguished general of western origins, who had never, so far as we know, even served in the east. In January 379, although his elevation was no doubt the result of much jockeying at court, Theodosius was starting essentially from scratch to govern the east.[43] A hostile account of the political activity this situation required can be found in Zosimus' picture (derived from Eunapius) of the early days of the reign. Great streams of people rushed to Thessalonica from all over the east, we are told in one passage, and all received favourable replies to their requests (4.25.1). In another passage, this huge generosity caused such an impoverishment of the imperial fisc that it became necessary to sell official positions to the highest bidders (4.28.1–4). Though deeply hostile, these passages capture something of the process of regime-building. On the one hand, important men wanting favours were themselves courted by Theodosius with gifts of money, title, and privilege. On the other, those wanting to carve out their own niches in the imperial administrative hierarchy came to court the emperor. However badly managed it may have been, this kind of political auction was unavoidable at the start of a reign which, because of the circumstances of Valens' death, could draw on no elements of continuity from the past.[44]

42  For full discussion, see the introduction to this chapter.

43  Vanderspoel, 1995, 191–5, unconvincingly argues that Theodosius had already started to create an eastern powerbase in late 378, visiting Constantinople in November. This is based on an obviously misdated reference in the *Chronicon Paschale* to Theodosius' first entry to the city (put in November 378 instead of November 380) in a passage which misdates other major events such as the death of Valentinian I (trans. Whitby and Whitby, 49 with nn.), and a forced reading of Themistius *Or.* 14.182a–b.

44  Constantine had similarly solved the same problem after 325: Heather, 1994. Ammianus similarly comments that the start of a reign was the perfect opportunity to press dubious claims before the regime had any real knowledge from which to judge their validity (30.9.3).

Oration 14 provided another vision of this activity, portraying it, of course, from a much less hostile perspective. It closed, indeed, with the plea that Theodosius should rival Constantine in his attentions to his new capital city, and in particular that he should make it an equal second Rome, not only in terms of its buildings, but also in its honours, by which Themistius specifically meant the numbers of its senators (183a–184a). As with most Themistian pleas, we find in the rest of the speech that Theodosius had already started implementing the recommended policy before Themistius spoke, having previously made some new senatorial appointments (183c; cf. Chapter 1 on pleas in general). Theodosius was probably using Themistius, therefore, to make the pronouncement that he was willing to increase eastern senatorial numbers until they were equal to those of the Senate of Rome itself. If such a view of the matter is correct, this would mean, interestingly enough, that Theodosius was here deploying a secular counterpart to the strategy he is well known for having employed in Church matters. For canon 3 of the ecclesiastical council Theodosius convened at Constantinople in May 381 formally declared the Patriarch of Constantinople to be the equal of the Bishop of Rome, and above all other patriarchs, because he ruled the Church in the city of New Rome. Themistius' evidence would suggest, therefore, that Theodosius wooed the east by offering its elites, secular and ecclesiastical, total formal equality with their western counterparts. The title of 'Senator of Constantinople' was clearly one of the major boons Theodosius was ready to dispense to the petitioners besieging him at Thessalonica.[45]

The speech's third major theme likewise went straight to the heart of the concerns of Theodosius' regime in these first few months of its existence: the Gothic war. In practical terms, the new emperor was faced with the problem of rebuilding the eastern field army which had been destroyed at Hadrianople. Themistius portrayed him recruiting and training peasants while encouraging the miners to produce more iron for military equipment. Other sources record that he also at this time recruited barbarians and transferred existing army units to the Balkans

---

McLynn, 1994, 107, suggests that *C. Th.* 10.10.12–15, dealing with vacant property, reflects such petitions. Libanius mentions two of his acquaintances who petitioned Theodosius: *Or.* 1.186, 196.

45 Constantine had originally founded the Senate of Constantinople for similar reasons: see further Heather, 1994.

from the east, while the law codes confirm his general recruiting activities, and contain further measures against deserters and to enlist the sons of veterans.[46] The overall message of this section of the speech, moreover, was very straightforward. Theodosius was a general of proven quality (esp. 181c) who had been made emperor to defeat the Goths. Themistius expressed this thought in a host of ways. In his opening paragraph, he hailed Theodosius with an epithet used by Homer of Ares, the God of war (180d). Just Theodosius' presence, he noted, was already enough to slow down the barbarians, and make the Romans recover their fighting spirit (181a–182a). Constantinople was preparing a victory crown for the emperor, to go with the crown of gold owed to him for his coronation (181d). The whole tone is nicely encapsulated in Themistius' vision of Theodosius ready for battle:

> What do we suppose those damned villains [i.e., the Goths] will suffer, when they see you raising your spear and brandishing your shield, the lightning flash from your gleaming helm close at hand (181c)?

The enthusiastic martial vigour of Oration 14 from spring or early summer 379 thus stands in marked contrast to the much more conciliatory tone towards the Goths that Themistius adopted in Orations 15 and 16 of respectively January 381 and January 383.

In the introduction to this chapter, we argued the case for supposing that the different tones reflect a major change of policy on the part of Theodosius, to which Themistius' speeches can be taken as an accurate guide. An alternative explanation, recently proposed by Malcolm Errington, is that Themistius was still unaware, in early summer 379, of how the new emperor was aiming to tackle the Gothic problem. The orator was still a political outsider at this point, Errington argues, and Oration 14, delivered at Thessalonica, should be seen as different in kind from Themistius' other speeches, being much more private in nature. Making his initial approach to Theodosius, Themistius had to guess what the emperor would do. In these circumstances, and faced with the rampant Goths, Themistius naturally resorted to a conventional account of Theodosius' martial prowess. The subsequent change of tone

---

46 Recruits: *C.Th.* 7.13.8–11; deserters: *C.Th.* 7.18.3, 5; sons of veterans: *C.Th.* 7.22.9–11; transfers: Zosimus 4.30–1. On all this, see, e.g., Hoffman, 1969, 460ff.; Errington, 1996b, 6–7.

in Orations 15 and 16 reflects the process by which Themistius became an insider, better equated with regime policy, but the fundamentals of that policy had not themselves changed. Theodosius was, therefore, a consistent advocate of a negotiated peace.[47]

This is certainly a possible argument, but we think it much more likely that Theodosius' policy actually changed between 379 and 381. There is no evidence, in fact, that Oration 14 was more private in nature than its two sequels. Like them, it was delivered in front of Theodosius' court. The court was situated at Thessalonica at the time, rather than Constantinople, but this hardly made it a private occasion. Apart from the full range of court functionaries, Theodosius' time at Thessalonica was spent, as we have seen, dealing with a multitude of landowning suitors from right across the eastern provinces. The Senate of Constantinople was not present in full formal session, but the context was nevertheless public, and given that Themistius came as a senatorial ambassador, this speech, like Oration 5 to Jovian, is likely to have had a second airing in Constantinople (see Chapter 3). Equally important, while Themistius may indeed have been ill, his delayed arrival fits a now well-established pattern of his career, whereby a considerable gap tended to ensue between the enthronement of a new emperor and Themistius' first speech on his behalf. In the case of Jovian, this gap was occupied by negotiations with the new regime, and there is every reason to suppose that this political rhythm also applied to Themistius and Theodosius.[48] Equally important, Errington's argument takes no account of the military disaster which befell Theodosius' army in the summer of 380, when it was finally committed to full-scale battle. As we have seen, it fell apart, and Theodosius was forced to rush to Sirmium to negotiate the handing back of the conduct of the war to Gratian's generals. This second Roman disaster provides a satisfactory explanation of the changing Gothic policy of Theodosius' regime. In our view, therefore, Oration 14 should be read like Themistius' other speeches: a rhetorically inventive but highly laudatory justification of the policies of the ruling regime.

---

47 Errington, 1996b, 8–9 (e.g., p. 9: 'Themistius' praise of the emperor here reflects the hopes and aspirations of his class, not the policy of the emperor').
48 On this repeated pattern of delay, see Chapter 1.

## ORATION 14
## EMBASSY TO THE EMPEROR THEODOSIUS:
## TRANSLATION

[180c] Up to now, your godlike majesty, I was unable to endure my illness, because I was compelled to lag behind those who share the embassy with me,[49] but now I am sensible of how much indeed my spirit's delight overcomes my physical infirmity. Indeed, it transforms my sickness to contentment and my old age to youth. Having had scant expectation of escaping from the cloud that enveloped this body of mine, I showed myself to be stronger than the sea, stronger than the mighty and swelling wave. I assumed my prime once again when I learned from the decree issued by the mightiest of our temple wardens[50] that we were to see the return of the golden age, [d] that we were to see the monarchy perfect and sound in limb,[51] illustrious in both forms of beauty, those of the spirit and of the body. Nor was this in fact an idle boast, for here there is an emperor to behold, for whom I had need of Homer's words

'Never did I look with my eyes on one so excellent
nor yet so noble – for you are like a king'.[52]

[181a] And so I am come to join in celebrating the first signs of the turning of the tide, towards which the eye of justice leads back the Romans and tips the scales to better fortune. You have appeared for us as one man in place of all others, we look to you in place of all others – Dacians, Thracians, Illyrians, men at arms and the rest of our armament all of which vanished away quicker than a shadow,[53] and we, who were

49  Themistius may well have been sick, but the delay in his appearance before Theodosius fits a general pattern in his relations with emperors suggestive of political negotiations: see Chapter 1.

50  ζάκορος – used by Themistius at *Or.* 4.53b of members of the Senate of Constantinople. The 'most powerful of the senators' who announced Theodosius' succession would be the urban prefect of the city and the senate's formal head. It is not known who was in office in January 379 (cf. *PLRE* 2, 1056). Note that Themistius did not take the opportunity to mention Gratian at this point: see the introduction to this chapter.

51  ἀρτίπους – used at Homer, *Odyssey* 8.310 of Ares, god of war.

52  Homer, *Iliad* 3.169f.: The Homeric lines have been modified to turn this into a first-person address. Themistius also used this passage at *Or.* 1.6b.

53  After the battle of Hadrianople in which two-thirds of Valens' troops fell on a single day: see the introduction to this chapter. Themistius used a similar phrase of the same event at *Or.* 16.206d (see below).

once ourselves pursued, drive on at full pelt. It is because of the hopes left to us in you that we have taken a stand, **[b]** that we draw breath and believe that you shall now check the impetus of success for the Scythians and quench the conflagration that devours all things, which neither the Haemus could halt nor the boundaries of Thrace or Illyria, a hard passage even for a traveller.[54] Now fighting spirit returns to the cavalry and returns to the infantry. Already you make even farmers a terror to the barbarian, and the miners too, whom you command to neglect gold and dig for iron. And this army which has not tasted the life of luxury has now come together voluntarily, **[c]** schooled to gain advantage from adversity.[55] It was not just a poet's tale that, by his war cry alone, Achilles struck dismay into the barbarians who were victorious up to that moment.[56] For if you, though not yet in the field against the guilty ones,[57] have checked their wilfulness merely by pitching camp nearby and lying in blockade, what do we suppose those damned villains will suffer, when they see you readying your spear and brandishing your shield, the lightning flash from your helm gleaming close at hand?[58]

**[d]** The city of Constantine owes you two crowns – one of gold, the other of goodwill; the Fair City is preparing the crown of riches for that day on which she shall place it on his brow when he returns in glory,

54 The junction of the western Haemus with the Rhodopes marked the boundary between Thrace and Illyricum. Traffic through this difficult region was confined largely to two routes: the Via Egnatia in the south and the famous military road in the north which in particular crossed the strategically vital Succi Pass between Naissus and Serdica. Before Hadrianople, Gothic raids seem to have been confined largely to Thrace; even when the Roman blockade of the Haemus failed in autumn 377, the Succi Pass was held against them (Ammianus 31.9; cf. 21.10.2–4). After Hadrianople, as Themistius tells us here, the Gothic war spilled into Illyricum: hence Gratian's grant of temporary control of Illyricum to Theodosius and the latter's residence in Thessalonica: see the introduction to this chapter.

55 The massacre at Hadrianople left Theodosius, the new eastern emperor, without an army. The sources record many of the different measures he took to put one together, especially in 379/80 at Thessalonica: for full refs., see the introduction to this chapter.

56 Homer, *Iliad* 18.215ff., where Achilles rallied the Greeks who were struggling to recover the body of Patroclus by sounding his war cry. Dismayed at his return, the Trojans gave ground, and the Greeks gained possession of the corpse. Themistius referred to this incident again at *Or.* 18.221a.

57 I.e., the Goths.

58 Themistius continued the Homeric theme, describing Theodosius in terms of a conventional Homeric hero (cf. 'Hector of the flashing helm') on the field of battle. In practice Themistius' hopes were dashed by the failure of Theodosius' army on the battlefield the next summer: see the introduction to this chapter.

bearing trophies of victory over the ill-starred barbarians.[59] The crown of goodwill, which it is proper for philosophy to administer, she both guards unsullied at home and yet has also sent out here both for those who genuinely bestow it and him who graciously accepts it.[60] **[182a]** For one might have offered up gold in fear, but goodwill cannot exist if not freely chosen. God prefers those who burn incense often, to those who dedicate tripods.[61]

Constantinople comes forward not only to seek what she wants but as the first to ratify the decree of proclamation. For it is doubtless proper for the city which rules cities to join in celebrating those who rule over mankind.[62] And yet of the two mother cities of the world – I mean that of Romulus and that Constantine – **[b]** it is ours, I would say, that is in greater harmony with you.[63] For she had no association of any sort with the race of rulers, and yet she became partner in empire with the great city through her virtue.[64] And it was not family connection which

59 On Crown Gold given to an emperor on accession, anniversaries, and triumphs, see the introduction to Chapter 3. Constantinople will present the gold at a later date, on Theodosius' triumphal entry into the city (so too Vanderspoel, 1995, 196). By then, two crowns would have in fact been owed: the original one for the accession, and a separate one for victory over the Goths. This thought perhaps stimulated Themistius' play on the two types of crown which immediately followed.

60 On Themistius' self-portrayal as 'philosophy', see Chapter 1. This passage picked up the point of the speech's opening lines. Themistius – 'philosophy' – has been sent by the city of Constantinople to reinforce the embassy that had congratulated Theodosius upon his accession. He was currently presenting one speech – the 'crown of goodwill' – to Theodosius, and promised that there would be another back in Constantinople, when the actual gold would be presented after Theodosius' promised victory over the Goths.

61 This sounds like a proverbial phrase, but we have not been able to identify it. Its point would appear to be that many small offerings are a better indication of true piety than an occasional showy one. Themistius may in part have been apologising for the brevity of his current speech, but at the same time stressed that his offering came from free will. On the general importance of free speech to Themistius' public image, see Chapter 1.

62 A difficult sentence which echoes Themistius' phraseology at *Or.* 3.41c. We follow Petavius' conjecture τῇ βασιλευούσῃ, and read βασιλεύοντας for βασιλεύσαντας. This gives the sense that it is right for Rome to join in Contantinople's salute to Theodosius, sustaining the overall point of Themistius' remarks, as the preceding and following sentences confirm, that Constantinople must in this case really be credited with taking the lead.

63 Themistius' comments here went beyond the virtual equality between the two capitals that he had noted in Rome in 357 (*Or.* 3.41cff.: Chapter 2); cf. Vanderspoel, 1995, 192–3.

64 I.e., before it became Constantinople and the second capital of the Roman Empire, Byzantium had had no particular historical relationship with Rome which might explain its unprecedented promotion.

advanced you to the purple, but virtue in superabundance, not close kinship but display of strength and manhood. Gratian acted wisely and in a way worthy of grey hairs rather than youth because he did not assume one of his nearest relations to be the best man but rather the best man to be his nearest relation.[65] Nobly, he has made the vote his own, [c] which circumstance had in anticipation carried. In this fashion, danger summoned Epaminondas the Theban to generalship when he was serving in the ranks.[66] And the Romans were summoning you to the kingship from that moment when you alone checked the raging Sarmatians as they overran the whole territory by the river, taking your stand with scant force and that not of your own choosing.[67]

And now that you have been called to the kingship on such an pledge, you are right to keep in sight no other thing, but to show all men that your virtue made you emperor, [d] and it was Gratian who proclaimed you. For indeed in the games it is physical strength which creates the winners of the victory crown and the heralds place it upon them. But in that instance, the herald does not share in the crown since he gives what he does not own. But a king who crowns a king is not diminished by the gift, but gains from it. For by giving the honour, he gains a sharing of responsibilities. [183a] Because of this, Gratian had no qualms about your age when he beheld your virtue nor did he reckon that as a younger man he was going to crown his elder, thinking rather that a father chosen with judgement is superior to a natural sire. Both men share equal praise, the one for proclaiming his elder, the other because being older he was entrusted with a son's goodwill.[68]

---

65 The audience would surely have understood this as an implicit criticism of Valentinian's promotion of Valens in 364, who was made emperor because of the family relationship rather than his virtues: cf. Ammianus 26.4.

66 The story of Epaminondas is recounted at Pausanias 9.5; Themistius also used it of the election of Jovian: *Or.* 5.66a–b (Chapter 3).

67 Theodosius' victory over the Sarmatians marked an important stage in his promotion: see the introduction to this speech.

68 Themistius here performed a careful balancing act, giving Gratian considerable credit for choosing Theodosius. Nonetheless, the latter's virtues and experience were emphasised, and the legal seniority of Gratian over Theodosius subverted by the carefully drawn picture of them as father and son. This was a foretaste of the lines of argument which would be developed further when Themistius was championing Theodosius' right to independence in *Or.* 16: see the introduction to this chapter. Vanderspoel, 1995, 197, detects an ominous tone to this section, translating ἐπιστεύθη as 'believed' rather than 'trusted'. We consider that reassurance was the necessary tone here, since the history of the

The Great City beseeches both, you because you have the power to give, and him because he has made you powerful, first that she receive her protector as soon as possible and meet him before the rest of the east,[69] and, **[b]** second, that all the gifts which your forefathers decreed might remain secure for her. And I name as your forefathers not simply every previous emperor but all those renowned for their gentleness and love of mankind whose true heir you show yourself to be.[70] Third, that the senate be exalted likewise with honours, seeking that most regal of all favours. For this alone is a treasure which does not diminish when it is spent; you need no contributions to it but the more liberally you employ this expense, **[c]** the more abundantly and greater it survives for you. Former kings gave us a multitude of columns and statues and an abundance of water, but you plant our senate thickly with honours and titles and cure this dearth which afflicts us no less than formerly the dearth of springs.[71] And those whom you have named conscript fathers, make worthy of the title![72] Nor yet shall you appear inferior to Constantine, whenever you set them up, if you should raise up the city with honours to a greater height than Constantine did with buildings. **[d]** Thus theatres, marketplaces and gymnasiums arose in mighty Rome too in the recent past, but honours, everlasting rule and sharing the stewardship of nations have been rooted in the city from its original foundation. Now we glory in the great size of our statues, but are not confident in the titles of our men: but if you, O divine eminence, should dedicate

---

4th-century Empire meant that an audience would need persuading that civil war would not follow a division of power. See also also the introduction to Chapter 3.

69  Vanderspoel, 1995, 192f., has suggested that, contrary to this statement, Theodosius had already paid a visit to Constantinople, but see note 43.

70  Themistius has in mind all the privileges granted to the city since Constantine's day. Vanderspoel, 1995, 198, suggests that in emphasising gentleness and φιλανθρωπία as essential ingredients for true imperial forefathers of Theodosius, Themistius may have been damning Valens by implication. This is possible: see the introduction to this chapter on Themistius' reconsiderations of Valens in *Orr.* 14–16.

71  Constantine and Constantius beautified the city with public buildings, Valens completed the massive engineering works required to produce more water. Until the completion of the latter, the city had been chronically short of water. See Mango, 1985, chs 2–3, and Mango's further article in Mango and Dagron, 1993.

72  The use of the perfect participle here (συγγεραμμένους) makes it clear that Theodosius had already started appointing new senators before Themistius spoke. What follows is thus a further instance of Themistius 'pleading' with an emperor for something that was already happening. On his use of this rhetorical device, see Chapter 1.

such prizes of victory to the great senate, then truly shall your city be a
second Rome, **[184a]** if indeed the city is its men. So now at least it is not
in an over-familiar fashion that we aspire to this name.[73]

## ORATION 15
## TO THEODOSIUS OR THE MOST ROYAL OF THE VIRTUES:
## INTRODUCTION

Indications within Oration 15 itself make the date of its delivery more or
less certain. It was given in winter, since, as Themistius tells us, the
season was not ripe for military campaigning (185b–c), and also in the
third year of Theodosius' reign: hence on or after 19 January 381. The
speech also contains a further passage which discusses the arrival in
Constantinople of the Gothic chieftain Athanaric (190c–191b). Other
sources indicate that he arrived in the city on 12 January 381, and died
there just under two weeks later, on 25 January. Since Themistius makes
no mention of the king's death, Oration 15 must have been given
between 19 January and 25 January 381. The likelihood is, indeed, that
Themistius delivered it precisely on the third anniversary of Theodosius'
elevation, 19 January itself, in the eastern imperial city, to the emperor
and his court (185a–b). Theodosius had formally entered his capital for
the first time the previous November.[74]

In its opening lines, Themistius noted that the army was in training,
in winter quarters, but held out the expectation that it would take the
field in due course (185b–c). Towards the end, the Goths were labelled
'the Hounds of Hell', and Themistius looked forward to the two
emperors, Gratian and Theodosius, inflicting such a defeat on the
Goths that it would be remembered, after Homer, in the 'far hereafter'
(197b–199a). Sandwiched between these relatively brief bellicose
remarks, however, was a long disquisition on the general nature of the
imperial office, and on Theodosius in particular, that gave the speech an
overall tone that differed markedly from that of Oration 14. Rather
than celebrating Theodosius' military capacities, Oration 15 concentrated instead on his possession of the moral qualities required to bring

73 On Theodosius' senatorial appointments and their political significance within his
overall strategy of making Constantinople the formal equal of Rome, both in secular and
ecclesiastical terms, see the introduction to this chapter.

74 Athanaric: *Cons. Const.* s. a. 381 (= *C.M.* 1, 243). This dating of the speech is generally
accepted: e.g., Scholze, 1911, 51; Vanderspoel, 1995, 199–200.

good civilian government to the eastern empire. In the speech, Themistius was quite explicit about this change of emphasis, noting right at the beginning that he would be combining the peaceful subject matter of Hesiod with Homer's grander rhetorical tone (184b–185a). In its central portions, he then went on to note that Theodosius' virtues had been displayed not only in his direct conduct of the imperial office, such as tempering justice with mercy and showing proper generosity to his subjects, but also in his ability to appoint officials who shared the same moral qualities as himself. Overall, Themistius argued, while it was all well and good for an emperor to be a capable general too, his chief job was good civilian government. Actually commanding troops in battle had become no more than an desirable extra, not an essential quality for the job (187b–d). This represents a strikingly different portrayal of Theodosius to that of Oration 14, which, as we have seen hailed him as the man who would put fight back into the Roman army and win the Gothic war.

The simplest and most likely explanation of this striking change was the course of the Gothic war itself. Defeat at the hands of Fritigern in summer 380 had forced Theodosius into a summit meeting at Sirmium with his western partner or the latter's representatives (see below), which clearly decided that administrative and military control of the war should be returned to Gratian. In its aftermath, Theodosius retreated to Constantinople and Gratian's forces carried on the war against the Goths. In January 381, Themistius' demilitarised account of the imperial office was simply attempting to find an alternative ideological justification for a regime whose initial self-presentation had been vitiated by the military disasters of the previous summer.[75] Portraying Theodosius as the upholder of divinely ordained civilised order exploited an alternative aspect of Roman imperial discourse. Emperors as triumphant conquerors of barbarians provided one of its central images, but no less important was the civilised, rational order at home which such conquests were designed to protect.[76] With the Gothic war still raging, Themistius could not afford entirely to abandon the image of Theodosius as general, but his rhetorical strategy was to concentrate instead on the

---

75 For further discussion, see the introduction to this chapter.

76 The moral education of individuals and the ordering of society according to written law were the central planks of this order (*civilitas*): see, for instance, Barnish, 1992; Heather, 1993a; 1993b.

other main set of Graeco-Roman ideological criteria by which Theodosius might be accounted a 'good' emperor.

   Within this overall strategy, the political context in which he and his
emperor were operating led Themistius to develop two more particular
themes: one implicit, the other quite explicit. Implicit in much of the
discussion of Theodosius' manner of government, as we have seen, is a
thoroughgoing critique of his predecessor in the east, the Emperor
Valens, based upon Theodosius' possession of the necessary experience
for high office and Valens' lack of it. Because of this imbalance, Valens
had suppressed proper freedom of speech (*parrhesia*), where Theodosius
now cherished it (190a–b). Valens had generated fear among his subjects
by sentences of exile, confiscation and death, where Theodosius had not
issued a decree of death in three years (190b–c), and had even returned
confiscated land to the heirs of those who had lost out under Valens
(192d, 194d). Valens had promoted unworthy subordinates, but Theodosius knew how to pick men who shared his own virtues (196c–d). As we
have seen, criticism of Valens was a marked feature of all three of the
orations translated in this chapter, and its point was very straightforward.[77]

   Cherishing freedom of speech, not resorting to fear to control one's
subjects, generosity, mercy, and picking good subordinates were all
highly traditional tests of good government within the established value
systems of the Graeco-Roman world. In the west in 379, for instance,
Ausonius had recently celebrated the Emperor Gratian in a discussion
framed according to exactly the same categories.[78] In general terms,
Themistius was trying to build consent by emphasising how superior
Theodosius' government was to its predecessor in areas that were generally recognised as being of fundamental importance in determining the
overall character of a regime. More particularly, his comparative
approach, holding Valens always before his audience, also reflected the
careful manner in which the new regime sought to appeal to its most
natural constituency: those who had lost out under its predecessor.[79]
Acceptance of this new ideological line also provided a good test of
loyalty to the new regime for the no doubt many proteges of Valens'

77 See the introduction to this chapter.
78 The *Gratiarum actio*.
79 For further discussion of the internal politics of Theodosius' early years, see the introduction to this chapter.

regime who retained office in the different levels of central and local government. The collapse of Theodosius' army in the summer of 380 merely added an extra urgency to what was anyway a natural propaganda line for Themistius to adopt.

The other, much more explicit sub-theme of Oration 15 is the relationship of Theodosius with his western counterpart, the Emperor Gratian. By and large, the speech presented them as equal partners. The Empire has two helmsmen, we are told. Both have climbed on deck and looked out over the stormy sea in order to decide what to do about the Gothic problem (194dff.). The two emperors are rivals only in doing good, and a single civilised order extends all the way from the [Atlantic] Ocean to the river Tigris (198b). Although relatively short, these passages are, as we have seen, very striking compared to Orations 14 and 16 for their highly positive assessment of Gratian. Oration 14 paid him some respect, Oration 16 none at all; neither portrayed anything like the active, equal partner, in both war and good government, who took the stage in Oration 15. Once again, the Gothic war provides the likeliest explanation for this short-lived change of tone. After his defeat in the summer of 380, Theodosius had been forced to hand back control of operations to Gratian, and needed his western colleague's military machine, so far largely untouched by the war, to bring the Goths to heel. In such circumstances, his propaganda had to be suitably respectful.[80]

Nevertheless, Themistius, as we have seen, stressed at some length the importance to an emperor of proper experience in official positions, such as Theodosius had enjoyed, without which he would be liable to many mistakes. The most obvious target for all this, of course, was Valens. At the same time, such thoughts were also applicable to Gratian. Raised to the purple aged 8, and still only 21 when the speech was given, he had never held any other administrative office. Themistius' choice, towards the end of Oration 15, of the noun *neanias* ('young man': 198b) to designate Gratian must have been designed to trigger further reflections in his audience about the wider applicability, beyond the figure of Valens, of problems associated with inexperience. The speech presented them as partners, but Theodosius' ambition was allowed to show through. Although formally the junior, having been

80 Themistius' overall treatment of Gratian in these three speeches is discussed in the introduction to this chapter.

promoted by Gratian, the stress on Theodosius' experience was meant to make the audience think of him as, de facto, the senior of the currently reigning emperors.

Aside from the broader themes of the speech and their historical implications, two more particular passages are also worth discussion for the important light they shed on different aspects of the Gothic war. First, following the defeat of his army earlier in the summer, Theodosius rushed to Sirmium in Pannonia in early September 380, for a meeting in which, as we have seen, he handed back control of the war to Gratian. He was in Sirmium on 8 September (*C. Th.* 7.22.1 and *C.J.* 2.47.2), but had been in Thessalonica on 31 August (*C. Th.* 10.10.13), and was back there by 20 September (*C. Th.* 10.10.14). It has often been suggested that he met Gratian himself there, but the issue has not generated scholarly consensus. Gratian had been at Aquileia in the summer of 380, and his troops, at least, went as far as Pannonia to deal with the Greuthungi of Alatheus and Saphrax. This makes a meeting at least possible, but no narrative source provides positive confirmation of such an encounter. On close inspection, a passage in Oration 15 perhaps sheds further light on the matter. This speech was given in January 381, and one would certainly expect it to have mentioned what would have been a very significant encounter between the two emperors, had it occurred, in its reasonably extensive discussion of their military cooperation (194ff.). The wording is a little evasive, but one passage, developing the ship of state metaphor, described the emperors as both climbing on deck, and both grasping the tiller while surveying the state of the sea (195a). If significant, the use of 'both' here might suggest that the emperors had indeed met.[81]

Second, as we have seen, one of the key pieces of evidence for dating the speech is provided by the passage which records the arrival in Constantinople of the Gothic king Athanaric (190c–191b). As has recently been argued, it may well be that Themistius' comments on this

---

81  Errington, 1996b, 25 n. 140, rightly corrects Heather, 1991, 153–4 (who at that point was also doubtful of a meeting) on the fact that the Codes do not show Gratian in Sirmium in summer 380. But Gratian's army at least went to Pannonia to fight Alatheus and Saphrax in that year, and the orders for the Church Council of Aquileia in 381 were given by Gratian from Sirmium, for which again the likeliest date is the summer of 380 (*Acts of the Council of Aquileia* 10; cf. McLynn, 1994, 111–12). There are sufficient gaps in Gratian's recorded movements for the summer to 380 to allow him to have made the relatively short journey to Sirmium from Aquileia in late August or early September.

episode were a late insert, skilfully woven into an already existing draft. The passage is short – half a page in the Teubner edition – and the argument before and after, concentrating on the beneficial effects of the justice of the emperor, would run together without interruption.[82] Apart from shedding light on how Themistius composed his speeches, the passage is also striking for what Themistius has to say about the Gothic king. His overall conclusion from Athanaric's arrival in Constantinople was that it proved that enemies were better subdued by persuasion than by force (190c–191a). As we have seen, this was a brief rehearsal of the argument which Themistius would deploy at much greater length in Oration 16 to justify the peace agreement of 382 with all the Goths. Its inclusion in Oration 15 suggests that, already by January 381, Theodosius and his advisors had begun to think the unthinkable: that a compromise peace might have to be made with the Goths.

The inclusion of such a highly charged thought in an official speech for such a grand occasion as Theodosius' third anniversary could not have been done without the emperor's express approval.[83] At the very least, therefore, the passage must rank as an example of what is known in British politics as 'kite flying': airing a possible policy change in public, via some less than direct means, in order to gauge the response to it of public opinion. And, more generally, once it became clear that a compromise peace was necessary, Theodosius would, as we have seen, have had to prepare public opinion carefully for the *volte face*. The Roman audience was expecting victory over the Goths, and the original presentation of Theodosius, as Oration 14 shows, emphasised that he was the man to provide it. If the outcome was going to be different, careful preparation was required. Even without the Athanaric insert, the switch between Orations 14 and 15 from martial emperor to civilian ruler, for whom military activity was but an optional extra, is already striking. Lip service was still being paid to victory in January 381, but for experienced pundits the switch would probably have been readable in itself as a signal of how the Gothic war might be expected to turn out. The arrival of Athanaric was no more than an opportunity to fly the kite a little higher.[84]

---

82 Errington, 1996b, 11–14.
83 So too Errington, 1996b, 12.
84 See the introduction to this chapter.

## ORATION 15
## TO THEODOSIUS OR THE MOST ROYAL OF THE VIRTUES:
## TRANSLATION

[184b] Surely, if a man is not competent to report wars and battles of men on an equal footing with the noble Homer and Thucydides the Athenian, such a one should pass into the palace in silence? One of them right at the beginning exhorted Calliope to sing of the wrath of Achilles,[85] and then goes through, one by one, all the evils which this same wrath bred for the Achaeans and how much the Greek army, as it was slaughtered by the Trojans, endured because of it. [c] But the other, making a more confident and splendid beginning to his story, does not hesitate to declare, as an enticement and allurement to his prospective audience, that he is going to relate in full the war between the Peloponnesians and the Athenians, judging it the greatest and most calamitous of all that had previously occurred, and he lists point by point how much greater and more worthy of note are the events of his own history than Homer's poem.[86] This was the way of these two men. Hesiod the Ascraean, on the other hand, did not think to introduce into his poetry bristling spears and clashing shields, men slaying and being slain, and the earth running with blood, [d] but rather these more humble subjects, both peaceful and more welcome to humankind: when to till the soil, when to sow, when to prune the vine, and how long to cut the axle and the mallet. And the Greeks lent their ears to him as he sang of these things from Helicon and were beguiled, thinking the advice of Hesiod no less useful that the manslaughterings of Homer.[87]

[185a] And so if I were some sort of teller of tales, one or other of these methods would for me too be the object of my study and the goal of my art.[88] But since I am able to contribute words that are more peaceful than Homer's, or more regal than Hesiod's, why shall my voice have been shut out of the great hall [of the palace] and why would

85 I.e., Homer, who (though not by name) invokes Calliope, the Muse of heroic epic, at the beginning of the *Iliad*.

86 Thucydides, *Histories* 1.1–3.

87 Hesiod's epic poem *Works and Days* combined moral instruction with practical advice on agriculture – lines 424ff. containing precise instructions on how to make various farming implements – and was considered a source of precepts on how best to live one's life. See Plato, *Republic* 363b.

88 The text is corrupt, but some sense can be made by reading ἢν ἄν after Jacobs.

⟨anyone⟩ not permit me, according to my custom, to cull virgin blooms from the meadows of Plato and Aristotle, virgin blooms which no blade has touched,[89] and to weave crowns of human happiness for the king? Nor is this theatre of yours, where I make an entrance to present my gift, any less lovely, any less cultivated or wise than the delightful one of olden times,[90] but at its head sits a man who, [b] unless I have failed to see that I am deluded

> 'is both a servant of the divine Enyalios and
> one who understands the Muses' lovely gift',[91]

while in a circle there stand and sit those who are fellow chorus members and fellow celebrants, every man exulting more in the Muses than in might.[92]

And so while the time is not yet ripe to rouse the battle line and the warband to answer the alarm call against the guilty Scythians,[93] when Terror and Fear take their ease because of the season [c] and it is not for the moment convenient to serenade Ares [the God of war], let the Muses lead in their dance for the king, bringing with them their leader Apollo to join in the dance. For that god is at once both Archer and Muse Leader and his array is twofold, for peace and for wars, and in both he is fit for a king. For a king needs weapons against his enemies

89  Themistius used this reminiscence of Euripides, *Hippolytus* 73, at *Or.* 4.54b giving thanks to Constantius for his favourable reception of Oration 1, an approval made tangible in the granting of a bronze statue. This reminder of his long experience in imperial affairs could be a response to some attempt literally to shut him from the palace, but was probably a further device to emphasise, to would-be detractors, Themistius' standing within the regime.

90  Where the Greeks had listened to Homer and Hesiod.

91  Archilochus fr. 1 ed. Diehl; Enyalios ('The warlike one') is an epithet of Ares, god of war. Compare *Or.* 4.54a where Constantius was described as both φιλόλογος [lover of reason] and φιλοπόλεμος [lover of war].

92  Themistius argues immediately that Theodosius and all his advisors delight more in peace and creativity than warfare. The speech was presumably given before Theodosius' consistory, the formal council of high civilian and military dignitaries of his regime: see Jones, 1964, 333–41; Matthews, 1989, 267–9. This was firmly in line with the regime's need, after the defeat of its army at the hands of the Goths in the summer of 380, to switch the emphasis of its propaganda from war to peace: see the introduction to this chapter. Themistius evoked a similar sense of an emperor surrounded by his councillors at *Or.* 5.67a–b (Chapter 3).

93  'Scythians' = Goths. The speech was given in January 381, well before it was possible to mount campaigns in the Balkans.

but the lyre for his subjects, with which he shall bring them together, render them harmonious and ready them for the contest, just as trainers not only give encouragement to athletes [d] when they are in the ring, when they box or contest the pankration,[94] but also when they spend time at home at leisure, and indeed especially then. It is during periods of leisure that the wise prepare for action, and although the trumpet's piercing note has not yet summoned them to Pisa, the Isthmus or to Delphi,[95] genuine competitors practise their exercises in the wrestling school as well as their diets, [186a] their hand-holds, and their weighted training jumps, choosing to shed much sweat before it is necessary to do so. And they endure all these things not for their children or their wives, not so that their native lands might remain unravaged, but with an eye to the crown of olive, wild celery or pine,[96] and nothing is important for them, neither instruction nor practice except that which leads to the crown and the victory proclamation. But one who rules over extensive tracts of land and sea, [b] who holds as subjects cities without number and countless peoples, must turn his thoughts not only to this – how he might drive the barbarians from that portion against which, already before his own governorship, they committed their drunken abuses[97] – but also to how he might regulate that area of the subject lands which they left unafflicted and unsullied, which is many times as large, and extends from the Bosphorus to the Tigris, and keep it completely untouched and inviolate not only from external but also internal afflictions. [c] In the same way, I think, shepherds and cowherds need to take some thought about dogs and sticks to fight off wild beasts, yet no less, indeed rather more, of healthy pasture and advantageous springs, the right time to milk, and the right time to shear. For negligence in this, and lack of consideration for what is suitable, is much more dangerous

94  The *pankration* was a dangerous combination of boxing and wrestling in which virtually every form of violence was sanctioned apart from biting and gouging. It was usually contested on the fourth day of the Olympic games.

95  The sites of the three Panhellenic athletic contests; Pisa was the area around Olympia where the games were held every four years until abolished by Theodosius in 393; the Isthmian games were held every two years at Corinth and the Pythian games at Delphi in the third year of each Olympiad.

96  The respective prizes awarded for success at the three games mentioned at 185d.

97  Themistius carefully pointed out here that the ravaging began before Theodosius' reign; i.e., it was in no way his fault. This was certainly true, but Themistius was also attempting to deflect potential criticism of his emperor after the debacle of the 380 campaigning season.

to cattle and flocks than wolves are. For wolves, once they have seized from the flock, like to flee the dogs and watchers, **[d]** but it is impossible for the fatted beasts to escape or be protected from a negligent or bad shepherd. Yet the shepherd of a flock and the shepherd of peoples do not have equal responsibility, but the skill of shepherding men, which it is right to call regal and political, has the management of a much more intricate and complicated creature than domestic beasts.[98] **[187a]** For beasts have no court cases against each other or laws or summonses, nor do they need law courts and decrees, but, in humans, there is greater struggle against their own kind than against the enemy, and he who would rule them with justice needs to be vigilant on both counts, and must be no less on guard against the wild beasts within the walls, which are more numerous, cunning, and implacable than those outside. For the chief officer and partner of kingship is the Law, which descended with it from the heavens for the salvation of mankind. Within the state, it exercises power over its subjects even at the frontiers of the realm, **[b]** and it is for these people that Right and Justice work together with the king, not for enemies outside.[99]

It seems to me that the marvellous Homer, even if he is rather more inclined towards Ares, nevertheless still realises, as do we, that a king should lay claim to be a king of Themis [Right] rather than of Enyo [War]. The one is his proper task, for which a king is called so by men, but the other, while not desirable, is necessary. **[c]** For in praising Agamemnon, he says that he is famed on both counts, as 'a good king and a mighty warrior'.[100] Speaking in this way, he seems to differentiate the regal from the martial art and not incorporate the mighty warrior in the good king. For he would not have applied both qualities to him if good government and excellence with the spear were not two separate things. But yet they are not mutually exclusive; **[d]** rather, it is appropriate for the king to command infantry, cavalry, generals and squadron commanders while also, as far as he himself is concerned, should it so happen, fight well on foot and on horseback, shoot arrows straight and

98  Themistius equated Constantius II with a shepherd of men at *Or.* 1.10a (see Chapter 2) in at least a partial echo of Christian imagery.

99  In Roman imperial ideology, written law played a critical role. It was seen as the ultimate civilising factor, established by the Divinity for humankind, which differentiated Roman society from the world of the barbarians. As such, it was a theme regularly revisited by Themistius; see, e.g., *Or.* 1.14b–15b (Chapter 2).

100  Homer, *Iliad* 3.179. The general point echoed *Or.* 13.176b to Gratian.

throw the javelin, as you and your ancestor did, both pre-eminent horsemen and archers

'warriors both, this fact all of us know'.

But both possessed these qualities perhaps as an additional qualification.[101]

[188a] Yet it would seem that Homer thought the task of a king, which defines a king, to be something else. For example each time he praises one of the generals, he confers on him, as a distinguishing mark, an epithet taken from his weapons, war cry or physique – Hector 'of the flashing helm', Diomedes 'of the great shout', Achilles 'swift of foot', Ajax, because he was a sort of giant, 'the hefty bulwark of the Achaeans'. For him good horsemanship, industry or endurance is sufficient for a general's praise. [b] Odysseus and Nestor gain their renown in his eyes from these praises. But whenever he admires someone as a king, praises him and posts his name in his poem, it is not his helmet, spear, or swiftness that causes him to be remembered there, but the fact that he is divinely nurtured and divinely born, and is 'equal to Zeus in wisdom'.[102] For this is his task by which he is defined as a king: to resemble Zeus. For, as his attendant and interpreter, [c] he is entrusted with no paltry portion of Zeus' realm in the flock of mankind.[103]

'And you, my friend – for you are indeed fair and tall to look on', and I shall not omit 'be valiant'.[104] These proofs are not in dispute, for the reasons I shall now reveal. For Gratian proclaimed with the crown of kingship a man who had in turn held the offices of squadron commander and general. But be sure, O noble man, that neither beauty, nor physical stature, nor swiftness, nor might makes a good king, unless he should

101  The quotation is from Homer, *Iliad* 7.281, referring to Ajax and Hector. Theodosius' ancestor was the elder Theodosius, Master of Horse (*Magister Equitum*) in the west from 369–375; hence Themistius' reference to him as a 'pre-eminent horseman'. The younger Theodosius was thus probably also *Magister Equitum* before his elevation to the purple. On Theodosius' accession, see the introduction to *Or.* 14 above.

102  Homer, *Iliad* 2.169, describing Odysseus.

103  As the Roman Empire was God-ordained to civilise humankind by upholding the rule of Law, so was the emperor, again at least according to the same ideology, directly appointed by a God who intervened actively in human affairs (see generally Dvornik, 1966). Themistius claimed as much for all the emperors he served, but the early death of Jovian caused him some subsequent embarrassment: see the introduction to Chapter 3.

104  Homer, *Odyssey* 1.301–2: Athena's words to Telemachus, Odysseus' son, encouraging him to take a stand against the suitors.

carry in his soul some form of resemblance to God. **[d]** So let us too make our own search from that source and call upon the poet to teach us how a man who walks upon the earth and is clothed in flesh can be thought to possess the form of Him who is seated beyond the furthermost vault and beyond everything that is.[105] Let us then listen to him. For he does not summon us to a long [speech] in which he thinks to discern the godlike king:

> **[189a]** 'Like', he says, 'some perfect king,
> who god-fearing maintains justice. The black earth bears
> wheat and barley, the trees are heavy with fruit,
> everything unfailingly brings forth, the sea gives up fish
> from his good leadership and the people thrive under him.'[106]

Justice and righteousness are the product of this art and from there comes the resemblance and similarity to the divine.

And the divine Plato is likely to have learned this lesson from Homer. For he states that justice combined with wisdom is resemblance to God.[107] **[b]** Thus for the man who holds fast to and restores this justice, Calliope says

> 'Oh, how many good things follow on: his crops flourish, his trees and vines flourish also, many animals are born and many men, all things which endure and live. Not only does the earth give its bounty of fruits but also the sea its fishes.'

Indeed, what power there is in righteousness whose benefit permeates not only the board of magistrates and the courts of justice but also all that lives and grows, what is sown and what is conceived. **[c]** How blessed is he to whom this righteousness belongs and has the same potency as Zeus, and is not only lord of mankind but indeed of the elements, so as

---

105  In line with his normal strategy of sticking to common ground in religious matters, Themistius used Platonising language of the relationship between man and the Divinity, which was acceptable to Christians and non-Christians alike. On the Platonic One and the spark of the Divine inside men, see Wallis, 1972, 61–89.

106  Homer, *Odyssey* 19.109–114 (omitting 110). These lines are quoted at Plato, *Republic* 363b where Plato reads πάντα (all) for μῆλα (sheep) in the penultimate line. Themistius preserved the Platonic version and, at 189b, puts a paraphrase of it into the mouth of Calliope, the Muse of epic (see note 85).

107  Plato, *Theaetetus* 176b; see also the previous note.

to make even these more fruitful, more fertile and of greater benefit to mankind.

Let us, my friend, hold fast to this goddess [Righteousness] who comes from Zeus himself, so that this unassailable chain of good things may be bestowed on us, and let us not allow her out of hatred of human affairs to fly up to heaven, but frequent the earth and seat herself beside you, a holy thing, upon a holy throne, joining with you in the management of human affairs. **[d]** And in her defence you shall have no need of soldiers, nor by Zeus, of slingers and archers, troops of Armenians and Iberians, shieldbearers and bodyguards, but you are sufficient in yourself. For intelligence alone is in charge of this task. There is no excuse for a king who takes no heed of justice, neither in the cowardice of soldiers nor the indolence of generals, but surely this is the proper task for you and you alone, **[190a]** so that it is possible when seated on the throne, both with small phrases and slight nods, to defend justice and with this defence to preserve the empire for all.[108] For see, O wisest of men, how I have come here today neither to flatter nor to fawn. It would not be proper for such a man who has already associated with such great emperors, both of recent and of more distant times, to dance attendance and fawn on one whom he knew to be the mildest of them all, the most tolerant and gentlest. When freedom of speech[109] is most secure, **[b]** then to choose base and unfree speech is absurd; just as one should check a thoroughbred colt when it is skittish, but he who attempts to break one which is naturally tame from the outset, without using its good breeding is absurd.

This then is already the third year in which the pen which issues death-dealing decrees is untouched by you.[110] So that while the black decree often makes its entrance as the law dictates, it always exits the palace transformed to white. For although in all other respects the most law-abiding of emperors, you know the occasions when it is more regal to violate the law than to uphold it. **[c]** No one comes into the palace

108  The central thesis of the speech. In complete contrast to *Or.* 14, Themistius argued here that warfare was not an emperor's core activity. The likeliest explanation of this change of mood is the failure of Theodosius' army in 380: see the introduction to this chapter.

109  *Parrhesia*: on the significance of this term, see Chapter 1. More generally, Themistius insinuated in this passage that freedom of speech had not existed under some of the previous emperors he had served. He never said so at the time: cf. Chapter 1 on his tendency towards *post mortem* criticism.

110  An important indication of date: see the introduction to this speech.

with pounding heart, chattering teeth and pale with fear but with confident and upstanding thoughts as if entering the sanctuary of a holy
place.[111] So mild are your eyes, so unperturbing your voice: calm
emanates from your entire visage. The very sight of you is enough to
dispel all fear from the spirit. So even he who was among your enemies,
long scorning your truce, and out of suspicion not daring to share your
table readily, now approaches unarmed and without his sword, [d]
giving himself to be treated howsoever you wish, knowing that you will
not want to treat him as an enemy, but as Alexander treated Porus the
Indian, Artaxerxes Themistocles the Athenian, and the Romans Masinissa the Libyan.[112] And so those whom we have not conquered by
arms, we attract voluntarily through faith in you and, as the magnetic
stone gently draws iron to itself, so you drew on the Getic chieftain
without effort and he comes to the royal city as a willing suppliant to
you, he who was once proud and haughty of spirit, [191a] whose father
the great and mighty Constantine won over with the statue which even
now stands at the rear of the Senate House.[113] Thus a good reputation is

111  On Theodosius' accessibility in his early years, his willingness to grant petitions, and
its relevance to regime-building, see the introductions to this chapter and *Or.* 14. Themistius
had earlier argued that Constantius II was similarly correct in mitigating the harshness of
the law: *Or.* 1.14c–15c (Chapter 2).

112  Porus, king of the regions east of Hydaspes river in North India, fiercely opposed
Alexander's attempts to cross it in 327 BC. His personal courage so impressed Alexander
that his kingdom was restored to him with some additions (see also *Or.* 7.88d–89c). Artaxerxes received Themistocles, the victor of Salamis, after his flight from Greece and made
him governor of Magnesia on the Meander. Masinissa, king of Numidia, initially fought
on the Carthaginian side from 212 to 206 BC but was persuaded by Scipio to change sides
and his cavalry played a decisive part in the Roman victory at Zama (202 BC).

113  The reference is to Athanaric, and again helps to date the speech. Athanaric surrendered to Theodosius and sought refuge in Constantinople on 11 January 381, dying there 14
days later (*Cons. Const.* s.a. 381 = *CM* 1, 243). He had been leader of the Tervingi (often, but
mistakenly, taken to be the same as the Visigoths), the Gothic confederation established
nearest to the Roman Lower Danube frontier before the arrival of the Huns (c.376). This
confederation had enjoyed semi-client status with regard to the Empire, hence Athanaric's
father, to whom the statue was raised, may have been the Gothic king's son who came to
Constantinople as a hostage under a peace treaty between these Goths and the Emperor
Constantine in 332 (*Anon. Val.* 6.31). By 381, Athanaric had lost most of his following in
two stages, one in c.376 (Ammianus 31.3.4–8, 4.13), the other c.380 (Ammianus 27.5.9).
Although his arrival in Constantinople represented a major propaganda coup, which Themistius tried to exploit in this passage, it thus did not, as has sometimes been thought (on the
basis of a confused report at Zosimus 4.35.2–5), represent the transfer of so many Goths to a
Roman allegiance that it helped end the Gothic war. See further Heather, 1991, ch. 3, App. B.

more powerful for a king than many shields and seduces as volunteers those who despise compulsion.[114] And it is not the case that [b] 'a wise plan defeats many hands'[115] but piety and love of mankind not only defeat many hands but preserve them too.

'I remember this deed from long ago and not as a recent event.'[116]

When the army of Antoninus, the emperor of the Romans – whose epithet was just this, the Pious – was suffering greatly from thirst, the king raised his hands to heaven and said 'I entreat you and supplicate the giver of life with this hand with which I have taken no life.' And he so shamed God with his prayer that rainbearing clouds appeared out of a clear sky for the soldiers. I have seen a representation of this act in a painting, the emperor offering up his prayer among his men, the [c] soldiers placing their helmets beneath the downpour and filling them with the god-given stream.[117] A leader's righteousness is just such a great boon to his subjects. In the opposite case, however, of one who is not pleasing to God and who does not perform pleasing acts, justice stems not from him but from his subjects.

'For nine days the shafts of the god visited the army',[118]

even though that army did not share Agamemnon's spleen against Chryses but on the contrary,

'all called out
that he should respect the priest and accept the glorious ransom'.[119]

114 Athanaric had previously resisted Valens' armies in the war of 367–9. On this war and Themistius' speeches, see Heather and Matthews, 1991, ch. 2. On the general significance of this passage for the evolution of policy towards the Goths, and the possibility that it was a hastily improvised insert, see the introductions, respectively, to this chapter and this speech.

115 Euripides, *Antiope* fr. 200.

116 Homer, *Iliad* 9.527.

117 Themistius appears to have confused Titus Aurelius Antoninus (Pius) with his son-in-law and successor Marcus Aurelius Antoninus. Dio Cassius relates how the latter conjured up a sudden downpour to refresh his troops who had run short of water while campaigning against the Quadi (71.8.3). Dio's account also contains the detail of the soldiers catching the rain in their helmets for the horses to drink.

118 Homer, *Iliad* 1.53.

119 Homer, *Iliad* 1.22–3. Agamemnon's refusal to ransom the daughter of the priest Chryses led to his calling on Apollo to inflict a plague upon the Greek army. This lasted nine days and struck the dogs and mules first.

**[d]** And if the army did indeed share the wrongdoing because it concurred, why then did the arrow [of disease] spread first of all among the mules and the guiltless dogs? Homer is teaching us, it seems, that while the sins of individuals fall on the sinners themselves, for the folly of kings it is their subjects who are called to account.[120] **[192a]** And so, like light which pours unsullied from the unsullied lamp, the good wrought by your thought shines on all, both far and near, but more clearly on those who stand close by.

Therefore neither this company which surrounds you nor the eminences of this company are difficult to approach, forbidding or entirely savage and untamed, as they say are the snakes which devour deadly poisons in their holes as they seek the means of destroying anyone they attack,[121] but your image has been made clear on all of them, as on coins, **[b]** and your stamp shows up for a single purpose, as an education in the good, each man imitating his leader as best he can, as the leader himself has imitated God.[122] For Pythagoras the Samian said that, for men, the only likeness to God seems to be right action, towards which your spirit naturally and unbidden wings its way, and one would sooner give up asking than you would granting and agreeing to requests.[123] Nevertheless, while you know both how to grant money

120  It would have been hard for an eastern senatorial audience presented with these reflections not to draw appropriately negative conclusions about the previous regime of the Emperor Valens who had died in battle, and passed on the highly destructive Gothic legacy. These comments fit a pattern of systematic denigration of Valens in *Orr.* 14–16 which was designed to cement loyalty to Theodosius: see the introduction to this chapter.

121  Reading ὀρέστεροι (literally 'of the mountains') for ῥαότεροι (after Cobet). The following simile is drawn from Homer's description of Hector preparing himself for the final showdown with Achilles (*Iliad* 22.93ff.). Mountain beasts were considered especially savage (see Euripides, *Bacchae* 1141; *Hecuba* 1059) and Plato speculates that the name Orestes may derive from his fierce nature (*Cratylus* 394e). The passage involves word play on κορυφή (mountain peak) and κορυφαῖος (leader) to promote the message that the 'people in high places' around Theodosius were not aloof or overbearing.

122  Themistius had earlier developed the same line of thought in relation to the regime of Valens despite his current denigration of it: *Or.* 8.118 (trans. in Heather and Matthews, 1991, 33). It was no abstract point. In the Roman world of centralised power but poor communications, imperial representatives exercised largely independent powers, and on their behaviour depended the happiness of local communities. A classic case from Tripolitana of Roman provincials being abused and then prevented by court officials from gaining access to the emperor to complain is recounted by Ammianus under Valentinian I (28.6).

123  On the political significance of liberality in the granting of petitions at the start of a reign, see the introductions to this chapter and *Or.* 14.

to your subjects and remove it from those called to account, **[c]** it is sweet for you also to waive the debts of bronze, weapons, horses and fabrics,[124] and it is only debts of words to which you make no concessions, or put off to some other time, but have been stubborn and implacable in this tax alone, not entrusting its exaction to any magistracy or soldier, but are yourself the general, yourself the keeper of these debts and their steward. You do not hand over to others the task of guarding whatever you exact, but seal up and hoard it in your own soul. **[d]** Because of this, a limitless and insatiable desire to do good is ingrained in you, because right and good action offers the opportunity for free and honest praises, with which you consolidate your reign every day and every hour. And hence if one were to count up all the perpetual exiles you have remitted, all those whom you have rescued from death, all those whose ancestral homes you have restored, all those in destitution for whom you have provided from your treasuries, he shall find the total to be not less than the days of your reign.[125]

**[193a]** You vie to surpass in deed the noble and royal saying of the Emperor Titus, contending that not just a day should pass which is unkingly because no good is done, but not even an hour.[126] For I do not omit the nights of your reign during which, although they are full of shadows and without light, it still is possible to sleep free from both fear and care. So if, as Titus believed, you are king for exactly as long as you are doing good, then you would be close to overtaking Augustus in extent of time.

**[b]** I do not think this total to be inferior to the triumphs of Alexander. For Antipater, Parmenio, the Companions and the Agrianes disputed them with him,[127] but you are the author and absolute master of this victory alone, and, in continually building up and increasing it,

124 The late Roman taxation system operated in both cash (Themistius' 'bronze') and kind as it suited the administration. Items such as horses and military clothing were levied by particular taxes, which, according to need or convenience, might be commuted into a money payment. See in general Jones, 1964, ch. 13 with, e.g., *C.Th.* 7.6 (clothing) and 11.17 (horses).

125 This would seem to be further implied criticism of the injustice of the previous regime, that of Valens: so too Vanderspoel, 1995, 201; cf. above notes 109 and 120.

126 Suetonius, *Titus* 8.1. A favourite Themistian aphorism, see *Orr.* 6.80b; 8.107a; 13.174c.

127 Antipater and Parmenio were generals of Philip II who helped Alexander in his conquests; the Companions were the mounted guard of the Macedonian kings. The Agrianes were a Thracian tribe who formed the crack troops of Alexander's army.

using these right actions like steps, you shall ascend on high and close to the hall of Zeus. For these are the only steps that lead up to heaven, not [c] Ossa, Olympus or Pelion,[128] but the divers plans and hopes of divers men. Heaven can be reached only by him who can construct this ascent through benefactions to mankind. This is the man of whom the Pythia should debate:

'I am uncertain whether I shall prophesy to you as a god or a man'

rather than Lycurgus the Spartan.[129] For Lycurgus, even though Lacedaemon was 'quite sundered with ravines',[130] harmonised albeit a single city, from disordered existence to good management, [d] but the cities that are subject to you exceed in number the men of Sparta and if you were to fill them up with happiness, we shall no longer flatter or deceive you when we apply to you the golden name of Divinity, but do so in all truth and without flattery. For the gods are givers of blessings, and by associating with them in the same task, you will be enrolled in their ranks, and all these epithets shall be yours from that time on, the saviour, the god of cities, the god of strangers and the god of suppliants,[131] [194a] names more elevated than Germanicus and Sarmaticus.[132] For titles such as these shall not pass on into the distant future but shall come to you with Terror and War, terrestrial spirits that pass their time on earth, which man's evil makes necessary. Neither Terror,

128  Peaks in the highest mountain range in Greece, which the giants Otus and Ephialtes piled upon each other to attempt to climb to heaven (Apollodorus, *Bibliotheca* 1.7.4).

129  The quotation is from Herodotus 1.65. Themistius had earlier applied the thought to Valens (whatever his implied judgements on him in this speech): *Or.* 7.97d.

130  Homer, *Iliad* 2.581; *Odyssey* 4.1.

131  See *Or.* 5 note 59 for the use of such epithets of Zeus.

132  The latter were official victory titles which late Roman emperors used as part of their official titulature to catalogue victories over neighbours. Every member of an imperial college had the right to adopt the title whether they had been personally involved in the action or not. On the principle, see Barnes, 1976a. Themistius had developed a similar line of thought in celebrating Valens' peace treaty with the Goths of 369: *Or.* 10.140a–d (trans. in Heather and Matthews, 1991, 48–9). Vanderspoel, 1995, 202, plausibly suggests that Themistius, although referring to the general practice of taking such titles, may also be accurately reporting the official titles of Gratian and Theodosius as they stood in January 381. If so, 'Germanicus' will have been adopted not after Gratian's operations on the Rhine in 379 (so Vanderspoel, 1995, 202), but after Gratian's victories over the Alamanni in 378 (Ammianus 31.10) which made Valens so jealous that he attacked the Goths unaided and lost at Hadrianople in the same year (31.12). 'Sarmaticus' presumably reflects the victory which catapulted Theodosius into power: see the introduction to this chapter.

War, nor indeed Turmoil or the Fates of Death are in heaven. For this
crowd has been driven far from where the springs of life and happiness
flow.[133] It is not the case that there are two jars placed at Zeus' threshold,
[b] filled with the fates of men, one of good the other of evil. For there is
no store of ills in heaven.[134] We ourselves fill up one of these jars and we
ourselves empty it. Should they show a jar of groans and tears in the
king's council, then I would have shown you the many great ones filled to
the brim with life, bounty, wealth, gentleness and good justice. Drawing
from and emptying these from the time he put on the purple, he does not
cease from irrigating and watering his subjects. He has no jar of blood or
fear or terror, [c] but, wherever it hides sunk in the earth, it lies mouldering
with its lid firmly on and closed up. Nor has hope alone been shut in, while
evils have poured out on mankind, but rather the opposite. It is these that
are locked away and have been sealed up with fetters that cannot be
loosed, and are indeed of adamant, while hope alone of good things has
flown free, so that everything is filled with hope.[135]

Orphanhood is a vanished name, and no one is without a father now;
even those innocents for whom some ill-starred necessity has spun this
evil destiny have got a king in exchange for their own father. [d] You let
children inherit everything from their parents, except the charges
against them, only these you do not allow, for they die along with those
who have done wrong and their lifespan does not extend beyond that of
the transgressors. You do not exact justice on those who were to be
punished for wrongs of previous generations.[136]

133 This vision of the sources of evil being driven from heaven recalls the Judeo-
Christian account of the Fall of the Angels much more than anything in classical mythol-
ogy; see, e.g., Revelation 12.7–9. This may well be another example of Themistius' willingness to adapt to the sensibilites of his Christian listeners. See further Chapter 1.

134 See *Or.* 6 note 183.

135 A variant on the story of Pandora, Hesiod, *Works and Days* 96ff. In the original,
Pandora released a swarm of evils into the world from a jar she had been forbidden to
open, only managing to prevent the escape of Hope.

136 Themistius was referring to Theodosian legislation of the previous summer, given in
Thessalonica, reflected in two surviving laws of the *Theodosian Code*. This allowed children
and other relatives of those sentenced to death or exile to retain part of the condemned
person's property (although half or more went to the fisc): *C.Th.* 9.42.8–9 (both 17 June
380); cf. Vanderspoel, 1995, 203. An interesting question is whether these new rules
applied to old cases. If so, as the wording of 9.42.8 might imply, then the measures would
have bought support among those who had lost out under earlier regimes. See also the introduction to this chapter.

It is as if we sail in a ship that is under the command of two helmsmen[137] on a voyage towards the storm which suddenly fell on it, [195a] and some of the waves are already stilled, while others are not so mountainous and raging.[138] Acting properly, both have climbed from the belly of the ship to the sterndeck, from where the whole ocean is visible, where the waves are rough, and where they begin to settle in a calm. Looking out and spying all around, both lay hold of the tillers.[139] For they have not assumed command of the ship as it rides peacefully at anchor in harbour nor sailing with a fair wind to swell the sails, but at a time when a tidal wave has mounted from every quarter, the sea boiling on this side and on that, and the ship's sides already labouring.[140] Both need the utmost skill and fortitude, [b] more even than Antiochus and Ariston.[141] For behold, how mighty is the ship they command, how many are those who sail in this ship, and how mighty are the squalls that loom over the barque. This is not yet time for sleep nor for taking one's ease, for songs and drinking – these are all the consolations and sweet accompaniments of calm, and when there is no danger both for the helmsman to be full of confidence and for the sailors to let go the oars, then it is not dangerous for the cook and the lower decksman to lay hold of the blades. For flat calm does not need precise skill. [c] But whenever

137 Gratian and Theodosius; the contrast between the complimentary treatment of Gratian here, and the more restricted and minor roles ascribed him in, respectively, *Orr.* 14 and 16 is striking, and indicative of the vicissitudes of the Gothic war. Having just seen his army fail in battle in the summer of 380, Theodosius currently stood in need of Gratian's support: hence Themistius' comparatively complimentary account of his emperor's western colleague.

138 Official imperial communiqués announcing victories were made in the autumns of both 379 and 380. The 'stilling' of 'some of the waves' may be a reference to a victory of Gratian's forces over one part of the Goths, those of Alatheus and Saphrax, but, more likely, he has in mind Athanaric, the Gothic king who fled to Constantinople. In general, Themistius was concerned to stress improvement, no doubt attempting to play down the fate of Theodosius' army in 380.

139 An important passage which may confirm that Theodosius met Gratian at Sirmium in September 380 after the defeat of his army by the Goths: see the introduction to this speech.

140 Compare *Panegyrici Latini* 10.4.2 where Maximian is described as grasping the helm of the ship of state at a time, similarly, of adverse winds.

141 Antiochus of Ascalon, a pupil and rival of Philo, founded the fifth Academy; Ariston of Chios was a pupil of Zeno.

'the East wind and the South blows with the stormy West',[142]

then, yes then,

'not every man gets to sail to Corinth'[143]

but only the most skilled and unflagging steersman, to whom the oarsmen are obedient and obedient is the officer at the prow, and to whose commands even the man who is in charge of the quarterdeck gives way; the reefs, the forestays and the sheets lie well and expertly disposed so that they are to hand for the coming need and the onslaughts of the gales.

[d] And so what in a ship is the skill of steering, is in a city the virtue of ruling. And it is necessary for this virtue to be willing to trust and unwilling to compel, in order not to fall far short in its care for public affairs. Virtue which is drawn into public affairs both grows greater and is brought to perfection. For what is always honoured is cultivated, but what is dishonoured is ignored. It is clear, then, that it is a wise saying that 'the people prosper under good kings'.[144] For swift was the progress towards what was held in honour for the masses too. [196a] Not only honour nurtures virtue, but study, hard work and devoting time to the task in hand. If it were to mount the tribunal and quit it again on the instant, shining out but for a moment and glorying in an evanescent and premature beauty, it would not move many devotees. And so it must be compared to a long-distance runner rather than a sprinter, and not stop right at the first turn, but press on over further circuits. In this way it would reveal its strength and splendour the more. [b] We see that charioteers too observe their horses over a period of time to find out what method should be applied to each.

But a man who steers cities and nations needs more experience of his subjects or he will be forced to change frequently between the bit and the reins, and not watch closely what is ahead, but always have his attention turned to those in pursuit, as to when, having run him close, they will cast him from the chariot board on which he is mounted. Therefore

142  Homer, *Odyssey* 6.295.

143  *Corpus Paroemiographorum Graecorum*, 591, no. 60; see also Aulus Gellius, *Attic Nights* 1.8.3, where the obscene origins of this proverb are illustrated by an anecdote concerning Demosthenes and the legendary Corinthian courtesan, Lais.

144  Homer, *Odyssey* 19.114; cf. Plato, *Republic* 551c. Some of the same line of thought reappeared at *Or.* 16.204a (trans. below).

he shall neither undertake a task that he knows requires time, [c] nor be gentle in his judgements or easygoing in his exactions. For haste and fear of those in hot pursuit on his heels will not accord with his being gentle in every case. Hence all the undertakings of such rulers are curtailed, incomplete, and utterly premature, since they are themselves also premature.[145] It is neither horses nor weapons so precisely scrutinised that you need, but men, who take as their share the governing of nations.[146] For God is not served by eyes, ears, or a mind bound to a body, but he is omnipresent, [d] completely untrammeled, and unbound, watching over the universe of which he is king. Because of this it is very easy for him, as he passes on his soundless path, to direct the affairs of men according to justice. But a mortal who commands and jointly rules virtually the whole earth and sea, needs to have many ears and eyes in his service. Otherwise he would not be equal to the great size of the empire. It is particularly necessary for the eyes of this man to be sound,[147] [197a] and so it is absolutely necessary for your[148] hearing and eyes to be sound also.[149] And so, as you are both defended to the east and to the west, and both go your way and keep your counsel in

145 ἠλιτόμηνος lit 'premature' – used by Homer of Eurystheus (*Iliad* 19.118ff.) whose birth after only seven months in the womb was engineered by Hera to foil Zeus' plans for Hercules. The preceding sentences would have again evoked Valens' inexperience in the minds of Themistius' audience: see the introduction to this chapter. Themistius here argued that this inexperience made Valens prey to and fearful of usurpers: the two most prominent incidents being the usurpation of Procopius (365/6) and (more relevant to Themistius' point here) the trials launched in Antioch in 371/2: Ammianus 29.1 with *PLRE* 1, 898 for further refs. If the legislation mentioned by Themistius just previously (note 136) did apply retrospectively then it was precisely the victims of Valens' various purges who gained. No doubt Themistius' emphasis on the importance of experience would have also been meant to prompt thoughts about the relative merits of Theodosius and Gratian, the latter's youth having been stressed in *Or.* 14 (see above).

146 Reading ἐθνῶν 'nations' rather than θεῶν 'gods' after Cobet. An emperor's need for excellent officials was a regular Themistian theme: see, e.g., *Or.* 8.117a.

147 There is a lacuna in the text at this point

148 Sing.: Theodosius.

149 The text is corrupt, but its general sense clear. Theodosius needs excellent deputies to ensure the excellence of his regime. Vanderspoel, 1995, 204, plausibly links this remark to the legislation Theodosius had issued the previous January and June from Thessalonica attempting to curb abuse of official power (*C.Th.* 9.27.1: 15 Jan. 380; 8.15.6; 3.6.1; 9.27.2; 3.11.1: all of 17 June), and notes the emperor's concern to limit the activities of informers: even those telling the truth were executed on the third occasion in which they acted in this manner (*C.Th.* 10.10.12–13: 30–31 Jan. 380).

equal measure, both fighting the good fight, may you both restore the Roman state with no great effort to its former position, and heal completely the wounds which it received before your stewardship,[150] having gone forth hither and thither, and having squeezed out whatever rebellious dregs of the ill-omened and lawless tribe that have remained at large.[151] One must be of good spirit. [b] The barbarians have not yet prevailed over the Romans; rather, order is manifestly stronger than disorder, system than chaos, valour than credulity, discipline than insubordination. These are the weapons with which men conquer other men. Gilded and silvered shields, glittering precious stones, a horse caparisoned with metal are surely not weapons but rewards for those who know how to conquer.

'The fiery Achilles carried off gold.'[152]

[c] And it is no wonder that the weapons of virtue are more potent and reliable than those crafted by shieldmakers and bronzesmiths. You two must bring order, daring and discipline back to the ranks, and, on their return, Victory will at once return with them. For, as sisters and fellow soldiers to each other, they generally camp together on campaign, and it is seldom that Victory and Virtue are not in the same tent.

Long ago when the Spartans were hard pressed in war by the Messenians, [d] the god bade them seek an alliance with Athens. But when the Spartans sent an embassy and sought the alliance that had been prescribed by the Pythia, the Athenians did not give them soldiers, cavalry, nor by Zeus, light troops or skirmishers but the poet Tyrtaeus.[153] For the Athenians knew in their wisdom that the Spartans were not being

150 Your = dual σφῷν; i.e., the troubles occurred before the stewardship of Gratian and Theodosius and were not their fault. Note the careful use of the dual throughout this passage; the contrast with the minimalist treatment of Gratian in *Orr.* 14 and 16 is striking, reflecting Theodosius' current need of Gratian's support, and hence temporary willingness to acknowledge his superiority.

151 I.e., the Goths: exiled from their homeland north of the Danube by the Huns. Themistius strikes a martial tone here and in what follows, which is worth contrasting with the entirely conciliatory tone of *Or.* 16. For the argument that Themistius' changes of general tone directly echoed Theodosius' changing needs, see the introduction to this chapter.

152 Homer, *Iliad* 2.875.

153 Tyrtaeus was a soldier and poet whose martial and exhortatory verses, some of which are still extant, encouraged the Spartans in the Second Messenian war (c.650 BC). There is a fanciful account in Plato, *Laws* 629a. 9 (embroidered by Pausanias 4.15.6) that he was a lame schoolmaster sent by the Athenians as a joke.

worsted by the Messenians in physical resources, but were superior both in enthusiasm and spirit when numbers were equal on both sides and even when they were greatly outnumbered, **[198a]** like those famous Spartans who were four hundred in number but did not yield to countless myriads of barbarians, as Lucullus did not yield to Tigranes, nor Pompey to Mithridates, nor Caesar to the Galatians, nor the *magister equitum* to the Sarmatians.[154] To raise up those cowering men, arousing their spirits and returning them to their former enthusiasm, Tyrtaeus was equal and philosophy is even more so.

'For long have I kept company with other kings, and never have they slighted me.'[155]

And so indeed with your leader too. And I am absolutely of the opinion **[b]** that the young man[156] is in all other respects admirable and especially a seeker of what is like himself, who considers kinship not to lie in closeness of blood ties, but in a nature that loves truth. Thus even if the two did not differ in physical beauty, I would have said that, as far as spiritual beauty is concerned, I have encountered a single king both by the Rhine and the Tigris. These two have extended order from Oceanus to the Tigris and, from the west to the east, like a single cornucopia of Amaltheia,[157] a single soul and a single thought, in an imperial chariot team, which the outrunner shall attend,[158] as

154 Examples of heroic resistance to barbarians. Leonidas and the Four Hundred held the pass at Thermopylae against the Persians in 380 BC; Tigranes I of Armenia (c.100–56 BC) and Mithridates VI of Pontus (120–63 BC) were successfully opposed by Lucius Licinius Lucullus and Pompey respectively. On Theodosius as *Magister Equitum*, see 187d above.

155 Homer, *Iliad* 1.260–1, spoken by Nestor, whose role as the aged wise counsellor Themistius appropriated here for himself (see also *Or.* 5 note 83). The Homeric original reads 'better men than you' rather than 'other kings' an interesting reversal of meaning given Themistius' history of service to other emperors.

156 Gratian. ὁ νεανίας is a significant choice of words, perhaps, given Themistius' previous emphasis on Virtue and experience going hand in hand.

157 Amaltheia was the nurse of Zeus characterised variously as a she-goat or a nymph. She provided Zeus with a goat's horn (and when herself a goat, one of her own) filled with fruit.

158 A fairly dismissive reference to Valentinian II (who was notionally Theodosius' senior, having been elevated before him): cf. Vanderspoel, 1995, 204. Valentinian was a half-brother of the Emperor Gratian, raised to the throne at the same time as the latter, but then gently retired. On his relations with Gratian and Theodosius, see now McLynn, 1994, 84–5, 163–9 respectively.

givers of life and of blessings, rival contenders with each other in doing good to mankind.[159] [c] But you, gentlemen, must remove the infection from us with the guardianship that you dispense,[160] an infection which still endures, is deep-seated and dies hard. Standing at the shoulder of Tyrtaeus and Homer, whose voice is yet greater than that of Tyrtaeus, I say

> 'Forsooth this is a great and strange wonder I see with my eyes, which I claimed would never come to pass – the Trojans coming against our cities, they who once were like fleeing harts',[161]

[d] and

> 'Son of Atreus, as before with unshakeable resolve, lead the Argives in doughty battles.'[162]

Exhort your soldiers on the one hand from Homer –

> 'Let him sharpen his spear well, and ready his shield well'[163]

– [199a] but on the other from philosophy. Let him indeed sharpen his spear well, but let him also, before his spear, sharpen his spirit; likewise, let him place his shield well, but let him also, before his shield, ready his stoutheartedness, and with these exhortations and encouragements

> 'you shall drive from hence the hounds of hell whom the Fates bring',[164]

and they shall carry them off to the Danube,

> [b] 'so that even someone born in the far hereafter may shudder at doing ill to the one who received strangers with friendship.'[165]

---

159 Themistius had earlier used this idea of two emperors with but a single soul of Valentinian and Valens: *Or.* 6.75d–76d (trans. in Chapter 3); cf. Vanderspoel, 1995, 204 n. 62, identifying Ael. Arist., *Or.* 27.22–39, as the source.

160 The text is corrupt, but this sense can be achieved by reading ἡμῶν after Harduin and ἃις ... κηδημονίαις after Reiske.

161 Homer, *Iliad* 18.99ff. The original reads 'ships' for 'cities'. The Goths are here cast as Trojans.

162 Homer, *Iliad* 2.344ff.

163 Homer, *Iliad* 2.382.

164 Adapted from Homer, *Iliad* 8.527ff.

165 Homer, *Iliad* 3.353–4: Menelaus' words referring to Paris, which are nicely applicable to the Goths who sought asylum in 376 and then rebelled.

## ORATION 16
## SPEECH OF THANKSGIVING TO THE EMPEROR FOR THE
## PEACE AND THE CONSULSHIP OF GENERAL SATURNINUS:
## INTRODUCTION

Oration 16 is among the easiest to date of Themistius' extant speeches. He composed it to celebrate the consulship of Flavius Saturninus, an imperial general (*Magister Militum*) and one of the architects of the peace deal concluded with the Goths in October 382 (cf. the title of the speech and 200a–c). Saturninus' year in office began on 1 January 383, and the oration was presumably delivered during the ceremonies of the day. As another passage makes clear, Themistius was speaking both in the Senate of Constantinople, and on its behalf, in the presence of the Emperor Theodosius himself and his assembled court officials (200c). Eighteen years previously, Themistius had delivered Oration 5 on a similar occasion marking the consulship of the Emperor Jovian.[166]

**Dynastic Policies**

This oration is also one of the most widely read in the Themistian corpus, primarily for the insights it provides into the peace treaty drawn up between Theodosius and the Goths, to which much of it is devoted. When read in conjunction with Orations 14 and 15, however, the silences and virtual silences of this speech are as historically significant as what it actually says, not least on the subject of the evolving relationship between Theodosius and his western partner, the Emperor Gratian. Of the three speeches, Oration 16, on the face of it, seems the least concerned with relations between Gratian and Theodosius. Just very briefly, in one passage, Themistius returned to the subject of Theodosius' elevation, noting that it was God who had actually chosen him for the purple, whereas Gratian's task had been merely to announce the decision (207b). Oration 16 offered no nod in the direction of Gratian's sagacity in spotting Theodosius' virtue, as Oration 14 had done, nor was there any treatment, as in Oration 15, of the theme of broadly equal imperial partnership. The speech thus demoted Gratian to a minor walk-on role as God's herald, and, more generally, the speech contained a number of other pointed remarks which were clearly aimed in Gratian's direction.

---

166  *Or.* 16.206.b–d further confirms the date, noting that it was also the fifth anniversary of the accession of the Emperor Theodosius, who had come to the throne in January 379.

Themistius made certain, for instance, that the audience understood that Theodosius had broken with the normal practice of the Valentinianic dynasty in awarding consular honours. Although it was the fifth anniversary of his accession, Theodosius had not taken the consulship himself, as it had become Valentinianic custom to do (202d–203b). Nor had Theodosius echoed a second Valentinianic custom, that of granting the consulship to minor sons. Theodosius had Arcadius (aged 5 or 6)[167] available (204b–d), but deliberately chose not to nominate him. Two recent eastern examples of the latter practice would have come to the audience's mind (Jovian's son Varronianus, and Valens' son Valentinian Galates, not to mention Valentinian II in 376, but he was already an Augustus), but Gratian himself, aged 6, had also been a child consul in 366.[168] According to Themistius' analysis, Theodosius' non-Valentinianic practice was much more generous and hence likely to generate greater political support among would-be non-imperial consuls, as well as showing greater confidence in future dynastic security than previous emperors who had rushed their sons into the office (203a–204b, 204d). A return to one of the themes explored in Oration 15, the bad effects of rushed promotions, similarly spat a certain amount of venom in Gratian's direction (205dff.; cf. *Or.* 15. 190a–194d, 196c–d). And, as we shall see, there was likewise no account of the latter's role in either the Gothic war, or the peace, a silence which does little justice to the other available evidence.

Compared to his earlier speeches, therefore, and especially Oration 15, Themistius was, by January 383, greatly downplaying Gratian's role in the momentous events of the recent past, and finding as many oblique ways as possible to criticise Gratian in particular and the Valentinianic dynasty in general, while emphasising the beneficial effects of Theodosius' contrasting behaviour. Such a previously loyal servant of Valens as Themistius would not have undertaken this assault on his own initiative, and Oration 16 contains important clues as to why Theodosius wanted an aggressive strategy pursued. Two passages were devoted to the five- or six-year-old Arcadius. The first commented that he would have been entirely worthy of the consulship, describing him as the 'beloved beacon of the world' and an Alexander in waiting (204c–d). These descriptions emphasised that Theodosius had shown truly great virtue in passing

167 Arcadius was 31 at his death in 408; hence he was born in c.377: *PLRE* 1, 99.
168 *PLRE* 1, 946, 381, 401 respectively.

him over as consul in favour of Saturninus. Significantly, Themistius then returned to Arcadius at the end of the speech, expressing the hope that the example of his father's virtue would shape the boy's character (213a–b). Eighteen days after Oration 16 was delivered, on the fifth anniversary of his own promotion, Theodosius raised Arcadius to the purple. He did so possibly without even consulting Gratian, although this seems unlikely, but certainly without his permission. The new Augustus remained entirely unrecognised on Gratian's coinage before the latter was killed the following summer.[169] Cause and effect seem clear. Downplaying Gratian's role in Theodosius' promotion, and stressing that the latter was God's choice, emphasised Theodosius' independent claim to the imperial office. This was entirely apposite at a moment when Theodosius was about to make overt his own dynastic ambitions by raising Arcadius to the purple without the prior approval of his western colleague. That his new practices in granting the consulship meant that more men could hope for this honour was equally to the point, since Theodosius was about to break with his imperial colleague and needed all the political support he could get.

## Peace Making

The strongly dynastic over- and undertones of Oration 16 have been little noticed in the past, but are also relevant to any understanding of Themistius' treatment of the other great theme of Oration 16: the peace agreement with the Goths of October 382. Oration 16 unambiguously describes Theodosius as the architect of the 382 peace agreement with the Goths, hailing him as the first to consider the idea of a negotiated peace (207b–c). This may be true, but since the statement occurs in a panegyric of Theodosius we cannot be certain. A more interesting question is whether Gratian and his advisors were involved at all in the adoption of the new policy. Oration 16 does not mention Gratian in the context of the peace, and barely, as we have seen, in any other. After 381, when Gratian's generals Bauto and Arbogast pushed the Goths out of Illyricum and back into Thrace, the Gothic problem was once again confined to territory belonging to the eastern Empire. Arguably, therefore, by 382 it had become Theodosius' problem alone.[170] On the other

169  *RIC* 9, xix–xxi, 72.
170  So Errington, 1996b, 17–18.

hand, there are a number of reasons for thinking that Themistius' silence over Gratian in Oration 16 – part of a wider strategy of Theodosian dynastic aggrandisement – has had, and was originally designed to have, a distorting effect. The contribution of the west to both war and peace was larger than the speech implied.

Ever since 376 the two halves of the Empire had at least attempted to agree a joint approach to the Gothic problem. Valens immediately negotiated for military aid from Gratian (very likely, as we have seen, linked to Themistius' dash westwards). Some aid came in 377, much more, if delayed, in 378. Theodosius' promotion was accompanied by a temporary transfer of Illyricum to him to facilitate the war effort, and Gratian's forces under Bauto and Arbogast rescued matters in 381, after Theodosius' makeshift army had collapsed in the summer of 380. After their great victory at Hadrianople, the Goths, like the Romans, had to be constrained militarily into making peace. If not destroyed themselves, they did have to be convinced that they could not defeat the Empire. Roman military action – as much as Theodosius' persuasion – was part of the peace process, therefore, and Theodosius did not have a functioning army.[171]

Gratian and his court, likewise, were near at hand during the campaigning seasons of the war subsequent to Theodosius' promotion. In 379, Gratian remained in the Balkans until midsummer, when his court moved briefly to Italy *en route* for the Rhine. In 380, his court was at Aquileia for most of the summer, an important base for controlling the Julian Alps. His forces intervened against Alatheus and Saphrax in Pannonia, and he himself, as we have seen, may have met Theodosius at Sirmium.[172] In winter 380/1, Gratian shifted the whole axis of his court, moving it lock, stock and mint from Trier on the Rhine to Milan in northern Italy. This more than anything else signals the greater degree to which his regime now felt driven by events on the Danube. In 381, the court oversaw events from Aquileia and travelled as far east as Viminacium in Moesia Superior in July.[173] For 382, we have little detail.

171 Heather, 1991, 175ff., commenting esp. on Ammianus 31.12.9.

172 Aquileia's strategic role: Ammianus 21.12.21; cf. McLynn, 1994, 100. Errington, 1996b, n. 140, corrects Heather, 1991, 171 n. 45, on its precise geographical position.

173 Milan: McLynn, 1994, 119–20. *C.Th.* 1.10, 1 and 12.1.89 have Gratian at Viminacium on 5 July 381 *and* 5 July 382 respectively. This coincidence is unlikely. Seeck corrected to 382, but other known imperial movements suggest 381: Errington, 1992, 458–9 (correcting Heather, 1991, 171).

Gratian oscillated between his new bases in northern Italy, but they had been established precisely to watch over Danubian events, and, at some point before 383, Gratian had come into contact with a large number of Alans whom he brought into his army.[174] These Alans were clearly drafted in from somewhere on the Danube.

It seems implausible to suppose, therefore, that in 382 Gratian and his advisors merely handed back the Gothic problem to Theodosius and washed their hands of it. As Themistius claims, Theodosius may have been 'the first' to advocate the new policy, but, as this statement actually implies, the policy was probably also followed by the western court. The end of the war, like its beginning and middle, is likely to have involved both halves of the Empire. In crediting the peace treaty entirely to Theodosius, Oration 16 has been generally followed by modern scholarship. We have, however, no panegyric from Gratian's court for 1 January 383. More than enough indications survive to show that such a speaker could have put together an entirely plausible account of how Gratian rescued Theodosius from disaster by constraining the Goths to surrender, and thus brought the war to a successful conclusion.

### Terms of Agreement

The actual terms of the Gothic peace, and their broader historical significance, have been often discussed, not least because no clear and precise account of them survives. As a result, Themistius' rather allusive and rhetorical accounts of the agreement, both in Oration 16 and again in Oration 34 (see Chapter 5), have been repeatedly mined for information, supplemented for some matters by other texts, especially the Latin prose panegyric of Pacatus from 389 and the *De Regno* of Synesius of Cyrene from about a decade later. Like Themistius' two speeches, Pacatus' panegyric was a rhetorical eulogy of Theodosius, while Synesius was concerned to mount an equally rhetorical assault on the policy of compromise with the Goths that the agreement encompassed.[175] By their nature, therefore, these texts – partial in one direction or the other – tend to provide contrasting images of different aspects of the peace agreement and its effects, rather than a straightforward account of its detailed provi-

---

174 Zosimus 4.35.2ff. seemingly dated to 382.

175 On Pacatus, see Nixon and Rodgers, 1994; nature and purpose of the *De Regno*: Heather, 1988, followed by Cameron and Long, 1993.

sions. Modern reconstructions of the latter, consequently, tend quickly to vagueness on matters of detail.[176] What, however, can be reconstructed?

In outward form, at least, the peace clearly took the traditional Roman diplomatic form of a *deditio* – surrender – of the Goths to the Empire. In both Orations Themistius consistently used language of surrender and subjection, and Oration 16 opened with a description of what would appear to be a formal surrender ceremony where barbarians were displayed in Constantinople giving up their weapons (199c). A later passage suggests, indeed, that some Goths were also present as Oration 16 was being delivered, again perhaps as a symbol of Saturninus' part in bringing about the peace (210d). Other sources confirm that this was how the peace was presented to the Roman public, and that this presentation was generally accepted. Orosius and other Latin chroniclers report that the Goths 'surrendered' (some using the language of *deditio*),[177] Pacatus referred to the Goths as 'in servitude' (*Pan. Lat.* 2.22.3), Libanius called them Theodosius' 'loyal slaves' (*Or.* 9.16), Synesius his 'suppliants' (*De Regno* 21.50.12). The point has significance because scholars have tended to believe the one ancient account which dissents from this picture. The sixth-century historian of the Goths, Jordanes, reports that the peace took the more equal diplomatic form of a *foedus* (*Getica* 27.141–29.146), and, on this basis, it has often been supposed that the treaty of 382 marked the first, or one of the first, occasions on which the Roman state was forced formally to acknowledge the decline of its strategic power by concocting a more equal form of diplomatic agreement with a group of intrusive outsiders. Jordanes' discussion of Gothic affairs is consistently anachronistic, however, so that his testimony is insufficient to counter the weight of more contemporary evidence. Formally, at least, the Goths surrendered unconditionally to the Roman state.[178]

176 Some modern discussions: Thompson, 1963; Stallknecht, 1969; Chrysos, 1972, 146ff.; Wolfram, 1988, 133–5; Heather, 1991, ch. 5; Cesa 1994; Wirth, 1997.

177 Orosius 7.34.7 (*Romano sese imperio dediderunt*); *Cons. Const.* s.a. 382 (*CM* 1.243); Hydatius s.a. 382 (*CM* 2.15); Marcellinus Comes s.a. 382 (*CM* 2.61).

178 Since Mommsen, 1910, it has been normal to view the treaty of 382 as the first occasion on which the diplomatic innovation of the *foedus* was used on Roman soil, although (again following Jordanes' anachronisms) it has been supposed that Constantine had previously tried it out with Goths north of the Danube in 332: e.g., Stallknecht, 1969, 26ff., 75ff.; Chrysos, 1972, 51ff., 146ff. More contemporary sources again make it clear that the treaty of 332 was likewise formally one of *deditio*: Heather, 1991, 107–15, 158–9; Wirth, 1997.

*Deditio* as a diplomatic form was admirably suited to Roman assumptions that theirs was an Empire teleologically sustained by the Divinity to bring humankind to proper perfection. Under this schema, barbarians were by definition inferior beings, and Romans expected their emperors to be triumphant, through divine aid, over them. Hence victory was the first virtue expected of any Roman emperor, and prone or supine barbarians were always portrayed pictorially in physical postures which captured the totality of their subjection. Hence too, the normal Roman response of fierce indignation directed against hostile barbarians, who could be thought of as having committed treason against this divine order.[179] From this perspective, total, unconditional surrender was the only reasonable form that relations could take between Romans and barbarians.

Unfortunately from the Roman point of view, the kind of expectations raised by presenting the peace of 382 in the overall guise of *deditio* were not entirely satisfied by its detailed terms. The hostile Synesius criticised Theodosius for allowing the Goths to continue to live under 'their own laws', by which he clearly meant that they had not become fully subdued imperial subjects (*De Regno* 19). Subsequent events confirm the substance of Synesius' remarks. After the treaty had been concluded, the Goths remained a distinct presence in the Roman Balkans. They participated *en masse* as a distinct military force in Theodosius' two civil wars against western usurpers (in 387 and 393/4), and revolted, again largely as one body, on Theodosius' death under the leadership of Alaric in 395.[180] Although presented as an unconditional Gothic surrender, the peace of 382 did not bring about the destruction of the Goths' independent identity, which was the object of normal Roman methods for resettling outsiders.[181]

This contrast, between normal expectations of *deditio* and the de facto survival of Gothic autonomy, lies at the heart of Themistius' presentation of the treaty of 382 in both Orations 16 and 34. Themistius

179 Expectations of victory: McCormick, 1986. Pictorial presentations: Calo Levi, 1952. A good example of Roman indignation when faced with revolting barbarians is Valentinian I: Ammianus 30.6.2–3. Themistius reflects the potency of such views in referring to the guilt of the rebellious Goths in *Orr.* 14.181c; 15.197b–198a; 16.210; 34.xx.

180 Heather, 1991, 181–99, arguing against Liebeschuetz, 1990, 48–85, who saw much greater discontinuity between the Goths settled under the terms of the 382 treaty and those who revolted under Alaric.

181 On these methods, see the introduction to this chapter.

himself acknowledged the problem, conceding, in one passage, that the Goths had not been wiped out (*Or.* 16.211a). He then attempted to satisfy public opinion by positing a range of arguments which cumulatively suggested that the best possible outcome had nonetheless been achieved. The least subtle of them was the claim that the Goths had been so thoroughly subdued that they might as well have been exterminated (210a). More fundamentally, Themistius argued that, even if the Goths could have been destroyed, it was much better overall that they had not. In making this case, Themistius came close to admitting that destruction of the Goths had not been a practical possibility after the Roman defeat at Hadrianople. To state this unequivocally, however, would have compromised the martial dominance expected of an emperor, and Themistius did not quite go beyond saying that defeating the Goths would have been very difficult (211a). Rather than focussing on the degree to which circumstance had constrained the Empire into a compromise peace, Themistius' argument concentrated instead on the positive virtues inherent in 'forgiving' the Goths. They were spared, he argued, so that they might serve the Empire in the guises of farmers and soldiers, increasing both imperial revenues by paying taxation and the overall military power at Theodosius' disposal. In Oration 16, the paying of taxes on agricultural production was put in the future, the speech concentrating on a description of the repopulation of Thrace after the devastations of war. Oration 34, however, declared the paying of taxes an established fact (*Or.* 16.211a–d; *Or.* 34.xxii). The basic point is confirmed by both Synesius who refers to Theodosius giving the Goths Roman 'land', and Pacatus who portrays Goths serving the Empire as farmers (*De Regno* 21; *Pan. Lat.* 2.22.3). None of these sources provides any detail on which lands were allocated, and to whom among the Goths, but the basic picture is clear enough.[182]

Gothic military service is likewise described in our sources only in rather general terms (Themistius, *Or.* 16.211a–d, *Or.* 34.xxii; Synesius, *De Regno* 21). One aspect of it, however, again seems clear enough. When required, the treaty Goths served *en masse* in expeditionary armies, such as those sent by Theodosius against the western usurpers Maximus and Eugenius. These seem to have represented only temporary

---

182 Clear enough to disprove, in this case at least, that the intrusive Goths were being supported out of redirected tax revenues (the influential argument of Goffart, 1980), rather than by grants of actual land that they had to farm themselves.

mobilisations for the duration of particular campaigns.[183] We also hear of Goths performing more regular military service. 'Tervingi' and 'Visi' are listed among the palatine auxiliaries of the two eastern armies under the command of *magistri militum praesentales* (*Not. Dig.* Or. 5.61, 6.61). The simplest explanation is that, in addition to occasional service *en masse*, some regular Roman regiments had also been recruited from among the Goths. This would be entirely in line with regular Roman practice.[184] Other pertinent details are not discussed. No reliable source tells us how many Goths were drafted in for the offensive expeditionary armies, nor how much they were paid. There are also hints that the Goths had some kind of general, defensive, military role on the Danube, but the indications are very unspecific.[185] There is no doubting the general point, however, that the peace left the Goths intact as a military force, whose potential was subsequently exploited by the east Roman state in a variety of ways.

Themistius' presentation of the Gothic peace in Oration 16 thus represented another careful rhetorical balancing act. His audience's expectations of victory were catered for by an emphasis on the Goths' subjugation, and also by a further passage, towards the end of the speech, where he looked forward to the assimilation of the Goths into mainstream Roman society, in the same way that Celts who had centuries earlier crossed over the Bosphorus had been absorbed into the general population of the province of Galatia which was named after them (211c–212a). The fact that the Goths had not been exterminated could not be hidden, however, and here Themistius' answer was to make virtue of necessity. Even though exterminating the Goths would have been difficult, he argued, it was much better not to make the effort, but to subdue them by persuasion so that they would survive to serve the Empire.

183 Implied particularly by Pacatus' account of the Maximus campaign: *Panegyrici Latini* 2.32.3–4. This aspect of Gothic military service is generally accepted, except by Demougeot, 1974; 1979, 154ff., who argues that Goths served in large numbers in the eastern field army up to 388, when Theodosius replaced them with westerners. Hoffmann, 1969, 469ff., showed that about 15 regiments were transferred from the west to the east in c.390, but Pacatus' evidence seems unambiguous that the mass of Goths served only irregularly in the Roman army even before this transfer.

184 Cf. most recently Liebeschuetz, 1990, 29ff.

185 Zosimus 4.34.5 (Scythians keeping watch on the Danube); cf. Zosimus 4.40 on a 'Scythian' force which clashed fatally with the regular Roman garrison of the city of Tomi in Scythia Minor.

But this was, of course, a presentation of the treaty, not straight-forwardly factual reporting of its detailed provisions. Themistius' discussion was carefully designed to cast the treaty in the most favourable light possible, and in particular to explain why it was a good thing that the Goths, who had beaten two Roman armies and ravaged the Balkans, had not been suitably exterminated. There is no reason to look further than the military situation to explain the change in Roman policy. As Themistius himself hinted, the Goths were not destroyed because the Romans could not manage it. The point is confirmed by subsequent events. In two major confrontations between 395 and 397, these Goths, now under the leadership of Alaric, could still not be destroyed. The policy change, moreover, affected only this group. More Goths, particularly those led by Odotheus in 386, and other groups of outsiders coming subsequently to the Danube were greeted in the traditionally martial Roman manner, and their overthrow suitably celebrated. There was no general change in policy, therefore, but only a specific alteration in relation to this one particular group of Goths.[186] In all this, as indeed in his denial of any role to Gratian, Themistius was seeking to continue the rescue of Theodosius' reputation, following his defeat at the hands of the Goths in the summer of 380, which had begun in Oration 15. It is a tribute to Themistius' skills as a propagandist that historians have been so ready to credit Theodosius' imagination, rather than the press of circumstance, for the compromise peace of 382, and to deny Gratian any part in the action. Oration 16 was, above all, an exercise in appropriating all possible credit for Theodosius from the outcome of the Gothic war, in preparation for the *coup d'état* represented by the unilaterial promotion of Arcadius which would follow only eighteen days after Themistius spoke. This dynastic context informed Themistius' presentation of the Gothic peace and must be understood by historians seeking to disinter the realities of the peace from the image of it so carefully erected in Oration 16.

186 On Odotheus and other Danubian intruders after 382, see Heather, 1991, 168–9; cf. Stallknecht, 1969, 78. Goffart, 1981, argues for a voluntary change in policy, but in our view the argument pays insufficient attention to the circumstances and limited nature of Theodosius' modifications.

## ORATION 16
## SPEECH OF THANKSGIVING TO THE EMPEROR FOR THE
## PEACE AND THE CONSULSHIP OF GENERAL SATURNINUS:
## TRANSLATION

[199c] I have often thought to myself that, since my body is worn out and old age advances,[187] now is the time to lay aside my writing tablet and cease from further wearying the king's ears with my speeches. For indeed if some contribution had to come to him from philosophy,[188] she has already made sufficient payment. But since I stood an eyewitness of that day on which he brought in peace quietly and calmly as if at a sacred rite, and, to those who were then in the deepest despair, presented the barbarians giving up their weapons voluntarily, and we saw clearly and in the flesh, what we had previously known through pictorial representations,[189] [d] I am unable to hold myself back and, in Euripides' words, do not disgrace my old age by intending to join the dance.[190] For it would be terrible to encourage him while he still resisted the enemy yet not to crown him once victorious, or to have admired him while he negotiated the peace but disregard him once he had completed the task, just as if I were to praise a competitor in the games while he fought his opponents in the arena, but then hesitate to proclaim his victory once he had thrown his man and gained the upper hand.

[200a] So being already eager for these reasons to reach out for my writing materials and make the attempt, if power to speak remained for

187 Themistius, probably born in the late 310s, would have been in his mid-sixties in 383.

188 Themistius' standard self-identification: Chapter 1. See also the opening of *Or.* 10 (trans in Heather and Matthews, 1991) for a similarly self-deprecating beginning.

189 Following Cobet's emendation γραφέντα ἐθεώμεθα misprinted (ἐδεώμεθα) in the Teubner apparatus. Themistius was contrasting standard imperial iconography of submitting barbarians, often represented (e.g., on coins: see Calo Levi, 1952) as kneeling under emperors' feet with the panorama of real barbarians submitting presented in the triumph Theodosius held in Constantinople after the peace with the Goths. This suggests that Theodosius held a real triumph (contra McCormick, 1986, 42) perhaps on 3 October 382 when *Cons. Const.* records the formal surrender of the Goths (*CM* 1, 243). Pictorial propaganda other than that on coins could play important roles; Eunapius fr. 68 records some inadvertently ridiculous effects of pictorial panels in the Circus at Rome depicting the hand of God driving off barbarians. Intermediate victory communiqués, such as those issued by Gratian and Theodosius in 379 and 380, may have been accompanied by appropriate illustrations for the masses.

190 Euripides, *Bacchae* 204: Tiresias' words on his intention to join the Bacchae in their ecstatic celebration of Dionysus.

me in such great physical storms, the king introduces another pleasant compulsion, proclaiming the general for the office which gives the year its name.[191] I have long been under an obligation to this man and was seeking a suitable opportunity for repayment. It was not just the common debt which words justly owe to the weapons which have stood in their defence and preserve them, [b] but there were also my more personal circumstances and an obligation which has grown greater over a total of more than thirty years in all.[192] For this man launched me when I was just beginning to make my way towards the palace, helped to correct me once I had established a reputation, and finally during this most happy reign, has omitted nothing, neither important nor trivial, with the king's enthusiastic help, to render me more honoured by [the few][193] and the many. And indeed it seemed strange to me that the Senate, convening at once when the emperor proclaimed him, gave the appropriate thanks, but I was at that time found wanting against my will, and who would willingly hold back, [c] save in one aspect of the present speech, that both the general and even more the king should receive praise together. For whenever the receiver of great things clearly deserves them, the judgement of the giver deserves admiration, and to achieve honour justly brings no greater[194] praise for the one who has achieved it than for the one who gives it.

But now the Senate convenes at our instigation, and adds, to the words then spoken as the occasion demanded, these which are the products of

---

191 The consulship; in Roman dating schemes, years were named after their two consuls. See, in general, Bagnall et. al., 1987, ch. 1. The general in question is Saturninus, on whom see below.

192 This would suggest that Saturninus first assisted Themistius' career in the early 350s. Saturninus was *cura palatii* under Constantius sometime before 361, which would have been a suitable position from which to accomplish this; see further the introduction to *Or.* 1.

193 There is a lacuna or corruption at this point. The sentence clearly requires something to balance 'the many'. We have supplied 'the few' which would also make the phrase balance with the preceding reference to things 'great and small'.

194 Reading οὐ μείζων; the same idea also appeared in *The Letter of Constantius*: Chapter 2. The Teubner text reads '. . . is less praise for the one who has achieved than for the one who gives it'. This is possible. In general terms, this paragraph makes it clear that there were two senatorial celebrations of Saturninus' consulship: one when he was formally designated consul for the coming year, the second when he assumed office on 1 January 383. The available evidence suggests that designations could be announced as little as one month or as much as six months before the assumption of office: Bagnall et al., 1987, 18–20. On this occasion, Themistius' illness seems to have been genuine rather than diplomatic.

reflection. For my voice must be considered the Senate's voice; **[d]** it sets me at its head for no other reason than for speeches. And while the words I utter are perhaps my own, their sentiment, because we all have one common sentiment, is also shared by those who hear them, and so we have convened.[195] Now it is said by many that the word is the deed's shadow,[196] and is in no way adequate as a thank offering. Yet whenever I look upon the assembled company **[201a]** and upon him who presides over that company, I would say that I make return not merely with like measure, but in fact with a much better one.[197] For I have not gathered together some random group of men, nor have I made my entrance into a repudiated theatre, like some rhetor or sophist, running through the set topic, but sacred is my speech, sacred the art that fashioned my words, and sacred also is the temple into which I have come.[198] Royal Zeus is my audience, and, with God, the king himself together with his whole entourage. **[b]** On the one hand, there are these offices which are forever the most mighty and equal rivals to each other,[199] on the other, there is the team of generals, one of whom yields to the privileges accorded to age and has considered this man's prior assumption of the honour a guarantee of his own, while for the other the reward is not unexpected.[200] Justice, king-

---

195 On the relationship between Themistius and the senate, infinitely more complex than this characterisation might suggest, see Chapter 1.

196 Plutarch, *On the Education of Boys* 1, 9, F: also used at *Or.* 11.143b.

197 Hesiod, *Works and Days* 349ff.

198 On sophists (display orators) and the charge levelled against Themistius, at different points in his career, that he was one, see the introductions to *The Letter of Constantius*, Chapter 1, and Chapter 5 on his assumption of the urban prefecture of Constantinople. In late Roman state ideology, the emperor was considered chosen by God and hence sacred, along with all his attributes and officials. Hence the senate and palace were both also sacred. For introductions to different aspects of this ideology, see Dvornik, 1966; MacCormack, 1981.

199 Reading πάρισοι as *A* and *Π*.

200 Saturninus the consul and Fl. Richomeres, who succeeded him as consul in the next year, 384. Richomeres had served in Gratian's forces up to Hadrianople, and, although present at the battle, had – like two other generals, Saturninus himself and Victor – managed to survive. Richomeres subsequently served Theodosius and the east: refs as *PLRE* 1, 765. The passage indicates that a future consulship for Richomeres had already been indicated, whether formally or informally. In January 383, it was important for political reasons for Theodosius to keep his two leading military commanders happy, since he was about to break with Gratian over the elevation of Arcadius: see the introduction to this chapter.

ship's lieutenant,[201] the government of the palace, the orchestrators of munificence and the dispensers of magnificence are also present.[202] Under such a chorus leader and in such a theatre, with the thank-offering making its entrance from philosophy, whose offerings are held in high regard even by kings themselves, the recompense cannot still be considered meagre, [c] nor numbered with the others or equivalent to talents of gold or silver or costly equipages. For neither Echepolus the Sicyonian who gave his mare Aithe as a gift to Agamemnon for military exemption, nor Kinyras, who gave his famous corslet,[203] wrote about the expedition, but it is Homer through whom the remembrance of those deeds has yet remained alive and undiminished.

[d] Now if it was prestigious for Alcibiades, Pericles and Themistocles to be crowned in the theatre at Athens by a public herald, and to have the Areopagus as witness or the Council of the Five Hundred or the mass of the people, how can it not be much greater and more prestigious to have the lord and master of all men as witness of both our words and actions, and audience of philosophy's proclamation, or rather him who first caused it to resound and shine out,[204] just as they inscribe the words 'Good Fortune' at the head of publicly proclaimed decrees.[205] [202a] For, indeed, who but the king has provided the actual impetus for these words? Who reminded us of the thanks owed to the general? Was he not the first to repay thanks to him? It is the prerogative of kingship and philosophy to reward virtue in fitting manner. For the witness from these sources is free and impartial. In contrast, all those ignoble flatteries expressed in complex and pretentious phraseology[206] are both distrusted and disbelieved by those who

201 At Hesiod, *Works and Days* 256, Justice sits by the throne of Zeus, as is implied by the term πάρεδρος here.
202 Respectively the *quaestor* (the emperor's chief legal officer), the *magister officiorum*, and the *comites sacrae largitionis* and *rei privatae* (chief financial officers). The sentence has no main verb; we have supplied 'are present'.
203 *Iliad* 23.293–300, 11.19–22. Echepolus' gift to Agamemnon allowed him to stay at home in Sicyon and not go to Troy. The story of Kinyras, king of Cyprus and son of Apollo, failing to keep his promise to assist Agamemnon is not recorded in the *Iliad*, which simply refers to his sending of a breastplate as a gift.
204 I.e., Theodosius whose appointment of Saturninus has caused philosophy (i.e., Themistius) to rejoice.
205 ἀγαθὴ τύχη: examples of imperial rescripts closing εὐτυχεῖτε (Millar, 1992, 222), suggest that this was probably a standard feature of imperial diplomacy.
206 Reading χρώμασι for χρήμασι after Doehner.

hear them.[207] **[b]** But this is truly the Olympic wild olive, the crown of Pisean Zeus.[208] For it is not right either for the man who holds sway over all things, or the man who pursues the truth, to be in any way insincere in giving thanks. And he who succeeds in this task shines out brightly like the Homeric star whose beams are seen from afar. And these neither darkness nor cloud obscure; but it is oblivion the great sun dispels rather than haziness.[209]

**[c]** And so Homer, when he asked the Muses who was the best man among the Greeks, did not reveal their opinion precisely but, by excluding Achilles on account of his wrath and awarding the first rather than the second place to Ajax, rendered the judgement equivocal. He weaves the same device for horses too, giving first prize to the mares of Eumelos but yet not excluding those of the son of Peleus.[210] But the king cast no darkness over his vote, nor presented it obliquely or ambiguously, when he had to proclaim the best man, but proclaimed who was in his mind in a clear voice. And what a difference in that declaration! **[d]** For instead of himself, he heralded this man, transferring the honour that had been offered to himself by his imperial partner onto a private citizen, and while confident that this prize lay within his power, sought a way that he might be seen to have discovered and bestowed such a gift as no king has ever bestowed on one highly honoured by him.[211]

**[203a]** Now, indeed, we know many emperors who have granted a consulship to several of those held in equal honour, but none, apart

---

207 I.e., panegyric. Themistius' career was based on distinguishing his own speeches from panegyrics and asserting that his efforts had much greater credibility because he was a truth-telling philosopher: see Chapter 1.

208 The wild olive was the prize awarded in the Olympic games; cf. above *Or.* 15.185d–186.

209 Homer, *Iliad* 5.6: the star is Sirius. 'Haziness' is an attempt to translate ἀχλύς, in Homer the mist which comes over the eyes of one dying or swooning, as opposed to λήθη, the total oblivion which follows death. Themistius was saying that the reputation of one legitimately praised by a truth-telling philosopher (such as himself) will be preserved forever.

210 *Iliad* 2.761ff. Achilles was the son of Peleus.

211 An important passage which has been taken as evidence that, in the 4th century, both consuls of each year were appointed by the senior Augustus: Palanque, 1944. It is clear, however, that Theodosius normally appointed one consul and Gratian another (cf. note 215 below). It was an established norm, rather than a real choice of Gratian, that Theodosius should have taken the consulship in the fifth year of his reign: Bagnall et al., 1987, 13–18. Ignoring a norm of the Valentinianic dynasty was probably designed to assert independence: see the introduction to this chapter.

from him, who has transferred to another man the consulship which had fallen to himself. Thus, if one were to say that this honour is greater than those taking the same rank and title by as much as a king is greater than private citizens, it would not be an error, or that it is the more prestigious and dignified, by as much as the honour bestowed with such remission has surpassed the one simply granted. **[b]** We shall discover no other private citizen in the whole of history who has assumed an honour set aside for a king. Consequently, I think, it is useless to do violence to the order of precedence of the titles even should we wish to, but he comes first who took the honour of the first man.²¹² O king who devised wonders that defy description: admired by those whom you have passed over, you are clearly admired still more by those to whom you have given a share.

**[c]** Now when Alexander of Macedon was asked where he kept his treasuries of money, he said, indicating his friends, 'in these men'.²¹³ But you have it in mind to treasure up in your friends the honours which belong to you, and, by giving, keep them safer. For honour is not used up like gold, but, if disposed after careful consideration, endures to an infinite degree both for the giver and the receiver, and is the greater for the giver, just as the giving of the greatest things is more blessed than receiving them. The greatest of all human honours is the consulship by which time itself is measured, **[d]** and without which it would pass without name or division like an unstamped coin.²¹⁴

By this measurement the name of your general shall be counted, and, after those who are your kin by blood, shall be listed he who is your kin in virtue. For although you honoured first your immediate family, I refer to your uncle and your in-law,²¹⁵ you did not make a distinction between

212 Saturninus was officially second in honour in 383 to his western partner Fl. Merobaudes, since the latter was consul for the second time in that year. Themistius is saying that Saturninus should really be viewed as the senior consul since he was standing in place of Theodosius. If the emperor had taken the consulship, he would have been senior to Merobaudes.

213 Stobaeus 214.

214 Consular lists provided one of the basic Roman dating system, events being dated according to consuls; the other, little used by the 4th century, was to date by years from the foundation of the city of Rome.

215 κηδεστής: usually father-, son-, or brother-in-law, but can have a more general meaning. After 380, when Gratian and Theodosius shared the consulship, the latter nominated one of the consuls: cf. Bagnall et. al., 1987, 15. In 381, he chose his uncle Eucherius (on whom see *PLRE* 1, 288). The two consuls for 382 were Cl. Antonius and Africanus

your gifts, but, by joining valour to kinship, made it clear by deed that the ruler of all things [Theodosius] is no less concerned to honour pre-eminence in virtue than proximity in family, **[204a]** and that he does not consider the closest to him to be best, but rather the best to be closest to him. For thus he shall inspire many others with the same enthusiasm. As the divine Plato says, what is honoured is practised but what is dishonoured is despised.[216] Kinship cannot be practised or studied, nor does it increase or flourish if it receives its own special honour. Someone who honours a brother, a connexion by marriage or son **[b]** does not create more brothers, in-laws or sons, but these continue to exist in the number fixed by nature. But, by exalting a good man and enhancing his reputation, you at once create a multitude of people who pursue the same goal.

Clear evidence can be shown that you yourself were aware of this first, and that I am not being sophistic. Supposing you did not judge the moment right to assume the honour yourself, **[c]** you could have appointed the beloved beacon of the world, whom I would make an Alexander, and philosophy would again boast to have fostered such as him.[217] It was possible to advance him in your stead, as has been the custom of past and recent emperors who placed the purple-edged toga on their sons before the full imperial purple, as if in prelude to their future reign. We will not call to mind ancient events but only just the other day, when one child in its swaddling put on the toga, and another who was virtually the same age as our shining light.[218] And no one would have been sick-

---

Syagrius, but which of the two was related by marriage to Theodosius has been disputed. The current consensus is for Cl. Antonius, whose sister perhaps married Theodosius' brother: Martindale, 1967; cf. *PLRE* 1, 77; Bagnall et al., 1987, 298–9.

216 *Republic* 551a.

217 Arcadius: Theodosius' son, who had been born in c.377 (*PLRE* 1, 99), and was thus about six. Alexander had been tutored by Aristotle. Themistius had written commentaries on some of the latter's work, and Alexander and Aristotle formed one of the archetypal pairings of ruler and philosophical advisor, popular in late antiquity (see Chapter 1). Themistius thus cast himself as Aristotle to Arcadius' Alexander, replaying virtually verbatim what he had previously said of Valens' son Valentinian Galates in 368: *Or.* 8.120a, trans. in Heather and Matthews, 1991, 36. See also the next note.

218 Varronianus, son of Jovian, held the consulship as a baby in 364, and Valentinian Galates, son of Valens, in 369 when he was about three years old. At the time, in *Or.* 5. (Chapter 3) and *Or.* 9 , Themistius had considered these appointments entirely virtuous. Gratian too had been a child consul, aged about seven, in 366, and this would seem to be one of several implied denigrations of Theodosius' western colleague: see the introduction to this speech.

ened by or pained at this. **[d]** Yet you choose none of these possibilities; nor, because you sought a more timely moment to assume the honour yourself, did you snatch it rashly for your son as if in doubt that you would have the power to accomplish this very thing hereafter. But with your beloved son before your eyes, already a boy, already a young man, already perfect in speech, soon able even to address the multitude – O what fortitude – you yielded to virtue, rather than nature **[205a]** just as your ancestor and forefather did. Although he had no children, there were the offspring of his brothers and nieces. Even so, he valued none of them above the esteem in which he held Lusius, a man who was not even Roman, not even a Libyan from the Libyan province, but from an obscure and remote borderland. He first proclaimed this man consul after his defeat of the Mardi and then appointed him successor to the throne.[219] Thus did the emperors of those days think it important that virtue never be deprived of its just rewards. **[b]** The Homeric examples I pass over as well worn and somewhat too ancient, that Agamemnon himself always held Ajax in greater esteem than Menelaus, and, when sharing the feast with his brother, gave precedence to the general.

Therefore this present honour is great indeed in the light of these considerations, but greater still in the light of what you shall hear. For it was always the custom of past emperors to hold the anniversary of five and ten years as sacrosanct, **[c]** and not concede to another the year's eponymous consulship. But this man has not only conferred this highest honour on him but also given a consulship which cannot be counted among all the rest, but surpasses them to the same degree that this five-year period has surpassed the years that have preceded it. This has never before come to pass for any man, that a private citizen lead the state during a royal anniversary, and not simply this, but the first of them, which by being first is the most welcome. **[d]** How then can one fail to envy the man whom he has set in his own place, whom with his own hand he has placed there in the first of his reign's anniversaries, since he surpasses by so great a degree all those who have achieved the same honour?[220]

219 Theodosius claimed descent from Trajan (Orosius 7.34.2), who in 117 appointed the Moor L. Lusius Quietus as consul.

220 Emperors did regularly take the consulship in quinquennial or decennial years, but not so invariably as the 'always' might imply. Such an anniversary was a specific, declared and celebrated event, which might be held a year early or late to coincide with other suitable events: Bagnall et al,, 1987, 15, 23–4. Such, however, had been the regular practice of

All this has come to pass in accordance with expectation. For he, practically alone of all the luminaries and celebrities of today,[221] is not assailed by the envious criticism which usually snarls at all those at the summit of power. That criticism yields to and casts its vote in favour of the sequence of honours. **[206a]** He did not make a great leap upwards, achieving sudden eminence from a mean or humble station 'to strike his head against the sky',[222] but as in geometrical propositions where the second part derives from the first and the third from both, each derivative element always being more perfect than its predecessor with no gap of understanding in between, so too did this man's honours follow each other in due order and unbroken succession, the next always more prestigious than the former. No aspect of military command was omitted, nor could anyone find a prestigious title that he has not surpassed under arms. **[b]** Envy does not come to meet those who have carried on according to destiny in this fashion and, without faltering, reached the summit from the foothills. But whenever an Agoracritus or a Hyperbolus or Demades achieves success, even comedy sets about them in splendid fashion,

'Yesterday a nobody but tomorrow a VIP'.[223]

Everyone finds the unexpected irksome but no one grumbles at what accords with their expectations. Since even if one were to consult those who from youth were his fellow soldiers **[c]** and who travelled the same path in imperial affairs, who long ago were quite rightly and properly

Valentinian and Valens, so that not to do so did mark a break with immediate precedents: cf. Vanderspoel, 1995, 206. Given that Theodosius was about to break with Gratian over Arcadius' promotion (see the introduction), showing unusual generosity with honours was presumably part of a strategy to establish solid political support among eastern landowners.

221 Themistius allowed the audience to draw its own conclusion about whether or not Gratian was included among the luminaries being condemned. Proclaimed emperor in 367, the pattern of his subsequent consulships – 371, 374, 376, 380 (with Theodosius) – suggest that, taking account of the option of holding anniversaries a year early or late (see above), Gratian had reserved a consulship for himself during anniversary celebrations.

222 Homer, *Iliad* 4.443, where these words refer to Strife, the sister of war.

223 Aristophanes, *Knights* 158. Agoracritus was Aristophanes' savage caricature of Cleon. Both he and Hyperbolus, another contemporary Athenian politician and frequent butt of Aristophanes' satire, were ridiculed for reputedly humble origins. Demades, an Athenian orator fl. 350–319 BC, is not known to have been the subject of comedy.

considered worthy of this honour, the charge us of being late rather than early would be laid against us.[224]

Although it is possible for me to go through the man's valorous exploits in the war, I think I will leave these for the poets and historians whose task it is to celebrate and exalt 'battles and slaughterings of men'.[225] For my part, inasmuch as I am a lover of peace and of peaceful and untroubled words, I will proceed to these things, **[d]** having first brought to mind some small matters, so that you may realise more fully the kind of circumstances from which, and to which, through the king's foresight we have passed. For after the indescribable Iliad of evils on the Ister and the onset of the monstrous flame, when there was not yet a king set over the affairs of the Romans, with Thrace laid waste, with Illyria laid waste, when whole armies had vanished completely like a shadow,[226] when neither impassible mountains, unfordable rivers, **[207a]** nor trackless wastes stood in the way, but when finally nearly the whole of the earth and sea had united beside the barbarians,[227] and, from here and there, encircling them on one side and another Celts, Assyrians, Armenians, Libyans and Iberians, as many (peoples) as faced the

224 The classic nobody appointed above his station was Theodosius' predecessor Valens, but Gratian too, Augustus from the age of nine, had not arrived at the purple through a steady progression of other offices, so that this passage contained implicit criticism of his qualifications to rule. This again fits the context of political conflict between the two imperial colleagues: see the introduction to this speech.

225 Homer, *Iliad* 7.237. One might contrast this with the martial tone adopted by Themistius towards Theodosius in *Or.* 14: see above. The approach here is consistent with, and deliberately recalled, that of *Or.* 15, where, as we have seen, the change of tone was forced upon emperor and orator by the former's defeat at the hands of the Goths in summer 380.

226 The aftermath of Hadrianople on 9 August 378, when two-thirds of the eastern Roman field army was destroyed, allowing the Goths to run loose over the eastern and western Balkans (Thrace and Illyricum respectively). Theodosius was not made emperor until 19 January 379. For more detail with full refs, see the introduction to this chapter.

227 By itself this sentence is ambiguous as to whether the list of 'barbarians' (i.e. foreigners) were fighting *for* or *against* the Romans: περιστάντων 'encircling' might have either meaning. Poetically at least, the list encompasses the major neighbours of the Roman state from the Rhine (Celts), to North Africa (Libyans), to the Caucasus (Armenians and Iberians) and Mesopotamia (Assyrians = Persians) and the rest of the sentence makes it clear that they are fighting against the Romans, since a) the sentence is cataloguing accumulating evils, b) it refers explicitly, just previously, to nearly the whole earth and uniting against the Romans, and c) the Assyrians (= Persians) can only be enemies, even if the others were sometimes allies. The idea that the reigns of Valentinian and Valens heralded the onset of a period of the Roman Empire *contra mundum* is also found at Ammianus 26.4.5.

Romans from one end of the earth to the other; when all these encircled them, it was then we thought we fared best when we had suffered nothing still worse.

And so when almost everyone, both generals and soldiers, had their wills overturned in the face of such great and momentous blows **[b]** and were wondering how this ill would turn out, with no one taking steps to prevent it, God summons to leadership the only man capable of resisting such an inundation of misfortune; while Gratian proclaims the decision from on high.[228] Earth and sea welcome the proclamation in preference to good hopes and good omens. Once he had taken up the reins, and, like the most experienced of drivers first tested his horses to gauge their strength and mettle in his hands,[229] he was the first who dared entertain the notion **[c]** that the power of the Romans did not now lie in weapons, nor in breastplates, spears and unnumbered manpower,[230] but that there was need of some other power and provision, which, to those who rule in accordance with the will of God, comes silently from that source, which subdues all nations, turns all savagery to mildness and to which alone arms, bows, cavalry, the intransigence of the Scythians, the boldness of the Alans, the madness of the Massagetai yield.[231]

228  See the introduction to this speech on the very limited role granted Gratian in *Or.* 16.

229  A euphemistic account of the events of 379/80 when Theodosius attempted to reconstitute the eastern army destroyed at Hadrianople, and then saw it fall apart again in battle. This certainly was the context which generated the decision to move towards a compromise peace with the Goths, as Themistius went on to say, but he did not make clear that the testing of the reins had ended in failure. For a more detailed account, see the introductions to this speech and chapter.

230  Themistius thus unambiguously gave Theodosius all the credit for the peace with the Goths. This may have been true, but he was carefully downplaying Gratian's role: see the introduction to this chapter.

231  Scythians are usually Goths in 4th-century classicising authors such as Themistius, Alans are Alans obviously enough, Massagetae often Huns. A separate group of Huns and Alans from north of the Danube joined the Goths in their revolt in autumn 377 and operated with them subsequently: Ammianus 31.8.4, 12.17 with Heather, 1991, 150–1, arguing against some modern interpretations, which consider one of the two groups of Gothic refugees, the Greuthungi of Alatheus or Saphrax, to have been a 'Drei-Volker Confederation' consisting of Huns, Alans, and Goths, entirely ignoring the sense of Ammianus' words. In 379, the imperial authorities also announced victories against Huns, Goths and Alans. Themistius' words here would imply that Huns and Alans were also party to the final peace treaty. It has usually been thought, by contrast, that they were settled separately in Pannonia by Gratian after his intervention there in the summer of 380, but the evidence

And it is this that the poets of old in their excellent writings teach us from our youth:

[d] 'One wise plan conquers many hands',[232]

and

'Calculation brings to nought many things, even the actions of the enemy's sword',[233]

and

'Better indeed is the woodman who uses skill not strength',[234]

and [208a]

'The wise mind leads all things from perplexity and charms all things, even if one should be under a sworn oath'.[235]

The tale has also been told by Aesop the storyteller of a contest between Persuasion and Force, and in the story, Persuasion achieves more than Force; the sun makes one shed clothes before the raging winds do.[236] In the same way, the poets tell that in their battle with the gods, the Giants resisted Ares to the utmost, but were sent to sleep by Hermes and his wand.[237]

The most wise king, finding that this was the only power left to the

---

for a Pannonian settlement is very unconvincing (Heather, 1991, App. B), so that there is no reason not to take Themistius at face value.

232 Euripides, *Antiope* fr. 200.

233 Euripides, *Phoenician Women* 516–7: a famous aphorism previously used of Constantius by both Themistius and Julian: *Or.* 2.37b; *Or.* 2.73b–c respectively.

234 Homer, *Iliad* 23.315.

235 *Tragicorum Graecorum fragmenta*, vol. 2, 566. It was believed by some Romans that the Goths had sworn a solemn oath by the Danube not to cease their activities until they had destroyed the Empire (Eunapius fr. 59). The extent to which this might be historical is hard to estimate (Heather, 1991, 139–40 with refs.), but such thoughts may have prompted Themistius to pick this particular passage with its reference to wisdom even having the power to overcome sworn oaths.

236 Aesop, *Fables* 46 Hausratt / Hunger = 73 Chambry.

237 The Gigantomachy – battle between the gods and the giants – was one of the most popular myths in Greece, with participants and details varying from one account to another. Hermes is chiefly famous in Gigantomachy for slaying Hippolytus, and no account of him putting all the giants to sleep appears in any surviving version. The scene may have figured in the bronze relief of the battle displayed in Constantinople which Themistius referred to at *Or.* 13.176d–177a. Alternatively Themistius may have had in

Romans unscathed and untested by the barbarians, **[b]** and recognising
that the more they did wrong, so the more they knew it would be to their
advantage, realised that forgiveness towards those who had done wrong
was better than to fight it out to the bitter end. And seeking someone
who would be of service to him in gaining this victory and winning the
day by his intelligence and goodwill, he lost no time in finding the most
suitable man, but appoints forthwith for this endeavour him [Saturninus]
who of his generals he had long known to have the same thoughts and
ambitions as himself, **[c]** and sends him out just as Achilles did his companion [Patroclus] but with better auspices, and better fortune both for the
despatcher and for the whole business, not to quench the flame of a
single Thessalian ship that had just been fired, not to scare the enemy
from where a single line of defence had failed,[238] but in case anything at
all had survived and escaped the previous attacks after the barbarian
thundercloud had loosed its bolt against it. He sent him as the son of
Peleus [Achilles] had done, arrayed in his own truly heavenly armour –
forbearance, gentleness, and love of mankind – **[d]** all of which fitted
him perfectly, rather than one part but not another, as for example the
Pelian ash spear in the case of Menoiteus' son.[239]

And he set out at once with confidence, with no company of foot
following, no troop of horse in escort, not with five subordinate generals
in tow,[240] but protected only by the king's instructions, which he used as
his escorts and heralds. **[209a]** He needed no time at all to achieve this
victory, but had only to reveal and proffer the goodwill of the man who
had sent him for the arrogance of the Scythians at once to bow before
him, their boldness to be cut short, their spirit humbled, the sword to
fall voluntarily from their hands and for them to follow as he led them
to the king as if in a religious procession or festival, respecting the land
which they had once drunkenly abused, and showing reverence towards
the dead as if they were sacred, carrying only their short swords which
they intended to present to the king in place of suppliant offerings. **[b]** In

---

mind Homer, *Iliad* 24, where Hermes put the Greek camp to sleep to allow Priam to approach Achilles.

238  The story is told in Homer, *Iliad* 16.

239  Cf. *Iliad* 16.13ff.: Patroclus (Menoiteus' son) put on Achilles' armour but was unable
to wield Achilles' spear of Pelian ash.

240  Patroclus was sent out with Achilles' five lieutenants – Menesthius, Eudorus,
Peisander, Phoenix and Alcimedon – and their troops.

other respects, they were unarmed and peaceable, beaten by intellectual not physical forces. What potion of Egyptian Polydamna was mixed in the wine bowl, or what girdle of Aphrodite was it, so potent and effective as to render towers more solid than adamant, softer than wax?

'Such were the skilful potions Zeus' servant had,
and benign, which the immortal king gave to him'[241]

[c] that restrain not grief or tears but the evils that cause them.

Once upon a time, the power of music, not of weapons, was to be found in Thrace, and it is no longer right to doubt that boars followed the strains of Orpheus and trees and rocks went wherever he might lead them with his songs. But while Orpheus, it seems, was capable of charming wild beasts, he could not charm the harsh nature of men. Rather the Thracian women discredited his art, and not only failed to be enraptured by his songs, [d] but were driven madder still by them, even to do to the singer himself what they in fact did do.[242] But this interpreter and disciple of the celestial Orpheus [Saturninus], using the god-given music – enchanting words flowing sweeter than honey – was sent out so equipped by the man who despatched him [Theodosius], and casting spells with these weapons, bewitching with them, exhorting with them, putting forward good hopes for the future and removing the suspicion about those they had wronged, [210a] wafting the king's love of mankind before them like an olive branch,[243] led them docile and amenable, all but twisting their hands behind their backs, so that it was a matter of doubt whether he had beaten the men in war or won their friendship.[244]

241  Homer, *Odyssey* 4.227. The original Homeric text has Διὸς θυγάτηρ: i.e., Helen. Themistius adapted the lines to make Theodosius the object. When Helen and Menelaus were entertaining Telemachus, Helen dropped into his wine a drug given to her by Polydamna, wife of Egyptian Thon, which removed grief and painful memories.

242  They tore him apart. The story of Orpheus' effect on their menfolk was often used in antiquity as a metaphor for the softening effects of civilisation upon barbarians; see, e.g., Cassiodorus *Variae* 2.40. In this case, the fact that the action occurred in Thrace will also have called this story to mind.

243  θαλλὸν: the olive-branch used as religious festivals.

244  Themistius thus claimed that conquest by *philanthropia* had won a more complete victory than one by arms since it had overcome the opponents' will to resist. This was part of his attempt to 'sell' the peace deal to landowning opinion. In reality, the Goths were left with much of their autonomy and military capacity intact, as subsequent revolts in 387, 391 and 395 showed. On the detailed terms of the peace, see the introduction to this speech.

Now Corbulo the general, having persuaded the Armenian Tiridates to entrust his affairs to Nero, a damned and tainted man and not worthy of such great goodwill, realised that he had revealed his qualities at the wrong moment, and, for the sake of glory, had espoused the cause of no true king.[245] [b] But he [Saturninus] is most fortunate in his zeal on behalf of such a one [Theodosius], most fortunate too in the thanks he receives from him – which is no surprise. For it was no Tiridates that he charmed for us, not some Armenian easily subdued and easily led, even among the barbarians of that place to whom haughty pride is second nature but so too subservience and servitude is not much different from liberty, but he charmed those in whom there is bred from childhood an unyielding spirit, and for whom the slightest submission is worse than death. We have seen their leaders and chiefs,[246] not making a show of surrendering a tattered standard, [c] but giving up the weapons and swords with which up to that day they had held power, and clinging to the king's knees more tightly than Thetis, according to Homer, clung to the knees of Zeus when she besought him on her son's behalf, until they won a kindly nod and a voice which did not rouse war but was full of kindness, full of peace, full of benevolence and the remitting of sins.[247]

'The son of Cronos spoke and assented with his dark brow. [d] The lord's ambrosial locks poured down from his immortal head; he made mighty Olympus tremble',

and no word of his is taken back, is false, or remains unfulfilled.[248]

But see how the most hated name of Scythia is now beloved, now

245 Tacitus, *Annals* 15.27–30.

246 An important phrase, which, together with the overall tenor of the speech, makes it clear that no king of all the Goths had survived the six years of war (376–82) to negotiate peace with the Romans. The main Gothic leaders at the time of Hadrianople – Fritigern especially of the Tervingi, but also Alatheus and Saphrax of the Greuthungi – are not heard of again after c.380, and it seems clear that their overthrow was either a condition of the peace or a product of the warfare which led up to it: Heather, 1991, 157–8, 173–4 with refs.

247 ὅλης ἀφείσης τὰ ἀδικήματα. This is not the precise wording of the Lord's prayer in either Matthew (6.12: ἄφες ἡμῖν τὰ ὀφειλήματα ἡμῶν) or Luke (11.4 ἄφες ἡμῖν τὰς ἁμαρτίας ἡμῶν), but, given Theodosius' strong public Christian stance, this may well be a deliberate echo of Christian rhetoric.

248 Homer, *Iliad* 1.528ff. Thetis' son was Achilles. She asked Zeus to punish the Greeks for Agamemnon's expropriation of Briseis, Achilles' prize, to replace the ransomed daughter of Chryses.

pleasant, now agreeable. They join together with us in the festive celebration of the general, by whom they had the good fortune to be captured,
and partake of the feasts that celebrate the triumph over themselves.[249]
[211a] If they have not been utterly wiped out, no complaint should be
raised.[250] For such are the triumphs of reason and universal love, not to
destroy but rather to make better those who have caused suffering. For
just suppose that this destruction was an easy matter and that we
possessed the means to accomplish it without suffering any consequences, although from past experience this was neither a foregone nor
likely conclusion,[251] nevertheless just suppose, as I said, that this solution
lay within our power. Was it then better to fill Thrace with corpses or
with farmers? To make it full of tombs or living men? [b] To progress
through a wilderness or a cultivated land? To count up the number of
the slaughtered or those who till the soil? To colonise it with Phrygians
or Bithynians perhaps, or to live in harmony with those we have
subdued. I hear from those who have returned from there that they are
now turning the metal of their swords and breastplates into hoes and
pruning hooks,[252] and that while paying distant respect to Ares, they
offer prayers to Demeter and Dionysus.[253]

249  The words 'the festive celebration' imply that Goths were present in some capacity at
the consular celebrations for Saturninus, as well as having participated in the triumph when
peace was formally made. It is uncertain whether such a participation of the defeated in a
celebratory feast for the victor was usual, or an outward sign of the break with tradition
encompassed in the Gothic peace agreement of 382. Subsequently, Theodosius continued
to use feasts for Gothic leaders as an important mode of political contact to make the agreement work: Eunapius fr. 59; Zosimus 4.56; cf. Heather, 1991, 186.

250  Here, as often, Themistius states one of the central arguments of his speech simply
and directly before going on in what follows to attempt to justify it. Although presented as a
*deditio*, the compromise peace of 382 departed sufficiently from established Roman imperial practice to require careful justification. See the introduction to this speech.

251  Quite an admission given normal expectations of imperial victory (on which see
McCormick, 1986). Themistius was referring to the defeats of Valens at Hadrianople and
Theodosius in Illyricum: see the introduction to this chapter.

252  Cf. Vanderspoel, 1995, 207 n. 75, this is surely a reference to the famous Old Testament image of returning peace (Joel 3.10; Micah 4.3). Other biblical references in Themistius, but not this one, are identified in Downey, 1962. On Themistius and Christianity, see
further Chapter 1.

253  Ares was the god of war, Demeter the goddess of corn and fruitfulness, and Dionysius the god of wine. Thus Themistius hinted that, although the Goths have been tamed,
their martial spirit might still be harnessed for the Empire's benefit, a point he expanded
on below.

Human existence has in the past brought forth many such examples, [c] and our times are not the first when it has come to pass that those who have transgressed have found forgiveness and thereafter been of use to those who had been wronged. Look at these Galatians, the ones on the Pontus. Yet these men crossed over into Asia under the law of war, and, having depopulated all the region this side of the Halys, settled in this territory which they now inhabit. And neither Pompey nor Lucullus destroyed them, although this was perfectly possible, nor Augustus nor the emperors after him; rather, they remitted their sins and assimilated them into the Empire. And now no one would ever refer to the Galatians as barbarian but as thoroughly Roman. [d] For while their ancestral name has endured, their way of life is now akin to our own. They pay the same taxes as we do, they enlist in the same ranks as we do, they accept governors on the same terms as the rest and abide by the same laws.[254] So will we see the Scythians do likewise within a short time. For now their clashes with us are still recent, but in fact we shall soon receive them to share our offerings, our tables, our military ventures, and public duties.[255] Yet if they had been utterly wiped out, [212a] we would have punished the Thracians as well as the Scythians.

When the Romans took the Libyan Masinissa alive, a man who had perpetrated many terrible acts against them, they preserved rather than destroyed him. And Masinissa became a bulwark and defence for them against future enemies.[256] Now the whole continent is settled, land and sea garland their leaders; the realm, like a great merchantman that has suffered much damage in storm and tempest, is righted and made

254 Cf. our introduction to this speech, Synesius reports that the Goths lived under their own laws after 382. In Graeco-Roman ideologies, living under a system of written law was the hallmark of civilisation, and it is this symbolic sense that both authors had in mind. In fact, the treaty of 382 allowed the Goths a tolerated autonomy, so that both views were perfectly correct, depending upon whether emphasis was placed on the toleration or the autonomy.

255 Envisaged, by careful use of the future tense, as a future development here (on 1 January 383), Goths as Roman soldiers and tax-paying farmers is presented as accomplished fact in Themistius Or. 34 of a year or so later (see Chapter 5). On the broader significance of this passage, see the introduction to this speech.

256 Cf. Vanderspoel, 1995, 207 n. 76, Themistius also used the example of Masinissa of Numidia in his ostensible plea to Valens for clemency for the followers of Procopius: Or. 7.94d. Themistius is the only source to report that Masinissa was captured by the Romans rather than won over to their side by diplomacy (see also Or. 6.190d in Chapter 3).

secure. Roads are open, mountains are free from fear, plains now bear fruit, **[b]** and the land around the Ister does not leap in the theatre of wars but devotes itself to sowing and ploughing. Road stations and lodgings come back to life and cover the ground providing rest as of old.[257] The whole realm draws common breath and has common feeling like one creature, and is no longer out of joint and scattered everywhere. Did Greece gain such a great boon from Aeacus' prayer when it was afflicted by drought, and not even all Greece but only the region around Aegina, compared to the light you have spread over the greatest part of the earth?[258] **[c]** You did not deliver this prayer on a single occasion, but your entire reign has been for us like a prayer. For the prayer is not just phrases and words, but piety, justice, and gentleness with which you are clearly always invoking God.

What other emperor has instituted milder laws, restored damaged houses, relieved disasters, lightened misfortunes, pitied youth, shown respect to age, and been a father to orphans? In whose reign has money been returned from the treasury to those unjustly brought down?[259] Who has raised a trophy to Persuasion? Who has granted the fruits of victory to Reason over the sword? **[d]** Who has won such a victory in which no soldier had a hand? What better refuge has been opened up for the unfortunate? For, to pass over other events, but only the other day the unfortunate Galatian youths, who had all but perished in accordance with the laws, you protected and preserved, not by breaking the laws but mitigating them, because you yourself are the living law and are superior to its written letter.[260] If we can accomplish these things, if we can do more things of this kind, **[213a]** just as we overcame the Scythians without shedding blood or tears, so too shall we ally the Persians to ourselves before long, so too shall we recover Armenia, so too shall we rescue all the territory of Mesopotamia that others abandoned, so too

257  We have translated this as referring to the *cursus publicus* – the network of post-stations, lodgings, and stables which allowed official traffic to move easily about the Empire – after the seemingly parallel passage at *Or.* 34.xxiv in Chapter 5.

258  Aeacus, son of Zeus and Aegina, prayed to his father to relieve the island of Aegina from drought: Pausanias 2.29.6; Isocrates, *Evagoras* 14ff.

259  See the notes to *Or.* 15.194c–d above.

260  This specific incident is possibly that referred to at *Or.* 34.xviii (Chapter 5). Themistius consistently viewed the emperor as law incarnate, echoing the norms of late Roman state ideology. See, e.g., *Or.* 1.15a–c (Chapter 2).

shall we proclaim many other consuls for their noble actions and fine service.[261]

May I rear on these examples the beloved star of the world [Arcadius], may I be his Phoenix, setting him on my knee, not glutting him with delicacies or honeycakes, **[b]** but singing of the glorious feats of men and the good deeds of kings, especially the many deeds of his father.[262] For these are sweeter to him and more familiar than all the others and these above all will stay before him and remain indelible and ineradicable in his remembrance.[263]

261 Much of former Roman Mesopotamia had been ceded to the Persians by Jovian in 363. Themistius was previously ready to see this treaty as a success (*Or.* 5: Chapter 3). Roman influence in Armenia had come under Persian pressure in the reign of Valens, and, faced with the Goths, Valens had been forced to come to terms in 377: Ammianus 31.7.1. Themistius thus looked forward to an end to the Persians' traditional hostility towards the Empire, and the reversal of major recent defeats. Cf. Vanderspoel, 1995, 208, it is just possible that Themistius knew that something was afoot. Shapur II, Persian victor in these encounters, had died in 379 and his successor Artaxerxes was so unpopular that in 383 he was ousted in a coup, an event which formed the precursor to an agreement over Armenia and a long period of peace between Persia and the Empire: see, e.g., Whitby, 1988, 202ff.

262 Phoenix the charioteer had been Achilles' guardian and sat him on his knee as a boy to feed him with portions of his food: Homer, *Iliad* 9.48ff.

263 Themistius here echoed the Graeco-Roman cultural topos that literary study shaped character by exposing the individual to examples of good and bad behaviour from which he could learn: see, e.g., Heather, 1993a; 1993b, with refs. Ending the speech with a reference to Arcadius suggests that Themistius knew that the prince was to be declared co-Augustus 18 days later. This was done without Gratian's prior approval, and marked a major break between the ruling Augusti of east and west: see the introductions to this speech and chapter.

# CHAPTER 5

# PHILOSOPHER PREFECT:
# THEMISTIUS ORATIONS 17 AND 34

For a few months in either winter/spring 383/4 or spring/summer 384, Themistius held formal administrative office for the first time in his life. The Emperor Theodosius appointed him urban prefect for the city of Constantinople.[1] The post had been created in 359 by one of Themistius' former imperial patrons, Constantius II, as part of his expansion of the Senate of Constantinople (see Chapter 2). Since the city was now to have a senate on a par with that of Rome, it was decided that it should be run, like Rome, by an urban prefect, and no longer by a pro-consular governor. The urban prefect was responsible for most aspects of administration and justice within the city; among many other things, he presided formally over meetings of its senate.[2] Themistius' tenure of office prompted a flurry of rhetorical activity on his own part, the orator producing three speeches in defence of his decision to accept the prefecture. Within a few days of his promotion, Themistius came to the senate to deliver a short speech on the subject, Oration 17, the first of those translated in this chapter. This was followed, while he was still in office by Oration 31.[3] Oration 34,

1 That the tenure of office was brief is made clear by *Or.* 34.xi. *Or.* 31, given while Themistius was still in office, was delivered during in either January or Lent 384 (see note 3). According to one's view on this, the prefecture would then be dated to winter/spring 383/4 (Scholze, 1911, 54–6; cf. Schneider, 1966, 44–54) or spring/summer 384 (Dagron, 1968, 11–12; Vanderspoel, 1995, 206–10). Seeck, 1906, originally placed the prefecture in autumn 384, on the basis of *C.Th.* 6.2.14, dated September 384, and ostensibly given to Themistius' predecessor in office, Clearchus; but he later accepted (Seeck, 1919, 514) that there was probably a mistake in the date. Penella, 2000, 35, lays out the alternatives.

2 See generally, Dagron, 1974, chs 7 and 9, esp. 226–9, where he largely follows the analysis of the Roman urban prefecture made by Chastagnol, 1960, pt. 2, chs 3–6.

3 Vanderspoel, 1995, 209–10, argues that references to the 'holy month' involving legal amnesties at *Or.* 31.352b mean Lent rather than January 384 (*contra* Scholze, 1911, 57) since Theodosius was in the process of transferring such matters from their traditional position at the start of the Roman year to the run-up to Easter: *C.Th.* 9.35.4 (cf. 2.8.19). *Or.* 18 which followed *Or.* 31 chronologically was given in the sixth year of Theodosius' reign (Jan. 384 to Jan. 385: 217d) while Themistius was still in office, so this cannot have been Lent 385.

the second speech translated in this chapter, represents a further, much more substantial offering on the same subject. It was delivered after Themistius had left office, but clearly not too long after, and hence at any point between early summer 384 to early 385, depending upon how one dates the actual prefecture.[4]

## CONTROVERSY

This rhetorical activity stemmed from the fact that Themistius' tenure of prefectural office gave renewed life to the controversies which had originally been generated by his successes in the reign of Constantius. The argument focussed not on the details of how he had fulfilled his duties as prefect, although one aspect of this, as we shall see, did come in for comment, but on the whole principle of his nomination to office. This criticism must be understood in the light of the social disengagement required of the true Hellenic philosopher. As we have seen, this kept a philosopher free from entanglement in wealth, office, and the other vanities of this world, and underlay his right to absolute freedom of speech (*parrhesia*). Throughout his life, Themistius had exploited these traditions as the basis of his public persona, and used them to justify the kinds of relationship he had developed with a string of emperors. Under Constantius, as we have seen, the extent of Themistius' successes had first occasioned the charge that he was not a true philosopher, but a sophist fundamentally interested only in material gain.

Themistius' urban prefecture raised the same issue, but with greater force, and criticism duly followed. It was one of the highest offices of the state, giving its occupant the many privileges of high status in an extremely hierarchical society, not to mention countless opportunities for amassing wealth and influence. Viewed from one angle, holding such an office thus appeared to give the lie to the whole image Themistius had presented of himself throughout his career. The potential for accusation was all the greater for three additional reasons. First, when faced with

4 Between *Orr.* 31 and 34, and before he left office, Themistius gave *Orr.* 18 and 19, which predate the birth of Theodosius' second son Honorius on 9 September 384, since the event is unmentioned at points where it would have been highly appropriate: Vanderspoel, 1995, 210–13. Summer 384 thus provides a *terminus post quem* for *Or.* 34. Dagron, 1968, 26, seems overly prescriptive in arguing that *Or.* 34 must have been given in early 385 rather than late 384. Having dated the prefecture somewhat earlier (see note 1), Schneider, 1966, 42–53, and Scholze, 1911, 57, consequently date *Or.* 34 earlier too, to the first half of 384.

accusations of worldliness in the 350s, Themistius had based his self-defence (especially in Oration 23 of probably 359) on the fact that, whatever other gains may have come his way, he had never accepted pay from the state, and had thus preserved a properly philosophical independence. By becoming urban prefect under Theodosius, Themistius thus crossed a line which he himself had previously drawn.[5]

Second, it was also general knowledge that Themistius had refused the prefecture on a previous occasion, and had claimed credit in public for so doing. This fact emerges clearly from *Or.* 34.xiii, although it had already been hinted at in Oration 17, the former passage indicating that the source of this knowledge was a no doubt highly laudatory letter from an emperor (probably Valens: see below) to the Senate of Constantinople. The letter had mentioned the offer of the prefecture, the emperor's determined efforts to persuade Themistius to accept the post (no doubt citing his many virtues), and the latter's eventual refusal. Such letters were themselves a great honour, as the same section of Oration 34 acknowledges. In other words, Themistius had previously claimed great credit by publicly refusing the prefecture, probably maintaining, although any reasons mentioned in the earlier letter are not referred to in the oration, that it was incompatible with his philosophical independence, as required by Hellenic tradition. In the past, therefore, Themistius had extracted credit from a refusal of the office he had now accepted.

Third, Oration 34 also makes it clear that there was a further line to the critique of Themistius' prefecture: the brevity of its duration. Themistius admitted in the speech that he had held the post for only a few months, and then went on to explain why this should not be considered a mark against him (34.xi). There was no set duration of office for the urban prefect of either Rome or Constantinople in the fourth century, but tenure tended to average out at a year or a little more, and, in Rome at least, was eventually formalised at twelve months.[6] Although we do

5  *Or.* 23.292c–d with Dagron, 1968, 46–8, 52–3, on the importance of being perceived to have moved from city representative to state functionary. One body of modern scholarly opinion continues to hold that Themistius had earlier held office as pro-consul of Constantinople in the late 350s: Daly, 1983, followed by Penella, 2000, 219 nn. 19 and 20. In our view, its non-mention in Themistius' own catalogue of his honours in *Or.* 34 is a decisive indication that he did not. For further argumentation and full refs., see the introduction to Chapter 2.

6  Chastagnol, 1960, 187–7: there were 129 urban prefects of Rome in the 133 years between 290 and 423 AD; by the 6th century normal tenure had been formalised at 12

not know exactly how long Themistius was in office, at a few months it was obviously for a rather shorter period than the average. His critics no doubt exploited this fact to argue that a short tenure showed that the underlying point of the job for Themistius had not been its practicalities, the chance to do good within Constantinople, but the perquisites of office. Themistius had done the job only for the shortest possible time, in other words, to pick up its attendant benefits and then retire.

These attacks came partly from inside the Senate of Constantinople, and partly from outside. Oration 17, certainly given within a few days of his appointment, was, as we shall see, noticeably defensive in tone, which might suggest that criticism of the appointment had already emerged in senatorial circles. In addition, Themistius' first attempt at a formal defence of his actions (in Oration 31) took the form of a public address to the senate, taking as its premise that some of its individual members had been criticising him in private.[7] In due course, however, adverse comment also came in the form of public ridicule. The *Greek Anthology* preserves the following epigram composed by a traditionally educated grammarian from Egypt, Palladas, resident in Constantinople by the early 380s:[8]

> Seated aloft at heaven's bar, you came to crave
> a silver car. What boundless shame that was!
> So high and mighty once, much lower you've become.
> The way back up is down, for now you've upwardly descended.

The nature of the attack is very clear: worldliness, and hence the betrayal of the philosophical vocation. Palladas drew part of his inspiration from Themistius' own, unfortunate reference to the silver-gilt carriage of the

---

months. The evidence for Constantinople is not so comprehensive, but likewise suggests normal tenure lengths of usually one, but not more than two years, with occasional exceptions like Cyrus and Proclus holding office for 4 years: Dagron, 1974, 278–80, 284–5. It has been suggested that Themistius was forced to resign from office early (Schneider, 1966, 15; Dagron, 1968, 49; cf. Penella, 2000, 39), but *Or.* 34 provides no explicit evidence to this effect.

7   *Or.* 31. esp. 352a–b, with the discussions of Dagron, 1968, 49–50 improving on the still useful Meridier, 1906, 93–100. Oration 31, together with 17 and 34, is now available in English translation in Penella, 2000.

8   A free translation which tries to preserve the word play around the terms for entering and leaving a chariot. A more literal version can be found in the Loeb edition of the *Greek Anthology* at 11.292. On Palladas, see Cameron, A. D. E., 1965.

urban prefect (*Or.* 31.353d), and the rest came from a famous passage of Plato which referred to the divine as the proper sphere of philosophy, not human affairs.[9] Not only did Oration 31 fail to silence the critics, therefore, but it provided them with further ammunition, and prompted a change in the nature of the attacks. It seems extremely likely, indeed, that Palladas' epigram was composed in the interval between Oration 31 and Oration 34. Oration 31 mentioned the epigram's punning accusation – that by ascending to the prefecture, Themistius has descended from his life's vocation – not at all. Oration 34, by contrast, made no less than seven explicit references to the charge of descent-by-ascent, the references marking, indeed, all the important points of transition in Themistius' argument. It is just possible that the word play on ascent and descent originated in another quarter, and that Themistius' attempted defence in turn prompted Palladas' epigram, but the more economic and likely explanation is that the epigram prompted the speech.[10]

## THEMISTIUS' DEFENCE

In the face of these charges, Themistius used three public occasions – and no doubt countless private ones lost to us – either to attempt to head off criticism or to defend himself more formally. On the first of these, he delivered Oration 17, which may well have been his speech of thanks for the appointment. Its tone, nonetheless, was already defensive. As might be expected, it began by paying homage to the Emperor Theodosius' understanding of the true importance of philosophy, namely that it should not merely watch and comment upon human affairs from the sidelines, but actually participate in political administration and action. The speech 'demonstrated' the truth of this proposition by examining briefly first Theodosius' own actions as ruler, and then picking out the fact that the emperor had considered it very important to offer the prefecture to Themistius, thus bringing the philosopher into active political life. Because of Theodosius' own philosophic virtue, Themistius concluded in this opening section, it would have been wrong for him to have rejected

9  Plato, *Republic* 362eff., referred to by Themistius himself at *Or.* 34.xxx.

10  Cameron, A. D. E., 1965, argued that the epigram was inspired by the speech; cf. Penella, 2000, 38, this could only work if another now unidentifiable critic had first used the 'ascent/descent' language. This seems unnecessarily complicated, and we are happy to endorse the general scholarly consensus that Oration 34 was a response to the epigram.

the offer (214c). This is a striking remark, and very much the pivotal sentence of the entire oration. Themistius' opening words led up to it, and what followed expanded on this centrepiece of self-justification. In other words, Themistius constructed the speech to counter an expectation among his audience, or some of it, that he should not have accepted the prefecture.

As we have seen, Themistius was certainly right to anticipate opposition. General expectations that a Hellenic philosopher should refuse office to preserve his complete independence, combined with Themistius' own very public refusal of the same office in the past, made it more or less inevitable. The basic argument put forward in Oration 17 to justify the present acceptance of an office previously refused was that conditions had changed. Theodosius was such an ideal philosopher king that this entirely validated a philosopher in accepting nomination to office. This was the subtext of his opening remarks, and the second half of the speech used historical *exempla* to show that there were many Graeco-Roman precedents for philosophers accepting employment under philosopher kings. Themistius offered only one, half-developed supporting argument. At 214b, he briefly referred to the ten embassies he had undertaken in the name of the Senate of Constantinople, and presented the prefecture as an extension of this established pattern of action on behalf of his city. As we have seen, it was part of Hellenic tradition that a philosopher could intervene in political affairs in support of his city's interests (see Chapter 1).

Oration 17 was not enough to quell the controversy. Private criticism by individual senators, as we have seen, brought Themistius back to the senate to give Oration 31.[11] Among other matters, however, the reference in the speech to the fact that opponents had accused him of holding 'false tablets' of office makes it clear that basic criticism had continued. As Dagron has convincingly interpreted it, the charge must have been that it was wrong in principle for a philosopher to accept appointment to formal office.[12] In other words, opponents had not been convinced by either of Themistius' arguments in Oration 17: neither the main one that a philosopher could legitimately accept office under a philosopher king,

11 Bouchery, 1936, 207–7, argued that Themistius had left office by the time he delivered Oration 31, but the speech contains no indication to this effect.

12 *Or.* 31.353b; cf. Dagron, 1968, 50 with refs., improving on the previous attempts to interpret the phrase by Harduin (706–7 in Dindorf's edition) and Meridier, 1906, 96–7, the latter seeming to us to come closer to Dagron's interpretation than Dagron thought. See too Schneider, 1966, 15–17.

nor the subsidiary one that the prefecture was merely an extension of Themistius' other acts of service to his city. To counter this continued criticism, Themistius deployed a range of arguments which attempted to justify his acceptance of office and also sought to raise the stakes involved in the hope of silencing the opposition.

The intellectual elements of his self-defence were straightforward. He claimed, first of all, in an argument which was to be more fully developed in Oration 34, that Hellenic tradition legitimised two forms of philosophical activity: not just the individual search for wisdom, but also his own type of socially active philosophy (352c–d). More than that, he said that he had never actively sought wealth and reward, but had merely acquiesced when emperors wanted to give him things in order to encourage others to follow a similar path to himself, secure in the knowledge that efforts in that direction would not go unrewarded (353a–c). The honour of which he was really proud was not the prefect's silver carriage, but standing in a 700-year line of principled social action which led back to Socrates and beyond (353c–354c). At this point the speech changed gear, its tone becoming noticeably more aggressive. Themistius noted that he would greatly appreciate the support of the senate, but, if this were not forthcoming, there were others who recognised his true value. Among these, he numbered the Senate of Rome, and, above all, a succession of five different reigning emperors who had all valued his advice, including in particular the currently reigning Theodosius (354c–355a). The speech closed by reiterating that if the senate did grant him its support, it would show itself a centre of wisdom (355a–c). What he seems to have tried to do, therefore, was first provide a plausible justification of his actions in the light of Hellenic tradition; then attempt to quieten criticism by recalling, second, his standing above all with the Emperor Theodosius; and, third, extract from the senate some sign of public consent to his prefecture.[13] The second strategy again prefigured Oration 34, which is even more explicit on the point that to criticise the emperor's choice of prefect was to criticise Theodosius himself. The nature of the consent Themistius was seeking to extract has occasioned much debate. The Greek word used (*psephos*) means 'vote' and by extension 'decree'. Dagron suggested, therefore, that the occasion of Oration 31 might have been some kind of contested vote over Themistius' presidency of the senate. But late Roman public life did not tolerate dissent

13 So too Meridier, 1906, 98–9.

in such obvious ways, and presidency of the senate was, as far as we know, de facto an attribute of the urban prefecture. Hence it could not have been separated from it and made the subject of a vote.[14] In any case, the start of Oration 31 is quite explicit that the criticism it aimed to counter was private. The key would seem to lie in the range of possible meanings of *psephos*, which, by the second half of the fourth century, could encompass something as informal as a very general indication of approval. In this context, senatorial approval could have meant no more than Themistius' speech not being greeted with any hostile response, as indeed it could not without the individuals concerned making themselves liable to the attention of the emperor.

As we have seen, however, Oration 31 failed to satisfy the critics, although the fact that opposition next surfaced in the shape of Palladas' epigram might indicate that it was enough to hush the mutterings in the senate. Hence Themistius returned to the subject again in Oration 34, given after he had left office, for a third attempt to silence the critics. By this point, the brevity of his tenure had added a further element to the basic charge against him. Dagron, indeed, was even led to wonder if the brevity of his tenure was a sign that Themistius had been forced to resign from office because of the criticism levelled at him. This is just about possible in theoretical terms, but Oration 34 contains no reference to such an event, the urban prefecture had no set term, and, as we shall see in a moment, there is some reason to suppose that Themistius had merely been going through the motions of holding office before effectively retiring from public life.[15]

In Oration 34, Themistius attempted to answer these general and specific charges in the context of an overall account of his career, which aimed to demonstrate its total consistency with long-established Hellenic traditions about how a philosopher might legitimately behave. The basic arguments offered in support of this proposition differed little from those deployed in Oration 17, but Themistius returned to them in much greater detail, and worked into them a response to Palladas' epigram which had appeared in the interval between Orations 31 and 34. He also showed a modicum of humility, which rendered the tone of Oration 34 somewhat softer than that of his previous defences. Oration 34 opened, for instance, with a highly conciliatory approach to those who, having

---

14  Dagron, 1968, 48–50; 1974, 253; cf. the criticisms of Vanderspoel, 1995, 105–6, 209.
15  Dagron, 1968, 49; 1974, 253, 276–7.

thought about the matter carefully, considered that no state office was sufficiently elevated for a philosopher to hold. Themistius declared himself highly respectful of such a line of thought, even if he ultimately disagreed with it (34.i). Right at the end of the speech too, Themistius modestly located himself in the earthly sphere, identifying himself as one who sought merely to bring some divine principles into play in the organisation of human society (34.xxx). The rhetoric of Oration 34 was thus in some ways softer than the uncompromising tone of his previous defences, which allowed of no legitimate opposition to Themistius' prefecture, and hence reached out to his more moderate critics.

In between, the counter-attack against those whom Themistius labelled as unthinking proponents of the idea that a philosopher should not hold office (34.i) – Themistus clearly had Palladas among others in mind – was as uncompromising as ever. The speech was essentially framed in three sections. The first comprises a lengthy, if selective and highly derivative, history of philosophy based on traditional sources, whose purpose was to 'prove' Themistius' central contention that the origins and developmental mainspring of philosophy had always been to place the practical organisation of human affairs on a sound and divinely inspired footing, rather than knowledge for its own sake or internal spiritual development (34.i–ix). This led into an account of Themistius' own career, which 'established' that its patterns conformed to those legitimated by the history of philosophy which preceded it (34.x–xiv). The third section comprised a lengthy panegyric of Theodosius which established in turn that the emperor really was the perfect philosopher king, and hence it was entirely legitimate for Themistius, as a philosopher, to serve him (xv–xxx). The argument, then, was essentially the same as that produced in Oration 17, but the historical *exempla* of philosophers in action, together with his own understanding that action was the mainspring of philosophy, were worked up in much more detail.

There were also some new specific twists. In Oration 17, the issue of why Themistius had previously refused but now accepted the prefecture was addressed only by implication. In Oration 34, Themistius faced it head on. The argument had to tread carefully since Themistius was known to have been a close associate of the emperor under whom he refused office, so that he could not damn him overly without damning himself in the process. Nonetheless, Themistius set about showing that Theodosius was a much better emperor than this earlier patron, so that

holding office under him was indeed legitimate.[16] Oration 34 also
attempted to deal with criticism that he had not held office for long,
arguing both that quality rather than quantity was what mattered, and
that the length of his service for the city should not be judged on the
basis of the prefecture alone. Any reckoning should rather take full
account of all the embassies and other services he had undertaken on its
behalf, and, on that basis, his service could not but be considered
substantial (34.xi–xiii).

Perhaps the most striking departure from Oration 17, however, is
Themistius' determined involvement of the Emperor Theodosius in the
argument. This started in the speech's first few sentences, which threw
out the thought that any criticism levelled against Themistius' prefecture
was also by implication a criticism of the emperor's decision to give him
the office in the first place (*Or.* 34.i). It also continued right through the
speech, in the sense that Themistius argued that it was Theodosius'
virtue which made holding office under him legitimate, so that any
denial of this point might be taken to imply that the emperor was not
Plato's ideal philosopher king. Apart from working up his general argument in more detail, and adding a few specific points, Themistius thus
followed a dual rhetorical strategy. On the one hand, he reached out to
more moderate critics by acknowledging that there was a real issue to be
addressed and respecting those who had, on reflection, come to a
different conclusion to his own. On the other hand, he deliberately
raised the stakes. Criticism of the sacred emperor was potentially liable
to a charge of treason under the fierce *maiestas* laws of the late Empire.
He adopted, overall, a rhetorical carrot and stick, trying to allay his
moderate critics while warning entrenched opponents that they were
running the risk of arousing imperial wrath.

How successful Themistius' defence of his prefecture ultimately was
is very difficult to say. We have no contemporary response to Oration
34. It was clear and learned, and the argument proceeded perfectly logi-
cally given its own assumptions. Aside from a few specific twists,
however, it was essentially the same argument that Themistius had used
in Oration 17, and that had clearly failed to satisfy the critics. This is
perhaps not too surprising. Institutionally and ceremonially, the urban
prefect did occupy an ambiguous position. Appointed by the emperor

---

16  *Or.* 34.xiii–xvi specifically, but the panegyric of Theodosius which comprised the rest
of the speech also implicitly addressed the point.

alone, he nonetheless had to undergo formal confirmation by the senate, and unlike Praetorian Prefects and their deputies, the vicars, who wore the military cloak (the *chlamys*), the urban prefect's ceremonial dress was entirely civilian.[17] More sympathetic ears might well have been willing, therefore, to view the prefecture as an extension of city service.

That said, Themistius' contemporary Libanius, whose reactions might be taken as a litmus test of traditional Hellenic opinion, maintained a very clear conceptual distinction in his works between services rendered to cities and services rendered to the state.[18] For people of this persuasion, there would have been no doubt that the urban prefect of Constantinople was the holder of a state office, rather than someone serving his city. For some, therefore, Themistius' acceptance of the prefecture would have led him beyond the boundaries of legitimate behaviour for a philosopher, and no amount of self-justification would have led them to think otherwise. For others, undecided on this issue, the success or otherwise of Themistius' arguments would have turned on whether they accepted the characterisation of the Emperor Theodosius as an ideal philosopher king, which, Themistius claimed, legitimated his service. Given the prevailing treason laws, anyone pressed on this point would have been advised to answer yes. Whether they would really have believed it, especially given the fact that all of Themistius' previous imperial employers had likewise been characterised by him as ideal philosopher kings up to the moments of their deaths, is quite another matter. On balance, Themistius' defence seems plausible rather than compelling. It is hard to imagine that it commanded total consent, although it was sufficient, perhaps, given the introduction of the emperor's reputation into the matter, to generate at least superficial public acceptance.

## THE PERQUISITES OF OFFICE

All this raises one obvious question. Given the definition of legitimate behaviour for a philosopher which Themistius himself had laid down in 359, and the credit he had taken for previously refusing the prefecture, why did he finally accept the post in 383/4? He really should have been

17 Chastagnol, 1960, 193–4, 197–8.
18 Linguistically, Libanius consistently distinguished between *politeuomenoi* and *archontes*: Petit, 1956, esp. 72–4; cf. Dagron, 1968, 52–3.

expecting the storm of criticism which came his way. Orations 17 and 34 preserve, of course, only Themistius' public utterances on the matter – that the appearance of a philosopher emperor demanded the service of philosophy – and there is no reason to suppose that these, any more than his public utterances on so many other matters, communicate the entire truth. No doubt one element of motivation was a kind of public service to Constantinople, his adopted city. The urban prefecture, as Themistius claimed in Oration 34, could, on one level, be seen as the most important post in city government, and hence a natural one for a good Hellene to hold, but this, as we have seen, certainly stretched traditional cultural boundaries close to, if not beyond, breaking point. On the other hand, Themistius had never been one to shy away from worldly success, despite his philosophical pose. He was careful throughout his career to parade any marks of public prominence which came his way, not least in Oration 34, which mentioned the statues raised to him, official imperial letters celebrating his activities, and his close association with a sequence of emperors (esp. 34.xiii). There is every reason to suppose, therefore, that Themistius would also have enjoyed the perquisites of the office.

Among his contemporaries, Themistius was hardly unique in this respect. Late Roman society was status conscious in the extreme. Complicated laws on precedence governed every aspect of public life, not least the operations of the Senates of Rome and Constantinople. As the Emperor Gratian had put it in the year 380, one's status within the senatorial order decided who would have the 'more prominent seats, and more distinguished place, and priority in deciding and speaking' (*C.Th.* 6.7.2 trans. Pharr). Being urban prefect was not only an important job in itself, but carried with it a pre-eminence, which remained with the appointee beyond departure from office. The operations of status in the political world of the later Roman Empire, in the latter part of Themistius' career at least, had been defined in a comprehensive piece of legislation issued by the Emperors Valentinian and Valens in 372. According to this law, former and current urban prefects of Rome and Constantinople ranked second of all in the senatorial order, coming after only former and current Patricians and Consuls, but ahead of even the most senior of imperial civil servants.[19]

---

19  *C.Th.* 6.7.1: other parts of the original law are preserved at *C.Th.* 6.9.1; 6.11.1; 6.14.1; 6.22.4; cf. Jones, 1964, 142–3. On the importance of status in general, see Jones, 1964, 543–5.

Why was Themistius ready to take the office in 383/4, but not before? The likeliest answer to this is provided by a combination of the storm of public controversy it provoked and how Themistius had actually structured his career. He was not shy of worldly success, but it had had to be expressed informally. The stance of independent philosopher interested in the affairs of his city, essential to the role he played for his string of imperial patrons, was, as the prefecture controversy shows, more or less impossible for him to maintain once he had taken office. For city-minded, traditional Hellenes, imperial offices were unpleasant and demeaning innovations. Themistius' correspondent and old sparring partner Libanius, for instance, reportedly refused a grant of the title of honorary Praetorian Prefect from Theodosius late in life, because he considered any honours not directly earned in his capacity as an orator 'vulgar and common'.[20]

For Themistius, the urban prefecture had the particular value of translating a pre-eminence which had been his since the 350s on an informal basis into a formally defined one. It also, however, blew his cover, making it difficult if not impossible for him to maintain his philosophical pose. Against this backdrop, it is very striking that Themistius disappeared from public life soon after the prefecture. A letter of Libanius suggests that he was still alive in 388 (*Ep.* 18), but no speeches of substance can dated after Oration 34 of late 384 or early 385.[21] By this date, Themistius was in his mid to late 60s,[22] having been born about 317, and had already, if one can really believe it, been complaining of ill health in Oration 14 of 379 and Oration 16 of January 383 (Chapter 4). It is a guess, but a far from unlikely one, that Themistius finally decided to take the prefecture (an office with which, as the imperial letter mentioned in *Or.* 34.xiii shows, he had previously toyed) when he was more or less ready to retire from public life. At that point, the limitations of informal pre-eminence would have become more problematic. If he were to stop speaking for emperors, his influence would cease to be

20 Eunapius, *Lives of the Sophists* 496; cf. Dagron, 1968, 53.

21 It is possible to argue that *Or.* 19 is later than *Or.* 34, but only because its contents are lacking in specific references to major public events. Even if Themistius continued to speak, therefore, it was no longer as an insider charged with crucial aspects of the regime's self-presentation, and most commentators would anyway place *Or.* 19 before *Or.* 34: e.g., Dagron, 1968, 24; Vanderspoel, 1995, 213.

22 At *Orr.* 17.214b and 34.xii Themistius emphasised that he was now in old age; cf. Penella, 2000, 35.

apparent and perhaps disappear entirely. To secure a cheerfully grand retirement, therefore, he was ready to take the criticism and enjoy both the prefect's silver carriage, and its comfortable aftermath: a guaranteed front seat in the Senate of Constantinople.

## ORATION 17
## ON THE ELECTION TO THE URBAN PREFECTURE:
## INTRODUCTION

Little need be said by way of particular introduction to Oration 17. This short speech cannot be dated precisely, but the general circumstances of its delivery are clear enough. As its contents indicate, Themistius was speaking to the assembled Senate of Constantinople, but not in the presence of the Emperor Theodosius. Two possible scenarios can be suggested for the circumstances of its delivery. On the one hand, its final paragraphs have led some to argue that the senate may have had a formal role in the appointment or at least the ceremonial induction of the urban prefect, who was its notional head, and that this speech belonged to those proceedings. Although the appointment of urban prefect was made by the emperor, the senate may, however, have been required to express its formal approval of the choice, perhaps even by some kind of vote or, more likely, ritual acclamation. Dagron suggested that Oration 17 was delivered as part of such an occasion, and the contents of the speech – praising Theodosius for the choice, alluding to Themistius' qualifications for office, and asking the senate for backing – make this an entirely plausible argument.[23] If not given in the course of such a ceremony, then the speech was clearly given on some other occasion

---

23 See esp. 215d asking the senate to follow the divine decree, and 216b–c asking for senatorial support. On methods of appointment, see Chastagnol, 1960, 194–4. *Or.* 17 has often been seen as part of such proceedings: Dagron, 1968, 23; Penella, 2000, 35. If so, Themistius may have been looking for senatorial approval such as that expressed by the carefully choreographed, shouted acclamations which greeted the publication of the *Theodosian Code* (see the *Minutes of the Senate* edited by Mommsen/Kruger and translated by Pharr in their respective versions of the *Code* itself). Dagron, 1974, 231–2, argues, on the contrary, that there was a formal vote, perhaps to make the new urban prefect president of the senate, on the basis of Themistius' reference to a *psephos*/vote at *Or.* 31.355a, and sees this as an institutional innovation of the Constantinopolitan senate. This is not impossible, but would be out of keeping with the concord expected on Late Roman public occasions (Matthews, 1974; MacCormack, 1981), and there is no other evidence for such a procedure.

within a few days of Themistius' appointment to office. In that case, it was a call for senatorial support of a more general and informal kind.

As this suggests, and as we have already seen, the speech is very striking for its defensiveness of tone. Themistius was clearly attempting – even so early in his tenure of office – to justify the change of position involved in his acceptance of an office which he had previously so publicly rejected. The wording of the oration suggests very firmly that Themistius was expecting to encounter, or indeed had already encountered, some criticism on this score.[24]

## ORATION 17
## ON THE ELECTION TO THE URBAN PREFECTURE: TRANSLATION

[213c] The god-like emperor has at long last restored philosophy once more to the care of public affairs and more prominently than those who have lately ruled. For they honoured [philosophy] just for her words and did not press her to return to action although that was often her preference,[25] but up to now she was involved in state affairs and gave her services to the commonwealth only to the extent of her embassies.[26] [d] But the king [Theodosius] not only places the office [of prefect] upon her but also commands her to take control of those things which he once deemed fit for others. It used to be that philosophy, having given instruction to the competitors, was herself able to watch the games of state quietly and without involvement. [214a] But the king leads her down from her spectator's seat to the arena and makes it possible for her to persuade men at large that philosophy is not indeed reasoning divorced from deeds but a display of deeds guided by reason, nor is it a risk-free instruction in how to rule but rather the practice of what it preaches.[27]

24  The crucial sentence occurs at 214c. Meridier, 1906, 91–2, suggested that the criticism was probably potential rather than actual, but there is no way to be certain.

25  Reading προελομένην see Hansen, 1967, 117; Penella, 2000, 231 n. 1.

26  In this opening sentence, Themistius adopted his normal personification of himself as philosophy, so that to promote himself was to promote the subject. Embassies, involving the hazards of travel and negotiation, were a traditional Hellenic measure of service, and their outcomes, if good, a measure of personal success. Themistius later specified some of his own successes at *Or.* 34.xiii, xxix (see below). At *Or.* 17.214b, he specified that he had undertaken ten embassies for Constantinople.

27  Reading ἀπόδειξις ('display') as *A* and *Π*. Themistius clearly acknowledged in this opening paragraph that taking the prefecture – i.e., holding an administrative office – repre-

And our age has brought in a kingship which is conversant with the thoughts of the ancients who understood that the affairs of cities would fare well at those times when the power of action runs together with skill in speaking, and both these things, political authority and philosophy, proceed towards the same place. And the most philosophical of emperors, [b] having been the first to show that these attributes combine in himself,[28] bids that we too, even in our old age, be guided by youth as it practises philosophy[29] and allots to us the most noble part of his own responsibilities, this august and venerable prefecture, to be ours, to follow the ten embassies and the sojourns aboard which we have accomplished on your behalf to the best of our ability, from our youth to this age, neither unworthily of your choice nor without advantage.[30]

And, instead of those two statues and the countless private consultations, he surpasses previous emperors by distinguishing us with a real and substantial honour,[31] and by bringing it about that it [the office] is necessarily distinguished [c] by not electing an alien or foreigner to have command of the ruling city, but a native who was raised with you and who grew up and lived among you, so that there is no benefit in this present office which is not manifestly shared by

---

sented a major new departure for his career. He sought to head off any potential charges of inconsistency by suggesting that he had always been ready to act as well as advise, but that previous emperors had not appointed him. See the introduction to this chapter.

28  Reading πρῶτος ('the first to') after Harduin. *Or*. 34.ix, xviff. argues the point in more detail. Because Theodosius is the ultimate philosopher king, Themistius the philosopher can actively serve him in good conscience.

29  I.e., Theodosius, who although about 37 when this oration was given is characterised as a 'youth' to make him conform to the first of Plato's criteria for the ideal king: see further *Or*. 3 note 270 and 215c below.

30  The ten cannot all be identified: Schneider, 1966, 194–5. Apart from the traditional reasons for emphasising ambassadorial service (see note 26), the embassies were important for Themistius' argument because they allowed him to claim that he had always been an active servant of the public interest, and hence that taking the prefecture was not such a large leap.

31  Themistius rightly acknowledged that, in the imperial scheme of things, the formal honour attached to prefecture ranked much higher than the rewards he had previously received, whether formal (statues, open imperial letters etc.: cf. *Or*. 34.xiii) or informal (different forms of privileged access to the emperor: audiences, meals etc.: see Chapter 1). See further the introduction to this chapter.

everyone.[32] And this is the reason why it was not right for me to reject this election.[33]

For a philosopher who rejects election to public office by a philosopher king straightway shows himself to be alien to his title, unless we consider our philosophy to lie only in the tongue rather than to a much greater degree in the soul – [d] whenever violent emotion is stilled and anger is bridled by reason, whenever avarice departs from the soul and savagery decamps to some far off place, but on each side Law and Justice and Right take their seats of honour.[34] He who considers that such a king is not a philosopher is heedless not only of Plato and of Pythagoras too, but also does not recognise this self-evident point, [215a] that philosophy is the absolute desire for virtue, and he perverts the most godlike of the sciences into hair, let's say, and a beard and a philosopher's cloak.[35]

And so let our age enjoy the return of the times of Trajan, Hadrian, Marcus [Aurelius] and Antoninus [Pius] which raised Arius and Rusticus from their books and made them participants and colleagues in the management of public affairs.[36] And these men were not innovating nor introducing something unusual into the state but were emulating the

32 Themistius' origins lay in Paphlagonia, but his father had taught in Constantinople, Themistius spent much of his childhood in the city, and in his adlection letter to the Constantinopolitan senate Constantius II had said that Themistius should be reckoned a native (see *The Letter of Constantius* in Chapter 2). This was an important element to his public image, since philosophers were traditionally expected to serve their cities: see Chapter 1.

33 Themistius was thus justifying himself against the expectation that he should have refused prefectural office. *Or.* 34.xiii shows that it was the orator's own behaviour, in taking public credit for refusing it on a previous occasion, which had sown this expectation.

34 Echoing the traditional Graeco-Roman view of civilisation: the development within the individual of reason (originally by education, but sustained subsequently by voluntary obedience to good laws) to control violent emotional impulses with their origins in the physical senses of the body: see further Heather, 1993a; 1993b with refs.

35 I.e., mistakenly judge who is a philosopher on the basis of the traditional exterior attributes (the τριβώνιον – the worn and threadbare cloak which was the badge of the true philosopher from Socrates onwards – combined with unkempt hair and beard) rather than on underlying action. Themistius would elaborate on what he saw in Plato's example as justifying his actions at *Or.* 34.v, vii, xvi, xxviii–xxx (see below). The later speech did not return to Pythagoras.

36 Trajan, Hadrian, Marcus Aurelius, and Antoninus were often picked out by Themistius as historical archetypes of the philosophical emperor: *Orr.* 13.166b (omitting Hadrian), 19.229b–c (omitting Hadrian), 34.vii (omitting Trajan). Themistius returned to the same linkage between Arrian and Rusticus and the emperors who appointed them at *Or.* 34.vii–viii.

ancient Romans, **[b]** in whose time the Scipios, the Varros and the Catos engaged in political affairs as philosophers and held the highest offices, and Thrasea, Priscus, Bibulus and Favonius exchanged the philosopher's and the senator's cloak in turn,[37] just like Xenophon and Socrates among the Greeks, the one holding the office of general, the other of prytani.[38] I omit the divine Plato who prayed that he would find such a king with whom he could share the care of state but who did not achieve this prayer and in seeking, as he himself says somewhere, **[c]** one who is young, learned, gentle, mild, great of spirit and greathearted[39] – in short a very Theodosius[40] – was cast up thrice on Dionysius and Sicily, and through love of true kingship was forced into a tyrant's company.[41] I let pass Pittacus, Bias and Kleoboulus, I let pass Archytas the Tarentine all of whom were more engaged in deeds than in writings.[42]

The present occasion is no less worthy of celebration than all of these because of both the man bestowing the honour and the man receiving it,[43] and it is necessary for you to join them in their task, O conscript

37  Scipio, Varro, Cato, Priscus, and Thrasea are all likewise mentioned at *Or.* 34.viii. Of the more obscure figures, Favonius Marcus was an admirer of Cato who conspired against and was later executed by Caesar; Clodius Thrasea Paetus was a philosopher and politician, who also wrote a biography of Cato, and was eventually executed under Nero; Helvidius Priscus was a philosopher and son-in-law of Thrasea eventually exiled and executed under Vespasian. We have followed Harduin and Dindorf in emending βίβος to βίβουλος. If so, the most likely candidate would appear to be L. Calpurnius Bibulus, who studied at Athens before joining his stepfather Brutus in the civil war. Later rehabilitated, he commanded the fleet and governed Syria for Mark Antony. For further comment and fuller refs., see Penella, 2000, 233 n. 5, who prefers M. Calpurnius Bibulus, Caesar's consular colleague of 59 BC.

38  Themistius returned to the practical achievements of Socrates and Xenophon at greater length at *Or.* 34.x: for details see our annotation below.

39  Themistius used this characterisation of Plato's political thought at several places, not least at *Or.* 34.xvi, where the argument was developed at greater length: see below.

40  Themistius was punning on the literal meaning – 'God-given' – of Theodosius' name: Penella, 2000, 233 n. 6.

41  Plato, along with Dion, encouraged Dionysius II, tyrant of Syracuse, in his passion for philosophy, but their attempts to guide his regime eventually led to failure and their estrangement; hence Dionysius' memory was disparaged in the Academic tradition. Plato's three visits are also mentioned at *Or.* 34.xxviii.

42  The practical achievements of Pittacus, Bias, and Kleoboulus were returned to at *Or.* 34.iii: see below. Archytas was a Pythagorean philosopher who was also elected general of Tarentum seven times.

43  Theodosius and Themistius himself respectively: both, according to Themistius, examples of active philosophers.

fathers. There is nothing glorious or great in your being first among all men in buildings, gold or silver. **[d]** But if we show clearly our desire to honour philosophy and to lead virtue to the fore, then we shall not be false to our title of 'fathers', then our senate shall stand in first place, then it shall be a temple of the Muses, not filled with bronze statues but loaded with their archetypes.[44]

Let us imitate our leader, ye guardians of the world, let us follow the decree bestowed by God, let us become day by day a greater source of pleasure to Him. **[216a]** The young man[45] does not love treasures, he does not love precious gems, he does not love richly woven fabrics. But he gladly uses these and lets them go. He loves one thing alone and is subordinate to it – that is virtue – and those things that virtue brings: love of mankind, gentleness, forbearance. Because of him no man puts on the black cloak,[46] because of him no one is fatherless, or completely an orphan but for those still young whom some cruel necessity [has made so] he turns aside this ill fate and they have a king in place of their own father. **[b]** He wishes the treasuries and the store of these good things to increase and grow large for him. And may he deem us worthy of being rich in those treasures which he has thus first hoarded in himself. For it is only by thus possessing these good things that we can show ourselves to be of greatest value to him.[47]

And so you must bring back discipline and order to the senate and respect for the office [of prefect], to which they have lent honour,[48] must

44 This paragraph makes it clear that *Or.* 17 was given in the Senate of Constantinople, and – cf. the introduction to the speech – that the occasion was some kind of confirmation of Themistius' appointment.

45 Theodosius: cf. *Or.* 17.214b. In this context, where it heightens the impression of his virtue, Themistius played on Theodosius' relative youth, since philosophical virtue was considered more remarkable in a younger person. In the context of justifying the emperor's position against Gratian during the Gothic war years and afterwards, Themistius had stressed Theodosius' experience: see the introduction to Chapter 4.

46 Black was the colour of death: cf. *Or.* 15.190b–c on the black colouring or edging of death sentences issued from the palace. It is unclear whether the black cloak was worn by the executed or the executioner.

47 Themistius returned in greater detail to Theodosius' gentle management of his population's problems at *Or.* 34.xvi–xix. From *Or.* 34.xviii it becomes clear that the reference to 'orphans' had in mind a specific *cause célèbre*, which, not surprisingly, involved members of the landowning elite, at whom most imperial actions were directed. Theodosius' skill in this area was an important topic of *Or.* 15.189c–194d and mentioned in *Or.* 16.212c–d.

48 ἣν ἐκόσμησαν: Penella, 2000, 234 (cf. note 23) translates this as 'who have given the honour', accepting the interpretation that the senate was in some way responsible for giving

be sought from its chief officers, and compliance from the people. And let it be thought that the great senate is in no way different from a healthy creature, [c] in which the rest of the body should follow the eyes' lead with neither the hands nor the feet anticipating [what] the eyes [see] but whenever each of the limbs enjoys its particular function, then all must be well with the whole creature.[49]

## ORATION 34
### IN REPLY TO THOSE WHO FOUND FAULT WITH HIM FOR ACCEPTING PUBLIC OFFICE: INTRODUCTION

In Oration 34 Themistius made a full-scale attempt, after he had left office, to still the criticism which his urban prefecture had continued to provoke. Its date depends upon when one places Themistius' prefecture, but most commentators argue that it was delivered in late 384 or perhaps early 385.[50] Like Oration 17, its contents make it clear that the intended audience was the Senate of Constantinople. As far as one can tell, it was a publicly delivered self-defence, rather than a literary exercise.[51] The great value of Oration 34 to the historian is that, in answering criticisms of his prefecture, Themistius reviewed his whole public career and attempted to demonstrate that it had consistently adhered to the principles of Hellenic *paideia*. The oration thus recapitulates, sometimes with interesting expansions, many of the themes which are characteristic of his other oratorical contributions, but also introduces some new

---

or confirming the prefecture. This is certainly possible, but the Greek seems to us a little less definite, and might also be a reference to the ex-city prefects in the senate, who had already lent the office honour by holding it themselves, and who, upon retirement, ranked high in the senatorial order (see the introduction to this chapter).

49 This paragraph suggests that Themistius was expecting or had already experienced some kind of hostile reaction to his prefecture: see the introduction to this chapter.

50 See the introduction to this chapter.

51 Cf. Schneider, 1966, 17–18; Maisano, 1995, 990. Penella, 2000, 38, argues that it had a more general audience on the basis of Themistius' frequent use of 'you' (pl.) and the fact that there were some orphans present (*Or.* 34.xviii). But if we are right – as seems likely – to identify these orphans as the *cause célèbre* mentioned also in *Orr.* 15 and 16, then Theodosius' rescue did indeed return them to the senate, and the second-person plurals make perfect sense for a senatorial audience.

information about himself. Both features make it fundamental to any understanding of his career.

## Rhetorical Structure

The rhetorical structure of Oration 34 has been convincingly analysed by Hugo Schneider, who demonstrated that Themistius had closely modelled it after the characteristic format of a piece of forensic oratory.[52] Schneider's analysis is generally persuasive, except that it labels two key points of Themistius' argument as 'digressions' (*egressiones*). What follows summarises Schneider's analysis, but also attempts to show how closely tied into Themistius' argument the so-called digressions actually are.

1. *Praepositio* First half of paragraph i: defines the purpose of the speech. Themistius has been ignorantly accused of betraying the true purpose of philosophy.

2. *Partitio* Remainder of paragraph i: summarises the approach Themistius will take. The true purpose of philosophy must be identified, and his career then measured against it. In addition, since the office was conferred on him in honour of philosophy by the Emperor Theodosius, it is necessary to consider the emperor's grasp of the true meaning of philosophy.

3. *Argumentatio* (consisting of positive arguments in favour of the case being made – *probatio* – and destruction of opposing arguments – *refutatio*). Paragraphs ii–viii: Schneider identifies here two digressions (*egressiones*): a) on the history of philosophy (ii–vi); b) on how rare it has been for past kings, unlike Theodosius, to recognise the value of philosophy (vii–viii). Here Schneider's analysis seems a little off-target. The history of philosophy was no digression but a partisan argument designed to show that true philosophy is not about detached analysis and theoretical contemplation, but a recipe for practical political action, of the kind Themistius has tried to pursue throughout his life. It also seems artificial to divide vii and viii from ix and x (see below). We would thus include ii–viii as part of the *probatio*.

---

52 Schneider, 1966, 19–22, for an outline. On the rhetorical theory behind such speeches, see, e.g., Leeman, 1963, 26–8, 49.

**3a.** ***Probatio*** Paragraph ix and first half of x: evidence in support of Themistius' case. Theodosius was really a philosopher disguised as an emperor and various other philosophers, even the great Socrates himself, had, like Themistius, engaged in public action. Schneider's analysis would again be more persuasive in our view if it kept paragraphs vii to x (first half) together. Between them, these established three connected points: a) Theodosius' grasp of the true meaning of philosophy; b) how rare such a grasp was among known rulers of the past; c) that philosophers had been known to engage actively in public affairs.

**3b.** ***Refutatio*** In 2 parts: paragraphs x (second half)–xiii, and xiv–xv. Down to xiii, Themistius refuted the accusations levelled at him by showing that his career as a whole entirely accorded with the true importance of philosophy and the examples of other active philosophers established in paragraphs ii–viii. Paragraphs xiv–xv answered the question why it was right to take office, when previously it had not been, in terms of the Emperor Theodosius' total embodiment of the ideal philosopher ruler.

**4.** ***Laudatio*** Paragraphs xvi–xxvii: a further digression in Schneider's analysis praising the good government of the Emperor Theodosius, and in particular showing how its decrees accorded with the principles of good government laid down by philosophy. Although long enough to be more reasonably thought of as a digression than paragraphs ii–vii, its argument was still very much to Themistius' point, since it reinforced the case that it was right to take office under Theodosius, where it had not been before.[53]

**5.** ***Peroratio*** Paragraphs xxviii–xxx: Afterword briefly recapitulating, with some different *exempla*, Themistius' overall argument.

Oration 34 was thus a carefully crafted speech designed to answer the charges laid against Themistius by a careful review of his entire career. Palladas' lampoon was not the only charge on his mind, but the

53  Cf. Penella, 2000, 39–40.

epigram was cited at many of the crux points in the argument: twice in paragraph i at the end of both the *praeposito* and *partitio*; in paragraphs ix and x in anticipation of the *refutatio*; in xii as Themistius introduced the analysis of his career; in xxvii at the end of the *laudatio*; and again in xxx at the conclusion of the *peroratio*.[54]

## The Refused Prefecture

Aside from its many items of individual interest, the account of Themistius' career given in Oration 34 includes one important incident which requires fuller discussion. One of the central accusations levelled against Themistius was inconsistency. Under a previous emperor, he was known to have refused the urban prefecture which he had so recently accepted from Theodosius. It emerges from paragraph xiii that the episode was public knowledge because the then emperor had mentioned the offer in an open letter to the senate. This letter recorded that the emperor had tried to persuade Themistius, and had nearly succeeded, but that, in the end, the philosopher had decided against taking the job. The accusation of inconsistency naturally centred, of course, on why, having previously refused the prefecture, Themistius had now accepted it. He attempted to justify himself, as we have seen, by claiming that the overwhelming virtue of Theodosius had simply compelled his acceptance. But which emperor had been less successfully persuasive in the past?[55]

The question has stimulated considerable debate, revolving around the following clues:

1. The emperor concerned was highly solicitous towards philosophy (paragraph xiv). Some have argued from this that he was himself a philosopher, but that is not what Themistius said. The sentence continues '[he] often made me his fellow counsellor in my philosopher's cloak'. Themistius was thus making his standard personalising equation of himself with philosophy. What he meant was that the emperor was very gracious towards Themistius himself.[56]

54  Cf. Dagron, 1968, 50–1.

55  The argument has sometimes been confused by an association of this incident with Themistius' self-defence in the 350s. See note 5.

56  The misinterpretation goes back to Mai, followed by Schneider, 1966, 124. Similar analyses of Themistius' meaning as argued here: Dagron, 1968, 58; Brauch, 1993a, 47.

2. As point 1 would anyway suggest, relations between the orator
   and the emperor were very amicable. Themistius often ate with
   the emperor, and travelled with him (xiv).
3. The emperor often listened to Themistius' advice, tolerating
   anything he had to say (xiv).
4. The emperor was extremely careful when it came to affairs of
   state, investigating determinedly before deciding what was
   the best course of action (xiv).
5. At the same time, the emperor could be considered the 'least
   amenable' of all those Themistius served (xiii).
6. The letter to the senate mentioning the offer was written at a
   moment when the pulse harvest had failed (xiii).[57]

Most previous discussions of the issue have wavered between
Constantius and Julian. Under Constantius II, there was a major crop
failure in 357/8 (6),[58] and Oration 31 celebrated the fact that Themistius had been invited to dine with that emperor (2). As we have seen,
Themistius also received many marks of favour from Constantius (1),
and gave many speeches in front of him (3: cf. Chapter 2). On the
other hand, the highly laudatory description Themistius gives of
Constantius' character in Oration 31 would hardly qualify him as the
'least amenable' of Themistius' emperors (*Or.* 31.353a). Likewise, the
description of the anonymous emperor's attitude to state affairs (4)
corresponds to nothing known of Constantius.[59] In favour of Julian
has been the misinterpretation of what Themistius says about the
emperor's attitude to philosophy (1), and the fact that he was a difficult
character (5). But, while there is reason to think that relations between
Themistius and Julian warmed up after some initial frost, nothing
suggests that he was closely involved enough in the latter's regime to
justify the characterisations at (2) and (3) (see Chapter 3). In addition,
no famine is known from the time of Julian (6), and his character
seems to have been prone to rashness rather than careful scrutiny
(4).[60]   Having made these observations, Schneider concluded that in

57 We take 5 and 6 to refer to the same occasion, but it is possible that there had been
more than one public offer of the prefecture to Themistius; see *Or.* 34.xiii with footnotes
below.
58 Schneider, 1966, 123.
59 Cf. Brauch, 1993a, 55–6.
60 Cf. Brauch, 1993a, 54–5.

character the anonymous emperor seemed to resemble Julian, but all the circumstances of the relationship suggested Constantius II. Most subsequent commentators have echoed this judgement, while opting for one or other of the two candidates.[61]

There is, however, one further candidate, who has largely gone unconsidered: the Emperor Valens.[62] And Valens, in fact, fits every aspect of the description. He could certainly be described as the 'least amenable' (4) of Themistius' imperial patrons. His purges after the usurpation of Procopius and in the treason trials of the early 370s have left graphic accounts of his ferocity, and one source even reports that he had threatened to destroy Constantinople should he get back safely from the Gothic war.[63] On the other hand, Ammianus records that Valens was extremely conscientious in the pursuit of state affairs (5).[64] The nature of his relationship with Themistius also satisfies the description. Themistius travelled with Valens extensively: to the Danube in 368 and Mesopotamia in the 370s. In Oration 31, Themistius records, likewise, how Valens often listened to his advice. Themistius was highly prominent under Valens' regime, and was himself shown many marks of favour;[65] it is likely, indeed, that Valens was responsible for the second of the statues erected to him (see below). Conditions (1), (2), and (3) are all satisfied, therefore, and there was also a major famine under Valens, in Phrygia in the year 370. Conditions were bad enough to force people to come to Constantinople, so that this was memorable enough for

---

61 Schneider, 1966, 124; echoed by Daly, 1983, 193–4; Vanderspoel, 1995, 111–3. Dagron, 1968, Notes II and IV (cf. 58–60) argued that it was Constantius, taking *Or.* 23.292b–c as Themistius' own reference to the matter. On the real significance of this text, see the introduction to Chapter 2. Vanderspoel, 1995, 112–13, slightly favours Constantius because of the amicable relations described between the emperor and Themistius. Daly, 1983, 194–204, opted for Julian on the grounds that the ambivalence in their relationship would have given Themistius cause to refuse.

62 The one exception to this is Brauch, 1993a (see below). Theoretically, the anonymous emperor might also be Jovian or Theodosius. But, as all commentators have agreed, Jovian did not hold power long enough to justify the kind of characterisation Themistius' gives. Likewise, Themistius justified his eventual assumption of office on the grounds that Theodosius was more in tune with philosophy than the anonymous emperor, so he too can be ruled out.

63 See Matthews, 1989, chs 8–9. The correspondence is noted by Brauch, 1993a, 52–3, 56–7.

64 Ammianus 31.14.2–3; cf. Brauch, 1993a, 49.

65 *Or.* 31.354d; cf. Brauch, 1993a, 47–9, 50–1.

Themistius, as a Constantinopolitan, to seize upon as a chronological marker (Socrates, *Ecclesiastical History* 4.6).

Every aspect of the description thus fits Valens. The one major study to consider seriously the case for Valens, and reject it, more or less accepted the strength of these correspondences, but raised one objection. Palladas' bitterness, it concluded, was only explicable if Themistius, a non-Christian, had accepted the prefecture from a Christian (Theodosius), while rejecting it from a fellow non-Christian (i.e., Julian). If the refused anonymous emperor were another Christian, then the vitriolic anti-Christian Palladas would not have cared so much.[66] Themistius' prefecture attracted criticism, however, not for any religious reasons, but because he had spent his entire career claiming to be an independent philosopher, commenting on events without fear or favour. He had also, in 359, maintained that his independence was secure so long as he did not accept state office, and clearly taken credit, in similar fashion, in an intervening imperial letter, for not taking the prefecture at an earlier point. It was thus the principle of taking office which was at stake, not the religious affinities of the particular emperors involved. Given everything he had previously said of himself, Themistius' acceptance of office in 383/4 looked like the grossest hypocrisy, and suggested that the public image of his entire life had been no more than a lie. No matter who the previous emperor might have been, Themistius' acceptance of the prefecture was bound to have aroused a storm. There is thus no reason not to accept what the weight of correspondence suggests: the anonymous emperor was Valens.

## ORATION 34
### IN REPLY TO THOSE WHO FOUND FAULT WITH HIM
### FOR ACCEPTING PUBLIC OFFICE:
### TRANSLATION

[I] Some people consider philosophy worthy of such great things that they think even the greatest office inferior to her; I have much praise for these men and love them. For to purpose the greatest things for the most divine of human pursuits, I deem the mark of a not ignoble nature. There are those, on the other hand, who have either never reflected on

---

66  Daly, 1983, 198–9; having noted on pp. 194–7 how well the descriptions in *Or.* 34 fit Valens.

the tasks proper to this art, or not thought it worthwhile to learn them, yet who all the same make a display what they think, and I consider this to be unworthy of the opinion they profess to have about her.[67] Now, if they were laying the present accusation against me alone, it would have been sufficient for me to talk with them elsewhere. But since the giver must undeservedly share the charge with the receiver, the shared accusation must be refuted before you [sing.] as judge. For either both of us raised up philosophy, by leading her from words to deeds, or both of us have cast her down.[68] So, first of all, it is necessary to make it clear both for all you who now listen to me,[69] and for all who will come upon this speech subsequently, what it is right to consider as philosophy's task, what it was she desired when she came forward into the life of man, how she was exalted in the beginning and loved, and how great is her kinship and affinity with kingship and how great her alienation from tyranny.[70] Thus you all might more easily understand whether I guarded her ancestral tenets when I undertook the office or whether I departed from them.

[II] Now if anyone were to ask you all in what respect man most differs from the rest of creation, and why he has dominion over the other creatures and is the mightiest of them,[71] who stands so far removed from reason as not to think that it is reason which is the most important part of this self-same nature?[72] For it is certainly not physical

67  Dagron, 1968, 50 n. 94, is surely correct that the critic unlearned in philosophy to whom Themistius addressed himself was Palladas whose lampoon is referred to at key points of transition in the argument of *Or.* 34: see the introduction to this chapter.

68  Themistius used 'you' singular to address the individual picked out to judge the 'case' for his self-defence laid out in *Or.* 34. This was clearly the Emperor Theodosius, who gave Themistius the gift of the urban prefecture, an identity confirmed by xxiff. below which praised 'you' singular for having ended the Gothic war of 376–82. The speech sometimes also referred to the emperor in the third person even while addressing him as judge, and also occasionally addressed a further group of individuals in the second-person plural (see the next note). Associating the emperor directly with Themistius' appointment, both as its author and as judge of the present speech, was designed to make people think twice about criticising it (cf. Penella, 2000, 209 n. 2).

69  We use 'all you' to translate the 'you' pl. addressed occasionally in the speech. Section xiii indicates that this broader audience was the assembled Senate of Constantinople.

70  Themistius characteristically used 'philosophy' as a synonym for himself, as well as in the abstract.

71  Recalls Gen. 1.26, perhaps deliberately; see also Isocrates 3.5: see the introduction to Chapter 2.

72  Schneider, 1966, 38–40, identifies the sources behind Themistius' account of the history of philosophy which follows.

strength, nor swiftness, nor excellence of perception. In all these things one cannot describe the extent to which we are inferior to wild beasts and birds.[73] And so this superiority in man, if it chance on a good education, produces a divine creature on the earth, but if a bad one, creates a beast more hard to overcome than bears and boars.[74] For reason serving evil is a weapon against which it is difficult to prevail. It was for this education that law was sought out, and a method[75] identified to be law's discoverer.[76] If you track down the first beginnings of philosophy, going as far back as possible, like those who trace the sources of rivers,[77] you will find it to be nothing other than this [lawgiving], and those who shone out and flourished when she had recently come into existence, have for this first deed alone become famous and celebrated.

[III] For the famous Solon and Lycurgus, Pittacus, Bias and Kleoboulus were called wise by the men of those times,[78] not because they twisted syllogisms this way and that, nor because they discoursed on forms, nor because they uncovered the veiled and the horned dilemmas, intractable and dangerous contrivances, hard to fathom and useless to understand, nor yet because they took the sun's measure-

73 A commonplace going back to the pre-Socratics: *VS* 59B 216; cf. Schneider, 1966, 95–6.

74 In the Graeco-Roman conception, an education in literature was a crucial factor in shaping morality, allowing individuals to learn from the centuries of examples of men behaving well and badly recounted in these texts. For an introduction, see Heather, 1993a; 1993b. On the dangers of improperly educated humans, see Plato, *Laws* 766a; Aristotle, *Politics* 1.2; cf. Penella, 2000, 210 n. 3.

75 τέχνη: a set of rules to define any given subject. It here designates philosophy.

76 It was another long-established commonplace that philosophy was required to establish laws: Schneider, 1966, 38–9; cf. Seneca, *Letters* 90.6; Cicero, *Tusculan Disputations* 5.5; *Laws* 1.17

77 A metaphor long applied to the study of philosophy: Schneider, 1966, 96–7; cf. Cicero, *Academica* 1.8.

78 The Greeks traced the history of philosophy back to the seven sages listed by Plato at *Protagoras* 343b: Solon, Pittacus, Bias, Kleoboulus, Thales, Periander and Chilon. Themistius omits the last three because Thales did not engage in practical matters (see note 79), Periander worked with tyrants, and Chilon was little known. Solon and Pittacus were semi-mythical Athenian lawgivers; less is known of Bias and Kleoboulus. Lycurgus, not normally reckoned one of the sages, has been added as the famous Spartan lawgiver, a move already made by Cicero, *Tusculan Disputations* 5.3.[7]; cf. Schneider, 1966, 97–8; Penella, 2000, 211 n. 4. Themistius had used the examples of Pittacus, Bias and Kleoboulus to the same purpose at *Or.* 17.215c.

ments or calculated the moon's course.[79] Rather because they set down laws, and taught what should and should not be done, what it is right to choose and what to avoid, and the fact that this creature [man] is not solitary and self-sufficient but social and civic, and because of this should attend to country, laws and constitution.[80] They did not hesitate not only to teach these things, but also to put them into practice, so that while you will certainly find the writings of each of these men to be formidable in expression, their deeds are equally extraordinary: embassies, generalships, liberations of homelands, acquisitions of territory.[81]

[IV] Such indeed was philosophy's first beginning. As time advanced, however, philosophy also underwent the same changes as the other arts. And just as these, even though necessity drove each one forward, did not halt as necessity directed, with building not progressing only as far as walls and a roof, nor weaving only as far as covering the body, but they advanced further and fashioned beauty to complement what was necessary and took care to apply ornament to their creations.[82] In the same way, philosophy was not content with 'Know yourself' and 'Recognise the moment' and 'Nothing to excess',[83] nor was satisfied with the actions and precepts that were necessary for human existence, but has put on a great deal of external embellishment: the study of nature, and the perfection of reasoning.[84] In the same way, before the banqueting

79  This recalls a similar list of theoretical philosophical subjects at *Or.* 2.30b. The references here are to Aristotle (syllogisms = formal logic), Plato (Ideas: not included in *Or.* 2), Diodorus Cronus (dilemmas), Thales (predicting solar eclipses), and Meton (calculating the lunar calendar); cf. Schneider, 1966, 98–100; Penella, 2000, 211 n. 4. As in the passage in *Or.* 2, Themistius wishes to point out the contrast between philosophy practised as a purely intellectual exercise and for the benefit of the state and people.

80  Another amalgam of commonplaces going back to Aristotle, *Politics.* 1.2, 3.6; cf. *Eudemian Ethics* 7.10. Further comment, see Schneider, 1966, 100–1; Penella, 2000, 211 n. 4.

81  For examples of (some of) the seven sages in action, see Snell, 1952, 1629. Bias served as ambassador to Samos; Pittacus commanded his city's army in the war against Athens and liberated it from the tyrant Melanthias; Solon acquired Salamis from the Megarians. See further Penella, 2000, 211 n. 4.

82  Cf. Schneider, 1966, 102–3, architecture and weaving were common metaphors in ancient discussions of the progress of knowledge.

83  These three sayings were attributed to respectively Chilon, Pittacus and Solon: Snell, 1952, 8–13, and referred to in general by Themistius at *Or.* 26.317a.

84  It was a long-established idea that necessity started, but did not fully account for, the progress of knowledge: Uxkull-Gyllenbrand, 1924, 36. The threefold division of philosophy was traced back to Plato: Schneider, 1966, 103; cf. Cicero, *Academica* 1.19.

hall and inner chamber, a house has outer gates and porticos,[85] tapestries and statues, which fulfill no need but are an ornament and enhancement to what is necessary.

[V] Because of this, the famous Socrates of old, whom one could call the father and originator of the more valuable wisdom, thought that certain matters did not need to be examined: some having no relevance to us, of others the understanding being beyond us, but yet he made a complete examination of good and evil, from what cause man might become happy, and from what cause comes the household and the city, and he praised Homer for deeming it right to examine before all else 'what good and evil had been done in the palace'.[86] And the true circle of Socrates – Cebes, Phaedo, Aristippus and Aeschines[87] – abided by these limits. But it was the divine Plato alone, being by nature the noblest and finest, who first embellished philosophy with his many offerings and added these branches of knowledge: arithmetic, music, and astronomy.[88] In his advance, he ascended even beyond heaven itself, and was bold enough to concentrate his attention upon discovering whether there is not something which is above nature itself, not to show that this superabundance contributes nothing to our commonwealth, but – and this was the special characteristic of Plato's thinking – to link together the mortal with the divine Good, and to fashion as far as possible the organisation of human affairs after that of the Universe. This is what the *Republic* and the famous *Laws*, the *Phaedrus* and the *Gorgias* intend, in all of which he is in fierce competition with himself in showing that justice should be chosen by men for its own sake, and wickedness shunned for its own sake: even if there is no reward for one and the other escape retribution entirely. This then is Plato,[89] but [VI] is

85  Reading στοὰς after Jacobs.

86  That Socrates heralded a new beginning was another commonplace: Schneider, 1966, 103–4; cf. Cicero, *Academica* 1.15. The quotation from *Odyssey* 4.392 was reputedly Socrates' watchword. In a different context, Themistius had previously made a much greater distinction between Socrates and his predecessors: *Or.* 26.317aff.; cf. Penella, 2000, 212 n. 6.

87  All four were known in antiquity as true followers of Socrates, and reference is sometimes made to their works. None have survived, although Phaedo relates Plato's dialogue of the same name. An extant dialogue under the name of Cebes should probably be dated to the 1st century AD. See further Schneider, 1966, 104–5.

88  On Plato's championing of these subjects: Marrou, 1948, 113–7.

89  This is a not unfair summary of one of the tendencies of Plato's work, but is certainly a selective reading, and one that did not go unchallenged in antiquity. The Middle Platonists

Aristotle any different? Certainly there is a greater versatility and subtlety to him, yet his extensive corpus and his entire system does not avoid the good of mankind but is directed towards and dependent on this. For him the summation of human happiness is the practice of virtue for a perfect existence, and the action of the soul according to virtue its guiding principles. We practice philosophy, he says, not in order to know what is just but as far as is possible in order to put it into practice.[90] For him the Good has been divided among the soul, the body and what lies outside them – and he would fill up human happiness from the first, second and third bowl, saying that while happiness is desirable in an individual, it is greater and more perfect in an entire city. For this reason he calls the method political and says that right action cannot happen without action, and that the God which directs this universe and those who accompany Him are practising an active and political philosophy, keeping the whole of nature unswerving and incorrupt throughout eternity.[91] Yet most people either do not know or choose not to learn that this art supports so many and such important deeds and undertakings for the sake of humanity and human happiness, but stand amazed at its approaches, friezes, precincts, groves and meadows. They do not welcome the fact that it has afforded sheltering quarters insusceptible to the blasts of fortune.[92]

[VII] But not the emperor, who is god-like indeed, and following these illustrious men, he brought forth philosophy, who had for a long time been confined to her quarters, into the national and political arena

---

argued against the whole view of Plato's works as a coherent corpus from which one doctrine could be derived. In Themistius' lifetime, the Emperor Julian likewise directly questioned his reading of Plato, arguing that the god-like ruler who, through philosophy, could learn to run human affairs as God wanted (customarily used by Themistius of the emperors he knew: Chapter 1) was a theoretical ideal rather than a practical possibility, and that men could not aspire to be god-like: *Letter to Themistius* 7.326a commenting on Plato, *Laws* 709.6; cf. Athanassiadi, 1992, 90–1 and the introduction to Chapter 3 above.

90 A line based on Aristotle, *Nichomachean Ethics* 1103b 27, which Themistius had used before: *Or.* 2.31c. The argument that Plato's teaching can be subsumed within the work of Aristotle was a characteristic view of the Peripatetic school; cf. Schneider, 1966, 106.

91 Cf. Aristotle, *Nichomachean Ethics* 1.2 1094b.7ff.; *Magna Moralia* 1184b.4ff.; *Eudemian Ethics* 1219b.1ff.

92 I.e., they are entirely absorbed in the ornaments of the discipline, and do not recognise its necessities: section iv above. Themistius' general argument in sections ii to vi and especially the latter echo *Or.* 17.214d (see above) and recall a passage from *Or.*1.2c–d.

and, rather as if he had acquired a sacred statue of the ancient art, has brought her out into the public arena instead of enjoying her alone.[93] If you have to name someone as heir to the precepts of the divine Plato, you should not name Speusippus nor Xenocrates thus,[94] but the one [Theodosius] who has reinforced the idea which that man [Plato] would have put into practice most of all, namely to see political power and philosophy converging, rather than thought and power moving in opposite directions. For it was a king who revealed to the men of today this sight that was looked for no longer, that of philosophy, together with the highest power, giving judgement on what is just, and demonstrating that the words which it has long been putting forward in its writings have life and power.[95] Those who are to come shall sing the praises of Theodosius for calling on philosophy to take part in public affairs, just like Hadrian, Marcus Aurelius, and Antoninus – his forefathers as well as citizens and ancestors – whose heir he was not content to be only in so far as [wearing] the imperial purple. Rather, by returning their statues after a long interval to the palace, he placed philosophy at his side as they did.[96]

[VIII] Cyrus the Persian could not make such a boast nor Alexander the Great who, although he thought his teacher Aristotle to be worthy of many great honours and repopulated Stageira for him, yet did not set him up in the glory of such an office.[97] Nor did Augustus for Arius, nor

93  I.e., Theodosius did not just draw on Themistius for counsel, but actually gave him office; cf. *Or.* 17.213c–214a. Themistius here maintained his usual equation of himself with philosophy.

94  Speusippus was Plato's nephew who succeeded him as head of the Academy (347–339 BC); Xenocrates was a close disciple and the Academy's next head (339–314 BC).

95  Theodosius, via philosophy, has become capable of running human affairs in a God-imitating manner, thus fulfilling Plato's desideratum. Themistius had applied the same characterisation to every emperor he served: see Chapter 1.

96  Themistius is probably referring to a metaphorical (rather than, as some have argued, an actual) return of these emperors' images; cf. Schneider, 1966, 111 with refs. The *Meditations* made Marcus Aurelius the archetype of philosophical emperors. Hadrian befriended, employed, and promoted the intellectual Arrian, who was known primarily as a philosopher in his own time. Antoninus Pius employed the philosopher Rusticus. The three are often used by Themistius as *exempla* of archetypically philosophical emperors: *Or.* 13.166b, *Or.* 17.215a (see above), *Or.* 19.229b–c. He also thought of them, along with Trajan, as sharing Spanish provincial origins with Theodosius: *Or.* 19.229c; Penella, 2000, 214 n. 10.

97  Plutarch, *Life of Alexander* 7.3, reports that it was Philip who repopulated Stagira, which he had previously destroyed, in order that Alexander could study there with

Scipio Panaetius, nor Tiberius Thrasyllus, but they kept them only as spectators of their own contests and were not able to draw them to the stadium or the wrestling arena, even though they may have had a great desire to do so.[98] But not so the fathers and ancestors of the king, great are their names. They raised up Arrian and Rusticus from their books and did not allow them to be mere pen and ink philosophers: to write about courage while sitting at home, to compose legal treatises but to flee from public affairs for which the laws exist, to decide on which is the best of political systems but to stand aloof from all politics. So they advanced these men not just as far as the speaker's platform but to the general's tent, and, as generals of the Romans, they traversed the Caspian Gates, drove the Alans from Armenia, established boundaries for Iberians and Albanians. In return for all of this, they enjoyed the office of eponymous consul, regulated the great city and presided over the ancient senate.[99] For these emperors knew that office is like a body, and that the greater and more noble it might be, the more it needs to be purified. They also recognised that the ancient Romans were of the same opinion, including Cato the lover of learning who was censor, Brutus who held the praetorship, Favonius who was tribune of the people, Varro who held the six-axed office,[100] and Rutilus the consulship. I omit Priscus, Thrasea and those of the same stamp of whom the historians shall give you your fill should you so desire.[101] For Marcus Aurelius himself was nothing other than a philosopher in the purple, so too

---

Aristotle. Other sources claim it was Alexander himself: Aelian, *Miscellany* 12.54; cf. Penella, 2000, 215 n. 11.

98  Panaetius was a Stoic philosopher from Rhodes who eventually moved to Rome and joined the entourage of P. Cornelius Scipio Aemilianus, famous conqueror of Carthage. Thrasyllus, from Alexandria, wrote on Plato, but is chiefly famous as the Emperor Tiberius' astrologer. Having himself now been promoted from counsellor to office holder, Themistius here argued, contrary to his normal usage of these *exempla* (*Orr.* 5.63d (Chapter 3); 8.108b (trans. in Heather and Matthews, 1991); 11.145b), that these rulers were actually deficient in their behaviour towards philosophy.

99  Arrian (see also note 96) was consul in 129, and then employed by Hadrian as legate for Cappadocia (133–137), writing a famous account of the tactics he used against the Alans. Rusticus was ordinary consul and urban prefect in Rome in 165 under Marcus Aurelius.

100  I.e., the praetorship.

101  Themistius also used these *exempla* at *Or.* 17.217b–c. For relevant details of their careers, see our annotations above.

Hadrian and Antoninus, and now indeed Theodosius.[102] [IX] Now, if you were to examine his belt and cloak,[103] you would number him with many kings, yet if you glance into his soul and thought, alongside those three. He should be placed among those of like mind, not among those who are similarly attired. Therefore this king alone is sufficient to call forth in me a desire for virtue,[104] and not an idle and impractical one, rather one which each day unravels not symbols and propositions, but deeds in accordance with the precepts of the Academy.[105] Can you[106] say, then, that I have descended out of ambition in undertaking the rule of the Fair City?[107] If I acted outside its precepts in any way, then I did descend. But if I guarded the laws of that body in every respect, I have not descended, my friend, but, without altering my position, have ascended.[108]

[X] The famous Socrates certainly did not descend from philosophy in holding the office of prytany in Athens. He held out against the Thirty.[109] The noble Xenophon did not descend from philosophy by being general of the ten thousand; indeed he saved the Greeks from extreme dangers. And Parmenides did not descend by establishing

---

102 Marcus' philosophical reputation was based on *The Meditations*, Hadrian's upon his philhellenic intellectual culture, Antoninus' on his upright character: Penella, 2000, 216 n. 14.

103 The χλαμύς was the military cloak, the ζώνη (= Lat. *cingulum*) the military belt. Theodosius dressed, as was traditional for emperors, as a soldier rather than in the philosopher's cloak, but Themistius argued that this outward appearance was deceptive.

104 With Schneider and Penella, 2000, 217 n. 15, an emendation of the MS σοι (you) to μοι (me) makes better sense of the passage.

105 The Academy was the philosophical school established by Plato in Athens. Themistius is thus repeating the point made in section v that to be politically active is to follow the precepts of Plato.

106 Sing. = Theodosius, the judge of the case Themistius was making: note 68.

107 καλλίπολις: the name of the Platonic ideal state (*Republic* 527c) often applied to Constantinople by Themistius (see *Or.* 3 note 242).

108 Themistius' references to 'ascending' and 'descending' deliberately reversed the motions ascribed to him by Palladas' epigram (see the introduction to this chapter); cf. Dagron, 1968, 50 n. 94.

109 The *pyrtanies* were Athenian magistrates who served by rotation; Socrates famously served his turn, voting by himself (against the other 49) against applying the death penalty to Athenian commanders who had abandoned the bodies of their dead after the battle of Arginusae in 406 BC. After Athens' defeat in the Peloponnesian War, he openly ignored an order by the Thirty Tyrants, who had taken power in Athens, to arrest innocent citizens: Plato, *Apology* 32b–d; cf. Themistius, *Or.* 20.239a–b.

laws for the Italiotes; rather he filled what is called Magna Graecia with good order.[110] Even so, if any good now comes from my office, it is not my doing but has been stamped by this example [i.e. of the Emperor Theodosius]. If I kept myself above personal gain, I was imitating the man who daily bestows riches. If I held my temper in check, I looked to the man who elected me. If I protected orphans, I imitated the father we have in common. If I did not allow the public bread distribution to be corrupted, this action too I drew from the same source. If I gave judgements in accordance with the laws, I looked to the living law.[111] And so, stretching out towards that object of emulation, I call on Adrasteia in what I am about to say,[112] and call to witness your judgement, [XI] that I have shown a few months to bring no less honour than many years, and that I did not leave those under my authority labouring under my rule but thirsting for it.[113] For it is not time which creates goodwill in subjects but forethought, industry, and thinking nothing to be more important than the common advantage: neither ambition, nor power, nor the pursuit of either enmity or favour. The man who guards these precepts does not need a multitude of years but rather shrinks from such a thing. For it is hard for man to preserve the good unblemished for long. But a few months, even days, are sufficient to display virtue. For we do not seek a multitude of deeds in any other art, but rather beauty and precision. I have marvelled at Pheidias for his Pisaean Zeus, and Polygnotus for the Hall at Delphi, and Myron for a single cow. The works of Pauson may exceed in number those of Zeuxis and Apelles, but who does not value a single painting of these two over the complete works of

110 Xenophon led the retreat of the surviving Greek mercenaries who served with Cyrus the younger's rebellion against his elder brother Artaxerxes II in 401 BC. In antiquity, he was primarily known as a philosopher: ὁ Σωκρατικός: Schneider, 1966, 118. Parmenides was the semi-mythical 5th-century BC lawgiver of Elea, a Greek colony in southern Italy.

111 νόμος ἔμψυχος (see *Or.* 1 note 138): Themistius' standard characterisation of the emperor as lawgiver, entirely in tune with imperial propaganda. At *Or.* 16.212d (translated above) and again later in this speech (section xviii) Themistius referred to what was clearly a *cause célèbre*, Theodosius' rescue of two senatorial youths from Galatia.

112 One of the names given to the goddess Nemesis 'to whom all must bow' (Plato, *Republic* 451c). To invoke her was supposed to protect the speaker against the wish being confounded as a direct result of having spoken it aloud (Aelius Aristides 20.1, 68.2). Themistius also invoked her at *Or.* 31.354c.

113 On the brevity of his tenure of office which stimulated a further charge against Themistius, see the introduction to this chapter.

Pauson?[114] **[XII]** But if you think time to be something glorious and worth seeking, I can also boast of all the time that I have been involved in the governmental affairs of the Fair City. For from the beginning, as a young man, I did not choose philosophy in an ivory tower but I have passed from childhood to youth, from youth to manhood, and from manhood to this honour with goodwill towards this city. And it is not with unwashed hands,[115] as the saying goes, that I took up her reins, but I accomplished this by long-standing and continuous preparation, and have climbed steadily from the foothills of the political art to the summit.[116] **[XIII]** I was engaged in this presidency from that time when you all elected me to be ambassador to glorious Rome and despatched me to the son of Constantine.[117] I have had the people in my care from that time when I restored the bread dole, I

114 Phidias' chryselephantine statue of Zeus at Olympia (cited also at *Or.* 25.310b and 27.337b) was one of the Seven Wonders of the world; Theodosius brought it to Constantinople in 392. Polygnotus was famous for paintings at Delphi depicting the fall of Troy (Pausanias 10.25.23). Myron's most famous sculptures included the Discobolus (which survives in copy) and a bronze cow (which does not). Apelles was renowned for portraiture and Zeuxis' forte was apparently hyperrealism: his painting of a bunch of grapes was said to have attracted hungry birds. Pauson's works were compared unfavourably with those of Polygnotus at Aristotle, *Poetics* 6.1448a; *Politics* 8.5 1340a 36.

115 Cf. Homer, *Iliad* 6.266–7.

116 On the perceived importance of steady rather than sudden promotion in the ancient world, see the introduction to Chapter 4 on Themistius' posthumous characterisation of Valens. This characterisation of his career as one of slow, steady promotion is a further argument against the idea that Themistius had held a job as prominent as the proconsulship of Constantinople in the 350s: see the introduction to Chapter 2.

117 'Presidency' translates ἡ προστασία. Much scholarly ink has been expended on identifying the position to which Themistius here refers. Vanderspoel, 1995, 105–6, interprets προστασία as a specific office, which, as the rest of the paragraph makes clear, Themistius would have had to have held for nearly 30 years since 357 (the date of the embassy to Rome), and suggests the post of *princeps senatus*. Others have suggested that προστασία was a reference to a proconsulship or urban prefecture held in the time of Constantius: Seeck, 1906, 298–9; Daly, 1983. But the passage is quite specific that προστασία here refers to something held continuously from 357 to the present, and there are other reasons for denying that Themistius held a proconsulship or prefecture under Constantius (see the introduction to Chapter 2). In our view, the keys to interpreting this interesting passage are a) that at *Or.* 34.xvi Themistius again used προστασία, this time unambiguously of his post as urban prefect (cf. Penella, 2000, 37) and b) in this passage Themistius was trying to defend himself against charges of having held this prefecture for an embarrassingly short period. We interpret Themistius' counterargument to mean that, if you understood his career properly, he had in fact been acting as prefect for the city in a non-literal, but nevertheless real way for nearly 30 years, so that any accusations based upon his brief

have been making provision for the senate in my thoughts from that time when I filled up the register of my fellow members from a scant three hundred to two thousand.[118] From these activities came these two bronze statues from two emperors,[119] and immense honours in the edicts,[120] and summonses to this office,[121] not once, not twice, but on many occasions.[122] And add to all these things the how and when [of the invitations]. I did not beg [for them], nor for anything except to speak,[123] in the time when there was no harvest of pulses under the man who was the least amenable,[124] who, in writing to the senate, expressly confirms this very point: that he partly and with difficulty won me over, but that I was not completely educated, and that I acquired nothing that was equal to what I had contributed, and had lent grandeur to the name of the office through my association with it.[125] **[XIV]** And if anyone were to ask me the reason why I hesitated

---

tenure of office were misplaced. There is thus no need to find a separate office for Themistius to have held between 357 and 384.

118 On these successes in the reign of Constantius, see the introduction to Chapter 2.

119 The first was a reward from Constantius for the delivery of *Or.* 2. The second is mentioned for the first time in *Or.* 11 of 373. Stegemann, 1934, 1644, argued that it was from Julian, but Valens seems a much more likely candidate.

120 One extremely complimentary edictal reference to Themistius survives in the *Theodosian Code* at 6.4.12. He will also have had in mind the letter of the Emperor Constantius adlecting him to the Senate of Constantinople (Chapter 2), and, in addition to the letter (probably of Valens) he was just about to discuss, elsewhere mentioned further letters of the Emperors Julian and Theodosius at *Or.* 31.354d–355a: cf. Schneider, 1966, 123; Dagron, 1968, 56 n. 129; Penella, 2000, 219 n. 20.

121 τὴν ἀρχὴν ταύτην: the urban prefecture.

122 On the (hotly disputed) circumstances of these previous invitations to the prefecture, see the introduction to this speech.

123 *Or.* 23.292b uses the same phrase to designate unsolicited honours: Dagron, 1968, 56 n. 131. See also *Or.* 16.200d.

124 We have taken 'no harvest of pulses' and 'man who was least amenable' as chronological qualifiers for the one and the same previous occasion when, from the imperial letter to the senate mentioned here, it was generally known that Themistius had turned down an offer of the prefecture. It is possible that these were separate occasions, however, since the speech refers to Themistius having been summoned to the prefecture 'not once, not twice. . .' Penella, 2000, 220 n. 21, sees the reference to beans as metaphorical, but this is unconvincing. The offer or offers had probably been made by Valens: see the introduction to this speech.

125 Themistius here apparently quoted, if indirectly, from the imperial letter, which set out the 'official version' of one of the offers of the prefecture, to back up his assertions that

then but now do so no longer, I will reply, making no reservations and with no caveats. On the one hand, I held that emperor[126] in reverence and he was worthy of every honorific remembrance. For he omitted nothing, neither great nor small, which raises philosophy on high, but often made me his fellow counsellor in my philosopher's cloak, as well as his table companion and fellow traveller, and gently bore my advising and was not annoyed at my admonishing, so that as far as my own personal affairs only were concerned ‹. . .›, but he was both secretive and immovable especially when scrutinising the advantage to be had in what in itself was generally popular.[127] However, the circum-

---

he had neither solicited such offers nor sought the rewards that office might bring. He thus sought to sustain his claim that, as a philosopher should, he had always preserved a proper independence of worldly gain. The letter seems to have presented Themistius' refusal of office as a whimsical reversal of the usual roles of emperor and advisor – pupil and teacher – with the emperor seeking to educate the philosopher who here proved an imperfect student.

126 The 'least amenable' one under whom Themistius had previously refused the prefecture; cf. Penella, 2000, 220. This was in all probability Valens: see note 124.

127 At the beginning of this section Themistius stated that he would set the record straight as to why he could now accept the prefecture where previously he refused it, thus implying that the 'official version' from which he quoted did not tell the full truth. The necessary antithesis is indeed prefigured at the beginning of the second sentence ('On the one hand, I held that emperor in reverence . . . '), but most editors and commentators and we ourselves mark a lacuna at the crucial point where it should have been fully developed. The general outlines of what must have followed are clear enough. Themistius needed to achieve a careful balancing act. On the one hand, he had to explain why he was willing to take office under Theodosius. As the latter part of section xiv onwards makes clear, he did this by concentrating on Theodosius' overwhelming personal virtue, which made him the perfect philosopher king. On the other hand, while he had not accepted the offer of the prefecture from the earlier emperor, probably Valens, Themistius was known to have been his close associate, and hence could not be overly damning of him either. Most editors supply οὐ within ὡς τ'αμὰ ἴδια μόνον to fill out a 'not only/but also' contrast, but this has the effect of making Themistius say nothing negative at all about Valens. Given the promise to come clean at the opening of section xiv, this seems to us unlikely. We suggest instead that this part of the text be allowed to stand unamended and interpret the passage, lacuna included, as making a contrast between how Valens treated Themistius personally and the emperor's general handling of public affairs, where he was notorious for the stubborn harshness of his response particularly to the usurpation of Procopius (cf. Ammianus 31.14.57). We have therefore given the negative connotations of 'secretive' and 'immovable' to στεγανὸς and σταθερός, and retain the ms text at the end of the sentence rather than emend as Penella, 2000, 220 n. 22 (following Cobet), to supply a positive judgement of Valens. Themistius' meaning would appear to be that, rather than doing good for its own sake, Valens had a

stances of human affairs cause many things to be understood differently from how they were in fact accomplished.[128] But in the face of this [i.e. Theodosius'] calm and gentle quality and in the face of outpoured persuasion, who could be harder than adamant so as to hold out, and not consider that it was philosophy herself sitting in state who proffered the tablets [of office]? It was from her own hand, over which the black vote[129] has no power, that I received the tablets, and from which each day proceed springs of goodness, the restraint of evils. **[XV]** It was right for Plato not to associate with Dionysius, for he enslaved Sicily. Right that Solon fled from Peisistratus, for he had removed freedom from the citizens. Right that Musonius turned away from Nero as he played his lyre. Right that Demetrius shunned Domitian in his wrath.[130] But what excuse could I give in reply to those who would have accused me, if I had not heeded? That he who summons me was difficult? Or stubborn? Or that he was hard to manage by reason? Or that he was not easily controlled by admonishing? Or because he rejects free speech?[131] Or none of these, but that he is of bad character, a cheat, a fraud? Or what, by the gods? **[XVI]** Moreover how could I still prevent[132] those who do not deal with philosophers from accusing them of uselessness, if, when summoned to the presidency[133] of the city that reared me by a man who loves philosophy with a holy love, I

---

tendency to seek out short-term popularity. This contrasts with the behaviour imputed to Theodosius, especially at section xviii below.

128  The Greek is difficult here; Dagron, 1968, 57 n. 137, suggests that the text may be corrupt. In our view, Themistius is commenting that the audience had thought that he had consistently sought the prefecture, when in reality the emperor had tried to thrust it upon him (cf. xiii above).

129  Of death; cf. *Or.* 15.190b and 17.216a.

130  For the uneasy relationships between Plato and Dionysius II of Sicily, and Musonius and Nero, see note 14 to *Or.* 6 in Chapter 3. Themistius follows Diogenes Laertius 1.49–50 in having Solon leave Athens out of opposition to the tyrant Peisistratus (Plutarch, *Solon* 30–2 has him remain). Demetrius of Sunium, the Cynic philosopher, was exiled from Rome under Nero, returning under Vespasian, and Philostratus, *Life of Apollonius* 7.10, has him fall foul subsequently of Domitian. See further Schneider, 1966, 125; Penella, 2000, 221 n. 23.

131  *Parrhesia*: the licence to speak frankly traditionally granted to philosophers (see Chapter 1).

132  Reading ἐκωλύομεν following Jacobs and Cobet.

133  ἡ προστασία: the urban prefecture; cf. note 117 above.

did not at once set out to join him.[134] I shall give you Plato as witness, that it is in accordance with his precepts that I gave in to the king. For the king for whom he asks in his writings from the gods for mankind is young, learned, magnificent and great-hearted. And even if he does not say his name, it is this man[135] he means, this man for whose appearance he prays. For no other man are the tokens of recognition more fitting.[136] And so, since this is the man for whom he prays, and his prayer being answered, would he not have jumped at the chance of the association? Would it not be uncharacteristic of Plato not to become involved, when he appears, with the man whom he seeks so earnestly? Through whom would he rather have secured the laws he wrote? Through whom could he have shown more clearly that it is excellently said that in the highest office one should use persuasion rather than force, and take up the sword as little as possible?[137] These things however we see and hear each and every day. Has not lamentation been driven from the magistrates' halls, and public executioner become an empty title? To inform, denounce, and accuse are now meaningless words. [XVII] No one fears a relentless assessor, a vengeful tax collector, the cursed informers, the eyes that cast an evil glance.[138] Our ears are full of it. This man has returned from exile; he snatched this man from the death-dealing law; this man has recovered

---

134  Themistius here seeks to bolster his position further by trying to present his action as the logical culmination of a Hellene's proper devotion to his native city; cf. Dagron, 1968, 52.

135  Theodosius.

136  Same phrase, different emperor. Based especially on Plato, *Republic* 487a, *Laws* 709e, Themistius had used such characterisations of most of the previous emperors he served. Constantius: *Or.* 3.46a (trans. in Chapter 2), 4.62a; Valens: 8.105b–c, 119d (trans. in Heather and Matthews, 1991, ch. 2); Theodosius: 17.213d–214a (trans. above). Themistius also here continued the pun on Theodosius' name ('god-given'): Penella, 2000, 222 n. 24.

137  The superiority of persuasion over force was an old chestnut going back to the Presocratics: Schneider, 1966, 126. *Or.* 16.207c–208a, 212c (see Chapter 4), presented Theodosius' solution of the Gothic problem in this light, but it was a thought which Themistius used frequently (cf. Penella, 2000, 222 n. 24): *Orr.* 1.10c–d; 3.46b, 48b; 5.67b–c; 7.96b–c; 9.122b.

138  Schneider, 1966, 127, suggests that ὁ λογιστής = tax assessor = lat. *curator civitatis*; ὁ ἐκλογεύς = tax collector = lat. *exactor tributum*; and οἱ πευθῆνες = lat. *delatores* = informers (legislated against by Theodosius early in his reign: *C.Th.* 10.10.12–13; cf. *Or.* 15.197a above with notes). For ὀφθαλμός 'eye' as one who conveys information to the king, see Aristotle, *Politics* 1287 b29. The most famous example was the 'King's Eye', the chief spy of the king of Persia: Aristophanes, *Knights* 92ff.; Xenophon, *Cyrus* 3.2.10ff. Thus Themistius probably means 'spies'. Penella, 2000, 222 (trans.) and 223 n. 25 is similar.

his patrimony; he provided an annual pension for that man; he helped give that man's daughters dowries; he helped that man pay off constraining debt.[139] Among the ancient Persians gifts were set before the man who discovered a new pleasure,[140] but royal prizes shall be set out before him who provided a new source of benefaction. What could be more novel than money going back along the same route from the Treasury to the man from whom unjust exactions were made? All past time did not hear this news; punishment was irreversible for those who had been wronged. But both in giving a gift to those who asked to use it, and, indeed, in giving a gift that was greater than they asked to have,[141] and, what is more, in erasing the request so that the gift was considered his own idea, does he not surpass an Alcibiades? Does he not show a Cimon to be a Smicrines?[142]

[XVIII] But seeing these very youths, even though my theme does not allow me to linger on them individually, I cannot pass on in silence. Orphaned sons and daughters of a house famous on the father's side did not even have that,[143] but, being unable to pay a fine which was beyond their means, were deprived of all their goods, and, gaping helplessly at the doors of other men, endured year after year, so that they reached adulthood among their misfortunes. But once the king had appeared to them, like a god in tragedy, all the terrible things vanished. No longer fatherless, no longer in dire need, no longer private citizens. And did he permit them to prosper through regaining their patrimony, but let those suffer from whom he took when he made the gift? Not at all: rather, he purchased love of mankind, he paid back gold in piety, he bought from those who have as a private citizen and gave to those who had lost it as a king. Now both parties are wealthy in unsullied riches: one group

---

139 Exile: cf. *Or.* 15.193d (trans. in Chapter 4). Deaths: cf. *Or.* 19.227d. Casting the emperor as 'living law' (see *Or.* 1 note 138) justified the mitigation of harsh written law. On the general political point of generous treatment of members of the landowning class, see Chapter 1.

140 Cf. Cicero, *Tusculan Disputations* 5.7[20]; Valerius Maximus 9.1, ext. 3; Athenaeus 4.144e–f, 12.539b, 545d; Plutarch, *Quaestiones Conviviales* 622b; cf. Penella, 2000, 223 n. 25.

141 Reading ἤτησαν, although the ms singular ἤτησε 'he asked' is not impossible.

142 Alcibiades and Cimon were well-known *exempla* of generosity, Smicrines a comic miser: Schneider, 1966, 130 with refs; Penella, 2000, 223 n. 26.

143 Themistius was playing on the two senses of house as 'family line' and 'family property'.

regaining what is their own property, the other obtaining just possession of much gold in place of the property they had held unjustly.[144]

**[XIX]** I know that many appear ungrateful to the king in not returning their goodwill in equal measure for the benefits they have enjoyed.[145] And for him who has done good, a lack of recognition from him who has benefited is indeed the sharpest pain. Even so, this man who is invulnerable in every way is not wounded by such a wrongdoing but pours out from the same jar even over those who are incapable of holding water.[146] But, as I have said, one argument leads me on to another and diverts me from my theme. For I have not made an entrance wishing to count up the emperor's praises but to show myself to have been well advised in this matter [accepting the prefecture], because, by associating with such a king in such an office, I did not bring down philosophy, but exalted her.[147]

**[XX]** I pass over Socrates' prytany, because lot bestowed it and not a count of votes. But I would boldly set myself up against Arrian and Rusticus as regards the virtue in their elections.[148] For whenever I see that the king's gentleness has such a power as is not possessed by all the combined arms of the Roman Empire, and those Scythians who did not yield to the two armies who beleaguered them from east and west, nor to those that joined together from the Tigris and Arabia,[149] but decided to

144 The sequence of events would appear to have been this. A fine devolved on some youngsters of senatorial family, who, not being able to pay, were sold up, with another party buying their estate. Theodosius then repurchased the estate from the latter and returned it to the youths, along with their status; hence they were no longer private citizens, but senators, and Themistius was able to see them as he spoke, that is, actually in the senate. If this, as seems likely, is a further reference to the incident Themistius mentioned at *Or.* 16.212d (trans. in Chapter 4), then the youths' estate was in Galatia. Cf. the introduction to Chapter 4, the political context may have been restoring the fortunes of those who had lost out in the reign of Valens.

145 This is an interesting and, in Themistius, unique reference to a regime enjoying less than total popularity.

146 On Themistius' rejection of the latter half following Plato of the Homeric image of Zeus pouring human fates out of two jars, one marked good, the other evil, see *Orr.* 6.79c; 15.194a–b with notes. The end of the sentence is corrupt. We read τοῖς στέγειν μὴ δυναμένοις as Mai and Cobet, the passage perhaps echoing Plato, *Gorgias* 493a where the souls of the thoughtless are compared to leaky jars.

147 See note 108.

148 See sections x and viii respectively.

149 A brief but perfectly accurate summary of the two main phases of the Gothic war: see Chapter 4. In 378, Valens approached from the east, and Gratian from the west, but

surrender to love of mankind alone, **[XXI]** I praise Euripides for prefer-
ring good counsel over many hands.[150] I bless the emperors, for whom
such a triumph shall be recorded in which no soldier enjoyed a share. I
contend with Antoninus. That man drew down water from heaven for his
troops who were sorely afflicted by thirst, but you yourself quenched a
flame that had spread over such a great part of the earth.[151] The clouds
also obeyed the king of Lydia once when he prayed to them,[152] but the
barbarians at the height of their dominion were never subservient to
anyone. They showed their arrogance towards our army, yet were
captured by the virtue of the king and brought themselves in willingly as
prisoners, even at the time when they were confident in their weapons.[153]
You, Theodosius, are become one man in place of many: in place of Thracians, in place of Celts, in place of Illyrians, in place of weapons, in place
of horses, in place of all other equipment, in place of impassable rivers.[154]

**[XXII]** Those many vanities have been found wanting by us. Your
counsel and intelligence alone held out unvanquished, with which you
won a fairer victory than if you had shown yourself superior by arms.
For you have not destroyed those who had done wrong but made them
yours; you did not punish the earth but have appropriated those who
will farm it;[155] you did not slaughter them like wild beasts but cast a

---

before the two could meet, Valens' army was destroyed at Hadrianople. Western forces continued to operate until the peace of 382, as did Theodosius' substitute eastern army put together from the garrisons and other troops of the east, including the Arab auxiliaries of
Queen Mavia.

150 I.e., masses of troops. After Euripides, *Antiope* fr. 200. 3; used previously at *Orr.*
15.191a; 16.207d (both trans. in Chapter 4).

151 Themistius here confused Marcus Aurelius Antoninus, the real wonder-worker, with
Antoninus Pius; see *Or.* 15 note 117; cf. Schneider, 1966, 133. The metaphor of war as a flame
originated in Homer, and was applied by Themistius to the Gothic war at *Or.* 14.181b (trans.
in Chapter 4), *Or.* 18.219b.

152 Croesus, sentenced to be burnt to death by Cyrus, was saved by a storm sent by the
gods: Herodotus 1.86.

153 I.e., they had not been decisively beaten in battle; see the introduction to Chapter 4.

154 Thrace, Gaul (the land of the Celts) and Illyria had become the traditional recruiting
grounds for the Roman army. The rivers are the Danube and the Hebrus (the latter a barrier
to Macedonia); Themistius also referred to the failure of natural defences at *Or.* 14.181b
(trans. in Chapter 4); cf. xxiv below.

155 Reading οὐδ' εζημίωσας ⟨τὴν⟩ γῆν. Penella, 2000, 225, suggests 'You did not punish
them by seizing their land', but this doesn't make sense of the treaty of 382 which dealt with
land inside the Roman Empire, rather than anything north of the Danube.

spell over their wildness, like one who, having ensnared a lion or a leopard in a net, did not butcher it but accustomed it to bear burdens. Now those who breathe fire, who were more troublesome to the Romans than Hannibal, come forward, gentle and tame, handing themselves over, weapons and all, for the king to use as he wishes whether as farmers or as soldiers.[156] And the consciousness of their enormous and manifold wrongdoings does not frighten them, nor produce distrust of finding mercy and love of mankind in those who had suffered the utmost wrong, but the king's gentleness stands as a stronger security for their safety than what they have acknowledged in themselves.

[XXIII] In the same way, the poets say that the Giants rose up against Ares, Enyo, Zeus' thunderbolt and the gods, and held out for some time. When, however, Apollo and Hermes appeared, young gods, beautiful and enchanting, they had no need for bow and arrows, but they [the Giants] were charmed by the staff and lyre.[157] Such are the triumphs of piety: not to destroy but to improve the vanquished. [XXIV] Come here you Thracians and Macedonians; take your fill of an unbelievable spectacle. The Scythians share our roofs and our libations and the feasts in celebration of the victory over themselves. They did not know, it seems, that they would encounter such a gentle man,[158] and become entangled in his nets. They fell suddenly on what were impregnable places as far as the Romans were concerned – the Haemus, the Hebrus and the wastes of Thessaly – but, having crossed over these,[159] were checked with no

---

156  On the image and reality of the peace terms, see the introduction to *Or.* 16. Errington, 1996b, 21 n. 117, argues that it is a 'misinterpretation' of this passage to suppose that it means that Gothic farmers were meant to pay tax to the Roman state: *contra* Heather, 1991, 159. The Goths may not in practice have paid tax, but Themistius' picture of 'farmers. . . bearing burdens' was surely meant to suggest to his audience that they were doing so or would do so in the future (see Chapter 4, esp. *Or.* 16.211d).

157  The Gigantomachy was one of the most popular myths in ancient Greece, reworked many times by different poets. This version of the myth, which has Apollo and Hermes enchanting rather than killing their opponents, would have been particularly familiar to Themistius because it was displayed in relief in Constantinople: *Orr.* 13.176d–177a; 16.208a; cf. Schneider, 1966, 135–6.

158  Reading ἵλεωι after Mai rather than adopting Jacobs' conjecture Ἰόλεωι which the reference to hunting may have prompted. Themistius in xxviii compares himself to Iolaus and is unlikely to have used the same image to refer both to himself and Theodosius in such close proximity. So too Penella, 2000, 226 n. 32.

159  Reading ἅς διέζοντες after Cobet. The text is corrupt at this point but some sense can be derived from the passage it recalls in *Or.* 14.181b.

great effort by divine defences: piety, justice, mildness, and love of
mankind. Come out now from your fortifications with confidence; it is
now time for you to leave your battlements and to look to your herds
and ploughs and sharpen the sickle rather than your swords and javelins.[160] The land is now open to travellers and there is no need to sail the
sea since there is no fear of going on foot. Road stations come back to
life, and stables and lodgings and they cover the ground providing rest
‹for travellers› as of old.[161] Such a great cloud of hail has suddenly
dispersed into the clear air, and the stormy sea into a flat calm, so
peaceful, so soundless that the whole affair can be compared to a riddle.
For we did not conquer those whom we fought, but, laying down our
arms, we won them over to ourselves. Once we counted up those whom
we were going meet in battle, now we count those over whom we will be
masters.[162] Then we were in trouble if they were many, now we are
worried if they are not. [XXV] Reflect, then, on how much more like a
king Theodosius has behaved towards those who angered him, than the
descendant of Pelops, the son of Atreus, Homer's Agamemnon of wide
dominion.[163] He reproved his brother when he was relenting towards
the suppliant, and sent up such a bitter, even barbaric prayer, that none
of the Trojans should escape, not even the male child whom his mother
carries in her womb, that not even he should escape but even those as
yet unborn should die before they come into existence.[164] But we are
gentle towards those who are suppliants; we nourish their sons and give
their daughters in marriage, not hating them as Scythians, but deeming
them worthy of mercy as human beings. For this is how things are. He
who visits the ultimate penalty on the barbarians in their wilfulness
makes himself king of the Romans alone, but he who conquers but is
merciful knows that he is the king of all men, whom one might address

160 Eunapius frr. 47–8; Zosimus 4.31.5–32 provide echoes of what would originally seem
to have been an extensive account of Roman city life in the Balkans under siege from the
Goths.

161 The restoration of the *cursus publicus*, with its network of *stationes*, *stabuli* and *man-
siones*, the communications system on which, however slow, imperial administration was
based; cf. *Or.* 16.212b.

162 Theodosius' propaganda consistently presented the treaty of 382 as a submission on
the part of the Goths, but it is clear that unprecedentedly generous terms had had to be
granted them: see the introduction to *Or.* 16.

163 Homer's standard epithet for him; cf. *Iliad* 1.102.

164 Homer, *Iliad* 6.55–60 (paraphrased); used also in *Or.* 10.132a.

with justice as one who truly loves all mankind. As for other rulers, you might call Cyrus a lover of Persians, but not a lover of mankind, Alexander a lover of Macedonians but not of mankind, Agesilaus a lover of Greeks, Augustus of Romans, and any other individual the lover of whatever race or tribe he happened to be king.[165] But a lover of mankind without qualification, and king without qualification is he who asks only this question: whether it is a man who craves fair treatment, and not whether it is a Scythian or a Massagete,[166] or whether he had done the first wrong in some way or other. For this, even if it is just, is not divine and in accordance with our[167] great name for divinity, but rather is the characteristic of those who 'go upon the earth'[168] for whom to be hostile or ill-disposed towards someone is not a source of blame, and to injure and give injury in return and to suffer something and to return in due measure has its pardon through the equal balancing of fortune and power.[169] **[XXVI]** But for a king in whom there is such a superiority over other men that it does not seem unfitting for him to have the name of divinity, it is not right either to be hostile or ill-disposed towards mankind, no more indeed than for a shepherd towards his flock, a groom towards horses, or a herdsman towards cattle.[170] Socrates son of Sophroniscus declared such a dominion to be much more fitting for those who are ruled. This same Socrates reworked the much repeated

165 Themistius had used this approach before, when Valens had made peace with the Goths in 369: *Or.* 10.132b–c (trans. in Heather and Matthews, 1991, ch. 2); cf. *Orr.* 8.114a; 13.166b. It was a clever play on the idea of imperial victory titles, which were very familiar to his audience.
166 Themistius' usual euphemisms for Goths and Huns. The sentence is notable for its implicit acceptance of the idea that Roman mistreatment of the immigrants of 376 had been at least partly responsible for the Gothic revolt. This is also strongly implied by Ammianus' account: 31.4–6.
167 Reading ἡμῶν as *A*.
168 Homer, *Iliad* 5.442: i.e., rulers who are not god-like.
169 A striking departure from the norms of imperial propaganda, where barbarian attacks were regarded with moral outrage. Compare the apoplectic rage at barbarian excuses of Valentinian I which led to his fatal stroke: Ammianus 30.6.25. Again, Themistius was probably deliberately deploying Christian ideas of divine forgiveness to good effect; cf. Schneider, 1966, 139, who cites Matt. 5.38–45, Luke 6.27–8, 1 Thess. 5.15, 1 Peter 3.9. On this, see further Chapter 2. To put the passage into perspective, it should be remembered that, whenever he could, Theodosius was as happy to destroy barbarians: see the introduction to *Or.* 16.
170 On Themistius' use of such religiously neutral imagery as the Good Shepherd, see the introduction to Chapter 2.

saying about the just man and justice; that one should do good to one's
friends and ill to one's enemies. And, preserving half the saying and
correcting the other, he agreed that one should do good to one's friends
but, rather than doing ill to one's enemies, make them friends, and thus
he improved it.[171] **[XXVII]** If, therefore, we know that one of those who
put on the philosopher's cloak obeys this, we shall praise him and
pronounce him happy, especially since it did not fall to Socrates himself
to enjoy his precept, nor was he able to win over Meletus or Anytus or
Lycon.[172] We, however, know the king, and see him doing good to his
friends every day and every hour, and transforming his enemies whole-
sale, by race and tribe, from hostility to goodwill. And so, having been
summoned by this king to share in the administration of public affairs, I
did that which both Socrates praised and Plato admired. And, having
taken charge of one of the eyes of the earth,[173] I did not, my friend,
become more earthbound, nor have I cast philosophy away but I have set
my hand to productive labour.[174] **[XXVIII]** You hear that Hercules the
son of Zeus was such a great man, not because he made precise distinctions between conclusive and inconclusive arguments, but because he
prevented lawlessness, [and] because he did not permit the bestial
elements of human nature to prevail.[175] I then imitated Iolaus and have
been for a time servant to Callinices, and had the common hearth in my
care.[176] I have not wasted my labour, nor is it less fitting for this to be the
case than for me to have persevered with geometrical diagrams. Plato
did not 'descend' by sailing three times over the Ionian sea for Dion,[177]

171 Based on Plato, *Republic* 335b–36a; *Critias* 49a–d. Hence Themistius made Socrates
agree with Christ that men must love their enemies, an imputed correspondence which goes
back to Celsus; cf. Schneider, 1966, 139–40. This is a further example of the religious strategy Themistius had adopted throughout his public life: see further Chapter 1.
172 The three Athenians who brought the action against Socrates (cf. also *Or.* 26.326c);
it draws on Plato, *Gorgias* 486a–b.
173 Constantinople: the other being Rome.
174 The key point in Themistius' self-justification that he has played an active and beneficial role in the city's affairs: see also *Or.* 17.214a.
175 Themistius also used Hercules as an exemplar of lawgiving at *Orr.* 13.169c–d,
20.240a.
176 καλλινίκης 'the gloriously triumphant one' is an epithet of Hercules, and a common
comparison for the emperor. Iolaus was the son of his half-brother Iphicles who assisted
him in certain of his labours. The common hearth is Constantinople.
177 It was Dion, his first minister, who called in Plato to influence Dionysius II of Syracuse. Dion was later discredited and fled to Athens, before returning to seize Sicily for
himself. He was later assassinated. See also note 130 above

nor did Aristotle by taking thought for the people of Stageira, nor did Carneades nor Critolaus on their embassies for Attica.[178] **[XXIX]** But I have long since, or so it appears, been rolling around on the ground, as a result of the circuits I made back and forth from east to west, bearing with me the city's high opinion. Nor would I exclude from the number of embassies bestowed upon me, my recent sojourn abroad in illustrious Rome. I was ambassador to your Fathers[179] then too, in presiding over concord between the cities and rendering you all honoured and esteemed by them. For the vote those men passed on your behalf to the emperors is itself a shared glory for the city. And, were I not to become wearisome in your eyes by the burden of reports enumerating the praises of myself, I would have read to you the acclamations of that senate through which you would thus benefit by learning how much more completely the Romans surpass others in honouring and praising virtue.[180] **[XXX]** Do not[181] therefore hold fast to the literal word, and do not, just because Plato in the Republic teases those who descend from the divine sphere of contemplation to the human with this clever little phrase,[182] think that it is of no importance to take part in public affairs. Rather, realise that 'up' and 'down' are not unqualified terms. Epicurus was of small account, together with any of his disciples who admires the pleasures of the flesh.[183] But

178 Carneades, head of the Academy, and the Peripatetic philosopher Critolaus were sent to Rome by Athens in 155 BC. 'Descend': as note 108.

179 The senators of Rome.

180 A strikingly uncompromising finale to Themistius' self-defence. He recalled here in particular his embassies to Rome, including the important mission of 376/7 (see the introduction to Chapter 4), and the praise which greeted him. Acclamations were formalised and repeated ritual shoutings (usually of praise, but they could be critical), cf. those for the publication of the *Theodosian Code*: trans. Pharr, 56. At *Or.* 17.214b, Themistius specified that he had undertaken a total of ten embassies.

181 Second-person singular. Themistius ended the speech by addressing himself once more to the judge he had appointed for the case he was trying to make, the Emperor Theodosius: see note 68.

182 ῥημάτιον (clever and deceptive phraseology; cf. Aristophanes, *Achainians* 444, 447). At *Republic* 520c, Plato said that it is necessary for the philosopher 'guardians' who were to govern the city to descend from the upper world into the cave to accustom themselves to the shadows, but Themistius denied here that this should be taken literally.

183 Epicurus taught that man is entirely mortal, that the universe is the result of an accident, and that there is no providential God. He thus represents the exact opposite of Themistius' professed world-view. Epicurus and his disciples were also quite ascetic in

Plato is always up, and so too he who follows Plato, in trying to become like God. We are in the middle ground,[184] happy if at one moment we may be up and at another down. Yet, for us, down is not completely so, but is dependent on and directed from above.

---

their lifestyle, rather than devoted to the pleasures of the flesh as they were commonly portrayed.

184 Between the flesh (Epicurus) and the divine (Plato).

# BIBLIOGRAPHY

## NOTES ON PRIMARY SOURCES

### Themistius

There are two main editions of the speeches of Themistius. Up to the 1960s, the standard edition was W. Dindorf, ed., *Themistii Orationes* (Leipzig, 1832). This includes the Petavius–Harduinus annotations (*Orr.* 1–33) and the notes to *Or.* 34 from A. Mai's edition of 1816. It has now been largely superseded by the Teubner edition of H. Schenkl, G. Downey, and A. F. Norman, eds., *Themistii Orationes*, 3 vols (Leipzig, 1965–74). Themistius' extant paraphrases of various works of Aristotle can be found in M. Wallies et al., eds., *Commentaria in Aristotelem Graeca*, vol. 5 (Berlin, 1899–1900).

For translations of some or all of the speeches into modern languages, see Downey, 1958 (*Or.* 1 into English), Heather and Matthews, 1991, ch. 2 (part of *Or.* 8 and all of *Or.* 10 in English translation), Kesters, 1959 (*Or.* 26 into French), Leppin and Portmann, 1998 (German translation of *Orr.* 1–19), Maisano, 1995 (complete Italian translation), Penella, 2000 (*Orr.* 17 and 20–34 into English, together with *The Letter of Constantius*), and Schneider, 1966 (*Or.* 34 in German). Themistius' paraphrase of Aristotle, *On the Soul* has been translated by Todd, 1996.

### Secular Texts

The non-Christian Classical sources cited by Themistius and discussed in the introductions and annotations can be consulted in the standard Classical series, most notably Oxford Classical Texts, Teubner, and Budé. Fragments of Greek tragedy are cited from *Tragicorum Graecorum fragmenta*. Where different standard editions have adopted different principles of organisation, as is the case with Aesop's *Fables*, we cite both. Many translations of these texts into English are available. The Loeb series is generally excellent, a smaller range is available in Penguin Classics, and we would particularly recommend the on-going Aris and Phillips editions of Euripides. Many late antique texts from the Latin west

336 BIBLIOGRAPHY

can be found in the Monumenta Germaniae Historica series, their eastern counterparts in the Bonn corpus of Byzantine historical sources. Aside from those in standard series, we have also used the following editions:

Eunapius of Sardis, historical fragments, see Blockley, 1983.
G. Kirk, *Heraclitus: The Cosmic Fragments* (Cambridge, 1954).
John of Antioch, historical fragments, in C. Muller, ed., *Fragmenta Historicorum Graecorum*, vols 4 and 5 (1868 and 1870).
Menander Rhetor, see Russell and Wilson, 1981.

**Christian Texts**

Christian sources of the Patristic and Late Antique periods are available in numerous standard series. The *Patrologia Graeca* and *Patrologia Latina* provide comprehensive but often outdated coverage. More recent (sometimes competing) editions of most of the texts cited in the introductions and notes can be found in *GCS* (*Die Griechischen Christlichen Schriftsteller der ersten Jahrhunderte*), *CSEL* (*Corpus Scriptorum Ecclesiasticorum Latinorum*), *CC* (*Corpus Christianorum*), and *SC* (*Sources Chrétiennes*). Some Christian authors can again be found in Loeb and Budé editions, or the Bonn corpus. Additionally, for the *Life of Daniel the Stylite*, see Delehaye, 1923.

## SECONDARY SOURCES

Alföldi, A., 1952, *A Conflict of Ideas in the Late Roman Empire: The Clash between the Senate and Valentinian I* (Oxford).
Ando, C., 1996, 'Pagan Apologetics and Christian Intolerance in the Age of Themistius and Augustine', *Journal of Early Christian Studies* 4, 171–207.
Arce, J., 1984, *Estudios sobre el Emperador Fl. Cl. Iuliano* (Madrid).
Armstrong, A. H., 1967, *The Cambridge History of Later Greek and Early Medieval Philosophy* (Cambridge).
Armstrong, A. H., 1979, *Plotinian and Christian Studies* (London).
Armstrong, A. H., 1990, *Hellenic and Christian Studies* (London).
Athanassiadi, P., 1992, *Julian: An Intellectual Biography* (London).
Bagnall, R. S., et. al., 1987, *The Consuls of the Later Roman Empire* (Atlanta).
Barnes, T. D., 1973, 'Porphyry *Against the Christians*: Date and the

Attribution of Fragments', *Journal of Theological Studies* 24, 424–42.

Barnes, T. D., 1975, 'Constans and Gratian in Rome', *Harvard Studies in Classical Philology* 79, 325–33.

Barnes, T. D., 1976a, 'Imperial Campaigns, A.D. 285–311', *Phoenix* 30, 174–93.

Barnes, T. D., 1976b, 'The Victories of Constantine', *Zeitschrift für Papyrologie und Epigraphik* 21, 149–53.

Barnes, T. D., 1982, *The New Empire of Diocletian and Constantine* (Cambridge, MA).

Barnes, T. D., 1987, 'Himerius and the Fourth Century', *Classical Philology* 82, 206–25.

Barnes, T. D., 1989, 'Christians and Pagans in the Reign of Constantius', in A. Dihle, ed., *L'Eglise et l'empire au IVe Siècle: sept exposés suivis de discussions* (Geneva), 301–43.

Barnes, T. D., 1993, *Athanasius and Constantius: Theology and Politics in the Constantinian Empire* (Cambridge, MA).

Barnes, T. D., 1995, 'Statistics and the Conversion of the Roman Aristocracy', *Journal of Roman Studies* 85, 135–47.

Barnes, T. D., and Vanderspoel, J., 1981, 'Julian and Themistius', *Greek Roman and Byzantine Studies* 22, 187–9.

Barnish, S. J. B., 1992, *Cassiodorus Variae*, trans. with commentary, Translated Texts for Historians (Liverpool).

Beard, M., et al., 1998, *Religions of Rome* (Cambridge).

Behr, C. A., 1981, *Aelius Aristides: The Complete Works* (Leiden).

Bidez, J., 1930, *La Vie de l'Empereur Julien* (Paris).

Blockley, R. C., 1983, *The Fragmentary Classicising Historians of the Later Roman Empire: Eunapius, Olympiodorus, Priscus, Malchus*, vol. 2 (Liverpool).

Blumenthal, H. J., 1979, 'Photius on Themistius (Cod 74): Did Themistius write Commentaries on Aristotle?', *Hermes* 107, 168–82.

Blumenthal, H. J., 1990, 'Themistius: the last Peripatetic Commentator on Aristotle', in R. Sorabji, ed., *Aristotle Transformed – the Ancient Commentators and their Influence* (London), 113–23.

Bonner, S. F., 1965, 'The Edict of Gratian on the Remuneration of Teachers', *American Journal of Philology* 86, 113–37.

Bowersock, G., 1978, *Julian the Apostate* (London).

Bouchery, H. F., 1936, 'Contribution à l'étude de la chronologie des Discours de Thémistius', *L'Antiquité classique* 5, 191–208.

Bradbury, S. A., 1987, 'The Date of Julian's *Letter to Themistius*', *Greek Roman and Byzantine Studies* 28, 235–51.

Bradbury, S. A., 1994, 'Constantine and anti-pagan legislation in the Fourth Century', *Classical Philology* 89, 120–39.

Brancacci, A., 1985, *Rhetorik Philosophousa: Dione Crisostomo nella cultura antica e bizantino* (Rome).

Brauch, Th., 1993a, 'The Prefect of Constantinople for 362 AD: Themistius', *Byzantion* 63, 37–78.

Brauch, Th., 1993b, 'Themistius and the Emperor Julian', *Byzantion* 63, 79–115.

Brown, P. R. L., 1961, 'Aspects of the Christianisation of the Roman Aristocracy', *Journal of Roman Studies* 51, 1–11.

Brown, P. R. L., 1967, *Augustine of Hippo: A Biography* (London).

Brown, P. R. L., 1976, 'Eastern and Western Christendom in Late Antiquity: A Parting of the Ways', in *The Orthodox Church and the West*, Studies in Church History 13 (Oxford), 1–24; reprinted in P. R. L. Brown, *Society and the Holy in Late Antiquity* (London, 1982), 166–95.

Brown, P. R. L., 1980, *The Philosopher and Society in Late Antiquity* (Berkeley, CA).

Brown, P. R. L., 1992, *Power and Persuasion in Late Antiquity: Towards a Christian Empire* (Wisconsin).

Brown, P. R. L., 1995, *Authority and the Sacred* (Cambridge).

Browning, R., 1975, *The Emperor Julian* (London).

Burgess, R. W., 1988, 'Quinquennial Vota and the Consulship in the Fourth and Fifth Centuries', *Numismatic Chronicle* 148, 77–96.

Butterfield, H., 1957, *George III and the Historians* (London).

Callu, J.-P., 1978, 'Denier et nummus (300–354)', in *Les 'Dévaluations' à Rome: Epoque républicaine et impériale*, Collection de l'Ecole française de Rome 37 (Rome), 107–21.

Calo Levi, A., 1952, *Barbarians on Roman Imperial Coinage and Sculpture*, Numismatic Notes and Monographs 123 (New York).

Cameron, A. D. E. [Alan], 1965, 'Notes on Palladas', *Classical Quarterly* 15, 215–29.

Cameron, A. D. E., 1968, 'Gratian's Repudiation of the Pontifical Robe', *Journal of Roman Studies* 58, 96–102.

Cameron, A. D. E., 1969, 'Theodosius and the Regency of Stilicho', *Harvard Studies in Classical Philology* 73, 247–80.

Cameron, A. D. E., 1970, *Claudian: Poetry and Propaganda at the Court of Honorius* (Oxford).

Cameron, A. D. E., and Long, J., 1993, *Barbarians and Politics at the Court of Arcadius* (Berkeley, CA).

Cameron, A. M. [Averil], 1991, *Christianity and the Rhetoric of Empire* (Berkeley, CA).

Cameron, A. M., and Hall, S. G., 1999, *Eusebius: Life of Constantine* (Oxford).

Cesa, M., 1994, *Imperio tardantico e barbari: La crisi militare da Adrianopoli al 418*, Biblioteca di Athenaeum 23 (Como).

Chadwick, H., 1967, 'Philo and the Beginnings of Christian Thought', pt. 2 in Armstrong, 1967.

Champlin, E. J., 1982, 'Saint Gallicanus (Consul 317)', *Phoenix* 36, 71–6.

Chastagnol, A., 1960, *La Préfecture urbaine à Rome sous le Bas-Empire* (Paris).

Chastagnol, A., 1976, 'Remarques sur les sénateurs orientaux au IVe siècle', *Acta Antiqua Academiae Scientiarum Hungaricae* 24, 341–56.

Chastagnol, A., 1982, *L'Evolution politique, sociale et économique du monde romain de Dioclétien à Julien: la mise en place du Bas-Empire (284–363)* (Paris).

Chrysos, E. K., 1972, *To Byzantion kai oi Gotthoi* (Thessalonica).

Colpi, B., 1988, *Die paideia des Themistios: Ein Beitrag zur Geschichte der Bildung im vierten Jahrhundert nach Christus* (Bern).

Dagron, G., 1968, *L'Empire romain d'Orient au IVe siècle et les traditions politiques de l'Hellénisme: le témoignage de Thémistios,* Travaux et Mémoires 3 (Paris).

Dagron, G., 1974, *Naissance d'une capitale: Constantinople et ses institutions de 330 à 451* (Paris).

Daly, L. J., 1971, 'Themistius' Plea for Religious Tolerance', *Greek Roman and Byzantine Studies* 12, 65–79.

Daly, L. J., 1972, 'The Mandarin and the Barbarian: The Response of Themistius to the Gothic Challenge', *Historia* 21, 351–79.

Daly, L. J., 1975, 'Themistius' Concept of *Philanthropia*', *Byzantion* 45, 22–40.

Daly, L. J., 1980, 'In a Borderland: Themistius' Ambivalence Toward Julian', *Byzantinische Zeitschrift* 73, 1–11.

Daly, L. J., 1983, 'Themistius' Refusal of a Magistracy', *Byzantion* 53, 164–212.

Dauge, Y. A., 1981, *Le Barbare* (Paris).

Delehaye, H., 1923, *Les Saints Stylites* (Brussels).

Demougeot, E., 1974, 'Modalités d'établissement des féderés barbares de Gratien et de Théodose', in *Mélanges d'histoire ancienne offerts à William Seston* (Paris), 143–60.

Demougeot, E., 1979, *La Formation de l'Europe et les invasions barbares: II. De l'avènement de Dioclétien (284) à l'occupation germanique de l'Empire romain d'Occident (début du VIe siècle)* (Paris).

des Places, E., 1966, ed. and tr., *Jamblique: Les mystères d'Egypte* (Paris)

Dillon, J. M., 1977, *The Middle Platonists: A Study of Platonism, 80 BC to AD 270* (London).

Downey, G., 1955, '*Philanthropia* in Religion and Statecraft in the Fourth Century after Christ', *Historia* 4, 199–208.

Downey, G., 1957, 'Themistius and the Defense of Hellenism in the Fourth Century', *Harvard Theological Review* 50, 259–74.

Downey, G., 1958, 'Themistius' First Oration', *Greek and Byzantine Studies* 1, 49–69.

Downey, G., 1962, 'Allusions to Christianity in Themistius' Orations', *Studia Patristica* 5, 480–8.

Drijvers, J. W., and Hunt, D., eds, 1999, *The Late Roman World and its Historian: Interpreting Ammianus Marcellinus* (London).

Dvornik, H., 1966, *Early Christian and Byzantine Political Philosophy: Origins and Background*, The Dumbarton Oaks Center for Byzantine Studies (Washington, DC).

Eck, W., 1971, 'Das Eindringend des Christentums in den Senatorenstand bis zu Konstantin d. Gr.', *Chiron* 1, 381–406.

Errington, R. M., 1988, 'Constantine and the Pagans', *Greek Roman and Byzantine Studies* 29, 309–18.

Errington, R. M., 1992, 'The Praetorian Prefecture of Virius Nicomachius Flavianus', *Historia* 41, 439–61.

Errington, R. M., 1996a, 'The Accession of Theodosius', *Klio* 78, 438–53.

Errington, R. M., 1996b, 'Theodosius and the Goths', *Chiron* 26, 1–27.

Fletcher, R., 1997, *The Conversion of Europe: From Paganism to Christianity 371–1386 AD* (London).

Fowden, G., 1978, 'Bishops and Temples in the Eastern Roman Empire', *Journal of Theological Studies* n.s. 29, 53–78.

Fowden, G., 1982, 'The Pagan Holy Man in Late Antique Society', *Journal of Hellenic Studies* 102, 355–59.

Fowden, G., 1986, *The Egyptian Hermes: A Historical Approach to the Late Pagan Mind* (Cambridge).

Fowden, G., 1987, 'Pagan Versions of the Rain Miracle of A.D. 172', *Historia* 26, 83–95.

Geffcken, J., 1978, *The Last Days of Graeco-Roman Paganism*, trans. S. MacCormack (Amsterdam).

Gerson, L. P., 1996, ed., *The Cambridge Companion to Plotinus* (Cambridge).

Gladiis, C., 1907, *De Themistii Libanii Iuliani in Constantii Orationibus* (Breslau).

Gleason, M. W., 1995, *Making Men: Sophists and Self-Presentation in Ancient Rome* (Princeton, NJ).

Goffart, W., 1980, *Barbarians and Romans AD 418–584: The Techniques of Accommodation* (Princeton, NJ).

Goffart, W., 1981, 'Rome, Constantinople, and the Barbarians in Late Antiquity', *American Historical Review* 76, 275–306.

Grumel, V., 1951, 'L'Illyricum de la mort de Valentinien Ier (375) à la mort de Stilicon (408)', *Revue des études byzantines* 9, 5–46.

Hall, S. G., 1998, 'Some Constantinian Documents in the *Vita Constantini*', in Lieu and Montserrat, eds, 1998, 86–103.

Hansen, G. Ch., 1967, 'Nachlese zu Themistios', *Philologus* 111, 110–18.

Hanson, R. P. C., 1988, *The Search for the Christian Doctrine of God* (Edinburgh).

Harries, J., 1999, *Law and Empire in Late Antiquity* (Cambridge).

Harries, J., and Wood, I., eds., 1993, *The Theodosian Code* (London).

Heath, M., 1995, *Hermogenes On Issues: Strategies of Argument in Later Greek Rhetoric* (Oxford).

Heather, P. J., 1988, 'The Anti-Scythian Tirade of Synesius' *De Regno*', *Phoenix* 42, 152–72.

Heather, P. J., 1991, *Goths and Romans 332–489* (Oxford).

Heather, P. J., 1993a, 'Literacy and Power in the Migration Period', in A. Bowman and G. Woolf, eds, *Literacy and Power in the Ancient World* (Cambridge),

Heather, P. J., 1993b, 'The Historical Culture of Ostrogothic Italy', in *Teoderico il Grande e i Goti d'Italia: Atti del XIII Congresso internazionale di studi sull'Alto Medioevo* (Spoleto),

Heather, P. J., 1994, 'New Men for New Constantines? Creating an Imperial Elite in the Eastern Mediterranean', in P. Magdalino, ed., *New Constantines: The Rhythm of Imperial Renewal in Byzantium, 4th–13th Centuries* (London), 11–33.

Heather, P. J., 1995, 'The Huns and the End of the Roman Empire in Western Europe', *English Historical Review* 110, 4–41.

Heather, P. J., 1996, *The Goths* (Oxford).

Heather, P. J., 1999, 'Ammianus on Jovian: History and Literature', in Drijvers and Hunt, eds, 1999, 105–16.

Heather, P. J., and Matthews, J. F., 1991, *The Goths in the Fourth Century*, Translated Texts for Historians (Liverpool).

Hoffmann, D., 1969, *Das spätromische Bewegungsheer und die Notitia Dignitatum* (Düsseldorf).

Honoré, A. M., 1981, *Emperors and Lawyers* (London).

Hunt, D., 1999, 'The outsider inside: Ammianus on the rebellion of Silvanus', in Drijvers and Hunt, eds, 1999, 51–63.

Janin, R., 1964, *Constantinople Byzantine: Développement urbain et répertoire topographique*, 2nd edn (Paris).

Jones, A. H. M., 1964, *The Later Roman Empire: A Social, Economic and Administrative Survey*, 3 vols (Oxford).

Jones, C. P., 1972, 'Aelius Aristides, *Eis Basilea*', *Journal of Roman Studies* 62 (1972), 134–52.

Jones, C. P., 1978, *The Roman World of Dio Chrysostom* (Cambridge, MA).

Kaster, R. A., 1988, *Guardians of Language: The Grammarian and Society in Late Antiquity* (Berkeley, CA).

Kennedy, G. A., 1983, *Greek Rhetoric Under Christian Emperors* (Princeton, NJ).

Kesters, H., 1959, *Plaidoyer d'un Socratique contre le Phèdre de Platon, XXVIe Discours de Thémistius: Introduction, texte établi et traduit* (Louvain and Paris).

Kopecek, T. A., 1979, *A History of Neo-Arianism* (Philadelphia, PA).

Lane Fox, R., 1986, *Pagans and Christians* (London).

Leeman, A. D., 1963, *Orationis Ratio: The Stylistic Theories and Practice of the Roman Orators, Historians and Philosophers* (Amsterdam).

Leppin, H., and Portmann, W., 1998, *Themistios Staatsreden*, Bibliothek der greichischen Literatur; Bd 46, Abteilung klassische Philologie (Stuttgart).

Lewy, H., 1886, 'Zu Themistius', *Rheinisches Museum für Philologie* 41, 307–8.

Liebeschuetz, J. H. W. G., 1969, *Continuity and Change in Roman Religion* (Oxford).

Liebeschuetz, J. H. W. G., 1972, *Antioch: City and Imperial Administration in the Later Roman Empire* (Oxford).

Liebeschuetz, J. H. W. G., 1990, *Barbarians and Bishops: Army, Church and State in the Age of Arcadius and John Chrysostom* (Oxford).

Lieu, S. N. C., and Montserrat, D., eds, 1998, *Constantine: History, Historiography and Legend* (London).

Lim, R., 1995, *Public Disputation, Power, and Social Order in Late Antiquity* (Berkeley, CA).

Lizzi, R., 1996, 'La politica religiosa di Teodosio I', *Rendiconti Accad. Naz. dei Lincei* ser. 9, vol. 7, 323–61.

Lyman, J. R., 1993, *Christology and Cosmology: Models of Divine Activity in Origen, Eusebius, and Athanasius* (Oxford).

MacCormack, S. A., 1981, *Art and Ceremony in Late Antiquity* (Los Angeles and Berkeley, CA).

McCormick, M., 1986, *Eternal Victory: Triumphal Rulership in Late Antiquity, Byzantium and the Early Medieval West* (Cambridge).

McLynn, N., 1994, *Ambrose of Milan* (Berkeley, CA).

McLynn, N., 1996, 'The Fourth-Century Taurobolium', *Phoenix* 50, 312–30.

MacMullen, R., 1984, *Christianising the Roman Empire (AD 100–400)* (New Haven, CT).

Mahoney, E. P., 1982, 'Neoplatonism, the Greek Commentators and Renaissance Aristotelianism', in D. J. O'Meara, ed., *Neoplatonism and Christian Thought* (Albany, NY).

Maisano, R., 1995, *Discorsi di Temistio* (Turin).

Mango, C., 1985, *Le Développement urbain de Constantinople (IVe–VIIe siècles)*, Travaux et Mémoires, Monographies 2 (Paris).

Mango, C. and Dagron, G., eds, 1993, *Constantinople and its Hinterland* (London).

Markus, R. A., 1974, *Christianity in the Roman World* (London).

Markus, R. A., 1990, *The End of Ancient Christianity* (Cambridge).

Marrou, H. I., 1948, *Histoire de l'éducation dans l'antiquité* (Paris).

Martindale, J. R., 1967, 'Note on the Consuls of 381 and 382', *Historia* 16, 254–6.

Matthews, J. F., 1967, 'A Pious Supporter of Theodosius I: Maternus Cynegius and his Family', *Journal of Roman Studies* n.s. 18, 438–46.

Matthews, J. F., 1971, 'Gallic Supporters of Theodosius', *Latomus* 30, 1073–1099 (= Matthews, 1985, no. IX).

Matthews, J. F., 1974, 'The Letters of Symmachus', in J. W. Binns, ed.,

*Latin Literature of the Fourth Century* (London), 58–99 (= Matthews, 1985, no. IV).

Matthews, J. F., 1975, *Western Aristocracies and Imperial Court A.D. 364–425* (Oxford).

Matthews, J. F., 1985, *Political Life and Culture in Late Roman Society* (London).

Matthews, J. F., 1989, *The Roman Empire of Ammianus* (London).

Matthews, J. F., 1993, 'The Making of the Text', in Harries and Wood, eds, 1993, 45–67

Mattingly, H., 1950, 1951, 'The Imperial Vota', *Proceedings of the British Academy* 36, 155–95; 37, 21–68.

Méridier, L., 1906, *Le philosophe Thémistius devant l'opinion de ses contemporains* (Rennes).

Millar, F., 1982, 'Emperor, Frontiers and Foreign Relations, 31 BC to AD 378', *The International History Review* 10, 1–23.

Millar, F., 1992, *The Emperor in the Roman World*, 2nd edn (London).

Mitchell, S., 1998, 'The Cities of Asia Minor in the Age of Constantine', in Lieu and Montserrat, eds, 52–73.

Moles, J. L., 1978, 'The Career and Conversion of Dio Chrysostom', *Journal of Hellenic Studies* 98, 79–100.

Mommsen, Th., 1910, 'Das römische Militärwesen seit Diocletian', in *Gesammelte Schriften*, vol. 6 (Berlin), 206–83.

Namier, L., 1968, *The Structure of Politics at the Accession of George III*, 2nd edn (London).

Nixon, C. E. V., and Rogers, B. S., 1994, *In Praise of Later Roman Emperors: The Panegyrici Latini* (Berkeley, CA).

Norman, A. F., 1992, *Libanius: Autobiography and Select Letters*, 2 vols, Loeb (Cambridge, MA).

Palanque, J. R., 1944, 'Collegialité et partages dans l'Empire romain aux IVe et Ve siècles', *Revue des Etudes Anciennes* 46, 47–64 and 280–98.

Pavan, M., 1964, *La politica gotica di Teodosio nella pubblicistica del suo tempo* (Rome).

Penella, R. J., 1990, *Greek Philosophers and Sophists in the Fourth Century A.D.: Studies in Eunapius of Sardis* (Liverpool).

Penella, R. J., 2000, *The Private Orations of Themistius* (Berkeley, CA).

Petit, P., 1956, *Les étudiants de Libanius* (Paris).

Petit, P., 1957, 'Les sénateurs de Constantinople dans l'oeuvre de Libanius', *L'Antiquité Classique* 26, 347–82.

Pichon, R., 1906, *Etudes sur l'histoire de la littérature latin dans les Gaules. Les derniers écrivains profanes: les panégyristes* (Paris).

Piganiol, A., 1972, *L'Empire chrétien* (Paris).

Portmann, W., 1988, *Geschichte in der spätantiken Panegyrik* (Frankfurt am Main).

Portmann, W., 1992, 'Zum Datum der ersten Rede des Themistius', *Klio* 74, 411–21.

Ramsay, A. M., 1925, 'The Speed of the Imperial Post', *Journal of Roman Studies* 15, 60–74.

Ritter, A. M., 1965, *Das Konzil von Konstantinopel und sein Symbol: Studien zur Geschichte und Theologie des II. ökumenischen Konzils* (Göttingen).

Roberts, C. H., and Turner, E. G., 1952, *Catalogue of the Greek and Latin Papyri in the John Rylands Library Manchester*, vol. IV (Manchester).

Roueche, C., 1989, *Aphrodisias in Late Antiquity*, JRS Monographs 5 (London).

Russell, D., 1998, 'The Panegyrists and their Teachers', in M. Whitby, ed., *The Propaganda of Power: The Role of Panegyric in Late Antiquity* (Leiden), 17–50.

Russell, D. A., and Wilson, N. G., 1981, *Menander Rhetor* (Oxford).

Rutherford, I., 1992, 'Inverting the Canon: Hermogenes on Literature', *Harvard Studies in Classical Philology* 94, 355–78.

Rutherford, I., 1997, *Canons of Style in the Antonine Age: Idea-Theory in its Literary Context* (Oxford).

Sabbah, G., 1978, *La Méthode d'Ammien Marcellin: Recherches sur la construction du discours historique dans les Res Gestae* (Paris).

Salzman, M. R., 1990, *On Roman Time: The Codex Calendar of 354 and the Rhythms of Urban Life in Late Antiquity* (Berkeley, CA).

Schenkl, H., 1898, 'Die handschriftliche Überlieferung der Reden des Themistius', *Wiener Studien* 20, 205–43.

Schenkl, H., 1899, 'Die handschriftliche Überlieferung der Reden des Themistius', *Wiener Studien* 21, 80–115, 225–63.

Schenkl, H., 1901, 'Die handschriftliche Überlieferung der Reden des Themistius', *Wiener Studien* 23, 14–25.

Schenkl, H., 1919, 'Beiträge zur Textgeschichte der Reden des Themistios', *Sitzungsberichte der Akademie der Wissenschaften in Wien, Philosophisch-historische Kl.* 192, 3–89.

Schneider, H., 1966, *Die 34. Rede Des Themistius (peri tes arxes)*, (Basel).

Scholze, H., 1911, *De temporibus librorum Themistii* (Göttingen).

Schroeder, F. M., and Todd, R. B., 1990, *Two Greek Aristotelian Commentators on the Intellect*, Medieval Sources in Translation 33 (Toronto).

Seeck, O., 1906, *Die Briefe des Libanius zeitlich geordnet* (Leipzig).

Seeck, O., 1919, *Regesten der Kaiser und Päpste für die Jahre 311 bis 476 n. Chr.* (Stuttgart).

Seeck, O., and Schenkl, H., 1906, 'Eine verlorene Rede des Themistius', *Rheinisches Museum für Philologie* 61, 554–66.

Settimane, 1982 = *Cristianizzazione ed organizzazione ecclesiastica delle campagne nell'alto medioevo: espansione e resistenze*, Settimane di Studio del centro italiano di studi sull'alto Medioevo 28 (1982), Spoleto.

Sidebottom, H., 1990, 'Studies in Dio Chrysostom On Kingship', DPhil thesis, Oxford University.

Sievers, G. R., 1868, *Das Leben des Libanius* (Berlin).

Sirks, B., 1993, 'The Sources of the Code', in Harries and Wood, eds, 1993, 45–67.

Sivan, H., 1993, *Ausonius of Bordeaux: Genesis of a Gallic Aristocracy*, London.

Smith, R. R. R., 1990, 'Late Roman Philosopher Portraits from Aphrodisias,' *Journal of Roman Studies* 80, 127–55.

Smith, Rowland, 1995, *Julian's Gods: Religion and Philosophy in the Thought and Action of Julian the Apostate* (London).

Smith, Rowland, 1999, 'Telling tales: Ammianus' narrative of the Persian expedition', in Drijvers and Hunt, eds, 1999, 89–104.

Snell, B., 1952, *Leiben und Meinungen der Sieben Weisen*, Munich.

Sorabji, R., 1983, *Time, Creation and the Continuum: Theories in Antiquity and the Early Middle Ages* (London).

Sorabji, R., 1988, *Matter, Space and Motion: Theories in Antiquity and Their Sequel* (London).

Stallknecht, B., 1969, *Untersuchungen zur römischen Aussenpolitik in der Spätantike* (Bonn).

Stegemann, W., 1934, 'Themistios', *PWRE* 5, A2 (1934), 1642–80.

Stein, E., 1959, *Histoire du Bas Empire*, vol. 1, trans. J.-R. Palanque (Paris).

Thompson, E. A., 1963, 'The Visigoths from Fritigern to Euric', *Historia* 12.

Todd, R. B., 1996, *Themistius on Aristotle On The Soul* (London).

Trombley, F., 1993, *Hellenic Religion and Christianisation c.370–529* (Leiden).

Uxkull-Gyllenbrand, W. v., 1924, *Greichische Kultur-Entstehungslehren*, Bibliothek für Philosophie 26, Beilage zu Heft 3/4 des Archivs für Geschichte der Philosophie bd. xxxvi (Berlin).

Vanderspoel, J., 1987a, 'Themistius and a Philosopher at Sikyon', *Historia* 36, 383–4.

Vanderspoel, J., 1987b, 'Themistius, *Or.* 4.58c: An Emendation', *Mnemosyne* 40, 149.

Vanderspoel, J., 1995, *Themistius and the Imperial Court: Oratory, Civic Duty, and Paideia from Constantius to Theodosius* (Ann Arbor, MI).

Von Haehling, R., 1978, *Die Religionszugehörigkeit der hohen Amtsträger des Römischen Reiches seit Constantins I. Alleinherrschaft bis zum Ende der Theodosianischen Dynastie* (Bonn).

Vogler, C., 1979, *Constance II et l'administration imperiale*, Université des sciences humaines de Strasbourg, Groupe de recherche d'histoire romaine: *Etudes et travaux* 3 (Strasbourg).

Wallis, R. T., 1972, *Neoplatonism* (London).

Whitby, L. M., 1988, *The Emperor Maurice and His Historian: Theophylact Simocatta on Persian and Balkan Warfare* (Oxford).

Wickham, C., 1984, 'The Other Transition: From the Ancient World to Feudalism', *Past and Present* 103, 3–36.

Wiles, M., 1967, *The Making of Christian Doctrine* (London).

Wirth, G., 1979, 'Themistios und Constantius', *Byzantinische Forschungen* 6, 293–317.

Wirth, G., 1997, 'Rome and its Germanic partners in the fourth century', in W. Pohl, ed., *Kingdoms of the Empire: The Integration of Barbarians in Late Antiquity* (Leiden), 13–56.

Wolfram, H., 1988, *History of the Goths*, trans. T. J. Dunlap (Berkeley, CA).

Woods, D., 1998, 'Valens, Valentinian I, and the *Ioviani Cornuti*', *Latomus* 244, 462–88.

Woods, D., 1999, 'A Persian at Rome: Ammianus and Eunapius, Frg. 68', in Drijvers and Hunt, eds, 1999, 156–65.

Wooten, C. W., 1987, *Hermogenes On Types of Style* (Chapel Hill, NC).

# INDEX 1

## PEOPLE, PLACES AND SUBJECTS DISCUSSED IN CHAPTER 1 AND THE INTRODUCTIONS TO THE SPEECHES

*see also* Hellenic culture; *paideia*
Rome  44, 57, 117, 118
  Constantius' visit to  44, 114–5,
    119
  *see also* Constantinople

sacrifice, blood  49–51, 155–6
Salutius Secundus, and Jovian  147
Saphrax, leader of Greuthungi
    199, 202, 206, 234, 258
Sarmatians  219
Saturninus, general and politician
    209, 255, 257
  and Gothic peace  207
  and Themistius  18, 73
Severus, emperor  2
Sextus, philosopher  15n.
Shapur II, Persian ruler  70
Sicyon, anon. philosopher of
    (Hierius?)  16, 103
Silvanus, usurper  116
Sirmium  206
  Theodosius at  234
Socrates, Church historian  155
Socrates, philosopher  15
  as model of active philosophy
    293, 306
  *see also* Themistius, Hellenic
    culture of
Sopater, philosopher  18, 21
sophist, as false philosopher  104–
    5, 286–8, 310–11
  *see also* Plato; Themistius,
    career of
Spartans  209
Stalin, Joseph  26
status, late Roman laws on  296–7
succession, and imperial stability
    26, 146–7, 175

*suffragium*, practice of  17
Symmachus  16, 22, 35
syncretism, religious  40, 60, 61–8
  *see also* Themistius, Hellenic
    culture of
Synesius of Cyrene, *De Regno* of
    259, 260, 261, 262
'Syrians' as Christians  156, 178

*Taurobolium*  51
teachers  43
Tervingi, Gothic grouping  199–
    200, 201–2, 263
tetrarchy, political problems of
    176, 220
  *see also* succession
Thalassius, friend of Libanius  32
Thatcher, Lady  68
Themistius, career of  28–9, 38–9,
    118–20, 124, 2020–3, 296–8,
    310
  chair of philosophy  75, 97,
    105–6
  as cultural talisman  21–4, 40,
    57, 61–8, 74, 143, 209–10
  as imperial propagandist  26–8,
    32–3, 119, 120, 147–8, 150–
    8, 179, 212–13, 215–18, 231–
    2, 235, 256–7, 263–4
  and political discontinuity  24–
    6, 30, 138, 142–3, 145–8,
    208–9, 224
  public persona of  4–5, 7, 12, 16,
    17, 19, 20–1, 21–4, 47, 57,
    73–4, 118, 119, 286–7
  rewards and dangers of  12–17,
    18–19, 44, 47, 97, 296, 310

# INDEX 2

## PEOPLE, PLACES AND DEITIES MENTIONED IN THE ORATIONS

The letter 'a' after a citation denotes an allusion rather than a direct mention, 'q' denotes a quotation, 'r' that the citation occurs in a rubric.